P9-CRK-114

switzerland

NATIONAL GEOGRAPHIC
TRAVELER

switzerland

by Teresa Fisher

National Geographic
Washington, D.C.

CONTENTS

Pages 2–3: The iconic Matterhorn
Opposite: The instantly recognizable Swiss flag is on show in every
town and village—and at soccer matches!

TRAVELING WITH EYES OPEN

Alert travelers go with a purpose and leave with a benefit. If you travel responsibly, you can help support wildlife conservation, historic preservation, and cultural enrichment in the places you visit. You can enrich your own travel experience as well.

To be a geo-savvy traveler:

- Recognize that your presence has an impact on the places you visit.

- Spend your time and money in ways that sustain local character. (Besides, it's more interesting that way.)

- Value the destination's natural and cultural heritage.

- Respect the local customs and traditions.

- Express appreciation to local people about things you find interesting and unique to the place: its nature and scenery, music and food, historic villages and buildings.

- Vote with your wallet: Support the people who support the place, patronizing businesses that make an effort to celebrate and protect what's special there. Seek out shops, local restaurants, inns, and tour operators who love their home—who love taking care of it and showing it off. Avoid businesses that detract from the character of the place.

- Enrich yourself, taking home memories and stories to tell, knowing that you have contributed to the preservation and enhancement of the destination.

That is the type of travel now called geotourism, defined as "tourism that sustains or enhances the geographical character of a place—its environment, culture, aesthetics, heritage, and the well-being of its residents." To learn more, visit National Geographic's Center for Sustainable Destinations at *www .nationalgeographic.com/travel/sustainable.*

switzerland

ABOUT THE AUTHOR

Author, photographer, and member of the British Guild of Travel Writers, **Teresa Fisher** has had a lifelong love affair with Switzerland since her first visit as a toddler to the ski slopes of Wengen. Since then, she has penned over 30 guidebooks and children's travel reference books on a wide variety of destinations worldwide, specializing in European city guides. She has written extensively on Switzerland for several publishers including Thomas Cook and Columbus. Teresa is featured periodically on BBC local radio as a travel advisor, and her photography and travel articles have appeared in British national newspapers including the *Daily Telegraph*, the *Sunday Telegraph,* and the *Sunday Times.* Fluent in both French and German, she lived for seven years in the Alps as a cross-cultural communications trainer for BMW and also, for a short spell, as a journalist in Zürich. Teresa has skied most Swiss resorts; hiked on many an alpine pass; herded goats; and made mountain cheese by hand. But she has yet to master yodeling.

Charting Your Trip

The popularity of Switzerland as a tourist destination is wholly deserved. This small landlocked country, located at the heart of Europe and bordering Austria, France, Germany, Italy, and Liechtenstein, is known first and foremost for its sensational mountain scenery. However, with its grand cities filled with fine museums and galleries, its fairy-tale castles, and its outstanding vernacular and ecclesiastical architecture, there's plenty to offer everyone.

It is not possible to see everything in one trip, so don't even try! Most visitors fall into one of two categories. Many seek sport and recreation, especially skiing, in the mountains. After all, Switzerland is both a summer and a winter sporting paradise—a veritable tourist idyll with its glistening white Alpine peaks and sparkling lakes. Others are cultural visitors, who focus mainly on the cities and the nation's staggering 980 museums and galleries. Most of these—along with most of the country's 7.5 million residents—are in the cities north of the Alps. The capital, Bern, is near the center of the country, and the other main population centers are Zürich (northeast of Bern); Luzern (due east); Basel (to the north); and Geneva and Lausanne to the west. Swiss cities are a pleasure to visit. The efficient public transport systems are easy to navigate and minimize the inner-city traffic, making sightseeing altogether more enjoyable and stress free.

How to Get Around

Switzerland boasts the best national public transport network in the world, with Geneva and Zürich as the main hubs. The country is small enough to get around with ease and relative speed, thanks to its unrivaled system of trains, buses, boats, funiculars, and cable cars—which all interlink like clockwork. Most major cities operate comprehensive tram systems, and Lausanne is the smallest city in the world with a metro system. If you intend to travel a lot, the Swiss Pass (see p. 272) gives excellent value: It entitles visitors to unlimited travel over most of the system, and discounts on the majority of the rest. Switzerland is world-famous for its spectacular train journeys, so why not sit back, relax, and enjoy the views!

Swiss cheese fondue and side dishes

A Weeklong Visit

There are, of course, various options for touring the country, depending on whether you choose to stay in one city or resort, to explore a region, or to attempt a whistle-stop tour of the whole country. If you are feeling ambitious, one week is just long enough to get acquainted with some of the most appealing cities. If you find the itinerary too rushed, simply skip a town or a sight and continue at a more leisurely pace.

Start in the trend-setting city of Zürich, located on its own lake in the northeast. Spend **day one** and **day two** here, to take in the nation's top gallery, the Kunsthaus (Museum of Fine Arts), and some of the world-class museums, including the Schweizerisches Landesmuseum (Swiss National Museum). Once you have a grasp of the nation's colorful history, your travels will be all the more rewarding. Be sure to see the Fraumünster church with its beautiful stained-glass windows and the bird's-eye views from atop the tower of the Grossmünster (Cathedral). Then treat yourself to some shopping in Bahnhofstrasse, the Confederation's most sophisticated shopping boulevard. By night, enjoy some of the best nightlife in Switzerland, or treat yourself to a night at the opera (book tickets well in advance; see Travelwise, p. 309).

On **day three**, take the train to the tourist mecca of Luzern (a trip of about one hour), which is also set on its own lake, the Vierwaldstättersee. This is William Tell country, where the seeds of the Swiss Confederation were sown. With its cobbled streets, frescoed houses, and graceful spires and turrets, Luzern represents the epitome of chocolate-box Switzerland. It is also home to the Verkehrshaus des Schweiz—one of the world's finest transport museums—and the acclaimed Sammlung Rosengart Luzern, with its exceptional collection of impressionist and modern paintings. If you have the time, consider extending your stay in this area by a day for a mountain excursion up Mount Pilatus (via paddle-wheeler and cog railroad) or Mount Rigi, for one of the finest mountain vistas in central Switzerland.

NOT TO BE MISSED:

Merry-making in Basel during Fasnacht carnival 53–54

The museums and galleries of Geneva, Basel, & Zürich 60–69, 88–93, 190–207

A cruise on Lake Geneva 73

Swiss chocolate 78–79

Savoring cheese fondue 128–129

A hike in the Jungfrau region 134–135

Skiing in fabulously beautiful Valais 153

A glimpse of the mighty Matterhorn 159

Tasting Swiss wines 210–211

Riding the Glacier Express 240–241

The Swiss National Park 243–244

Visitor Information

A good source of information for those planning your trip to Switzerland is **My Switzerland** (www.myswitzerland.com), the website of the national tourist board. Here you'll find details of attractions, events, and activities in every canton. Each section is updated by cantonal tourist boards and contains links to regional information sites. To find out how to get around the country, the website of the **Schweizerische Bundesbahnen** (Swiss National Rail; www.sbb.ch) contains a useful route planner.

Driving in Switzerland

Most Swiss prefer to use public transport rather than drive. However, car rental is straightforward, and the roads are well maintained. The narrow, winding mountain roads are not for the faint-hearted, but they do offer some of the most scenic drives in Europe. The most spectacular and beautiful include the routes over the Great St. Bernard, Furka, Bernina, St. Gotthard, and Simplon passes. It is expensive to hire a driver.

On **day four**, continue on to the diminutive capital city of Bern—around one hour from Luzern by train—and take a walking tour of the medieval cobbled Altstadt (Old Town) before exploring one or two of the sights which most appeal to you: perhaps the heraldic bears in the BärenPark (Bear Park), or the Museum Paul Klee—a must-see for all art aficionados. Spend **day five** in the Bernese Oberland, one of the best-known Alpine regions due south of Bern. Interlaken, about one hour by train from Bern, makes an excellent base here. If you only take one mountain excursion during your stay in Switzerland, make it the Jungfraujoch, the highest railway station in the world. On **day six**, continue by train to Geneva—a trip of around three hours, including changing trains at Bern—Switzerland's best-known city, positioned at the tip of idyllic Lake Geneva in the southwest of the country. Geneva is home to a number of unique and inspiring museums such as the Musée International de la Croix-Rouge, devoted to the work of the Red Cross. Here too you can explore the ancient cobbled city center or tour the Palais des Nations, home to the United Nations Office. Tired of sightseeing? Head to Carouge to shop for souvenirs and gifts to take home. Or simply kick back with the locals relaxing on the beaches, swimming in the lake, and admiring the impressive Jet d'Eau water jet, set against the grandiose architecture of the lakeside quays. Spend **day seven** on a full-day paddle-wheeler tour of Lake Geneva. Cruise along the vine-clad Swiss Riviera to lively Lausanne, characterful Vevey, and ritzy Montreux, home to the world-renowned annual Jazz Festival. Return to Geneva, the gourmet capital of Switzerland, for a late dinner.

If You Have More Time

To get a real taste of Switzerland, you need to explore beyond the cities and experience all the different regions. This takes time, but you should consider a trip to the east—to the lush rolling countryside of picturesque **Appenzellerland**, with its vehement adherence to folkloric traditions, or to the *sgraffito*-adorned

What's in a Name?

You will see CH all over the place in Switzerland—on postal addresses, vehicle registration numbers, on Swiss website addresses (which are suffixed .ch), and in numerous other situations. Contrary to popular opinion, it does not stand for "CHocolate" but rather Confoederatio Helvetica—the Helvetic (or Swiss)

Confederation—the Latin title first given to the nation in 1291 (see p. 34) when an alliance was forged between three rural communities, Uri, Unterwalden, and Schwyz. These people collectively became known as Schwyzers (Swiss), giving rise to the nation's name: Schwyz (Switzerland).

A traditional folk festival at Urnäsch in the most traditional canton, Appenzellerland

houses of the **Engadine** valley in Graubünden. Alternatively you can head south to marvel at the iconic **Matterhorn** and other high Alpine peaks encircling Valaisan resorts such as **Zermatt** and **Verbier,** and travel to the glittering lakes and vineyards of **Ticino.**

In western Switzerland you can easily extend the One Week itinerary to two weeks or longer by adding additional excursions. Take the **Chocolate Train** from Montreux to the velvety green hills of the Gruyères region, for instance. There you can visit the eponymous medieval town, taste the local cheese, and visit a chocolate factory at nearby **Broc.** Alternatively, some of the often-overlooked regional towns and cities make excellent bases for a short break. Try **Fribourg** with its beautiful medieval center; **Neuchâtel,** the gateway to the Jura mountains; **St. Gallen** with its renowned rococo abbey library; or **Basel,** bastion of modern architecture on the Rhine River.

For those in search of peace and solitude, the high Alps offer almost limitless possibilities for exploring the great outdoors, especially in Graubünden, home to the wild, deserted valleys of the **Swiss National Park.** The canton of Valais also offers plenty of long, lonesome country walks, together with some of the nation's best skiing. Bordering Valais is Ticino, a canton centered on the historic towns of **Locarno** and **Lugano,** which combines Swiss efficiency with Mediterranean *joie de vivre.*

Ultimately, it's up to you to tailor your trip according to the regions which appeal most. One thing's certain: When you visit Switzerland and uncover some of its idiosyncrasies, it will simply whet your appetite and lure you back for more! ■

History & Culture

Twilight outside Zürich's busy railroad station

Switzerland Today

Switzerland is a small country, divided by its landscapes, its languages, its history, and its customs. Yet it is a great nation, united by its people and representing the perfect balance between northern efficiency and southern vitality. Whether Swiss-German, Suisse-Romand, Romanches, or Tessinois, all barriers fall away when it comes to their collective pride.

Everywhere imaginable the national flag is flown as a symbol of their patriotism. It is the world's only square flag, red with a white cross. Remove it from mountaintops, private gardens, and official buildings and something essential will be lacking from the landscape. The flag was originally created to identify mercenaries on the battlefield. Today it is virtually a Swiss brand, adorning everything from T-shirts to beer mugs. Even the best-selling postcard in Switzerland is the Swiss flag.

However, it is the nation's great diversity that impresses its visitors above all. You can travel just a few miles from one village to the next and find yourself in a new region with a complete change in language, but always with the unerring cordiality and generosity that has made the nation world-famous for its hospitality. The extraordinary variety of vistas—from the rounded forms and dense forests of the Jura chain to the lakes, vineyards, orchards, and historic châteaux of the plain—are set against a ubiquitous backdrop of the jagged Alps. These mountains form a grandiose amphitheater of glaciers clad in eternal snow. In the countryside, clusters of simple sun-faded wooden chalets, the color of honey or toffee, and the distant sound of cowbells lure visitors with their rustic appeal. Whether the Swiss like it or not, the "chocolate-box" image of Switzerland abroad—of white-capped mountain peaks set against cloudless blue skies, quaint chalet villages, flower-filled meadows, and yodeling cowherds dressed in traditional attire—is not unfounded.

> **You can travel just a few miles from one village to the next and find yourself in a new region with a complete change of language.**

However, there's much more to Switzerland than this. In perfect juxtaposition, the large, bustling cities with their world-class museums, cutting-edge architecture, jewelers, and luxury hotels serve as a reminder that this nation is also renowned for its enviable standard of living. The ultra-efficient transport system is second-to-none. Indeed, Switzerland boasts the densest network of public transport in the world, meshing the nation together with its punctual and comprehensive schedule of trains, boats, and PostBuses, which extends to the remotest of Alpine villages.

Switzerland's unique location has shaped the nation in many ways: politically, culturally, and linguistically. It has long been a melting pot for different cultures, located as it is at a crossroads for trade and intellectual exchange between the Latin and Germanic worlds, at a point where the German, French, and Italian language areas collide. It therefore comes as no surprise that Switzerland has not one, but four national languages. The majority of the population (63.7 percent) speak *Schwyzertütsch* (Swiss-German), an

The super-modern Westside shopping complex in Bern

Flower-filled Jardin Anglais in central Geneva

oral language with no standard written form. Its large variety of melodic regional dialects have developed because of the isolating effect of the mountains. Schwyzertütsch is written as *hoch Deutsch* (high German). French is spoken in western Switzerland by just over 20 percent of the population. The term used to refer to the French-speaking region is Swiss Romande. Swiss-French is very close to standard French, although there are some unique local expressions, accents, and vocabulary. The purest French is spoken in Neuchâtel. The invisible yet much vaunted *Röstigraben* (Rösti ditch; see sidebar p. 19) still divides French- and German-speaking parts of the country. Italian is the language of Ticino (6.4 percent) in the south of the country, while Romansh (see p. 49), a derivative of Latin, is spoken by around 1 percent of the population (in certain remote valleys of Graubünden, in the southeast). Three cantons (Bern, Fribourg, and Valais) are bilingual; and Graubünden is trilingual (German, Italian, and Romansh). English is widely spoken in all the major towns and cities (as the language of national and international commerce), as well as in some rural regions. Somewhat controversially, in a few German-speaking regions children are taught English at school before they study French.

Politics & Economics

Given Switzerland's melting pot of languages and cultures, its peaceful political situation is admirable. The Swiss political system is unique and relies on consensus-building. It is a "direct democracy" system, which has changed little since the signing of the 1848 Swiss Federal Constitution (see pp. 37–38). However, its roots go back to the Reformation in the 16th century, and the influence of Zwingli, Calvin, and Luther (see pp. 35–36), who envisioned the church as a meeting place for parishioners to worship as equals rather than regarding it as a hierarchical organization. This paved the way for an equal opportunity system of national referenda.

Government & Political Divisions: Switzerland has three different levels of government: the Confederation, the cantons, and the communes. The Confederation, at the highest level, has three branches of power: the executive, legislative, and judicial. The executive branch is formed by the Swiss Federal Council, which wields executive power, and a Federal Assembly, which is entrusted with legislative power. These federal bodies, based in the capital Bern, have jurisdiction over matters of common interest such as defense and foreign policy. The constitution limits federal influence in the formulation of domestic policy, emphasizing the roles of cantonal governments. However, in recent years, the Confederation has been compelled to enlarge its policymaking powers to cope with such national problems as energy, environment, and organized crime. The Swiss Federal Council is a seven-member executive cabinet formed by a "concordance system" (a coalition of the major parties elected in the same ratio as their ballots in the general election). It is chaired by the President of the Confederation, a more or less ceremonial position as head of government.

At cantonal level, the corresponding bodies are the Cantonal Council and the Cantonal Government, which both address such local issues as education and public health. The nation is divided into 26 cantons. Of these, 20 are "full" cantons and six are "half" cantons for purposes of representation in the federal legislature. These represent the original states that combined, in 1848 and in the ensuing decades, to form the Helvetic Confederation (see p. 37). The cantons regulate local government, and are further divided into communes which, as well as being given responsibilities by the Confederation and their respective cantons, also have limited powers of their own.

The entire system endorses people power. In some regions (including Appenzellerland and Glarus; see pp. 228–233), annual meetings of the cantonal parliaments still take place in the main squares in ceremonies little changed for centuries. Then, national costume is de rigueur, and locals vote by a show of hands or, in the case of the men, by raising a short dagger. What's more, any citizen is entitled to propose amendments to the Federal Constitution. Gather 100,000 signatures and you can put to the vote a change in the constitution.

Women's Voting Rights

Given the importance of Swiss democracy, it is surprising how long it took for women to gain the right to vote. As early as 1886, they petitioned unsuccessfully for it. It wasn't until 1957 that progress was made, when Basel allowed women to vote, but only at local and cantonal levels. This example was followed gradually by the French-speaking cantons of Geneva, Neuchâtel, and Vaud, and then by German-speaking Zürich seven years later. But, it wasn't until 1971 that women's right to vote in federal elections was accepted nationally by a two-thirds majority—much later than most other countries. Some cantons continued to resist, most notably Appenzell-Inner Rhoden, which didn't permit women to vote on local issues until as recently as 1991.

If you gather 50,000 signatures, you can block any law passed by the Swiss Parliament and force a national referendum. But with votes and polls taking place every couple of months on various municipal and cantonal issues, voters get tired of their duties and the turnout is usually only around 30 percent. A majority of both the cantons and the popular vote is needed for a change in law to be implemented. All national decisions go to a referendum, where voter turnout is greater. Referenda in recent years have rejected membership of the European Union (EU) in 2001 yet voted to aid new member states of the EU in 2006.

> Traditionally, Switzerland has avoided alliances that might entail military, political, or direct economic action.

In foreign affairs, the Swiss have been neutral for centuries. Indeed, the nation's financial prowess and famed political neutrality have enabled it to play a safe but key role in European and world affairs. As American actor and comedian Larry David (b. 1947) said, "Switzerland is a place where they don't like to fight, so they get people to do their fighting for them while they ski and eat chocolate." Their reluctance to join the EU is based on a number of factors: They would lose their Swiss franc; their effective system of initiatives and referenda would need radical reform and possibly curtailment to comply with EU rules; Swiss trade and industry is not convinced of the benefits of membership; and there are doubts whether their status of neutrality would be compatible with EU policy. Worse still, as a nation of four subcultures, the Swiss fear losing their cultural identity altogether if they merge with their big neighbors,

New Federal Council members are sworn in at the Federal Palace in Bern.

Germany, France, and Italy. To mitigate possible adverse effects of nonmembership, Swiss practices and legislation in many fields—including trade—have moved in line with that of EU directives. After all, nearly two-thirds of its exports go to EU countries. In 2008, Switzerland became the 25th country to sign the Schengen Agreement, which abolished border controls and enabled passport-free movement between some EU member countries. However, the Swiss government no longer talks of membership of the EU as a "government goal," but rather as "an option."

Switzerland on the World Stage: Switzerland was among the first nations on the continent to adopt and implement a modern democratic constitution, and their politicians, philosophers, and scientists have made major contributions to the common European heritage over the centuries. Swiss economic relations with the United States are also strong. The U.S. is the largest foreign investor in Switzerland and also the largest single destination of Swiss foreign investment.

Swiss neutrality, coupled with their long history of democracy and diplomacy, has been key to the country's international success. Traditionally, Switzerland has avoided alliances that might entail military, political, or direct economic action, preferring to serve as an intermediary and host to major international treaty conferences. Their eventual membership in the United Nations in 2002 marked the end of centuries of Swiss isolation.

The Swiss Constitution declares the preservation of the nation's independence and welfare as the supreme objective of Swiss foreign policy. Thereafter, its five main foreign policy objectives are: to further the peaceful coexistence of nations; to promote respect for human rights, democracy, and the rule of law; to alleviate need and poverty in the world; to preserve natural resources; and to promote Swiss economic interests abroad. To this end, Switzerland (particularly Geneva) is home to many international governmental and nongovernmental organizations, including the World Health Organization and the International Red Cross (whose flag is essentially the Swiss flag with the colors reversed). Switzerland is also a member of a number of international economic organizations, including the World Trade Organization (WTO), the International Monetary Fund (IMF), the World Bank (WB), and the Organization for Economic Cooperation and Development (OECD).

In 2010 the Swiss economy shrank by 1.5 percent as a result of the global economic slowdown. However, this would appear to be just a minor setback: Switzerland led the rankings of the World Economic Forum's Global Competitiveness Report 2010–2011, reflecting the country's sound infrastructure, efficient markets, and high levels of

The Röstigraben

The Röstigraben is an invisible internal border between French- and German-speaking regions of Switzerland. This linguistic and cultural frontier takes its name *Rösti Ditch* from a Swiss-German speciality dish *(rösti)* made with grated potatoes. It starts in the north, just east of Delémont in the Jura and west of Laufen, and crosses the cantons of Bern, Fribourg, Vaud, and Valais, with road and rail signs frequently showing both languages: for example, Basel/Bâle, Murten/Morat, and Biel/Bienne. Nowhere is the divide more pronounced than in Freiburg/Fribourg, where residents on the west bank of the river speak French, and those to the east speak German.

scientific research and technological attainment. They have the lowest inflation and unemployment rates of all the industrialized countries. Crime rates are among the lowest in the world and the Swiss legal and judicial systems are highly developed. The nation is politically stable, the Swiss franc remains one of the world's soundest currencies, and the country leads the world in its high standard of banking and financial services. Tourism, engineering, and insurance are also significant sectors of the economy. And the best national public transport system in the world, combined with a highly developed tourism infrastructure, makes travel and vacationing a pleasure for its visitors.

Tourism

Swiss tourism began in the early 19th century with the first ascents of the main Alpine peaks (mostly by upper-class British mountaineers accompanied by local guides), including the Jungfrau in 1811, Monte Rosa (at 15,203 feet/4,634 m, the highest mountain in Switzerland) in 1855, and the Matterhorn in 1865. This era became known as the Golden Age of Alpinism and led to the construction of mountain huts for expeditions and of grand hotels—not just in the mountain villages but also in the cities. Many were family-run, and each offered the highest levels of comfort to the intrepid, affluent explorers. Such tourism also called for the development of a basic transport infrastructure, and by the late 1800s major mountain train lines had opened at Pilatus, Gornergrat, and— most remarkably—the Jungfraubahn. The last went all the way up to the Jungfraujoch (see pp. 136–137), the highest train station in Europe, and is still the number one tourist excursion in Switzerland. As the American author and humorist Mark Twain (1835–1910) remarked in 1891: "There isn't a mountain in Switzerland now that hasn't a ladder railroad or two up its back like suspenders; indeed, some mountains are latticed with them."

The Swiss like everything to be spotlessly clean and tidy. Little wonder then that they are champion recyclers.

Rail communications were swiftly extended across the country and were electrified as early as the 1950s, forming the backbone of today's ultra-efficient, punctual, and fully-integrated Swiss Travel System. As the nation became the holiday playground of Europe, these grand hotels began to attract the attention of the rest of the world, marking the start of Switzerland's legendary reputation for hospitality. This reputation is based on consistently high standards, maintained to this day in the country's various celebrated schools of tourism and hospitality management.

Before long, mountain resorts realized that they could appeal in summer as well as during winter months. However, mass tourism didn't begin until well after World

Alpine skiing at Kleine Scheidegg in the Bernese Oberland

War II. Even as late as the 1960s and 1970s, the now internationally renowned resorts of Grindelwald and Zermatt were still just small, humble Alpine villages. Nowadays, the Swiss countryside is a giant year-round recreation area for tourists and, in the 21st century, its cities have become increasingly popular short-break destinations. The mountains still attract a large number of alpinists from around the world. And the winter ski and snow-sport resorts are also popular destinations in summer, offering some of Europe's finest walking and a host of other outdoor activities to suit all ages and abilities (see pp. 212–213).

The Swiss are fastidious about preserving their beautiful countryside and have some of the world's strongest environmental legislation (see p. 31). On a more personal level, they follow a strict series of unwritten rules and expect their visitors to do the same: These include never picking Alpine wild flowers, staying on marked paths when hiking, lighting fires only in permitted locations, and taking all rubbish home. The Swiss like everything to be spotlessly clean and tidy. Little wonder then that they are champion recyclers, leading the way in Europe. Everyone is encouraged to recycle as much as possible and, in many cantons, householders pay a tax according to the volume of garbage they create. On average, 70 percent of paper, 95 percent of glass, 71 percent of plastics, 90 percent of aluminum cans, and 75 percent of tin cans are reprocessed. It is not only individuals who collect the garbage. Companies also have stringent policies, including Swiss Federal Railways (SBB), which gathers and recycles 2.5 million plastic bottles, 2 million aluminum cans, 1 million glass bottles, and 2,875 tons (2,608 tonnes) of newspapers and magazines left on their trains every year. Environmental concerns always take high priority and, although tax-paying is no more popular in Switzerland than elsewhere, the Swiss electorate are happy to invest heavily into their ultra-efficient railway infrastructure in an attempt to reduce road haulage and commuter traffic.

What Makes the Swiss So "Swiss"?

Think Switzerland, and you think cheese, alphorns, cowbells, Heidi, and chocolate. The Swiss would call the discussion of such social stereotypes "hiking the ridge," a practice bound to result in prejudice. Although there is no such thing as the "typical Swiss," there are some character traits that are common to large groups of the population (currently just under 8 million people) and may help you understand the nation. Admittedly, they are not based on any socioeconomic facts or figures, and so they should perhaps be taken lightly.

Most Swiss would agree that small is beautiful, from the size of their nation to the tiny petals of their national flower, the edelweiss, and the intricate workings of their watches. Precision is key and perfection is striven for to maintain their fabled reputation

Crowds throng Zürich's main shopping street, Bahnhofstrasse.

EXPERIENCE: Learning French While Trekking

For a perfect way to improve your French in a relaxing yet invigorating environment, **Le Français en Marchant** (*Château-d'Oex, Vaud, tel 023/342 2267, e-mail: info@francaisenmarchant.ch, www .francaisenmarchant.ch, $$$$$*) offers week-long immersion courses in Vaud canton, at an elevation of 3,150 feet (960 m).

Three hours of language tuition each morning in small groups are combined with afternoons hiking in the pictur-esque Préalpes Vaudoises region (see pp. 146–149) and *chambres d'hôtes* accommo-dation in the village. While trekking, you will find plenty of opportunities to try out your newly acquired language skills.

for Swiss quality, although this may sometimes convert into impatience and pedantry in the eyes of the beholder. The Swiss possess a strong sense of identity and patriotism, and they have good reason to be proud. They are a prosperous nation. They are also very thrifty and rarely ostentatious with their wealth. In the cities, per capita income is among the highest in the world, as are salaries. The Swiss also enjoy an excellent education system and an efficient health service, and they are masters in the art of com-promise, instead of making only majority decisions. Though often criticized by political commentators as being slow and inefficient, the Swiss realize that long-term stability and broad acceptance of laws are better for the economy than frequent change. As a result, they are a generally harmonious, tolerant, and smoothly functioning nation. They rarely break the rules, and the electorate have a high acceptance of decisions taken for them. While key concepts such as human rights and asylum have long been associated with the Confederation, the Swiss are sometimes less tolerant of the many immigrants currently enjoying the Swiss lifestyle. More than 20 percent of the population is foreign and, while Swit-zerland has the highest rate per capita of political refugees in Europe, views on immigration laws remain divided.

> When in Switzerland, never be late! The Swiss are the undisputed masters of precision-timing and punctuality.

The Swiss work hard to preserve their unique identity, nurturing their traditions, customs, and folk traditions. Even in the technological world of the 21st century—where 94 percent of the population regularly use the internet—the alphorn remains one of the nation's key symbols (see p. 50). Although you are unlikely to hear one being played from the mountaintops to round up cattle as in the past, the alphorn remains an important part of Swiss heritage, still played recreationally in mountain bars or on the snow slopes. Yodeling too remains a vital element of traditional music and has seen something of a revival in recent years. Finally, when in Switzerland, never be late! The Swiss are the undisputed masters of precision-timing and punctuality. Trains depart on time, and people often turn up early to make sure they are not late. They even have a special word to describe this common Swiss practice : *Überpünktlichkeit* (over-punctuality).

There's no denying that everything ticks along like clockwork in Switzerland. It all sounds too good to be true, but this is how it is: The Swiss really are law-abiding, effi-cient, hard-working, clean-living, courteous, and thoroughly likeable. They work hard but they also play hard. And "Swiss made" is synonymous with quality worldwide. ∎

Land & Environment

Despite its small size, Switzerland boasts more than its fair share of dramatic scenery, from verdant, rolling lowlands, expansive lakes, and gently flowing rivers to precipitous Alpine peaks, glaciers, crashing waterfalls, and lush mountain valleys. With picture-postcard vistas at every turn, its unique and varied landscape makes it a nation of breathtaking beauty.

Geographical Divisions

The countryside of this landlocked nation is divided into three main geographical areas: the two mountain ranges of the Jura (in the northwest) and the Alps (in the south and east), and the comparatively low-lying Mittelland (Middle Land) or Swiss plateau, sandwiched between. The Mittelland is the most densely populated region, embracing several major cities and stretching diagonally from Lake Geneva in the southwest to Bodensee (Lake Constance) in the northeast. The mountains occupy almost two-thirds of the nation's 15,940 square miles (41,284 sq km), and reach a maximum height of 15,203 feet (4,634 m) at Monte Rosa in the canton of Valais. Despite this disadvantage, just under one-third of Switzerland's area is used for agriculture, industry, and urban areas.

The entire country has been shaped largely by glaciation. This can be seen especially in the Alps, where all the major valleys are U-shaped due to glacial erosion. During the Würm Glaciation, glaciers completely covered the Swiss plateau. After it retreated, 18,000 years ago, it left icy remnants in the form of glaciers in the high mountains. These are mostly situated in the Pennine and Bernese Alps, although most are now retreating due to global warming. They include the Aletsch Glacier (see p. 137) just south of the Jungfrau—the largest and longest glacier in the Alps. The Jungfrau–Aletsch region is the largest glaciated area in western Europe. It was designated a World Heritage site in 2001.

> **The Jungfrau–Aletsch region is the largest glaciated area in western Europe. It was designated a World Heritage site in 2001.**

The Swiss Plateau: The Swiss plateau's landscape, including the many lakes that help make up the country's spectacular scenery, was also formed by glaciation. The Swiss plateau forms a basin, and it is mostly undulating rather than flat. The plateau ranges in height between 1,300 and 2,300 feet (400–700 m) above sea level and represents around 30 percent of Swiss territory. The Seeland (Lake District), comprising the lakes of Neuchâtel, Murten, and Biel, marks the largest flat area within the Swiss plateau. Geologically, the Swiss plateau forms part of a larger basin extending at its southwest end as far as Chambéry in France, and into the German and Austrian Pre-Alps to the northeast. Within Switzerland itself, the plateau is approximately 186 miles (300 km) long, and gets progressively wider from the west to the east. It is sharply delimited geographically and geologically by the Alps to the south and the Jura Mountains to the north and northwest.

The Jura: The Jura mountain range is densely forested, and undulating. Occupying about one-tenth of the Swiss land surface, it dates from the Jurassic period (hence the name) and straddles the French border, separating the Rhine and Rhône Rivers. It also contains an impressive array of natural wonders (see p. 103), such as the Creux du Van cirque and the Taubenloch Gorge and, with its gentle hilly terrain, is a paradise for walkers, mountain bikers, canoeists, and cross-country skiers.

(continued on p. 28)

A bridge in the Gorges d'Areuse, near Couvet in the Jura

Summer in the Mountains

The unparalleled vistas of the Swiss Alps are famous the world over, from thrilling stunt scenes in James Bond movies to the distinctive Toblerone chocolate bar, shaped in the form of the nation's most iconic mountain—the Matterhorn.

For many of Switzerland's visitors, the country's mountains are things to ski or slide down, seen only when they are covered by snow and criss-crossed by ski-lifts. In the spring, however, when the snows melt and the skies clear, a landscape of breathtaking splendor and natural diversity is revealed. For those who come to the mountains during the spring and summer there are a multitude of possible activities and things to see.

Flora & Fauna

Thanks to tough environmental laws, wildlife thrives in the mountainous regions. Their fragile ecosystems shelter some rare plants, especially in the Alpine meadows, which are ablaze with colorful flowers from April to July. Look for early white crocuses and violet-blue gentians in springtime, which give way to dwarf Alpine orchids, tiny rock jasmine, yellow glacier buttercups, and bright pink *alpenrosen* (miniature rhododendrons). As a general rule, the higher the altitude the rarer the plant. The best known Alpine flower, but also one of the most elusive, is Switzerland's national flower, edelweiss. With its tiny star-shaped white flowers, it grows at altitudes of up to 10,170 feet (3,100 m).

The ibex (a type of mountain goat with curved, ridged horns) and the chamois (a horned antelope) count among the most distinctive animals at high altitudes. Ibex were extinct in Switzerland for over 100 years, until they were reintroduced in 1906. The same mammal recolonization program has since resulted in the successful reintroduction of the European lynx, mountain hare, ermine, weasel, and even a handful of wolves and European brown bears. Easier to see is the marmot

(a chunky squirrel-like rodent) which lives in underground burrows on the slopes and emits a loud shrill whistle if it senses danger.

Overhead, especially in southeast Switzerland, you may be lucky to spot the elusive but majestic golden eagle and the lammergeier, or bearded vulture, with its 10-foot (3 m) wingspan. The black Alpine chough (a mountain-dwelling crow with a yellow beak) and the extraordinarily hardy rock ptarmigan are other birds you should look out for on the slopes above the treeline. Distinctive birds of the forested mountain slopes include the noisy brown and white-speckled nutcracker, a denizen of aleppo pine forests, and the black grouse, whose early morning leks (mating "showgrounds") are an amazing sight. Contact the Swiss Association for the Protection of Birds (*www.birdlife.ch*) for additional information.

Hiking & Mountaineering

With mountains covering more than half Switzerland's area and with some of the finest Alpine Walking in Europe, it comes as no surprise that the Swiss love hiking, an enthusiasm they share with more than 120 million visitors each year. There are more than 39,146 miles (63,000 km) of designated hiking paths (marked *wanderweg* in German, *sentier* in French, and *sentiero* in Italian). This figure is not far off the length of the Swiss road network.

Mountaineering did not really catch on in the Alps until the mid-19th century, although a handful of major peaks were scaled before then, including Mont Blanc in 1779 and the Jungfrau in 1811. Mountaineering first became a popular pursuit after the founding of the English Alpine Club in 1857, the first of several

The mighty Matterhorn looms over a flower meadow in the Valais region.

clubs that brought together climbers from across Europe. The next 20 years marked the golden age of alpinism, with many first ascents, including the Eiger in 1858, the Weisshorn in 1861, and the Matterhorn in 1865.

Switzerland's largest mountaineering club, the Swiss Alpine Club (*Monbijoustrasse 61, Bern, tel 031/370 1818, www.sac-cas.ch*), was founded in 1863. As rough camping is prohibited, the club maintains 150 mountain huts to provide accommodation for hikers and climbers at high altitudes. Facilities vary from hut to hut, but all offer cheap, simple accommodation, and some offer a hot meal and shower facilities. Smaller, more remote huts are often unsupervised and rely on honesty for payment.

Sure-footed wild ibex are sometimes encountered in the Alps.

The Alps: The Alps form one of the largest and highest mountain ranges in the world, stretching in an arch from Slovenia in the east, through Austria, Germany, Italy, Liechtenstein, and Switzerland to France in the west. The Swiss Alps form the centerpiece of the range. They contain Europe's highest elevations (with the exception of France's Mont Blanc), with approximately 100 peaks close to or higher than 13,125 feet (4,000 m) above sea level.

These high mountain areas are generally sparsely populated, in comparison with the Swiss plateau. However, many mountain resorts have been developed, and a comprehensive network of trains, cog railways, buses, and aerial cable cars provides easy access to high altitudes. Mountains are the nation's main tourist attraction, in summer for hiking and climbing and especially during winter months for skiing and snow sports, in such world-famous resorts as Wengen, Zermatt, Saint Moritz, Davos, Klosters, and Verbier.

The Alps are made up of three main altitudinal zones. Below the treeline, the sub-alpine zone contains most of the mountain villages and hamlets. The forests here consist mainly of deciduous trees at lower elevations, giving way to conifers such as larch and

arolla pine from around 3,900 feet (1,200 m). The upper limit of the zone varies regionally, but is at about 5,900 feet (1,800 m) on the north side of the Alps and about 6,560 feet (2,000 m) on the south side. In the second—Alpine—zone, above the treeline, bushes and scrub give way to meadows of grasses and mountain flowers which make excellent grazing pastures. The extent of this zone is determined by the altitude of the first permanent snow and varies from region to region from 9,190 to 10,500 feet (2,800 to 3,200 m). The final, glacial, zone is the area of permanent snow and ice. There are no settlements here except high-altitude research stations, including the Jungfraujoch's Sphinx Observatory and the astronomical observatories near the Matterhorn at Gornergrat.

Alpine Passes & Tunnels

The lofty *alpenpässe* (mountain passes) offer some of the nation's most grandiose scenery for those willing to navigate their windy, narrow, and circuitous routes. With Switzerland's strategic location at the crossroads of Europe, these high mountain passes—including the Great St. Bernard (see pp. 150–151), the Simplon, and St. Gotthard passes—were first constructed centuries ago to link northern and southern Europe. Most routes are only passable from April or May to October depending on the snowfall, but some—including the Bernina, Maloja, Lenzeheide, and Simplon passes—stay open all year. Nowadays, however, most possess impressive road and/or rail tunnels through the mountains to reduce mountain traffic volume and journey times; each is an impressive feat of engineering. The very first tunnel in the Alps, the Urnerloch, was built in 1708 to ease the journey over the St. Gotthard Pass. It was just 210 feet (64 m) long. The first road tunnel through a pass was the Great St. Bernard in 1964. The 10.5-mile (17 km) Gotthard railway tunnel, bored in 1881, was the longest tunnel of its kind until 2007 when the 21.5-mile (34.6 km) Lötschberg base tunnel was opened. To date, it is the longest land tunnel in the world, accommodating both passenger and freight trains. Work on the Gotthard base tunnel is now underway. Due to open in 2016, it will be 35 miles (57 km) long. Both are part of the NRLA (New Railway Link through the Alps) project aimed at building faster north-south train connections across the Swiss Alps. Air pollution has long been a major concern, and recent changes in Swiss legislation have attempted to halt road building in the Alps and shift transportation policy off the transalpine roads and onto rail transport. Two major Alptransit rail links will help to accomplish these environmental goals.

> **The lofty *alpenpässe* ... offer some of the nation's most grandiose scenery for those willing to navigate their winding, narrow, and circuitous routes.**

Rivers & Lakes

Switzerland boasts more than 20,000 miles (32,000 km) of rivers and streams and 521 square miles (1,349 sq km) of lakes. The landscape is carved up by the great valleys of the Rhône in Valais; the Rhine and the Inn in Graubünden; and the Ticino in Ticino canton. Each river drains into a different sea: the Rhine to the North Sea; the Inn to the Black Sea; the Rhône to the Mediterranean; and the Ticino (which joins the Po River in northern Italy) runs down to the Adriatic Sea. Switzerland's lakes range from extensive Lake Geneva and Bodensee to hundreds of tiny crystal-clear lakes in the mountains. Fishing is permitted in most waters. Licenses are required, and are available through local tourist offices or municipal authorities.

Some of the larger lakes have been dammed to drive the water turbines of hydroelectric power plants, Switzerland's most efficient natural resource. These high mountain reservoirs, such as the Lac de Mauvoisin in the upper Val de Bagnes (see sidebar p. 160), are stunning feats of engineering, usually set in steep-sided rocky valleys. More than 60 percent of the nation's electricity is produced by hydroelectric power; making Switzerland one of the greenest countries in Europe. Most of the nation's remaining energy needs are met by nuclear power. The nation began researching nuclear energy (for purely peaceful purposes, of course) in the late 1950s and had developed its first nuclear power plant by 1969. Today, Switzerland remains at the forefront of hydroelectric and nuclear power development. In a national referendum in 2003, Swiss voters firmly rejected proposals to phase out nuclear power by 2014. With few material resources, the government adopted a new energy policy strategy in 2007, emphasizing the need to replace existing nuclear units with new power plants

Exploring the Countryside by "Yellow Class"

The Swiss travel system is world-famous with its efficient network of trains, funiculars, and aerial cable cars. Even so, with such mountainous terrain, not every town or village can be reached by train. Instead, bright yellow PostBuses, operated by Swiss Post, take passengers up steep mountainsides, over vertiginous passes, and to hamlets tucked at the ends of the remotest valleys—often to hidden areas that the vast majority of tourists never see.

The PostAuto (PostBus) service was established in June 1906, when three polished yellow vehicles were introduced to replace the horse-drawn carriages of the time. After initial skepticism, the vehicles soon gained an excellent reputation. More vehicles were added, the network was extended, and the PostBus

service reached its heyday between the two World Wars. Now, every village is serviced by distinctive buttercup-yellow PostBuses with their unmistakable three-tone horn (based on Italian composer Rossini's *William Tell* overture). Their network of 783 routes covers more miles than the Swiss railroad and carries more than 115 million passengers a year.

The PostBus network is an ideal way to access some of the most remote nature-watching sites. One example is the Marmot Trail (*Val Bregalga, Graubünden*), which is reached by the service between Avers and Juf, and where these cute mammals can be watched during the summer. Check Das Offizielle Kursbuch (official timetable; www.post.ch) for routes, timetable information, and money-saving day passes and travel tickets.

by 2030 to avoid a future energy gap. Switzerland does have some coal, but has to import most raw materials due to its lack of natural resources.

Climate

Switzerland offers a surprising variety of climates. The Atlantic Ocean influences the weather in the west, bringing winds, moisture, and rainfall, while eastern areas tend to have less rain, more sun, and higher temperatures. In balmy Ticino, the climate is warmer and almost Mediterranean, but precipitation is high due to the immediate vicinity of the Alps to the north. Since they are at very high altitudes, temperatures in the high Alpine regions are usually lower than in the northern and Mittelland regions, with more snowfall in winter and cooler summers.

Summer in the Alps is the best time for hiking, mountain biking, and other outdoor sports amid a profusion of wildflowers.

Switzerland has four distinct seasons, each with its own charm and appeal for travelers. Spring (March–May) is mild but sometimes changeable and rainy. It is nonetheless an ideal time to visit, before the summer crowds arrive. The snow is melting, the rivers and waterfalls are at their most dramatic, the countryside is lush and green, and the mountains still have their winter caps of snow. Summer (June–August) tends to be warm and dry, with temperatures averaging around 71°F (22°C) in the lower valleys and cities. This is the season of balmy evenings, al fresco dining, and swimming in the lakes. In the mountains, the weather is slightly cooler, with the zero line (32°F/0°C) sometimes as high as 13,124 feet (4,000 m). Summer in the Alps is the best time for hiking, mountain biking, and other outdoor sports amid a profusion of wildflowers. The Alpine passes are open, making it easy to explore the more isolated villages and valleys. However, the mountains are prone to sudden, unpredictable weather changes, even in summer, so always check a local forecast before setting out.

In the fall (September–November), days are frequently crisp, clear, and sunny but also quite a bit cooler than in summer, with the zero line dropping to around 6,560 feet (2,000 m) in the mountains. This is a popular time to visit the countryside for its russet and gold colors. The cities are generally quieter after the main summer tourist throngs have departed, making sightseeing more enjoyable. Winter (December–February), with its heavy Alpine snowfalls, beckons the winter sports enthusiasts heading to the slopes for some of Europe's best skiing (see pp. 246–247). Temperatures often drop below 32°F (0°C) throughout the land, bringing an occasional dusting of snow to settlements at lower elevations, too.

Environmental Protection

The Swiss have some of the world's most rigorous environmental laws. One of the world's earliest acts of environmental legislation was the Swiss Federal Forestry Law of 1876 prohibiting deforestation and, as a direct consequence, the forested areas of the nation have been expanding for more than one hundred years. The Swiss also lead the world in recycling (see pp. 21–22), and various effective environmental groups have been set up over the years, including the Swiss League for the Protection of Nature, established in 1909, and the Swiss Foundation for the Protection and Care of the Landscape, founded in 1970. ■

History

Given its neutral, peacemaking status in the modern world, it may come as a surprise to discover Switzerland boasts a surprisingly colorful past, with centuries of border disputes and internal conflicts. The history of human settlement in Switzerland dates back to the Stone Age from when various bones and flint tools have been found in the regions of Neuchâtel, Appenzell, and Schaffhausen near the Rhine.

The Romans & the Dark Ages

Around 1500 B.C. Celtic Rhaetian and Helvetii tribes settled on the Swiss plateau and on the banks of Lake Geneva. The Romans, led by Julius Caesar, arrived around 50 B.C. and remained until about A.D. 400. They founded settlements at Basel, Chur, Geneva, Lausanne, and Zürich, and built a line of fortifications along the Rhine to protect their new territory. Keen to control the Alps, Caesar attempted to open the Great St. Bernard Pass but failed, due to robust opposition by the local Veragri tribe. His successor, Augustus, succeeded in eventually gaining control over the Alpine region, thereby opening up a direct route from Rome to Gaul. The Roman era was one of peace and prosperity, as native tribes and Roman officials lived side by side. Agriculture flourished; and the Romans introduced such luxuries as vines, baths, and underfloor heating, utterly Romanizing the country and conferring on its citizens the right to vote.

> The Romans introduced such luxuries as vines, baths, and underfloor heating, utterly Romanizing the country.

By the fourth century A.D., however, the Romans were coming under increasing pressure from Germanic tribes that were migrating south. Finally, in A.D. 401, the Romans decided their position was no longer viable, and they retreated south of the Alps. During the next few centuries, Switzerland's population was supplemented by migrants from neighboring regions. The western territories were home to the Latin-speaking Burgundians, while the northern and central regions were populated by Germanic Alemans. In this way, the divisions of language seen in modern-day Switzerland started to develop. Indeed, the border between the Burgundian territory and the Alemanic lands survives today as the frontier between French- and German-speaking Switzerland (see p. 19). Rhaetia, in the south, maintained its Roman traditions and linguistic links longer than the rest of the country, and to this day a Latin-based dialect, Romansh (see p. 49), is still spoken in some parts of Graubünden. During the Dark Ages (from around 500–1000) Switzerland was a predominantly feudal society, where ownership of both the land and its inhabitants was divided between noblemen and the church. The influence of Christianity increased during this time, especially after Charlemagne (Charles the Great, 742–814) absorbed the country into his Holy Roman Empire, leading to the founding of numerous monasteries, including those still flourishing at Einsiedeln, Engelberg, Romainmôtier, and St. Gallen.

Basel's 16th-century City Hall

RENOVATUM ET AMPLI
FICATUM ANNO DOMINI
MDCCCCI

The Middle Ages

Switzerland thrived in medieval times, as various noble dynasties founded towns and fortresses to show off their wealth and assert control. The Zähringen family founded Bern, Fribourg, and Murten and constructed a castle at Thun. The Savoys built a series of castles around Lake Geneva, including the celebrated Château de Chillon. The Habsburgs, who later came to rule most of Europe, established their mighty fortress in the Aargau.

In 1220, the road over the St. Gotthard Pass was opened for trade, establishing a fast route from the Mediterranean to northern Europe. Overnight, such communities as Uri and Schwyz, situated on the northern approaches to the pass, became trading centers of great strategic importance. This sparked a series of local disputes over land ownership and government rebellions, which eventually forced the Holy Roman Emperor to intervene, granting to Uri in 1231 (and to Schwyz nine years later) the privilege of freedom from feudal rule. In 1273, Rudolph I of the Habsburg dynasty became Holy Roman Emperor. He heavy-handedly took control of much of northern Switzerland, introducing heavy tax demands and creating strong resentment among the Swiss.

The Pontifical Swiss Guard

Swiss mercenary soldiers were first invited to guard the Vatican in Rome by Pope Julius II in 1506. On January 22 that year, 150 mercenary soldiers from the canton of Uri entered the Vatican for the first time, to be blessed by, and to swear an oath of loyalty to, the Pope. Their much-photographed uniform—a flamboyant striped jacket, doublet, and hose in the Medici colors of blue, red, and yellow with a metal morion helmet adorned with an ostrich-feather—has changed little over the centuries. The Swiss soldiers at the gates of the Vatican still wear this uniform.

Birth of the Swiss Nation

The year 1291 is one of the most important dates in Swiss history, marking the start of the Swiss Confederation. It is the year that the mighty Habsburg ruler Rudolph died and the people of Switzerland took it upon themselves to secure their own destiny. Rudolph's death provoked a variety of popular revolts which, in turn, led to the forging of new partnerships between a number of Swiss communities to safeguard against an uncertain future. The most important of the alliances forged that year was the League of the Three Forest Cantons, which brought together Uri, Schwyz, and Unterwalden. This union of three wealthy and powerful cantons created a political force that would later become the core of the Swiss Confederation. The events of this period are shrouded somewhat by patriotic myths and legends, such as that of William Tell (see pp. 182–183), which make it hard to be sure about any of the details. Nonetheless, it is widely agreed that the representatives of Uri, Schwyz, and Unterwalden forged the alliance during a meeting at the Rütli Meadow on the western shore of the Urnersee.

The combined armies of the three forest cantons were a formidable military force. In 1315 they secured a historic victory at the Battle of Morgarten, in which they defeated a much larger Habsburg army that had been sent to quash the increasing tide of Swiss nationalism. Thereafter, the three cantons' union was recorded in the Federal Charter as the "Swiss Confederation." They collectively became known as Schwyzers; and the nation became known as Schwyz. Support grew steadily over the next two centuries, as more and more communities signed their pledge of eternal mutual defense and became part of the Swiss Confederation. Its Latin name, *Confoederatio Helvetica,* survives to this day in the "CH" abbreviation used to denote Switzerland. The Habsburgs then tried to force the canton of Luzern to fight the Schwyzers, but instead the lakeside neighbors joined the Confederation in 1332. The Habsburgs withdrew altogether by about 1350. Even in areas that hadn't yet joined the Confederation, the feudal system was beginning to collapse. In Zürich, for example, the newly founded workers' guilds had already overthrown the city's ruling nobility by the time they joined the Confederation in 1351. They were followed by Glarus and Zug in 1352; Bern in 1353; and Fribourg and Solothurn in 1481.

[The shock defeat at the Battle of Marignano in 1515 caused the Swiss] to withdraw from the international scene and declare their nation's neutrality.

As the Confederation grew, so did its military prowess. One noteworthy victory, in the Swabian War of 1499, brought complete Swiss independence from the Holy Roman Emperor Maximilian I. In 1512 as allies of Pope Julius II, they helped to shape Italy's destiny and were granted the title of "Defenders of the Church's freedom" by the Pope. Basel and Schaffhausen joined the Confederation in 1501, followed by the two tiny half-cantons of Appenzell in 1513. The first Swiss parliament—the Diet—was formed in Baden and, from the start, it introduced a system of government based on the peoples' vote.

In 1515, Swiss troops were caught short in the battle of Marignano, losing to a combined French and Venetian force. This shocking defeat prompted the Swiss to withdraw from the international scene and declare their nation's neutrality for the first time. For several centuries afterward, the highly-acclaimed Helvetian troops—feared throughout Europe for their loyalty and bravery—were used solely for mercenary purposes. Some were even employed to train the French and Spanish armies. Given the precarious economic conditions of the times, there was extensive poverty in Switzerland. Becoming a mercenary soldier abroad was not only commonplace but was also one of the most profitable jobs. Regarded as the best troops of the time, and always in demand, Swiss mercenaries played a key role in the creation of modern Europe. The tradition is maintained by the Swiss Guard who protect the Pope (see sidebar opposite).

The Reformation

The 16th century was a time of religious discontent in Western Europe. Beginning with the rise of Martin Luther (1483–1546) in Germany, Protestants proposed a "reformation" of the Catholic Church and denounced the rule of the Pope. Christendom became divided. A lay priest, Huldrych Zwingli (1484–1531), led the Swiss Reformation from the Grossmünster (cathedral) in Zürich. He translated the Bible into Swiss-German and set about changing church rituals with his new Protestantism. His motto "pray and work" was to have a profound effect on the development of modern Switzerland, as his beliefs were soon adopted in Zürich, Basel, Bern, and half the nation's cantons. The more conservative rural cantons of central Switzerland remained staunchly Catholic, causing a split in the country. This rift was exacerbated by Zwingli's controversial proposal to reorganize the

The French-born Protestant leader John Calvin refuses Holy Communion to his opponents (the "libertines") in Saint Peter's Cathedral, Geneva, around 1550.

Confederation under the twin city leadership of Zürich and Bern. This ignited a vicious sectarian conflict within Switzerland that saw the Catholic and Protestant cantons turn against each other. Zwingli was killed during a battle between Zürich and Schwyz in 1484. The Reformation continued to spread, spurred on by the arrival of the priest John Calvin (1509–1564), who was fleeing Catholic reprisals in France, in Geneva of 1536. With the spread of Calvinist doctrine, Geneva soon became one of the most zealous strongholds of Protestantism in Europe, regarding itself as the New Jerusalem. In a bid to preserve Catholic territory and reassert Catholic rights, a counter-reformation was launched in the 1550s and 1560s, but the progressive Protestant cities still held sway, thanks to their political and economic authority. In the end a peace treaty was signed that enabled the confederates to stay together by allowing each canton to practice its own faith. In 1597 Appenzell split into two half-cantons, one Protestant and one Catholic, in order to retain their religious independence. Nonetheless, during the early part of the 17th century, no new regions were admitted into the Confederation for fear they would upset the delicate balance between Catholic and Protestant cantons. Today 55 percent of the Swiss consider themselves Protestant, and 43 percent Catholic.

Economic Boom & Neutrality

The nation's domestic tolerance was to pay off. During the Thirty Years War of 1618–1648 the Swiss were unable to decide who to support in the various conflicts, and so remained neutral. As civil wars raged all around them, the members of the Confederation realized that, despite their ideological differences, they were stronger if they remained within their alliance rather than going it alone. This solidarity resulted in an agreed policy of neutrality. Indeed, the Treaty of Westphalia, which ended the 30-year conflict, officially acknowledged that Switzerland was a neutral state, independent from the Holy Roman Empire.

At the same time, the nation was experiencing an economic boom, driven by the thriving textile industry in the northeast. Once again, it relied on tolerance and cooperation, with predominantly Protestant merchants in the cities supplying raw materials to mostly Catholic peasants in the countryside who created the products before delivering them to city merchants for trade or export. During the 18th century, Geneva and Zürich enjoyed a golden age, as industries such as watchmaking and banking flourished. The second half of the century saw the liberal Enlightenment replace the rigorous ideals of Calvinism. The famous Swiss-born writer and philosopher Jean-Jacques Rousseau (1712–1778) was living in Geneva at this time. His writings, extolling universal liberty and equality, sowed the seeds of the American and French Revolutions.

In 1789, at the start of the French Revolution, Geneva and some other key parts of western Switzerland became annexed to France. Ten years later, the French under Napoleon Bonaparte (1769–1821) overran Switzerland, seizing Bern and Zürich. Within a week, the centuries-old cantonal system of the Confederation was dissolved, replaced by Napoleon's short-lived Helvetic Republic. The Swiss soon rebelled against its centralized government, resulting in a civil war which forced Napoleon to withdraw his troops from the country. In 1803, he reinstated the former confederation of cantons, but with France retaining overall jurisdiction. At this time the old Confederation was augmented by the cantons of Aargau, St. Gallen, Graubünden, Thurgau, Ticino, and Vaud (which had previously been considered to be allies or territories, rather than full members). When Napoleon fell from power at the Battle of Waterloo in 1815, the Swiss returned to the old system, joined by the cantons of Geneva, Neuchâtel, and Valais. In the aftermath of Napoleon's defeat European leaders fixed the present borders of Switzerland and formally acknowledged the nation's independence and neutrality.

> **The members of the Confederation realized that . . . they were stronger if they remained within their alliance.**

Establishing the Constitution

Switzerland remained prosperous in the early 19th century, when a rail network was established and the banking system flourished. However, in 1847 seven Catholic cantons attempted to sever themselves from the rest of the country. This so-called Sonderbund ("separate alliance") threatened to destabilize the entire country. The rebellion was quickly thwarted by the federal army under the leadership of General Henri Dufour (1787–1875). The postwar Federal Constitution of 1848 emulated that of the United States of America, with 25 more or less autonomous cantons. By dividing power between the cantons, it defused the deeply rooted Catholic fears of Protestant domination. For the first time, Switzerland had a central government, with a directly elected parliament seated in the capital of Bern. The cantons reluctantly relinquished their rights to print money, run postal services, and levy customs duties, transferring them to the centralized government, but they maintained legislative and executive control over local matters. In 1874 the constitution was revised as Swiss citizens formally adopted the referendum for local, cantonal, and national matters, in a move toward greater democracy. This same constitution (further revised in 1999) still prevails today.

In the second half of the 19th century, Switzerland's internationally recognized independence and neutrality led to it being associated with several important humanitarian movements. The first, and best known, of these was the Red Cross, founded in Geneva in 1863 by Swiss businessman Henri Dunant (1828–1910). The same spirit of humanitarianism led to the development of the first Geneva Convention in 1864, which established rules for the humane treatment of prisoners of war and refugees. At the same time, Switzerland's economy was booming thanks to the development of tourism in the Alps (see pp. 26–27).

Switzerland & the World Wars

Switzerland remained officially neutral in World War I, limiting its involvement in hostilities to the deployment of Red Cross units. The allegiances of the Swiss people, however, were sharply divided along linguistic lines, with many German-

EXPERIENCE: Hiking the Historic Swiss Path

The *Weg der Schweiz* or **Swiss Path** (www .weg-der-schweiz.ch) is an ingenious long-distance hiking route, inaugurated in 1991 to commemorate the 700th anniversary of the founding of the Swiss Confederation with the signing of an oath of eternal alliance between the cantons of Uri, Schwyz, and Unterwalden.

The 22-mile (36 km) trail aptly starts at the **Rütli Meadow**—the symbolic birthplace of Switzerland—and circumnavigates the Urnersee (Lake Uri), ending at the lakeside village of **Brunnen.** The path is in 26 sections, each representing a different canton. Along the path you'll see stone plaques identifying each canton in the order in which they joined the Confederation. The length of each section is directly proportionate to the size of each individual canton's population, so that every fifth of an inch (5 mm) of your

route represents one Swiss citizen. The longest section—representing Zürich, the most densely-populated canton—is 3.8 miles (6.1 km), while the tiny, sparsely inhabited half-canton of Appenzell Inner-Rhoden is just 233 feet (71 m) in length.

The walk is clearly indicated by yellow markers and is easily manageable in two days, with an overnight stop at Flüelen, or at Altdorf—the venue of William Tell's legendary apple-shooting stunt (see pp. 182–183). Alternatively, it can be broken down into smaller sections: Rütli to Bauen (5 miles/8 km, initial climb, then undulating, 3 hours); Bauen to Flüelen (7 miles/12 km, flat, 2.75 hours); Flüelen to Sisikon (5 miles/8 km, mostly flat, 2.5 hours); and Sisikon to Brunnen (5 miles/ 8 km, up and down, 5.5 hours). Local tourist offices stock English-language guide maps of the route.

German soldiers close the border between Switzerland and France at Pontarlier in 1940.

speaking Swiss publicly supporting Germany and Austria-Hungary. This resulted
in considerable tension between Switzerland's two biggest linguistic communities. The biggest impact the war had on Swiss society, however, was the influx of
refugees from elsewhere in Europe. These included the artists who established the
Dada movement (see p. 47), as well as the Russian communist agitators Vladimir
Lenin (1870–1924) and Leon Trotsky (1879–1940), who both took up temporary
residence in Zürich in 1914. In November 1918, news of the Russian Revolution
inspired Swiss workers to call a general strike—the first and only one in the history
of the nation. With Switzerland at a standstill, the Federal Council was forced to
accept some of the strikers' demands, including an extensive welfare system and
the adoption of proportional representation in national elections. After the war, in
1919 Switzerland joined the League of Nations as a neutral member on a purely
non-military basis, and subsequently provided space for the League's headquarters
in Geneva.

Europe's economic boom of the 1920s and the ensuing depression of the 1930s
did not leave Switzerland untouched. With Hitler's rise to power in Germany and the
prospect of war increasingly likely, Switzerland devalued the franc in 1936 to boost
the economy, and attempted to assert its national identity. It endorsed the status of
Romansh as a national language, and authorized the official usage of Swiss-German
in an attempt to distance itself from the High German of the Third Reich. It also set
up anonymous numbered bank accounts to protect the savings of German Jews
from the grasp of the Nazis. Despite the emergence of various political factions, the
commander-in-chief of the Swiss army, General Henri Guisan, invited all his officers to

the Rütli Meadow on 25 July 1940 to reaffirm the Swiss commitment to neutrality and resistance, and to establish the mindset of "Fortress Switzerland." As a consequence, and apart from a handful of accidental bombings, Switzerland remained remarkably unscathed during World War II, despite being surrounded by warring nations. It suited both allied forces and Nazi Germany to have a neutral nation in the midst of the conflict through which they could negotiate with each other.

Switzerland as a Special Case

The term *Sonderfall Schweiz* (Switzerland as a Special Case) was often used to refer to the nation during the second half of the 20th century, as Switzerland basked smugly in the glory of its insular neutrality and political isolationism.

> **Having avoided invasion in the world wars, its population believed themselves to be superior to the rest of Europe.**

Having avoided invasion in the world wars, its population believed themselves to be superior to the rest of Europe. While the rest of Europe licked its wounds, the Swiss economy continued to thrive, unemployment was virtually eradicated, and most citizens grew in prosperity, enjoying a high standard of living as one of the world's richest and most respected nations. The Geneva Convention's foundations of international humanitarian law led to the city becoming the European headquarters of the United Nations in 1945, even though its neutrality led it to decline membership. The headquarters of the World Health Organization was also founded in Geneva in 1948.

It was not until the 1980s and 1990s that an introverted, staid, but very affluent, Switzerland finally fell into line with other more forward-looking European countries. This was typified by the launch of Swatch in 1983, which catapulted the traditional watchmaking industry into the 21st century with its cutting-edge designs. Women were finally granted the vote in the canton of Appenzell Innerhoden in 1991 (see p. 17).

In the 1990s a series of banking scandals rocked the very bedrock of Swiss economic society when it was revealed that vast fortunes had been lying dormant in prewar accounts belonging to Holocaust victims and survivors, without any real attempt to trace their owners. After considerable bad press, the three largest banks—Union Bank of Switzerland, Swiss Bank Corporation, and Credit Suisse—ended up having to pay $1.25 billion in compensation to the families of Holocaust survivors. It was later revealed that Switzerland's wartime role was highly controversial in more ways than one. Although Switzerland provided a safe haven for hundreds of wartime refugees, it has subsequently been criticized for turning thousands of Jews back at the border to certain death; for supplying ammunition to the Third Reich in exchange for essential raw materials; and for harboring Nazi assets in anonymous accounts at certain Swiss banks. These events marked the demise of *Sonderfall Schweiz.*

A 21st-century Nation

The new Switzerland that has emerged in the 21st century is a more modest, humble country. In 2001, Swiss pride and self-confidence was further shaken by the financial collapse of the national airline and iconic company Swissair. In 2002, a national referendum finally voted (with a majority of just 54.6 percent) to join the United Nations as its 190th member state—a hugely significant event, as it marked the end of centuries of Swiss isolation. Today's Switzerland still enjoys its financial role as a tax haven and its political status of neutrality. Zürich leads the world in banking affairs; the country leads the world's pharmaceutical industry; while Geneva continues to play a key role in world affairs with its numerous international organizations. Swiss asylum and immigration laws remain highly contentious, however, and possible membership in the EU remains the subject of heated debate, with repeated rejections at national referenda. ■

The Celestial Sphere, sculpted by Paul Manship, outside the Palais des Nations, Geneva

Food & Drink

Swiss cuisine remains a well-kept secret. In this land bordered by France, Italy, Austria, and Germany, the very best culinary traditions and specialties from each of these countries have been absorbed into the Swiss kitchen. Alongside these dishes are local recipes steeped in the traditions of the Swiss people.

Swiss cooking is closely linked with the geographical characteristics of the country. In the high Alps, a unique Swiss style of cuisine has developed. This is the simple yet nourishing *cuisine de terroir* (country cooking), which has grown both out of the agriculture sustainable on the mountains and the locals' need to eat heartily to withstand the hard winters. In more remote valleys, the farmers and mountain folk will often make do with a nourishing bowl of soup, or just one course, or even simply a dessert. The cows on the mountain pastures provide rich, creamy milk for countless dairy-based specialties and a remarkable variety of cheeses, many of which are still traditionally made and preserved.

Typical dishes in this region include comfort foods like *älpler magrone* (macaroni and cheese served with bacon, onions, puréed apples, and cinnamon); *rösti* (similar to hash browns); and *birchermüseli* (oats, nuts, and fresh fruit blended with yogurt into a mousse-like consistency, and generally eaten as a daytime snack). The most Swiss of these comfort foods, however, are hot melted cheese fondues and *raclette*—melted cheese piled high on new potatoes, pickles, and pearl onions. In the central and southern valleys many dishes are based on potatoes, pasta, or dumplings, such as *spätzli* or *knöpfli* (tiny noodles made using flour, eggs, and water), which are served either as a substantial dish with cream and melted cheese or, more often, as an accompaniment to a sauced dish.

Swiss Cheeses

The Swiss have been making cheese for thousands of years. Indeed, by the time Roman travelers described Swiss cheesemaking, it would seem that it was already an important local industry. Today there are 450 officially recognized varieties of Swiss cheese, ranging from the hard and eye-wateringly powerful **sbrinz** (which medieval physicians prescribed as medicine) to soft, mild **vacherin mont d'or** (made in the Jura Mountains). The best known types of Swiss cheese are **emmentaler,** the holey firm cheese that is most commonly associated with the country; **gruyère,** a slightly salty cheese made in western Switzerland; and the dense, rich **appenzeller,** made in the northeastern Appenzellerland region.

Foreign Influences

Neighboring countries have also considerably influenced Swiss cooking. Step into any local supermarket and, alongside an assortment of high-quality breads, cheeses, wines, and vegetables, you will be impressed by the range of produce from France, Germany, Austria, and Italy. Those cantons closest to Germany and Austria feature numerous meat-heavy dishes—often ancient recipes originating in poor, remote regions—such as *weisswurst* (white veal sausages) and *leberknodli* (liver dumplings), and St. Gallen's ubiquitous *schublig* (sausages baked in bread dough).

Geneva and surrounding French-speaking cantons are influenced by the cuisine of France. Geneva, the nation's culinary capital, offers a host of bistros and restaurants serving French-style haute cuisine. However, nowhere is Swiss cuisine more influenced by its international

A selection of Swiss cheeses in Chas Barmettler, Luzern

neighbors than in Ticino. The canton's proximity to the northern Italian regions of Lombardy and Piedmont, and its geographical isolation from the rest of Switzerland by the Alps, has led to the creation of an entirely different cuisine, based on such wholesome staples as pasta, polenta, potato gnocchi, and risotto rather than fondue and raclette. Rabbit, salami, and *cicitt* (goat sausages) are local delicacies, but save room for *amaretti* (almond macaroons), chestnut vermicelli, *torta di pane* (bread cake), and other mouthwatering desserts.

Regional Specialties

Many other cantons have also developed distinctive regional dishes. Soups are especially popular, and often a meal in themselves, so keep an eye out for such specialties as *basler mehlsuppe* (onion soup thickened with toasted brown flour); *appenzeller bierrahmsuppe mit käseplätzchen* (beer soup with cheese croutons); *busseca* (similar to minestrone but with tripe as the main ingredient) from Ticino; *kabissuppe* (rice and cabbage soup) in Schwyz; and Fribourg's famous *soupe de châlet* (chalet soup), containing potatoes, cream, cheese, and macaroni.

Sausages form another staple with regional variants, with the pork-and-beef *cervelat* considered the "national sausage." Try also the *genevois longeole* (pork with wild fennel and garlic); veal-and-pork *emmentalerli* sausages; and Lausanne's *papet vaudois* (mildly smoked pork and beef sausage, served on a bed of leeks and potatoes). Valais is especially rich in culinary specialties. It is the most important wine canton

and is also renowned for its huge selection of mountain cheeses and the finely-cut *viande séchée* (air-dried beef), which is marinated in a brine containing aromatic spices and mountain herbs before being pressed between wooden planks and left to dry in the mountain air.

With all of Switzerland's lakes and rivers, it's no wonder fish features on most menus. Mountain streams are home to abundant trout, and the Rhine's *rheinäsche* (grayling) is delicious when baked. Also quite tasty is the *omble chevalier*, a salmon-like fish also known as char, and of course Lake Geneva's perch fillets—reputedly the nation's tastiest fish and a Swiss delicacy. The numerous lakes of central Switzerland provide an opportunity to try some lesser-known white fish such as the bondelle, féra, coregonus, and dace.

A Sweet Tooth

Switzerland's dairy produce provides the foundations for its countless gooey desserts and rich, flaky pastries and cookies. There

---

EXPERIENCE: Follow a Wine Trail

Many wine-producing villages have community cellars to showcase the local reserve, and some regions offer special walking routes and tasting trails. Here are some of the best:

The 20-mile (32 km) **Lavaux Vineyard Trail** (Lausanne to Villeneuve), with its terraced vineyards, affords unrivalled vistas of Lake Geneva with the Alps beyond. A special wine train, the Lavaux Express, meanders from village to village (see p. 83; *www.lavauxexpress.ch*).

The well-signed **Valais Wine Trail** (46 miles/74 km, Martigny to Leuk) has tasting opportunities at more than 150 wine cellars en route. There are also parallel cycling and driving routes.

Hikers on the **Wy-Erläbnis** (Wine Experience, 1.8 miles/3 km, Buus to

Maisprach, near Basel; *www.daswyerlaebnis .ch*) can stop to savor local wines and hors d'oeuvres.

On the family-friendly **Vully Wine Trail** (3 miles/5 km, Sugiez-Môtier), children enjoy an educational hike around Lake Murten with Wistenlach Vineyard's mascot, Viny, while parents enjoy a glass of wine.

The 90-minute **Werdenberg Grape Trail** ("Trübliweg," 3 miles/5 km, Werdenberg, near Liechtenstein) leads visitors past nine illustrated information stations about viticulture.

The first of three **Mendrisiotto Wine Trails** (7.5 miles/12 km, circular walk from Mendrisio) traverses the rolling vine-clad hills of Ticino at the southern end of Lake Lugano (see pp. 262–263).

Sealing the bottom of a wine cask in a Rigi cooperage

are few cantons that don't have a unique pastry to commemorate a local historical or religious event. Most noteworthy are Luzern's *lebkuchen*–a spiced Christmas cookie made with treacle and candied fruit–and Geneva's *tarte aux poires* (a kind of pear flan), which is specially made for the celebration of L'Escalade. Fruit tarts show the influence of French patisserie: Try the cherry cake in Basel, elderberry syrup tart in Bern, and the *zugerkirschtorte* (a tart laced with cherry brandy) in Zug.

Wine or Beer?

Swiss wine, while exceptional, is rarely found internationally simply because local demand for it is so high. At least 50 varieties of grape are cultivated here, with local specialties naturally varying according to climate and altitude. Some are unique to Switzerland, such as Petite Arvine, Completer, and Amigne whites, and Humagne Rouge and Cornalin reds (see www.swisswine.ch).

The main wine-growing areas are in Vaud and Valais. Valaisan wines include the well-known Fendant dry white and Dôle smooth reds. Along the northern slopes of Lake Geneva, La Côte and Le Lavaux vineyards produce subtle Chasselas white wines and fruity Pinot Noir reds. Ticino, with its mild Mediterranean climate, produces some outstanding red Merlots. In recent years, the slightly sparkling white wines of Bodensee and the Blaugunder reds of Schaffhausen have also gained a big following.

The Swiss take pride in their beers, especially in German-speaking regions. Feldschlösschen is the nation's largest brewer, while the oldest is St. Gallen's Schützengarten–whose dark, slightly sweet *schwarzer bär* beer is worth a try. Spirits are popular, and include schnapps, Xellent triple-distilled vodka (made with Swiss rye and Alpine glacier water), and the potent *appenzeller alpenbitter* (Alpine bitters, produced from the essence of 67 different flowers). Fruit liqueurs are often served as a digestif. Try *kirsche* (made from cherry pits), *williamine* (from pears), *damassine* (from prunes), *pflümli* (from plums), or fiery *marc* (which is made from grape skins).

Arts & Folklore

As a country Switzerland manages to be both socially conservative and culturally liberal. While it is in general a rather staid country with a strong sense of tradition, it encourages cultural innovation and experimentation. As a result visitors to Switzerland can experience everything from modern performance art to traditional rural entertainments.

Art

Switzerland has the most museums per capita of any country in the world—nearly a thousand in total. Thanks to an efficient funding system, recent decades have seen the nation's established institutions joined by a variety of quirky, independent art

"Safari Death Moscow" (1989) by the artist AurelioZen, in Basel's Museum Tinguely

galleries and private collections. According to Switzerland Tourism, it is possible to find an art institution worth visiting every 18 miles (30 km) between Geneva and St. Gallen. From west to east, top venues include the Musée d'Art et d'Histoire in Geneva; Fondation Pierre Gianadda in Martigny; the Kunstmuseum, Kunsthalle, and Fondation Beyler in Basel; Bern's Zentrum Paul Klee; the Sammlung Rosengart in Luzern; Zürich's Kunstmuseum; and the Oskar Reinhart collections in Winterthur.

Switzerland has also been the home of many notable artists, with prominent figures in almost every artistic epoch hailing from one of the cantons. Significant figures in the history of Swiss art include Konrad Witz (1400–1445), a painter of religious scenes; Henry Füssli (1741–1825), an imaginative Romantic painter; and Ferdinand Hodler (1853–1918), whose work gradually progressed from 19th-century realism to impressionism and finally to expressionism and art nouveau. The best known Swiss artist of the 20th century was Paul Klee (1879–1940), famous for his bright and colorful abstract paintings. During World War I neutral Switzerland was home to a large community of expatriate artists, who had fled the war in their home countries. Many of them settled in Zürich, where they founded the rebellious and surreal "anti art" movement known as Dadaism (see p. 199). Many Swiss artists received prestigious commissions from the state to design public works of art, or to design decorative elements for public buildings. The work of the sculptors Alberto Giacometti (1901–1966), famous for his elongated human sculptures, and Jean Tinguely (1925–1991), who designed constantly moving mechanical sculptures, are common sights in many Swiss cities. One contemporary Swiss artist who rarely gets asked to produce public artwork, however, is the sculptor and graphic designer H. R. Giger (b. 1940), a disturbing sculptor and graphic artist, best known as the artistic director of the 1979 sci-fi horror movie *Alien*.

Switzerland has the most museums per capita of any country in the world—nearly a thousand in total.

In the summer numerous international art fairs and events are held in cities around Switzerland. The most prestigious of these is Art Basel (*www.artbasel.com*), which is held in the northern city every June. This festival is centered on the world's largest temporary exhibition space, and attracts around 60,000 visitors each year.

Architecture

When most people think of Swiss architecture, they picture cute sun-faded wooden chalets festooned with geraniums or Emmentaler farmhouses with steep roofs that reach almost to the ground. There's more to Swiss architecture than these clichéd images: Since the early 20th century, Switzerland has been the home of many bold and innova-

The wellness complex at Tschuggen Grand Hotel, designed by Swiss architect Mario Botta

tive architects, starting with the most influential figure in modern architecture, Le Corbusier (1887–1965), who was born Charles-Édouard Jeanneret in La Chaux-de-Fonds, near Neuchâtel. Although Le Corbusier's works are dotted around the globe—from India to Argentina—Switzerland is home, fittingly, to the first building he ever designed (the Villa Jeanneret-Perret) and the last (the Heidi-Weber Haus). Le Corbusier's radical ideas have influenced a whole new generation of Swiss architects, most notably the Basel-based partnership Herzog & de Meuron, whose striking postmodernist style has won them numerous international awards. Notable projects include the Tate Modern art gallery in London and the "Birds Nest" national stadium in Beijing.

In recent years a number of high-profile public projects in Switzerland have been entrusted to innovative modern architects. Bern has Renzo Piano's wavelike Zentrum Paul Klee while Basel has Herzog & de Meuron's Schaulager art museum, Renzo Piano's Fondation Beyeler, and Mario Botta's Museum Jean Tinguely. Much of the nation's new architecture is unostentatious, and many noteworthy edifices are located off the beaten track. Two notable examples of this new Swiss architecture are Mario Botta's futuristic churches, the Santa Maria degli Angeli (see p. 261) at Monte Tamaro and San Giovanni Battista (see p. 261) in Mogno. Botta, a former pupil of Le Corbusier, is arguably Switzerland's most famous living architect. His home in Lugano is a showcase of his work and ideas, and the Ticino School of Architecture epitomizes his innovative and ambitious style.

Literature

Switzerland's literary heritage is a complicated and often confusing subject. Thanks to its multilingual population there are several different literary traditions within Switzerland that have evolved largely independently of one another. While there is a history of Romansh and Italian literature in Switzerland, the two main branches of the country's literary canon are in German and French.

Swiss history and culture in general is marked by an independent, almost isolationist tendency, but its literary culture has always faced outward, engaging more with the German or French traditions rather than forging one of their own. As a result it can often be difficult to define what constitutes a Swiss writer.

The most prominent historical figures in Swiss-German literature are the novelist Jeremias Gotthelf (1797–1854), often regarded as the first distinctively Swiss writer; Gottfried Keller (1819–1890), who is best known for his novel Der Grüne Heinrich (1880); and Conrad Ferdinand Meyer (1825–1898), a poet who also wrote historical novels that traced the development of Switzerland. In the 20th century, German-speaking Switzerland has produced several critically acclaimed writers, including the avant-garde playwright Friedrich Dürrenmatt (1921–1990) and the novelist Peter Stamm (b. 1963). The best known Swiss-German literary creation, however, is Heidi by Johanna Spryi (1827–1901). This charming children's story remains by far the most famous Swiss novel. Already a worldwide success by the end of the 19th century, it has been translated into more than 50 languages and adapted for the screen at least 12 times.

The Romansh Language

Romansh is the fourth language of Switzerland, but it is spoken by less than 1 percent of the population, mainly in the canton of Graubünden. It is a linguistic relic derived from Latin that, together with Friulian and Ladin (two languages spoken by around 750,000 people across the border in the extreme north of Italy), have survived in a handful of isolated mountain valleys. Even from valley to valley, the language varies considerably, and the online English–Romansh dictionary (www.mypledari.ch) contains five main dialects plus a standardized variation, Rumantsch Grischun. In 1996 Romansh was endorsed as a semi-official federal language, guaranteeing its promotion and preservation.

The parallel history of Swiss-French literature includes such distinguished names as the Genevese philosopher Jean-Jacques Rousseau (1712–1778), the realist novelist Edouard Rod (1857–1910), and Charles-Ferdinand Ramuz (1878–1947), whose novels and poems portray Swiss rural life. In more recent years the Swiss-French literary scene has produced writers like the acclaimed poet Jacques Chessex (1934–2009) and the poet and satirist Maurice Chappaz (1916–2009).

In addition to its native literature, many foreign writers have resided in Switzerland or been inspired by visits to the country. Some of them, such as the German-born author Herman Hesse (1877–1962), settled permanently in Switzerland and became full Swiss citizens, while others stayed only for a few months. Visitors who have been influenced by Switzerland's landscape and history include Lord Byron (1788–1824), whose famous poem *The Prisoner of Chillon* (1816) was inspired the Château de Chillon on the shores of Lake Geneva; Mary Shelley (1797–1851), who wrote *Frankenstein* (1818) during a wet, stormy summer near Lake Geneva, and Sir Arthur Conan Doyle (1859–1930), who used the dramatic Reichenbach Falls (see pp. 138–139) as the setting for Sherlock Holmes' death in "The Final Problem" (1893).

The most common reason writers had for settling in Switzerland was its neutral status. The first foreign writer to seek asylum in Switzerland was Voltaire (1694–1778), who lived in Geneva for a few years after his scathing satires got him exiled from France. During the World War I numerous writers sat out the war in Zürich and Geneva, including the poets and humorists associated with the Dada movement and the Irish modernist novelist James Joyce (1882–1941), who wrote his best known work, *Ulysses* (1922) while living in Zürich. With the rise of the Nazi party in the 1930s, the German writer Thomas Mann (1875–1955) fled across the border and settled near Zürich.

Authors from all four Swiss language regions, together with Swiss writers and poets living abroad, gather each year at the Solothurn Literary Workshop to present their latest texts, and to work together in discussions, workshops, performances, and exhibitions. At the same time, an annual anthology *New Swiss Writing* is published, containing around 40 texts in their original language with English translation.

EXPERIENCE:
Learn to Play the Alphorn

The alphorn is not an easy instrument to master, but with the mountains as your performance venue and cows for your audience, it's definitely worth a try. The **Swiss Alphorn School at Schönried** *(tel 033/744 58 35, www.alphornatelier.ch)* in the Bernese Oberland offers a variety of annual music courses run by a renowned alphorn teacher and player, Fritz Frautschi. Suited to all abilities, the courses range from one-day taster experiences and weekend courses to more intensive weeklong instruction on the appropriately named Hornberg (Horn Mountain). Instruments for beginners can be rented for a nominal fee.

Performing Arts

Visitors to Switzerland have a wide variety of options when it comes to live music. In the cities you can watch highbrow opera performances, energetic rock shows, or attend an effortlessly cool jazz festival, while in the mountains you can experience such authentically Swiss events as alphorn festivals and yodeling competitions. Every main city has a symphony orchestra and program of concerts. Among the best orchestras are the Bern Symphony Orchestra *(www.bsorchester.ch)*; the Zürcher Kammerorchester *(www.zko.ch)*; the Geneva-based Orchestra de la Suisse Romande *(www.osr.ch)*; and the Musikkollegium Winterthur *(www.musikkollegium.ch)*, renowned for its contemporary classical repertoire.

Several major music festivals take place throughout the year. The best known is the

Alphorn blowers prepare to perform at the annual Shepherd Festival in Valais.

Montreux Jazz Festival *(www.montreuxjazz.com;* see p. 83) in July, with its world-famous stars performing in a relaxed and intimate setting on the shores of Lake Geneva. Over the years, the festival's definition of what constitutes jazz has broadened to include high-profile rock bands and iconic soul and blues artists. The Lucerne Festival *(www .lucernefestival.ch)* dates back to 1938 when Arturo Toscanini conducted a gala concert in front of Richard Wagner's former residence in Tribschen (see p. 168) near Luzern. Since then, it has expanded into three festivals, one in the spring, one in the summer, and one devoted to piano pieces in November. These three events collectively attract around 150,000 visitors a year, and are mostly staged at the futuristic KKL concert hall. Many of the concerts feature the Lucerne Festival Orchestra. Founded by Italian conductor Claudio Abbado (b. 1933) it is one of the world's top-tier orchestras, formed by members of Abbado's Mahler Chamber Orchestra, and reinforced by internationally renowned soloists and chamber musicians.

Most Swiss theater is in French, German, or Italian and therefore often not especially appealing to the majority of overseas visitors, although there are a handful of high-quality English-language amateur groups in the main cities—especially Geneva—due to their large expat population. Puppet theater is also worth looking out for, as these shows seem to transcend language barriers and are popular with children. The content of these shows is often much-loved Swiss fairy tales and legends.

There is one enduring theatrical production that has appeal to many visitors, however. The Tell Freilichtspiele (Tell Open-Air Theatre, *www.tellspiele.ch*, see p. 132) in the Rugen wood near Interlaken, has staged Friedrich Schiller's celebrated William Tell story every summer (late June–early September) since 1912, in a lavish production which includes a cast of over 200, together with horses, goats, and cows.

Switzerland's most famous theater is the Schauspielhaus Zürich (Zürich Playhouse, *www.schauspielhaus.ch*), one of the most prestigious in the German-speaking world. It is renowned for its ground-breaking productions of classical and contemporary drama. These are staged in two separate venues: a traditional theater in the city center and the Schiffbau in Zürich West, an avant-garde arts center contained within a 19th-century redbrick warehouse. The theater gained its reputation in the 1930s and 1940s when many talented Austrian and German actors moved to Switzerland to escape Nazi persecution. During these years the theater was the largest free stage in the German-speaking world and staged many anti-fascist productions, including the world premieres of several plays by Max Frisch, Friedrich Dürrenmatt, and the Bavarian playwright Bertolt Brecht (1898–1956).

Switzerland is a nation known for its love of folklore and traditional Alpine culture.

Zürich also boasts the nation's finest opera company, which is housed in the beautiful neo-baroque Opernhaus (Opera House, *www.opernhaus.ch*) beside the lake. Built in 1891, it was the first opera house in Europe to have electric lighting. Many notable conductors and composers have been involved in Zürich's opera scene over the centuries, including Germans Wilhelm Furtwängler (1886–1954), Richard Wagner, Richard Strauss (1864–1949), Paul Hindemith (1895–1963), and the Swiss composer Arthur Honegger (1892–1955). The Opernhaus is currently regarded as one of the top opera venues in the world and an important ballet stage. Opera, ballet, and contemporary dance are also performed in the Grand Théâtre de Genève (*www.geneveopera.ch*) and at the Stadttheater Bern (*www.stadttheaterbern.ch*). However, it is the Béjart Ballet (*www.bejart.ch*), a world-famous dance academy in Lausanne, which leads the way in Swiss dance. The troupe was founded by Erasmus Prize–winning choreographer Maurice Béjart (1927–2007), whose exciting and innovative productions earned global critical acclaim and attracted new audiences for ballet. In Bern, each summer the annual Bern Dance Days festival showcases a whole range of dance genres at various venues, including the Kulturhallen Dampfzentrale (*www.dampfzentrale.ch*), an important center for contemporary music and dance.

Folklore & Traditions

Switzerland is a nation known for its love of folklore and traditional Alpine culture. Each region enjoys its own collection of local stories, celebrations, and customs. The most common and enduring characters in Swiss folklore are "Jack o' the Bowl," a friendly house spirit who looks after the inhabitants in exchange for a bowl of cream left out at night; and the "Barbegazi," small, shy, white-furred men with long frozen beards who live in the mountains. It is said that they travel from town to town using their enormous feet as skis. In Valais it was once thought that *gogwärgini* (wild gnomes) lived in the Fieschertal, helping villagers with their daily chores. Tales of these tiny, bearded folk still live on in the valley, and there is even a special *Gogwärginiweg* (Gnome Trail) in their memory.

Seasonal Festivals: In an age where most countries have turned their back on traditional entertainments, almost every town and village in Switzerland has at least one ancient festival that they continue to observe. Not surprising, considering how extreme the changes in weather can be over the course of a year, these festivals often mark the transition from one season to another. In many cases, these celebrations appear distinctly strange to modern visitors—involving activities like cow wrestling, cow beauty pageants, or cowbell-ringing competitions (almost all traditional rural festivals seem to involve cows in some capacity).

The *Fasnacht* (carnival) is a time-honored celebration of parades and merry-making

A performance of *The Count of Monte Cristo* at Theater St. Gallen

A colorful float in the *Basler Fasnacht* (Carnival of Basel)

that takes place in towns and cities across the country prior to Lent. Basel stages the largest carnival with flamboyant fancy-dress parades, street entertainments, and fireworks. In Bern, a captured "bear" is awakened from his winter sleep in the Prison Tower by the Ychüblete *(www.fasnacht.be)*, an impressive parade of drums. In Solothurn, the city is renamed Honolulu (directly opposite Solothurn on the other side of the world) for the day, and citizens parade through the streets with masks and fancy dress, all making as much noise as possible with percussion instruments. Zürich's spring festival, *Sechse-lauten* (Six O'Clock Chimes), features the ignition of the Böög—a snowman figure made of straw and fireworks, who represents winter. Locals say the faster his head explodes the better the summer will be.

In the weeks before Christmas, the cities are filled with festive cheer. There are twinkling lights, colorful themed window displays, and Christmas markets selling all manner of seasonal treats and decorations. In Fribourg on December 6 (St. Nicholas' Day), Sami-chlaus (the Swiss Santa Claus) leads a donkey laden with candy and gingerbread through the town. He gives these treats to the good children, while his scampering soot-covered

helper, Schmutzli, chases off the naughty ones. The New Year is heralded in with nationwide Silvester celebrations (New Year's Eve, www.silvesterzauber.ch). Zürich hosts the nation's largest party in a park by the lake, with great revelry and fireworks, while the villagers of Urnäsch in the Appenzeller hinterland celebrate twice (on December 31 and again on January 13) in accordance with the ancient Julian calendar.

Folk art: This art form is expressed primarily through music and song, poetry, wood-carving, embroidery, and in country dances such as the *schuhplattler*, with its rapid jumping and hopping sequences. The best example may be in Appenzellerland, where local crafts and music portray a way of life, and where traditional costume is de rigueur. Note the women in stiff-winged tulle caps and lace-edged dresses, and men in yellow breeches, embroidered scarlet waistcoats, and a silver earring in their right ear. The Lower Engadine villagers are especially proud of their robust and unique Romansh (see p. 49) heritage. They keep it alive through festivals like Mattinadas (January 2), when children parade through the villages with decorated sledges; and the popular spring parade of Chalandamarz, when children carry giant cowbells and singing traditional songs. Throughout the Alpine regions, another excuse to don traditional dress comes at the annual Alpauffahrt and Alpabfahrt, the seasonal migration of cattle between the valleys and high pastures. Each village celebrates this event with a grand procession of cows decorated with floral wreaths, embroidered bridles, and giant ornamental bells. Cows are awarded bells according to their annual milk production. The best milk-producing cow, the *kranzkuh*, leads the flamboyant procession through the village wearing the largest bell.

These festivals spurred the popularization of *jodeln* (yodeling) and the alphorn. Alphorns, originally used to round up the cattle on the upper pastures, are now played as musical instruments, typically to accompany yodeling. Some are over 10 feet (3 m) long and require a special breathing technique to play. Yodeling evolved as a means of communication from peak to peak and become an integral part of traditional Alpine music. Most yodeling is now for the benefit of tourists, although there are a few regional and cantonal festivals, and even a national Swiss Yodeling Festival. Staged once every three years in June, and hosted by a different town each year, this attracts over 200,000 visitors keen to enjoy the various traditional and modern incarnations of this rarified art, which nowadays include jazz- and rock-yodeling. ∎

Zürich's spring festival features the ignition of the Böög—a snowman figure made of straw and fireworks, who represents winter.

A historic French-flavored city on a beautiful lake, with parks galore, watersports, and acres of sun-warmed vineyards nearby

Geneva & Lake Geneva

Even from the other side of the lake the Jet d'Eau looks awesome.

Geneva & Lake Geneva

Geneva is the least Swiss of all Swiss cities. Of its 186,000 inhabitants, around 40 percent are foreigners, representing 190 nations. The capital of a small eponymous canton, Geneva is located in a particularly favorable geographic position. It is at the southernmost end of Lake Geneva (Lac Léman), where it joins the Rhône River, and it sits right on the border with France. The city is a veritable melting pot of cultures, surprisingly diverse and cosmopolitan—a small city with big ideas.

The City of Geneva

Geneva captivates visitors with its beautiful lake, more than 50 parks, and its alluring vistas of snow-capped Alps on the horizon. It is undoubtedly the nation's grandest city, and one of the safest in the world. Charming, elegant, and heavily influenced by neighboring France, it is celebrated for its watchmaking and banking and is second in size only to Zürich. Geneva boasts a long and eventful history, reflected in its many museums and galleries. It is also the culinary capital of the Confederation, with more Michelin-starred restaurants than any other Swiss city and, thanks to its multi-ethnic population, a glut of tiny cafés and restaurants serving specialties from around the world.

The lake and the river bisect Geneva into the grandiose Rive Droite (Right Bank), defined by major international organizations and attractive parks, and the artistic Rive Gauche (Left Bank), with its numerous museums, galleries, and glamorous shopping streets. Geneva's heart beats loudest in the knot of pedestrian streets and fountain-splashed squares that form the picturesque Vieille Ville (Old Town), where trendy boutiques, cozy restaurants, farmers' markets, and traditional festivals bring its historic mansions to life.

Geneva's compact size makes it easy to explore on foot, and the lakeside promenades are especially pleasant for a stroll. The bus and tram network is fast and efficient, and the small yellow *mouettes genevoises* (water taxis) that ply the lake (departing every ten minutes between 7:30 a.m. and 7:30 p.m.) are a fun and effective way to cross the lake. Bikes are available to rent for free from Genève Roule (*www.geneveroule .ch*), whose distribution stands are located at convenient points throughout the city.

Thanks to Geneva's strategic location at the heart of Europe, and at the crossroads of many ancient commercial, cultural, and spiritual routes, it has been the cradle of some of the greatest humanitarian ideas, attracting such luminaries over the centuries as John Calvin, Jean-Jacques Rousseau, and Henry Dunant,

NOT TO BE MISSED:

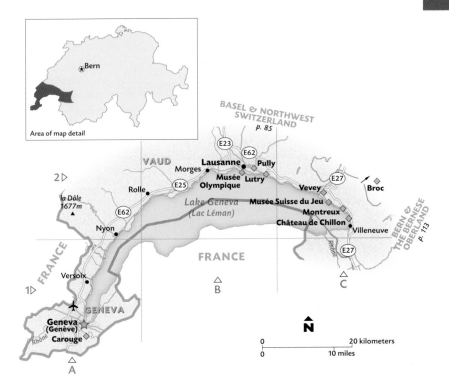

who founded the Red Cross organization and drafted the first Geneva Convention. Many major international treaties have been signed and numerous global organizations have established their head offices in Geneva (including the United Nations and the World Health Organization), contributing to its reputation as a city of enterprise, a meeting place for currents of opinion, and a window on the future.

Beyond the City

The region has more to offer than just the city of Geneva, and it is worth exploring the northern shore of Lake Geneva, including the rich wine country of the Pays de Vaud, which stretches to Lausanne and beyond. This area is also known for its culinary riches, including lake-caught fish and traditional sausages and stews.

The journey to Lausanne can be made by road, rail, or boat. Get the best out of the trip by driving in one direction—to stop off at the sights en route—then cruise back across

the lake for the full relaxation experience. Hilly Lausanne is an interesting city in its own right, with the old streets of its Vieille Ville, an impressive cathedral, a 14th-century chateau, and several high-quality museums. One of these—the Olympic Museum—is a must for anyone with an interest in sport. The Lavaux Wine Trail stretches from the museum to Château de Chillon and provides an excellent opportunity to combine some healthy walking, close contact with some of the vineyards, and some wine-tasting. The trail also passes close by the lovely spa resort of Vevey—with its elegant lakeside promenade, craft shops and boutiques, and Charlie Chaplin's former house—and Montreux. The latter is renowned worldwide for its annual jazz festival, but it's worth a visit at any time of the year. In this area there are plenty of reminders of one of Switzerland's great industries—even if you don't visit one of the chocolate manufacturers, you will find innumerable opportunities to purchase some as you travel from town to town. ■

Geneva

Visitors arriving by plane at Geneva's international airport or Gare de Cornavin rail station will first see the elegant northern half of the city, the Rive Droite. Across the Rhône River, in Rive Gauche, is Geneva's historic Vieille Ville, or Old Town. Its steep cobbled streets and clutch of historic museums portray the city's colorful past. Those prepared to wander farther will be rewarded with fine parks, galleries, and lakeside beaches.

The spire of Geneva's cathedral is a well-loved landmark.

Geneva
 59 A1

Visitor Information

✉ Geneva Tourism, rue du Mont-Blanc 18, Geneva

☎ (022) 909 70 00

🚋 Tram 1 (Mont-Blanc)

www.geneva -tourism.ch

Rive Gauche

The old heart of Geneva's Rive Gauche is a fascinating blend of Gothic, Renaissance, and baroque architecture. Just outside the city walls, beneath the Vieille Ville, lies the elegant, spacious square of **place de Neuve**, a good place to start a tour of

the city. Together with a statue of General Dufour, co-founder of the Red Cross, the square is surrounded by some fine old buildings. These include the majestic **Grand Théâtre** *(box office: place Neuve 5, tel 022/418 31 30)*. This, the city's opera house, was finished in 1879 in the same Second Empire style as Paris's then newly completed Opéra Garnier. Note the fine marble statues on the central facade representing drama, dance, music, and comedy. A fire partly destroyed the building in 1951, but it reopened 11 years later, rebuilt grander than ever and boasting the largest stage in Switzerland. Flanking the Grand Théâtre is the world-class **Conservatoire de Musique** *(rue de l'Arquebus 12, tel 022/319 60 60)*, with its large concert hall and dazzling Byzantine-style facade, and the **Musée Rath.** The latter, the first Swiss museum devoted to the fine arts, is an imposing neoclassical building gifted to the city by two sisters, Jeanne-Françoise and Henriette Rath, in 1826. The museum serves as a venue for prestigious exhibitions of international and Swiss art.

Across the square, the **Parc des Bastions** is a popular place in which to relax. Play on the giant

INSIDER TIP:

Take advantage of the
benches in the Parc
des Bastions to enjoy
a baguette stuffed
with a chocolate bar,
as the natives do.

—CAROLINE GRAVES
National Geographic
Books contributor

chessboard or enjoy coffee and
cake in the atmospheric **Café du
Parc des Bastions** *(promenade
des Bastions 1, tel 022/310 86
66)*, which is housed in a former
bandstand and winter garden. The
park was the city's first botanical
garden, and it contains more than
50 varieties of rare trees, as well
as statues and fountains. You are

now on the edge of the Vieille
Ville (see pp. 64–65). On one
flank of Parc des Bastions, the
impressive 298-foot-long (91 m)
**Monument International de
la Réformation** (International
Monument of the Reformation)
lines the city ramparts. Created in
1917 in honor of the founders of
Protestantism, it features the four
Genevese reformers (Farel, Calvin,
Bèze, and Knox) as its centerpiece, alongside Cromwell, Luther,
Zwingli, and the Pilgrim Fathers
(see pp. 35–37).

Beyond the park, the **Musée
d'Art et d'Histoire** (MAH;
Museum of Art & History) counts
among Geneva's most important
museums. It contains everything
from ancient Greek statuary and
medieval stained glass to canvases
by Rembrandt and Monet. Due

Musée Rath

- 61
- place Neuve 2
- (022) 418 33 40
- Closed Mon.
- $$$
- Bus: 3, 5, 36
  (Place Neuve);
  Tram: 12 (Place
  Neuve)

www.ville-ge.ch/mah

**Musée d'Art et
d'Histoire**

- 61
- rue Charles-
  Galland 2
- (022) 418 26 00
- Closed Mon.
- $$ (temporary
  exhibitions only)
- Bus: 3, 5, 36
  (Athénée)

www.ville-ge.ch/mah

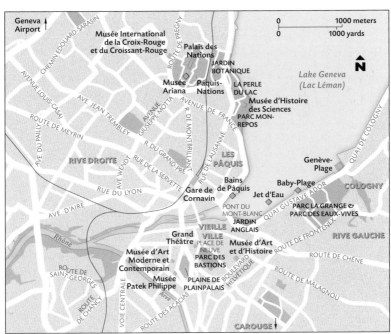

Musée Patek Philippe

🄰 61

✉ rue des Vieux Grenadiers 7

☎ (022) 807 09 10

🕐 Closed Sun. & Mon.

💲 $$

🚍 Bus: 1 (École-de-Médecine); tram: 12, 13, 14, 15 (Rond-Point de Plainpalais)

www.patekmuseum.com

Musée d'Art Moderne et Contemporain

🄰 61

✉ 10 rue des Vieux-Grenadiers

☎ (022) 320 6122

🕐 Closed Mon.

💲 $

🚍 Bus: 1 (École-de-Médicine); tram: 12, 13, 14, 15, 17 (Rond-Point de Plainpalais)

www.mamco.ch

west of the park, it is perhaps surprising to find another large open space so close to the city center. This is **Plaine de Plainpalais,** an area that has long been a place for recreation. As early as 1637, the ancient game of *mail* (similar to croquet) was played here and, over the centuries, Plaine de Plainpalais became popular for shooting contests, gymnastics competitions, and soccer matches. Today it is occupied by a skateboard park, *boules* pitches, and a children's playground. It hosts a fruit and vegetables market on Tuesdays, Fridays, and Sundays. And on Wednesday and Saturday mornings there's a flea market.

West of Plainpalais, the **Musée Patek Philippe** contains the most prestigious and complete watch collection ever assembled. No other Swiss city has been as closely associated with luxury watch manufacture as Geneva, and the local Patek Philippe company counts itself among the world's finest watchmakers. There is a collection of more than 200 machines and tools used by such craftsmen as engravers and goldsmiths on the ground floor, together with a brief film "A Legacy of Genius" (every 30 minutes). The Patek Philippe Collection occupies the second floor; the Antiques Collection of 16th to 19th-century European and Swiss watches is on the third floor; and on the top floor holds a library devoted to the measurement of time. Highlights include intricately enameled, filigreed, and bejeweled watches in the shape of animals, musical instruments, and guns in the Antiques Collection. And don't miss the Calibre 89 on the second floor—the most complicated (and expensive) watch ever made.

Toward the Lake: Farther along rue des Vieux Grenadiers, the **Musée d'Art Moderne et Contemporain** (MAMCO; Museum of Modern & Contemporary Art) is Geneva's leading modern art gallery, showcasing a variety of art, photography, sculpture, and video installations created during the past half century. They are displayed in a striking setting inside a converted former factory building.

In this part of Geneva, museums come thick and fast. The **Musée d'Ethnographie** (Ethnography Museum) reopens in 2014. Until then its impressive displays of human cultures from around the world are housed a little to the east in Conches.

From MAMCO, it's a brief walk north along rue des Bains to the Rhône River. When you reach the

---

Bohemian Carouge

South of the Old Town, the tiny residential Carouge offers a taste of bohemian Geneva, brimming with laid-back street cafés, a lively arts scene, and a glut of charming specialist boutiques. This attractive suburb developed as a town in the 18th century when it was annexed to the Kingdom of Sardinia. As a consequence, it has a distinctly Mediterranean feel, thanks to its Italianate architecture; its facades painted in shades of apricot, peaches, and cream; and its microclimate, which enables palms, oleander, and olive trees to flourish. Visit on a Wednesday and Saturday for the farmers' market.

The Musée d'Ethnographie has exhibits from every continent.

riverbank, head east and after the fifth bridge—Pont du Mont-Blanc—the river officially becomes Lake Geneva. On the lakeshore, the **Jardin Anglais** (English Garden; see p. 64) is celebrated for its floral clock. Directly in front of you, to the northeast, you'll see the spectacular **Jet d'Eau,** Geneva's best-known landmark. This jet of water was originally a pressure release for a hydro-powered factory, but the Genevese liked it so much that in 1891 the city made it into a fountain. The jet reaches a height of 460 feet (140 m) and pumps around 7,925 gallons (30,000 l) into the air every minute—that's five bathtubs of water every second! By day its spray creates a rainbow, and by night the plume is floodlit.

Parks & Beaches: Just along the quayside to the east,

beyond a clutter of fishermen's huts and boatsheds, lies **Baby-Plage.** This small, sandy beach is popular with city-dwellers for sunbathing and swimming during the summer months.

Near Baby-Plage are a couple of fine parks. The extensive **Parc la Grange** (quai Gustave Ador), with its centuries-old trees, orangery, and impressive vistas, is the city's largest and possibly most beautiful park. It also contains the nation's finest rose garden, some Roman remains (from the summer estate of a first-century Roman civil servant, Titus Riccius Fronto), and an elegant 18th-century mansion. Free concerts are staged in the park in the summer. The park closes at night (hours vary according to the season). The neighboring **Parc des** (continued on p. 66)

Musée d'Ethnographie
61
boulevard Carl-Vogt 65–67
(022) 418 4550
Reopens 2014
$

Musée d'Ethnographie (Conches)
rue Calandrini 7, Conches
(022) 346 0125
Closed Mon.
$$
www.ville-ge.ch/meg

Jet d'Eau
61
quai du Général-Guisan

Baby-Plage
61
Port des Eaux-Vives Ador

Walk Around the Vieille Ville

Geneva's long and eventful history is reflected in the museums and monuments of the Vieille Ville. No visit is complete without exploring the narrow streets and fountain-filled squares of this picturesque district, with its tempting specialist boutiques and its array of cozy cafés, bars, and restaurants.

A supersize game of chess in the Parc de Bastions

Start your walk at **quai Gustave-Ador** beside the **Jardin Anglais ❶**. This small park is best known for its working **Horloge Fleurie** (Flower Clock), comprising more than 6,500 flowers. The clock honors the two Geneva specialties of watchmaking and botany. From here there is an excellent view of the **Jet d'Eau** (see p. 63).

From place du Lac, at the western end of the park, head south across the city's main shopping area. First you will cross glitzy rue du Rhône with its uninterrupted parade of haute couture boutiques, jewelers, and watchmakers. Then pass the more affordable rue du Marché shopping precinct. Head up rue de la Fontaine to the photogenic **place du Bourg-de-Four ❷**, one of Geneva's most historic squares. This was where the Roman forum once stood and where Rousseau (see p. 37) spent his childhood

(at number 40). This remains the geographical and spiritual heart of the city, with galleries, antique shops, cafés, bars, and bistros.

Turn right along rue de l'Hôtel-de-Ville, then right again along place de la Taconnerie to the **Cathédrale de Saint-Pierre ❸** (*Cours St. Pierre 6*), a pleasing mix of Romanesque and Gothic features, built between 1150 and 1232. In 1536, during the Reformation, locals voted to make it Protestant, stripping all the decoration from the once ornate interior. A climb up the tower affords sweeping views of the region. Beneath the cathedral, and worth a visit, is an **archaeological site** dating from Roman times.

From the cathedral, follow rue Otto-Barblan to rue de Puits St. Pierre, where Henri Dunant, co-founder of the Red Cross, once lived. Also here, the city's oldest private house, **Maison Tavel ❹**, contains the **Museum of Ancient**

Geneva *(Maison Tavel, rue du Puits St. Pierre 6, tel 022/418 3700)*, with its fascinating model of 19th-century Geneva on the third floor. Up the hill, a 17th-century former **arsenal** *(rue du Puits St. Pierre)* has mosaic tableaus depicting scenes from Geneva's history.

At the Grand-Rue crossroads, note the **Hôtel de Ville** (City Hall) to your left, where the Red Cross was founded in the 19th century, and where the first Geneva Convention was signed in 1864. Pass through an archway and into a spacious square that boasts the longest wooden bench in the world, and a **statue** of statesman Charles Pictet de Rochemont (1755–1824), who instigated the nation's neutrality at the end of the Napoleonic wars.

Descend steep Rampe de la Treille to visit **place de Neuve ❺** (see p. 60), the nerve-center of Genevese cultural life. Look into

NOT TO BE MISSED:

Horloge Fleurie (flower clock)
• **Chapelle des Macabées inside the Cathédrale de Saint-Pierre**
• **Tour de l'Ile**

the neighboring **Parc des Bastions** with its celebrated **Monument International de la Réformation ❻** (see p. 61). Then climb the steep rue de la Tertasse and turn left down cobbled rue de la Cité, admiring its fine ancient houses, shops, and galleries. Continue to the river and the **Tour de l'Ile ❼** on the bridge. This is all that remains of a medieval bishop's château. From here it is a short riverside walk back to your starting point.

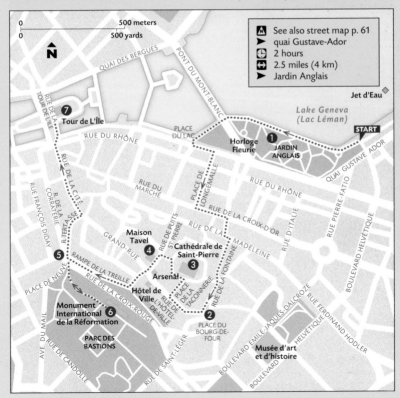

If the weather is fine, the Jardin Botanique is a great place to while away an hour or two.

Genève-Plage
- 🅰 61
- ✉ Port-Noir, Quai de Cologny
- ☎ (022) 736 24 82
- 🕐 Closed Oct.–April
- 💲 $
- ⛴ Mouette Genevoise 3, 4 (Port Noir)

Rive Droite
- 🅰 61

Bains de Pâquis
- 🅰 61
- ✉ quai du Mont-Blanc 30
- ☎ (022) 732 29 74
- 🚌 Bus 1 (Pâquis)
- ⛴ Mouette Genevoise 1, 2, 3 (Pâquis)

Eaux-Vives *(quai Gustave-Ador)* is at its best in May and June, when its many rhododendron bushes bloom. The Dutch government presented the city with these plants to show their gratitude for the humanitarian aid they received from the Swiss during World War II.

Farther east, **Genève-Plage** is the city's oldest public swimming pool. In addition to its Olympic-size pool, it features a water sports center, beach-volleyball, petanque, playgrounds, and restaurants—making it a prime spot for leisure and relaxation during the summer months. Beyond, on the hillside overlooking the lake, **Cologny** is Geneva's most sought-after suburb, commanding the highest real estate prices in the Confederation.

Rive Droite

Stately boulevards, five-star hotels, lakeside promenades, and extensive parks are the hallmarks of Geneva's opulent Rive Droite, on the northwestern shore of the bay of Lake Geneva. Away from the lake, the area is cosmopolitan and elegant—if a little staid—with a large number of international governmental organizations, and the headquarters of the United Nations at its heart.

The northern riverbank of the Rhône and the lake are fringed by elegant avenues called *quais* (quays) and beautiful *belle époque* mansions (several containing luxury hotels). These are set against a backdrop of the Jura Mountains. In their midst, a pier juts out into the lake, with a lighthouse and the

Bains de Pâquis (Pâquis Baths).

The latter have been a favorite Genevese haunt since 1932, offering swimming pools, beaches, tai chi, massage, and a simple café bar (which offers superb weekend brunch). There is even a sauna and Turkish bath to warm you after a chilly swim. The lively Pâquis district here epitomizes the cosmopolitan nature of Geneva, with its up-and-coming bars and clubs, and a plethora of multiethnic restaurants serving exotic cuisines from around the world.

Heading North: A short distance north of here the lakeshore gives way to parkland, making it a popular area for promenading. Geneva is often described as the "city of parks" with more than 50 occupying around a quarter of the city's total area. Many of them have magnificent lake and mountain vistas. **Parc Mon-Repos** is among the city's most popular, extending for over 1 mile (nearly 2 km) along the lake. It has swimming pools, sunbathing areas, and shady groves for picnics. The 19th-century mansion in the park belonged to the scientist Phillipe de Plantamour (1816–1898), who also established its rare trees and plants. Today the mansion houses the Henry-Dunant Institute, a center for humanitarian dialogue.

The neighboring park, **La Perle du Lac** (The Pearl of the Lake), is a picturesque area of paths, statues, clipped box hedges, and brightly colored flower beds, all with impressive views across the lake to Mont Blanc (15,781 feet/ 4,810 m), the highest of the Alps. The **Musée d'Histoire des Sciences** (History of Science Museum), with an impressive collection of ancient scientific tools and instruments, is housed in a beautiful neoclassical mansion (1830) in La Perle du Lac.

The vast **Conservatoire et Jardin Botanique** (Botanical Conservatory and Garden), one of Geneva's most visited sites, is another ideal spot for a leisurely stroll. Its collection of 16,000 plant species from all over the world is divided into various sections. In the gardens you'll find an arboretum, a "scent-and-touch garden," and the Botanicum, a family space featuring playful, sensory interactions with the plant world.

Facing the Botanical Garden, just across the avenue de la Paix, the **World Meteorological Organization** (www.wmo.ch) is housed in a massive glass-fronted

Musée d'Histoire des Sciences

🗺 61

✉ Villa Bartholoni, rue de Lausanne 128

☎ (022) 418 50 60

🕐 Closed Tues.

🚌 Bus: 1 (Sécheron); tram: 13, 15 (Butini)

🚢 Mouette Genevoise 4 (Perle du Lac)

www.geneve-tourisme.ch

Conservatoire et Jardin Botanique

🗺 61

✉ chemin de l'Impératrice 1, Chambésy-Geneva

☎ (022) 418 51 00

🚌 Bus: 1, 11, 28 (Jardin Botanique); tram 13, 15 (Nations)

www.ville-ge.ch/cjb

Themed Walks

To explore Geneva off the beaten track, watch for a series of ten *Genève à Pied* self-guided thematic walks, each with its own fold-up route details, map, and anecdotes *(available from the Tourist Office)*. These include "Walking Downstream" (4 hours); "From History to Modernity" (3 hours); and "Spirit of Geneva" (3 hours). Alternatively, follow a 2.5-hour audio-guide *(available from the Tourist Office for a small fee and a deposit for the MP3 player)*; or participate in an official guided walk. Featured themes are "The Old Town," "The Escalade" (see p. 68), and "In the Footsteps of Jean Calvin."

Palais des Nations

🏛 61

✉ Parc de l'Ariana, avenue de la Paix 14

☎ (022) 917 48 96

🕑 Tours daily April–Sept., Mon.–Fri., Oct.–March. Reservations essential.

💲 $$

🚌 Bus: 8, 28, F, V, Z (Appia), 5, 11, 14 (Nations); tram: 13, 15 (Nations)

www.unog.ch

building (designed by local architectural business, Brodbeck & Roulet), which appropriately mirrors the sky. This intergovernmental organization is the United Nations' scientific authority on climate change, air pollution, and ozone layer depletion.

Palais des Nations: In 1919 Geneva was chosen as the home of the League of Nations, a now-defunct organization established to prevent a recurrence of war on the scale of World War I. Since 1966 the Geneva office (UNOG) of its successor,

employees. Its conference center is the largest and most active in the world, with more than 10,000 meetings a year. Numerous UN bodies have their headquarters here, including those that work in the fields of peace and disarmament, human rights, humanitarian assistance, science, and technology.

As you pass through the gates to UNOG, you leave Switzerland and enter international territory—so remember to bring your passport! Book in advance for one of the compelling hour-long tours (in any of the UN's official languages).

Party-time Geneva

There's always something to celebrate in Geneva, from the feasting and fancy-dress parades of February's Carnival season to the sophisticated partying of the International Motor Show in March. There are fireworks and frolics on Independence Day (the world's largest celebrations of this kind outside the United States), and historical processions during the Escalade festival.

For the rest of the year, Geneva enjoys a lively yet sophisticated night scene. Top haunts include chic Capocaccia (rue de la Confédération 8, tel 022/310 15 15) for

cocktails, or the ultra-hip bar Le Glow (quai Wilson 41), overlooking the lake; Le Rouge et Le Blanc (quai des Bergues 27, tel 022/731 15 50), a trendy wine bar on the Rhône; La Clémence (place du Bourg-du-Four 20, tel 022/310 24 98) for cozy, old-town atmosphere; Alhambar (rue de la Rôtisserie 10, tel 022/312 13 13) and La Bohême (boulevard Helvétique 36, tel 022/700 46 00) for clubbing; and Au Chat Noir (rue Vautier 13, tel 022/343 49 98) or Gabs Music Lounge (rue de Zürich 12, tel 022/732 31 32) for live jazz and blues.

---

the United Nations, has been housed in the enormous Palais des Nations (Palace of Nations). This was built in the 1930s on the Varembé estate, an extensive plot of land bequeathed to the city by local arts patron Gustave Revilliod (1817–1890), the founder of Musée Ariana. The building is 1 mile (1.6 km) long and has 4,000 permanent

Visitors can see the vast **Assembly Hall,** the **Court of Honor,** the **Human Rights & Alliance of Civilizations Room,** the **Council Chamber,** and the **Salle des Pas Perdus** (Hall of the Lost Footsteps). From the last you can see the **Armillary Sphere**—the symbol of the UN—and the **Conquest of Space monument,** both set in the parkland surrounding the building.

In the Place des Nations (Nations Square), opposite a colorful avenue of flags, the enormous **Broken Chair sculpture** by Swiss artist Daniel Berset (b. 1953) symbolizes opposition to cluster bombs and land mines.

Just a few minutes' walk from the UN complex, **Musée Ariana** is one of Europe's top porcelain, glass, and pottery museums. Its artifacts span seven centuries from the Middle Ages to the present day. Musée Ariana is housed in a sumptuous neo-Renaissance edifice built by local collector Gustave Revilliod, and is named for his mother, Ariana de la Rive. The museum is also the headquarters of the International Academy of Ceramics. Nearby, the **Musée International de la Croix-Rouge et du Croissant-Rouge** (Red Cross & Red Crescent Museum) provides a poignant record of the heroic deeds of these two organi-

zations. It is contained within the headquarters of the International Committee of the Red Cross, which has provided humanitarian aid in times of crisis since its creation in 1864.

The Red Cross was founded by Genevese social activist and the first Nobel Peace Prize winner Henry Dunant (1828–1910), who was appalled by the horrors of war following a visit to the battlefields of Solferino, Italy. Today, the museum rouses powerful emotions with its vivid interactive displays and nonstop film footage portraying the extraordinary humanitarian missions carried out in times of war and natural disaster.

Farther north is the head office of the **World Health Organization** *(www.who.int)*, founded to promote international cooperation in the field of health. The office is not open to the public. ∎

Musée Ariana

🄰 61

✉ 10 avenue de la Paix

☎ (022) 418 54 50

🕓 Closed Tues.

💲 $ (temporary exhibitions only)

🚌 Bus: 8, 28, F, V, Z (Appia), 5, 11, 14 (Nations); tram 13, 15 (Nations)

www.geneve-tourisme.ch

Musée International de la Croix-Rouge et du Croissant-Rouge

🄰 61

✉ 17 avenue de la Paix

☎ (022) 748 95 06

🕓 Closed Tues., Sat., & Sun.

💲 $$

🚌 Bus 8, F, V, Z (Appia)

www.micr.org

The Council Chamber of the Palais des Nations, with wall murals by José Maria Sert

Lake Geneva

Lake Geneva (known locally as Lac Léman, or Genfersee in German-speaking regions) is the largest of the Alpine lakes. Idyllically located between the Alps and the Jura mountains and stretching northeast from the city of Geneva, the lake is the heart and soul of French-speaking Switzerland. It adds a touch of Mediterranean flair to the Alps, so little wonder it has been described as the most elegant lake in the world.

Sailboats vying for a breath of wind on Lake Geneva

Versoix

◪ 59 A1

Pays de Vaud

◪ 59 A2, B2, C2

Visitor Information

✉ Office du
   Tourisme,
   Canton de Vaud,
   avenue d'Ouchy
   60, Lausanne

☎ (021) 613 2626

www.region-du-leman.ch

Lake Geneva serves as a gateway to an entire region. Its shores fringe two countries (Switzerland to the north and France to the south) and three Swiss cantons (Geneva, Vaud, and Valais). On the Swiss side, Geneva, Lausanne, and Montreux are the largest lakeside cities. Opposite, the main French resorts are Thonon-les-Bains and Evian-les-Bains, easily reachable by ferry for a day trip.

Northeast of the city of Geneva, the eponymous canton stretches in a narrow band between the lake and the French border. About 7 miles (10 km) from downtown Geneva, and only a 15-minute drive away, is **Versoix,** which has a beautiful lakeside promenade and an annual one-day chocolate festival *(tel 022 775 66 08, place de la Gare, Versoix, www.versoix.ch/fdc.php).* There is a rail link between Versoix and Geneva.

Pays de Vaud

Beyond Versoix, heading north the traveler passes into Vaud

canton. The Vaudois countryside affords grandiose lake and Alpine vistas, lush forests, some of the nation's finest vineyards, tiny beaches, and sun-baked stone villages. A cruise along the shoreline (see sidebar p. 73) reveals glimpses of castles, palatial residences, lively towns, and alluring *belle époque* resorts.

The settlements strung out along the lake's shore—such as **Nyon, Rolle,** and **Morges**—are renowned for their hospitality. This region has more than its fair share of five-star deluxe hotels, world-renowned thermal spas, and internationally acclaimed health and beauty clinics, devoted to restoring the harmony and well-being of body and mind.

The Pays de Vaud has long been an area of great culinary riches, embracing the cuisine of the lake, the fertile slopes of the shoreline, and the mountains. From the lake, perch, whitefish, arctic char, trout, and pike grace local menus. The latter also feature such hearty country fare as *papet vaudois* (a leek and potato stew), accompanied by a variety of sausages: *saucisse aux choux* (sausage filled with cabbage), *saucise vaudois* (local pork sausage), or *boutefas* (smoked port prepared with spices and schnapps). For dessert, try the local *tarte à la raisinée*, a delicious tart filled with a gooey fruit concentrate made from pears and quinces cooked in wine. The regional cheeses are splendid: Look for those labelled Produits du Terroir Vaudois (*www.terroir-vaudois.ch*). Finally, with the major

wine-producing areas extending from Geneva to Lausanne, the wines produced from the steep south-facing slopes are among the finest in Switzerland.

Lausanne

The young, lively, French-speaking city of Lausanne is the sporting center of Switzerland. It is the world's "Olympic capital," headquarters of the International Olympic Committee (IOC) and 15 other international sports federations.

INSIDER TIP:

For one day in the middle of Lent, forget that resolution and visit the Versoix chocolate festival. At other times you can sample chocolates at Cartier-Chocolatier, beside the lake.

—CLIVE CARPENTER
National Geographic contributor

Lausanne also boasts more than 300 active sports clubs, ranging from water sports on the lake to cross-country skiing and hiking in the surrounding hill country.

However, there's more to the city than sport. Lausanne is a laid-back university city of 130,000 inhabitants, which rivals Geneva as the intellectual and cultural center of the Suisse-Romande region. It has long attracted luminaries to its

Nyon
🄰 59 A2

Rolle
🄰 59 B2

Morges
🄰 59 B2

Lausanne
🄰 59 B2
Visitor Information
✉ Office du Tourisme, Lausanne, Rail Station, place de la Gare 9 *&* place de la Navigation, Lausanne
☎ (021) 613 73 73
www.lausanne-tourisme.ch

Cartier-Chocolatier
🄰 59 A1
✉ Route de Suisse, Versoix
☎ (022) 755 10 05
www.cartier-swiss.ch

Inside the Cathédrale de Notre-Dame in Lausanne

Cathédrale de Notre-Dame

✉ place de la Cathédrale 4, Lausanne

☎ (021) 316 71 61

🚇 Metro: 2 (Bessières); Bus: 14 (Pierre-Viret)

shores, including the celebrated writers Voltaire, Jean-Jacques Rousseau, Victor Hugo, and Charles Dickens. And with its plethora of museums, stylish shops, gastronomic restaurants, theaters, the world-renowned Béjart Ballet, and the nation's best nightlife away from Zürich, the Lausannois also know how to play hard.

Lausanne can be challenging to explore: It spreads across three steep hills, and encompasses a height difference of 1,575 feet (480 m) between the lakeside district of Ouchy and the northern suburbs. Getting around Lausanne has been easier since the opening of the city's metro system in 2008. Its 14 stations are arranged along two lines, which together cover almost the entire city. People staying in the city's hotels can use the metro free of charge with a Lausanne Transport Card,

available from hotel reception desks. The card also covers travel on local buses and trains. The shoreline is ideal to explore by bike, using a Velopass. This simple system allows bike rental for a nominal charge from self-service depots around the city (www .lausanneroule.ch).

Cathédrale de Notre-Dame: Atop one of Lausanne's three hills, the atmospheric, ancient district of Cité comes as a surprise amid the modern metropolis. It is a largely pedestrianized huddle of medieval buildings housing shops, galleries, cozy bars, and restaurants. Its crowning glory is the 13th-century Cathédrale de Notre-Dame, Switzerland's largest cathedral. With its beautifully preserved medieval *imago mundi* rose window and glorious painted portal, the cathedral is a real Gothic

EXPERIENCE: Cruising & Watersports on Lake Geneva

The most romantic way to explore the Lake Geneva region with its vine-clad hillsides, castles, and mountain backdrop is by boat. You'll find plenty of options from steam-powered paddle-wheelers to pedal-powered paddle boats. And for those who want to do something more energetic on the lake, there are several watersports options.

Sailing

Sailing is an enormously popular activity on Lake Geneva, which has dozens of marinas and yacht clubs lining its shores. The most famous, the **Société Nautique de Genève** (www.nautique.org), frequently competes in the world's most prestigious yacht races. They operate a large **sailing school** (Port-Black, Cologny, tel 022/707 05 00, ecoledevoile@nautique .org, $$$$$) in the town of Cologny. The school offers courses for children as young as 6, as well as advanced courses for adults. If you're lucky you might catch sight of one of the club's massive and astonishingly fast ocean-going racing yachts undergoing trials on the lake.

Alternatively, Lausanne is home to two smaller sailing schools, **Ciels Bleus** (place du Vieux-Port, Lausanne, tel 076/366 39 49, www .cielsbleus.ch) and **Ecole de Voile d'Ouchy** (Chemin des Pêcheurs 7, Lausanne, tel 021/635 58 87, www.ecole-de-voile.ch, $$$$$). The former offers waterskiing lessons as well as sailing courses.

Watersports

If you're looking for something a little more exciting than sailing, you can try your hand at wakeboarding, an activity that combines waterskiing with surfing—pulling you behind a fast-moving boat on a short, surfboard-like board. The boats of the **Wake Sport Center** (quai de Cologny 9, Cologny, tel 079/202 38 73, www.wake.ch) go out on the lake every day in the summer, and can be rented with a professional instructor.

Just off the lake, on the fast-flowing waters of the Arve River (which joins the Rhône in Geneva), local company **Rafting.ch** (tel 079/301 41 40, www.rafting .ch) runs rafting trips down the Arve's cascades and rapids. These trips typically start from the Pont de Sierne, right in the center of the city.

Cruises

For those who'd rather just admire the view, several companies offer cruises on Lake Geneva. You can take a short themed cruise (including "Famous Lemanic Vineyards" and "Wonderful Alpine Scenery"). Or enjoy a daytrip that embraces all the main sights of the lake (including Geneva, Lausanne, Vevey, Montreux, Château de Chillon, and even the French town of Evian). Most lake cruises are operated by **Compagnie Générale de Navigation** (CGN; avenue de Rhodanie 17, Lausanne, tel 0848/811 848, www.cgn.ch, $$$$–$$$$$), with their fleet of 20 boats (including eight belle époque paddle-wheelers), and with departures from various resorts along the route. The cruise time from Geneva to Lausanne is 3 hours 45 minutes.

INSIDER TIP:

Renting a paddle boat for a small fee will provide you with a downtown river tour among the city's native swans.

—CAROLINE GRAVES
National Geographic Books contributor

Tour the region on a 3-hour mini-cruise aboard *La Vaudoise,* the last flat-bottomed barque with Latin sails on the lake. *La Vaudoise* was launched in 1932 as a vessel to transport stone and gravel and is now moored at the port of Ouchy (Les Pirates d'Ouchy, tel 079/446 2118, www.lavaudoise.com).

Hôtel de Ville
- ✉ place de la Palud 2
- ☎ (021) 315 25 55
- 🚇 Metro 2 (Bessières); Bus 14 (Pierre-Viret)

Musée Cantonal des Beaux-Arts
- ✉ Palais de Rumine, place de la Riponne 6
- ☎ (021) 316 34 45
- 🕐 Closed Mon.
- 💲 $$
- 🚇 Metro: Rippone-Maurice Béjart. Bus: 1, 2 (Rue Neuve); 8 (Riponne)

www.musees
.vd.ch/en/musee-
des-beaux-arts

masterpiece. Lausanne is the last city in Switzerland to keep alive the medieval tradition of the night-watchman who calls the hour from the tower every night between 10 p.m. and 2 a.m.

Behind the cathedral, the squat 14th-century **Château Saint-Maire** (St. Maire Castle) is the highest point of the old city and the seat of the cantonal government. Also nearby you'll find the **Musée Historique de Lausanne** *(place de la Cathédrale 4, Lausanne, tel 021/315 41 00, closed Mon. except July & Aug., www.lausanne .ch/mhl)*, housed in the former medieval Bishops' Palace. It relates the city's history from its prehistoric beginnings, and includes a vast 1:200 scale model of 17th-century Lausanne. The terrace affords sweeping city vistas toward the lake and across to the trendy Flon quarter to the west. Flon was once an industrial district, but its warehouses have been

converted into alternative cafés and bars, trendy dance clubs, and experimental theater spaces.

Near the cathedral entrance, the medieval **Escaliers du Marché,** a photogenic covered flight of wooden steps, leads down to the ancient market square, **place de la Palud,** the 16th-century **Fountain of Justice,** and the **Hôtel de Ville** (City Hall). The fine dragons atop the roof of the last are symbols of former trade links with East Asia. There are markets here on Wednesday and Saturday mornings.

Centre-Ville: The Centre-Ville district, or city center, brims with chic boutiques and prestigious art galleries, intermingled with high street fashions. Above place de la Palud, the vast Florentine-style neo-Renaissance **Palais de Rumine** (1900) was where the Treaty of Lausanne was signed in 1923. This treaty finalized the partitioning of the Ottoman Empire after World War I. Nowadays it hosts several museums, including the impressive **Musée Cantonal des Beaux-Arts** (Cantonal Museum of Fine Arts).

South of place de la Palud, across rue Centrale, the streets climb toward place Saint-François and its 13th-century church, **Église Saint-Francois** *(place Saint-Francois).* The church has a graceful bell tower, originally constructed alongside a Franciscan convent. A short walk from here, the tranquil **Parc Mon-Repos,** with magnificent trees, statuary, and an aviary, contains **Villa Mon-Repos,** the

---

The Modern Olympics

Baron Pierre de Coubertin (1863–1937) is credited with establishing the modern Summer Olympics. A French aristocrat and historian, Coubertin was a great believer in physical development partnering intellectual development. He romanti-cized ancient Greece and worked hard to establish the Olympics as an international competition. His wish was fulfilled in 1896 when the first Olympics of the modern era took place in Athens. Coubertin was the first President of the International Olym-pic Committee (IOC), which has continued to organize the games ever since and which met in Lausanne's Villa Mon-Repos between 1922 and 1967.

The Olympic flame burns at the Musée Olympique at Ouchy, near Lausanne.

former residence of Baron Pierre de Coubertin. Coubertin who founded the modern Olympics.

Down by the lake, the former fishing village of **Ouchy** (the "Lausanne Riviera") has grand hotels, a yachting harbor, manicured parks, and tree-lined promenades that stretch to Lutry. The striking waterfront **Musée Olympique** is the world's leading center of information and research on the Olympic movement, and Lausanne's most visited museum. It charts the development of the Olympic movement from the first games in ancient Greece (said to have taken place in 776 B.C.) to the present day. State-of-the-art 3D audiovisual and robotics technology enables visitors to experience at first hand the experiences of Olympic athletes.

Toward the East: East of Ouchy, the lakeside Vidy district

is popular for recreation, with its pool, sandy beaches, a yachting haven, and waterside bars and restaurants. The **Musée Romain de Lausanne-Vidy** (Lausanne-Vidy Roman Museum; *Chemin du Bois-de Vaux 24, tel 021/315 4185, www.lausanne.ch/mrv*) traces the history and lifestyle of the bustling Roman port of Lousonna on the shores of Lacus Lemannus from the first century B.C. to the fourth century A.D. The modern headquarters of the IOC occupies Château de Vidy, an 18th-century stately home. A 2.5-mile (4 km) "sports trail" loops through the district, with 22 markers en route explaining the history of the Olympics.

On the northern fringes of Ouchy lies one of the area's finest art galleries, the **Fondation de l'Hermitage** (Heritage Foundation). This institution

Musée Olympique
- ✉ quai d'Ouchy 1
- ☎ (021) 621 65 11
- 🕐 Closed Mon. Nov.–March
- 💲 $$$$
- 🚇 Metro 2 (Ouchy), Bus 8, 25 (Musée Olympique)

www.olympic.org

Fondation de l'Hermitage
- ✉ route du Signal 2, Bellevaux
- ☎ (021) 320 50 13
- 🕐 Closed Mon.
- 💲 $$$
- 🚌 Bus 16 (Hermitage)

http://en.fondation-hermitage.ch

Cyclists at the La Fourchette work of art by Jean-Pierre Zaugg, Vevey

Vevey

🗺 59 C2

Visitor Information

✉ Montreux-Vevey
Tourisme,
Grande-Place
29, Vevey

☎ (084) 886 84 84

🕐 Closed Sun.

**www.montreux-
vevey.com/en**

hosts exhibitions of paintings and sculptures from the late 19th and 20th centuries.

Swiss Riviera

East of Lausanne, as the north shore of Lake Geneva begins to follow a course to the south-east, and the lake itself starts to narrow, lie the towns of Vevey and Montreux. This is the Swiss Riviera. Like its French Riviera counterpart, it has a long-standing tradition of tourism. For decades it enjoys enticed the rich and famous to its shores. Visiting luminaries have included the wordsmiths Victor Hugo, Ernest Hemingway, and Graham Greene; French Impressionist artist Gustave Courbet; and actors Noel Coward and Charlie Chaplin. Today this area

is the home of pop stars, fashion designers, and sports stars including Formula 1 racing drivers Michael Schumacher, Alain Prost, and Lewis Hamilton.

The Swiss Riviera makes an excellent base for touring the surrounding countryside and marks the departure point for luxury GoldenPass Belle Époque panoramic train rides (see p. 111) to the Bernese Oberland. It takes less than an hour to reach the nearest ski resorts in the Alpes Vaudoises (see p. 153). If you intend to travel widely in the region, consider purchasing a five- or seven-day regional Lake Geneva-Alps pass, which offers unlimited travel on two (or three) freely chosen days, and a 50 percent reduction on the remaining days. This pass is available from tourist offices, train stations, and ship booking offices.

Vevey

The gracious spa resort of Vevey is one of the main towns on the Swiss Riviera and a popular destination for travelers. It has a lot going for it including a stunning lakeside location at the heart of the Lavaux vineyards and a pleasant climate known for its mild winters. Milk chocolate was invented in Vevey, which is also the home of Nestlé chocolate.

The Vieille Ville: The attractive cobbled streets of the Vieille Ville, between the railway line and the lake, are dotted with historical monuments and museums bearing witness to Vevey's rich heritage. This is also the place to visit quality boutiques and shops specializing in regional wines, cheeses, chocolate, arts, crafts, and antiques. A large, colorful food market fills the main square, **Grand Place** (also known as the place du Marché), every Tuesday and Saturday morning. From mid-July to the end of August, the **Marchés Folk-**

loriques (Folkloric Markets) draw thousands of visitors to watch local craftsmen, listen to traditional folk music, and taste regional wines and delicacies. Dominating the square, the **Market Hall** was financed by local businessman Henri Nestlé, and modeled on Paris's Les Halles. It now houses the tourist office. Here, too, the **Musée Suisse de l'Appareil Photographique** (Swiss Camera Museum) celebrates the printed image, with a display of cameras from the 1920s to the present.

Take time to stroll along the elegant lakeside promenade with its neatly manicured flower beds. Here stands a statue of the English comic actor and film director of the silent movie era, Charlie Chaplin (1889–1977), who lived for 25 years at **Manoir de Ban** in the Vevey suburb of Corsier. The refurbished house is set to open as a museum commemorating Chaplin's life and work in 2013. Other celebrated residents of Vevey have included French Impressionist artist Gustave Courbet (1819–1877) and exiled Russian author Fyodor Dostoevsky (1821–1888). French

(continued on p. 80)

Musée Suisse de l'Appareil Photographique
- ⊠ Grande Place, Vevey
- ☎ (021) 925 34 80
- 🕐 Closed Mon.
- 💲 $$
- 🚆 Train (Vevey)

Manoir de Ban
- ⊠ Route de Fenil 2, Corsier-su-Vevey
- 🕐 Due to open spring 2013
- **www.chaplin museum.com**

Celebrity Who's Who

Over the years, numerous poets, philosophers, writers, politicians, actors, artists, and musicians have stayed in the Montreux–Vevey region and have been inspired by the beauty of the Swiss Riviera. The ingenious Poet's Ramble (www .montreuxriviera.com/en/culture_leisure), a walking route incorporating 25 "talking benches," follows the tracks of those illustrious guests, recalling the thoughts, words, and verses of such luminaries as Charlie Chaplin, Graham Greene, Ernest Hemingway, and Victor Hugo. The benches describe the significance of the places where you have chosen to rest (free booklet available at tourist offices).

Swiss Chocolate

Eating chocolate is a way of life in Switzerland. In towns and cities, every street seems to have at least one chocolate shop to lure you in with its tantalizing aromas and its mouth-watering window displays. And hot chocolate is served on every café menu, especially during winter months. Little wonder, then, that the Swiss lead the world in chocolate production.

Chocolate samples at Chocolaterie Rapp

Most people would agree that the Swiss produce the finest chocolate in the world. And they are also true chocoholics, eating a remarkable 23 pounds (10.5 kg) of chocolate per capita a year. This is roughly equivalent to one average-size chocolate bar per person daily, making them the greatest consumers of chocolate in the world.

Swiss chocolate-making is a true art. Alongside all those truffles, pralinés, and hand-filled luxury chocolates, not a season goes by without some novelty temptations, too: chocolate flowers in spring, chocolate eggs at Easter, chocolate chestnuts and mushrooms in fall, and chocolate Santas at Christmas. There are regional specialties, as well: chocolate bears in Bern and chocolate watches in the Jura.

A Chocolate History

The Confederation has a long tradition of chocolate production, although chocolate's origins are much, much older. The Mayans of Mesoamerica were eating chocolate in the sixth century, and the tradition was later revived by the Aztecs. The Spanish conquistador Hernan Cortez took cocoa beans from Mexico back to his native land in the early 16th century; drinking chocolate was first introduced to France in the following century; and solid chocolate was eaten in Italy before it reached Switzerland. However, once François-Louis Cailler began Swiss production in Vevey in 1819, having acquired the skill from Italian confectioners, there was no looking back. Cailler was the first to

INSIDER TIP:

If the chocolate on its own isn't Swiss enough for you, head to Geneva's Edelweiss Restaurant *(place de la Navigation 2)* where you can fill yourself up with chocolate fondue while listening to authentic live yodeling.

—CAROLINE GRAVES
National Geographic Books contributor

invent the process of making chocolate into bars. He was followed soon after by Philippe Suchard in Neuchâtel, who made strides in improving production methods and making chocolate more affordable. Around 1870, Cailler's son-in-law, Daniel Peter of Vevey, invented milk chocolate by adding powdered milk (recently invented by his neighbor Henri Nestlé) to the cocoa paste. Such was his success that, in the 1880s, the entire chocolate industry had adopted his methods, thereby establishing the reputation of Swiss chocolate as the best worldwide: rich in cocoa butter, smooth, and extremely creamy.

Famous Names

Further innovations followed. In 1879 Rodolphe Lindt created "conching" (a mixing process resulting in smooth, liquid chocolate) in Bern, and in 1898 the Cailler company established the first large chocolate factory, at Broc. In 1909, the first chocolate patent by Bernese chocolatier Jean Tobler introduced "Toblerone" to the world. This triangular-shaped bar, containing honey and nougat, was inspired by the shape of the Matterhorn mountain. Another Swiss, Jules Sechaud of Montreux, developed a technique for making chocolate shells filled with other confections in 1913, ensuring

Switzerland's place as the market leader.

Nestlé, Suchard, Lindt—still today the great names in chocolate live on; and two of the most highly regarded Swiss chocolatiers are Sprüngli and Teuscher. However, don't just concentrate on the big brands or you will be missing out on the very finest of Swiss chocolates. Some of the top confectioners are small family concerns with just one or two outlets where exquisite, handcrafted creations are lovingly handmade daily. Be sure to try some before you leave Switzerland!

The Cailler Chocolate Factory Tour *(Maison Cailler, 7 rue Jules Bellet, Broc, tel 026/ 921 5960, $$$)* provides a useful introduction to the manufacturing process. Visitors can smell the aromas and taste the flavors of different kinds of cocoa beans and see the different processes along the way to making a bar of chocolate. The tour ends in a tasting room. Broc is easily accessible by road or rail from Lausanne and Montreux.

EXPERIENCE:
Making Chocolate

To try your hand at chocolate-making, reserve a place for a course at Chocolaterie Durig *(avenue d'Ouchy 15, Lausanne, tel 021/601 24 35, www.durig.ch, $$$$$).* **Master chocolatier Dan Durig's tasting course (30 minutes) and chocolate-making workshop (90 minutes) involve making your own seasonal chocolates, plus tastings of such unusual creations as chocolate vinegar, Mexican spiced cocoa, and chocolate with Alpine flowers. Alternatively, Chocolaterie Rapp** *(rue des Alpes 6, Prangins, tel 022/361 79 14, $$$$$),* **midway between Geneva and Lausanne, has day courses that last five hours. At Broc, 15 miles (24 km) northeast of Montreux, the Cailler Chocolate Factory** *(Maison Cailler, rue Jules Bellet 7, Broc, tel 026/921 59 60, $$$$$)* **offers two hour-long chocolate-making courses.**

Alimentarium

✉ quai Perdonnet, Vevey

☎ (021) 924 11 11

🕐 Closed Mon.

💲 $$$

🚌 Bus 1 (Court-au-Chantre)

⛴ Ferry (Vevey Marché)

www.alimentarium .ch

Musée Historique du Vieux Vevey

✉ rue du Château 2, Vevey

☎ (021) 921 07 22

🕐 Closed Mon.

🚌 Bus 1 (Ste-Claire)

⛴ Ferry (Vevey-La Tour)

The Lavaux vineyards are renowned for their Chasselas grapes, which produce a subtle white wine.

structural engineer Gustave Eiffel (1832–1923) had a holiday home here, and the English novelist Graham Greene (1904–1991) died here. The German pharmacist, Henri Nestlé (1814–1890), founder of the world's largest food company, moved to Vevey in 1839 and developed the first baby milk formula here in 1867. The headquarters of this famous multinational is still on the lake to the west of the town. The fascinating **Alimentarium** (Food Museum) analyses various aspects of food and nutrition in a lively,

fun way, with plenty of interactive activities and even an opportunity for kids to cook.

The **Musée Historique du Vieux Vevey** (Historical Museum of Old Vevey), housed in a beautiful 16th-century mansion, documents the region's colorful past, with special emphasis on the unique Fête des Vignerons (Winegrowers' Festival). This takes place here every 25 years, most recently in 1999. Near the rail station, an impressive neoclassical temple houses the resort's top-notch museum of fine arts,

Musée Jenisch, with its changing exhibitions of Swiss art. Its permanent treasures include important pieces by Dürer, Rembrandt, Corot, Picasso, and Le Corbusier. The Oskar Kokoschka Foundation contains the largest collection of the work of the Austrian expressionist who spent the last 26 years of his life in nearby **Villeneuve.**

Vevey eventually merges imperceptibly with its eastern neighbor, the photogenic villageport of La Tour-de-Peilz. Its lakeside château contains the entertaining **Musée Suisse du Jeu** (Swiss Games Museum), with a host of hands-on games to play.

The Lavaux Vineyards

The picturesque Lavaux vineyards, which cling to the shoreline of Lake Geneva, are mirrored in its calm waters as they slowly evolve from the browns of winter, through the vivid greens of spring and summer, to the russet shades of fall. In their midst, beautifully preserved villages, where the vintners live and press their grapes, provide a host of scenic walks and wine-tasting opportunities in the local *caveaux des vignerons* (wine cellars).

Wine production in Pays de Vaud dates from Roman times. It is now Switzerland's second largest wine region, producing a quarter of the nation's wines. Of its six main areas, the most famous is Lavaux *(www.lavaux.com),* the largest contiguous vineyard region in Switzerland, with a high yield of refreshingly dry fruity wines. Since

2007, it has been classified as a UNESCO World Heritage site. The wine area fringes the southfacing northern shores of Lake Geneva between the village of **Lutry** *(www.lutry.ch)* and the glamorous resort of Montreux, to the west. A wide variety of grapes are grown, including the smooth, light Pinot Noir, fruity Gamay reds, and subtle Chasselas whites (the main grape variety cultivated here). These are produced around the villages of Féchy, Epesses, Dézaley, Mont-sur-Rolle, and St. Saphorin. The wines draw their distinctive

INSIDER TIP:

The Lavaux are some of the steepest vineyards in Europe. Watch for the vintners using tiny funiculars and pulley systems to harvest the grapes.

—VINCENT COLLETTI
Valais wine expert

flavors from a combination of the high mineral content of the soil and the region's favorable climate, particularly its "three suns." This expression refers to the heat of the sun itself, the sunlight reflected off Lake Geneva, and the warmth absorbed in the 248 miles (400 km) of stone walls framing the vineyards, which is released at night.

The area is easy to explore, thanks to a variety of walking

Musée Jenisch
- ✉ avenue de la Gare 2, Vevey
- ☎ (021) 921 29 50
- 🕐 Closed Mon.
- 🚌 Bus 1 (Hôtel-de-Ville)
- ⛴ Ferry (Vevey)

Musée Suisse du Jeu
- ✉ Au Château, 1814 La Tour-de-Peilz
- ☎ (021) 977 23 00
- 🕐 Closed Mon.
- 💲 $$
- 🚌 Bus 1 (La Tour-de-Peilz)
- ⛴ Ferry (Vevey-La Tour)

www.museedujeu .com

Villeneuve
- 🗺 59 C2

Lutry
- 🗺 59 B2

Pully
◪ 59 B2

and cycling trails and even mini-train tours that crisscross the vineyards. The 20-mile (32 km) Lavaux Wine Trail stretches from Lausanne's Olympic Museum (see p. 75) to Château Chillon. It can easily be broken into shorter sections, such as the popular

stone villages of St. Saphorin, Rivaz, and Epesses. Most villages have *caveau des vignerons* to showcase local produce, usually open from Easter until October. There, you can meet winegrowers and taste local wines. A list of Lavaux cellars that offer tastings

Billy Idol performing at the 2010 Montreux Jazz Festival

Vinorama
✉ route du Lac 2, Rivaz
☎ (021) 946 31 31
🕒 Closed Mon. & Tues.
www.lavaux-vino rama.ch

Montreux
◪ 59 C2
Visitor Information
✉ Montreux Tourisme, place de l'Eurovision
☎ (084) 886 84 84
www.montreux-vevey.com/en

three-hour hike from St. Saphorin to the charming medieval town of Lutry on the lake near Lausanne. Neighboring **Pully** (*www.pully .ch*) is also worth a visit for its tiers of houses tumbling down to the shoreline and its delightful cobbled streets. Pully also has a tiny, atmospheric harbor and a fascinating Roman villa.

Every inch of the surrounding countryside is covered in vineyards and dotted with pretty hamlets such as Le Châtelard and Savuit. If you have the time, explore the beautiful golden-

is available at *www.lavaux.ch*. Most open at around 4 p.m. or 5 p.m., so plan your itinerary carefully. The **Vinorama** at Rivaz unites all the regional appellations of Lavaux under one roof. Around 200 wines are on display, and a different selection is available for tasting each week.

The **Train des Vignes** (Vineyard Train, *www.vins-vaudois .com*), runs hourly from Vevey to Puidoux. It passes through Chexbres, from where a miniature **tractor-train** (*www.lavaux-pan oramic.ch*) offers circuits around

INSIDER TIP:

On summer evenings, one of the best places to go in Montreux is the Promenade Fleuri, where you can sit in the shade of the trees and watch the little sailboats on the lake.

—BEN HOLLINGUM
National Geographic contributor

the villages of Rivaz, St. Saphorin, and Chardonne in the summer. The tiny **Lavaux Express** *(www .lavauxexpress.com)* explores the vineyards from Lutry to Grand-vaux, and from Cully to Riex and Epesses. Book in advance.

Montreux

Thanks to its Mediterranean-style microclimate and its spectacular location, the chic resort of Montreux has been a popular health resort since the late 19th century. But this gracious spa town is perhaps best known for the **Montreux Jazz Festival** (see sidebar), the largest and most prestigious of its type in the world. Each July, this festival draws jazz legends and other unmissable stars. Miles Davis, B.B. King, Herbie Hancock, James Brown, Eric Clapton, and David Bowie have all headlined. Montreux has long attracted the rich and famous—Jean-Jacques Rousseau, Ernest Hemingway, Igor Stravin-sky, and Freddie Mercury, to name but a few. Their memories

of Montreux can be traced in Montreux–Vevey's unique walking route, **The Poet's Ramble** (see p. 77). The small **Musée du Vieux Montreux,** on the upper slopes of the city, portrays the history and customs of the region in an attractive group of 17th-century winegrowers' houses.

A 45-minute stroll east along Montreux's palm-lined lakeside promenade leads to the resort's main attraction and one of the Confederation's most visited sights, the **Château de Chillon.** This beautiful medieval castle, built on Roman foundations and romantically sited on a rock beside the lake, has been immortalized by countless artists and writers, including Lord Byron in "The Prisoner of Chillon." ∎

Musée du Vieux Montreux

✉ rue de la Gare 40, Montreux
☎ (021) 963 13 53
🕐 Closed Mon. & Nov.–March
💲 $
🚌 Bus 4, 5, 6 (Rue de la Gare)

Château de Chillon

✉ avenue de Chillon, Veytaux
☎ (021) 966 89 10
💲 $$$
🚆 Train (Veytaux-Chillon); Bus 1 (Chillon)
www.chillon.ch/en

EXPERIENCE: Jazz in Montreux

Each July Montreux is transformed into a musical mecca for the annual Montreux Jazz Festival. More than 220,000 jazz aficionados squeeze into the Stravinsky Auditorium and the Miles Davis Hall at the Montreux Music & Convention Center for 16 days of world-class music.

There is really no substitute for being at one of the gigs. Get tickets for the festival at *www.montreuxjazz.com.* Alternatively, enjoy the full program of gigs in local bars, on street corners, and at festival stages dotted around the resort—all free of charge. Posters and DVDs can be purchased at *www.montreuxjazzshop.com;* Bazar Suisse *(Grand Rue 24, Montreux, tel 021/963 32 74);* or the Montreux Jazz Boutique *(avenue de Chillon 70, Territet).*

Traditional dairies, chocolate factories, and centuries-old watch manufacturers set in rolling country dotted with medieval towns

Basel & Northwest Switzerland

Kinetic artist Jean Tinguely's fountain in Basel

Basel & Northwest Switzerland

Northwest Switzerland is a land of gentle landscapes, lakes, forests, and traditional villages. It stretches from the Jura Mountains—cradle of the Swiss watchmaking industry—to the verdant rolling hills of Swiss cheese country, the Pays du Gruyère. A melting pot of French and German cultures, the region is rich in museums, galleries, and fascinating architecture. And Basel is its main focal point.

Detailed fresco on a facade in Basel

Basel (*Bâle* in French, and often anglicized to *Basle*) is perhaps best known beyond Swiss borders for its traditional Christmas market during Advent, and its flamboyant *Fasnacht* (carnival; see pp. 53–54) celebrations during Lent, known locally as *die drey scheenste däg* ("the three finest days"). However, it also counts among the nation's leading cultural centers, world-renowned for its wealth of galleries, art events, and museums, as well as for its adventurous modern architecture.

Basel is commercially important as Switzerland's main river port. The Rhine River forms the city's backbone, plied by trade barges yet also providing a place to relax at the very heart of the city. Basel enjoys good relations with neighboring Alsace (France) and has the Black Forest (southern Germany) virtually on its doorstep. The proximity of the three nations meant Basel was the only German-speaking region with a clear majority voting in favor of membership of the European Union in the 1994 referendum. For visitors, this gives the city—a wonderful melting pot of cultures and cuisines—a really cosmopolitan vibe.

Around Basel, you'll find plenty of varied

NOT TO BE MISSED:

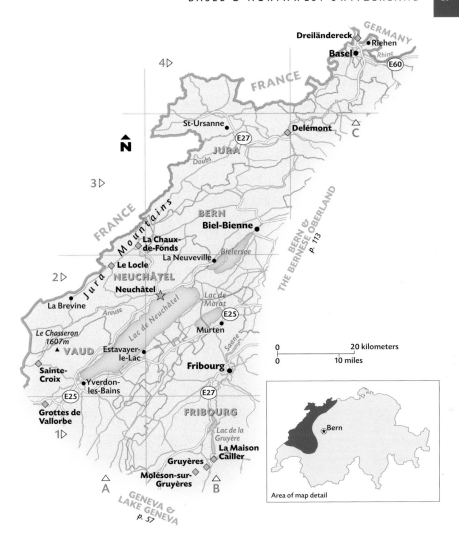

Dreiländereck
GERMANY
Riehen
Basel
Rhine
E60
4▷
FRANCE
St-Ursanne
Delémont
C
E27
N
JURA
Doubs
3▷
FRANCE
Jura Mountains
BERN
Biel-Bienne
La Chaux-
de-Fonds
Bielersee
BERN &
BERNESE OBERLAND
P. 113
THE BERNESE OBERLAND
La Neuveville
Le Locle
NEUCHÂTEL
2▷
Neuchâtel
La Brevine
Areuse
Lac de
Morat
E25
Lac de Neuchâtel
Le Chasseron
1607m
VAUD
Estavayer-
le-Lac
Murten
Saane
0   20 kilometers
0   10 miles
Sainte-
Croix
Yverdon-
les-Bains
Fribourg
E25
E27
Grottes de
Vallorbe
FRIBOURG
1▷
Lac de la
Gruyère
Bern
La Maison
Cailler
Gruyères
Moléson-sur-
Gruyères
A
B
GENEVA &
LAKE GENEVA
P. 57
Area of map detail

countryside to enjoy. Sports fanatics will enjoy the Jura Mountains, which run along the northwestern Franco-Swiss border. Somewhat off the beaten tourist track, the Jura are a nature-lover's paradise and hugely popular for walking and cross-country skiing.

Picturesque Neuchâtel, situated amid the vineyards on the northern shore of Lac de Neuchâtel, makes a perfect base for exploring the many local watchmaking museums and natural wonders of the Jura, as well as the historic towns and villages of the Trois-Lacs (Three Lakes) district.

To the south, the ancient, art-filled city of Fribourg is one of Switzerland's best-kept secrets, with its immaculately preserved medieval center and lively, college-town atmosphere. The Fribourg region is at the heard of the Pre-Alps, with their picture-postcard wooden chalets and bucolic hilly pastures, splashed with wild flowers and dotted with cows with clattering bells. This is archetypal Switzerland, perfect for gentle hiking and bike trails. Here too is the photogenic town of Gruyères, famed for its eponymous cheese, and the nearby Maison Cailler, an absolute must for chocoholics. ■

Basel

Switzerland's third largest city, Basel is on the banks of the mighty Rhine at the point where the Swiss, French, and German borders converge. Thanks to its large river port, it has been a hugely wealthy and important commercial city since medieval times, though today it owes much of its prosperity to its thriving pharmaceuticals industry. Basel is considered by many to be the cultural capital of Switzerland.

Mittlere Brücke in Basel, one of the oldest bridges over the Rhine

Basel

⚑ 87 C4

Visitor Information

✉ Basel Tourismus, Stadt-Casino, Barfüsserplatz, Steinenberg 14

☎ (061) 268 68 68

🚊 Tram 3, 6, 8, 11, 14, 16 Barfüsserplatz

www.basel.com

Basel is one of the world's greatest art cities. Barely 166,000 people live here, yet Basel has more than 30 world-class museums and galleries, including the fêted Fondation Beyeler (see p. 90). The city boasts a long history of artistic patronage, closely linked to its glorious past.

A Little History

Basel's history dates back to 40 B.C., when the Romans settled here, naming their town *Basilia*.

A Celtic town later developed on the site, but this was destroyed by the Huns in 917. During the Middle Ages Basel slowly regained its prominence, a process helped by the building of the first bridge across the Rhine in 1225. The settlements either side of the river (Grossbasel and Kleinbasel) joined forces as a single city shortly after the catastrophic plague of 1349, which killed around 14,000 people. Basel enjoyed its heyday in the 15th century—Pope Felix V was crowned there in 1440, and its population began to swell rapidly as emperors, princes, bishops, philosophers, and merchants took up residence. The University of Basel—the nation's oldest center of learning—was founded in 1460 and remained Switzerland's only official university for three centuries. The city became a major center for humanist ideas, spurring the growth of papermaking and printing. Great minds came to live here. Among their number were the Dutch humanist Erasmus (1466–1536), the German artist Holbein the Younger (ca 1497–1543) and, centuries later, German philosopher Friedrich Nietzsche (1844–1900).

Basel continued to be an important trading center, its port flourishing as the Confederation's gateway to the North Sea.

Modern Basel

Today the city remains a center of learning, printing, and finance—and also an international marketplace for art and antiquities. While Baslers are proud of their history, they are at the same time very receptive to new ideas. As a consequence, their beautifully restored medieval buildings stand side by side with modern structures designed by world-famous architects. This unique amalgam makes exploring Basel especially rewarding.

However it is the city's position on the Rhine which defines Basel more than anything. It is strategically located at the point where the river makes a sharp bend northward. The Rhine is Switzerland's only outlet to the sea and its gateway to northern Europe. Little wonder then that Basel's voters are the most pro-European of all the German-speaking cantons. Much of the city's daily life revolves around this broad, milky-turquoise river, from fishing to rowing, water-taxis to freight-barges, floating concerts, and hydroelectric power stations.

Closer to the center of town, the docks and warehouses of the working river give way to lovely riverside parks. In the summer months these tranquil spaces are home to al fresco cafés, bars, and riverside restaurants. There is also plenty of action on the river as dozens of barges travel through the city daily, passing narrowly under the various bridges. In summer, join locals at one of

EXPERIENCE:
Stand at Dreiländereck

Dreiländereck (Three Country Corner) is the point where the borders of Switzerland, Germany, and France meet in the middle of the Rhine. To get here, take a boat tour with **Basler Personenschifffahrt** (see p. 90) or catch tram number 8 to Kleinhüningen tram-stop. It is then a 15-minute walk: along the northern shore of the Wiese River to the Rhine, past Basel's major freight depot. Turn right and follow the river downstream alongside Kleinhünigen port to the border triangle. The Dreiländereck is marked by a small but sleek tri-point sculpture by local architect Wilhelm Münger (b. 1923).

Museum Tinguely

- ✉ Paul Sacher-Anlage 1
- ☎ (061) 681 93 20
- ⊕ Closed Mon.
- $ $$$$
- 🚌 Bus 31, 36, 38 (Tinguely-Museum)

www.tinguely.ch

Fondation Beyeler

- ✉ Baselstrasse 101, Riehen-Basel
- ☎ (061) 645 97 00
- $ $$$$$
- 🚌 Tram 6 (Fondation Beyeler)

www.fondation beyeler.ch/en

the dedicated *badis* (swimming platforms) and take a traditional dip into the Rhine at Birsköpfli, where the swift current will sweep you downstream past the Altstadt (Old Town). Remember to buy a waterproof swimming bag for your clothing from your hotel reception beforehand, as it's a one-way sport! In August the *kulturfloss* (culture raft) moors up opposite Hotel Krafft (see p. 282), with an exciting nightly lineup of live musical events.

North of the Rhine: The city is divided into distinctive districts, with the Altstadt bisected by the Rhine to create Kleinbasel (Small Basel) and Grossbasel (Big Basel). North of the Rhine, the main tourist area is Altstadt Kleinbasel, with its magnificent river frontage of beautiful old mansions. This is a popular residential district and one of the most multicultural areas of town, with myriad small restaurants, cafés, and shops. It has an edgier feel than Grossbasel, south of the river, and contains considerably fewer tourist attractions. Nonetheless

it is an excellent place to start your sightseeing. Stroll along Kleinbasel's lime-tree-shaded riverside promenade, with its magnificent views of Grossbasel and the cathedral (see p. 92), which dominates the skyline, across the river. The promenade leads west to the Dreiländereck (see sidebar p. 89; allow one hour on foot) and east to the **Museum Tinguely.** This curvaceous pink-stone building beside the Rhine, designed by celebrated Ticinese architect Mario Botta (see pp. 260–261), perfectly juxtaposes with the postmodernist mechanical sculptures within, created by local kinetic artist Jean Tinguely (1925–1991). Tinguely was famed for his colorful, clanking creations shaped from scrap metal, old wheels, and bits of everyday junk. South of the river, the **Tinguely Fountain** outside the Kunsthalle delights visitors with the twists and turns of its madcap metal contraptions.

Farther northwest is Basel's top gallery, **Fondation Beyeler** (Beyeler Foundation). The building

Rhine River Cruises

A boat trip on the Rhine is a highlight of any visit to Basel, providing an alternative and exciting perspective of the city's fine old river frontage. Basler Personenschifffahrt (*Westquaistrasse 62, Basel, tel 061/639 95 00, www.bpg.ch*) runs various cruises from mid-April to mid-October, departing from the Schifflände ticket booth and jetty in the city center.

Cruises range from city and harbor tours to lunch cruises. There are short hops upstream to Museum Tinguely (see this page) and downstream to the Dreiländereck (see p. 89) and Weil am Rhein. If you have more time, longer excursions pass eastbound through the locks along the Swiss-German border to Rheinfelden and back (allow 4 hours).

alone is worth the 10-minute tram trip from the city center to the suburb of Riehen. It is a striking glass-and-red-porphyry edifice designed by Italian architect Renzo Piano (b. 1937), which blends perfectly into sculpture-studded gardens and the landscape beyond. Within this modern, light-filled art temple is the small but select collection of local art-lover Ernest Beyeler (1921–2010). This includes works by some of the 20th century's most celebrated artists, including Matisse, Monet, Miró, Klee, Rodin, and Picasso. It was Beyeler who organized the very first Art Basel (see p. 47) in 1970. This is now the world's most influential annual contemporary art show.

South of the Rhine: Basel's main tourist zones lie south of the Rhine, and are easily accessible from Kleinbasel via three bridges, including one of the oldest, the 13th-century **Mittlere Brücke.** An alternative, more entertaining way to cross the river is to join locals on the four unusual *fähri* **cable-ferries** *(www.faehri.ch),* which have plied the river since the mid-19th century. Small and wooden, they are powered solely by river currents and are operated by a strong cable stretched from bank to bank. To hail a fähri, simply sound the jetty bell, wave to the ferryman, and jump aboard.

Once on the other side, set about exploring Grossbasel's Altstadt, the historic heart of the city. It has fine medieval buildings,

The Rhine viewed from the top of Basel's Münster

brightly painted (drinking-water) fountains, and quaint lanes with specialist galleries and boutiques (which become increasingly expensive the higher up the hill they are). This is also where you will find the daily food market at **Marktplatz.** Here, stalls sell mouthwatering Alpine herbs and honey, local cheeses, cherries (a Basel specialty), and wines. The fresco-adorned, 16th-century **Rathaus** (Town Hall) looks down on the market, which is the start point for five self-guided color coded walking tours. Each of these

Kunstmuseum

⊠ St. Alban-
Graben 16

☎ (061) 206 62 62

🕐 Closed Mon.

💲 $$$$ (includes
Museum für
Gegenwarts-
kunst)

🚊 Tram 2, 15
(Kunstmuseum)

**www.kunstmuseum
basel.ch/en/home**

Barfüsserkirche & Historical Museum of Basel

⊠ Steinenberg 4

☎ (061) 205 86 00

🕐 Closed Mon.

💲 $$

🚊 Tram 3, 6,
8, 11, 14, 16
Barfüsserplatz

depicts a different historic figure associated with the city, including Hans Holbein and Erasmus (contact the tourist office for details and an accompanying iguide).

A few hundred yards southeast of the Rathaus is the real highlight of the Altstadt—the imposing red-sandstone **Münster** (Cathedral). This former episcopal seat is a clever fusion of a Gothic exterior and a Romanesque interior. It features a dazzling colored-tile roof, serene cloisters, and a viewing balcony with sweeping views over Basel and the Rhine.

Many of the city's numerous museums can be found within easy walking distance of here. If you intend to visit several, purchase a 24-hour Basel Card from the tourist office. This covers admission to all city museums,

a guided walking tour, and a handful of further discounts. Several of the most interesting museums are in a cluster just south of the Münster. One not to miss is the **Kunstmuseum** (Fine Arts Museum). This is one of Switzerland's most important art museums, containing the world's largest collection of works by the Holbein family, as well as many 19th- and 20th-century canvases, including several by Cézanne, van Gogh, and Picasso.

Nearby, the **Barfüsserkirche** (Barefoot Church) contains the **Historical Museum of Basel,** and the **Cathedral Treasury.** Also close is the **Antikenmuseum** (Museum of Ancient Art, St. Alban-Graben 5, tel 061/201 1212, closed Mon., www.antikenmuseum basel.ch/en, $$), which is the only

Pondering the significance of a work in Basel's Kunstmuseum

EXPERIENCE: Brew Your Own Beer

The **Bräuerei Unser Bier** (Our Beer Brewery; Gundelgingerstrasse 287, tel 061/ 338 83 83, closed Sun., www.unser-bier.ch) was formed by a small group of home-brewers in 1998. They began by offering fellow Baslers small home-brewing courses. Such was the response, they founded a brewery. Their popular beers, all brewed in Basel, can be obtained at the **Bräustube** (Brewery Pub; Dornacherstrasse 192, open Thurs. & Fri. 5–8 p.m.), and in many local restaurants. Unser Bier also runs "Beer Experience" evenings (reservations essential), that give groups of 12 to 20 people a chance to brew their own beer. As the locals say "Zum Wohl!"

Swiss museum devoted exclusively to ancient Mediterranean civilizations. The small **Schweizerisches Architekturmuseum** (SAM) features various aspects of Swiss contemporary architecture. You can book architectural tours here to discover some of the city's hidden gems.

Basel's chemicals industry developed as an offshoot of its thriving textiles industry in the late 18th century. The production of chemicals later spawned the manufacture of pharmaceuticals, an enterprise that has contributed greatly to the city's wealth. To this day Basel plays a key role in the Swiss economy as a world leader in pharmaceutics. The **Pharmazie-Historisches Museum** (Pharmaceutical Museum, Tottengässlein 3, tel 061/264 9111, www.pharmaziemuseum.ch, closed Sun. & Mon., $$), set in a rambling medieval townhouse a little west of the heart of the Altstadt, illustrates the history of this industry.

St. Johann & Sankt Alban:

Northwest of the Altstadt, St. Johann is known for its cutting-edge architecture, with buildings by invited architects from around the globe. The site is centered around the former factory of the pharmaceutical giant Novartis, which is being converted into a research center.

East of the old town, beside the river, romantic Sankt Alban resembles an ancient village with its quaint half-timbered houses, narrow alleys, and streams. A center for handicrafts, it is home to a charming medieval watermill containing the **Basler Papiermühle** (Basel Paper Mill), where you can watch artisans at work, and even make your own paper and print on it. Sankt Alban also has the fascinating **Museum für Gegenwartskunst** (Museum of Contemporary Art). Farther south, Basel architectural duo Herzog & de Meuron designed the **Schaulager** (Haus zum Kirschgarten, Elisabethenstrasse 27, Basel, tel 061/335 32 32, open for special events only, www.schaulager.org), which is a new kind of art venue. Neither museum nor traditional warehouse, it houses contemporary artworks from the Emanuel Hoffmann collection stored and displayed simultaneously in concrete cubicles. ■

Schweizerisches Architektur-museum (SAM)
- ✉ Steinenberg 7
- ☎ (061) 261 14 13
- 🕐 Closed Mon.
- 💲 $$$
- 🚋 Tram 3, 8, 10, 11, 14 (Bankverein)

www.sam-basel.org

Basler Papiermühle
- ✉ St Alban-Tal 37
- ☎ (061) 225 90 90
- 🕐 Closed Mon.
- 💲 $$$
- 🚋 Tram 2, 15 (Kunstmuseum)

www.papiermuseum
.ch/en/the-museum

Museum für Gegenwartskunst
- ✉ St Alban-Rheinweg 60
- ☎ (061) 272 81 83
- 🕐 Closed Mon.
- 💲 $$$$ (includes Kunstmuseum)
- 🚋 Tram 2, 15 (Kunstmuseum)

www.kunstmuseum
basel.ch /en/home

Northwest Switzerland

Southwest of Basel, the relatively gentle green slopes and thick, dark forests of the Jura Mountains stretch out along the French border. This is the historic center of the watch-making industry, which is still thriving in La Chaux-de-Fonds and Le Locle. Neuchâtel, the biggest city in the area, sits beside the beautiful lake of the same name, while to the south are the charming medieval towns of Fribourg and Gruyères.

The Neuchâtel Artplage, an over-the-water architectural whimsy built in 2002

Neuchâtel

🄰 87 B2

Visitor Information

✉ Tourisme
Neuchâtelois,
Hôtel des Postes

☎ (032) 889 68 90

🕓 Closed Sun.
Sept.–June

**www.neuchatel
tourisme.ch/en/
home.html**

Neuchâtel

Just over 50 miles (80 km) southwest of Basel, and easily accessible from that city by rail and road is Neuchâtel. This small university town is the capital of the eponymous canton and sits at the foot of the Jura Mountains on the northwestern shore of Lake Neuchâtel.

The French novelist Alexandre Dumas (1802–1870) described the medieval town of Neuchâtel as "a toytown carved out of butter," because of the ancient artisans' houses of yellow limestone which flank the car-free streets and picturesque, fountain-filled

squares. Just a stone's throw from the Franco-Swiss border, French influences are strong in Neuchâtel, both architecturally and culturally. The town has long been an important center for watchmaking and precision engineering. It is also famed for its textile industry, introduced by Huguenot refugees from France during the 16th century.

The old town is easy to explore on foot, although some streets are quite steep. Keen sightseers will enjoy the eight *promenades touristiques* (tourist trails) signposted around the town, with an accompanying illustrated booklet available from the tourist office.

The Town Center: High above the town stand two major landmarks, the Renaissance château—once home to the Counts of Neuchâtel, and now the seat of the cantonal government—and the predominantly Gothic church, **Église Collégiale.** The church interior is striking for its painted vaulting (resembling a starry night sky) and a medieval polychrome cenotaph of the Counts of Neuchâtel (to the left of the main altar), comprising 15 carved and painted statues of knights and ladies. Walking downhill from the church square, you will pass the medieval **Prison Tower** *(open April–Sept.)* to your right, which affords sweeping vistas over the rooftops to the lake and beyond.

Neuchâtel is surrounded by vineyards. Wine tastings take place Monday through Friday at the **Caves de Neuchâtel** (Neuchâtel Cellars) adjoining the elegant French-style 19th-century residence Hôtel Dupeyrou (in the town center). Farther down the hill, the ornately painted **Fontaine du Griffon** (Griffon Fountain) is said to have gushed thousands of gallons of wine in 1657 to welcome the king of France. Near the lake, the **place des Halles** is the venue of a farmers' market (Tues., Thurs., & Sat. mornings), although its turreted 16th-century **Maison des Halles** (Covered Market) is now a restaurant *(rue de Trésor 4, tel 032/724 31 41).*

Neuchâtel also boasts a clutch of noteworthy museums, including the **Musée d'Art et d'Histoire** (Museum of Art & History) adjacent to the port. Alongside ceramics, timepieces, and canvases by Anker, Hodler, and other Swiss artists, there is a fascinating collection of 18th-century clockwork automata by local watchmaker Pierre Jaquet-Droz. These are set in motion on the first Sunday of each month at 2 p.m., 3 p.m., and 4 p.m.

In the northern outskirts of town, the striking **Dürrenmatt**

(continued on p. 98)

Neuchâtel Château
- ☎ (032) 889 40 03
- 🕑 Polyglot guided tours daily, April–Sept.

Caves de Neuchâtel
- ✉ avenue du Peyrou 5
- ☎ (032) 717 76 95
- 🕑 Closed Sat. & Sun.

Musée d'Art et d'Histoire
- ✉ esplanade Léopold-Robert 1
- ☎ (032) 717 79 20
- 🕑 Closed Mon.
- 💲 $$ (free on Wed.)
- **www.mahn.ch**

Pays de Trois-Lacs Ferry Tour

The area around Neuchâtel and south of the Jura Mountains is known as the Pays de Trois-Lacs (Drei-Seen-Land in German, or the Land of the Three Lakes). Lac de Neuchâtel, the "blue lung" of the city, is linked via two canals to Lac de Morat (Lake Murten) and Bielersee (Lac de Bienne or Lake Biel), and the ships that sail here are also floating restaurants. A combined tour of all three lakes is offered daily from late May to late September *(also weekends mid-April–mid-Oct.; Sun. Nov.–March).* The tour calls at various towns and villages, including the arcaded medieval town of Murten/Morat; Biel-Bienne (see p. 125); the picturesque wine-producing villages of Ligerz and Twann; and the nature reserve of St. Petersinsel/Île de St. Pierre *(Navigation Lacs Neuchâtel et Morat, Port de Neuchâtel, tel 032/729 96 00, www.navig.ch; Bielersee Schifffahrtsgesellschaft, tel 032/329 8811).*

Drive: Lac de Neuchâtel & the Roman Jura

This drive encircles Lac de Neuchâtel, the largest lake entirely within Switzerland, and skirts Lac de Morat. The route—against the backdrop of the Jura Mountains—is a voyage of discovery, passing historic fairy-tale castles, medieval towns, vineyards, and wine-growing villages. There's also an opportunity for some well-earned relaxation at the spa resort of Yverdon-les-Bains.

The historic town center of Yverdon-les-Bains

Head southwest out of **Neuchâtel,** following signs for Lausanne and Yverdon-les-Bains. You pass through the suburb of Auvernier, which is famous for its excavated Neolithic and Bronze Age lake dwellings, to **Colombier ①**. The high, turreted **Château de Colombier** (rue du Château, Colombier,

tel 032/889 54 99, closed Mon., $ for some exhibitions, www.chateau-de-colombier-ne.ch/eng) dates from the 12th to 16th century and houses a military museum with an impressive collection of weapons and uniforms; a small chintz museum; and the police museum.

Continue southwest, parallel to the lake on the A5. Take a slight detour off the main route to visit the market town of **Boudry ②**, birthplace of the chocolate manufacturer Philippe Suchard (1749–1884), with its picturesque peaches-and-cream-colored houses. The medieval **Château de Boudry** (Clos du Château, Boudry, tel 032/842 10 98) atop the town contains a museum devoted to the 2,000-year-old vineyards and wines of the Neuchâtel region. Highlights include a beautiful mosaic illustrating a Roman banquet.

Back on the A5, continue along the castle-lined route, past Bevaix's Baroque château and the medieval **Château de Vaumarcus ③**. Badly damaged after the Battle of Grandson (1476), the castle was rescued from ruin in the 1980s. Farther along at Grandson, is the 13th-

Jules Verne

Yverdon-les-Bains' eccentric museum, the **Maison d'Ailleurs** (House of Elsewhere; place Pestalozzi 14, tel 024/425 64 38, closed Mon. & Tues., www.ailleurs .ch), is devoted to science fiction and the paranormal, with eclectic displays of pulp sci-fi magazines (some as much as 100 years old), toys, models, and artworks.

The museum has recently been extended in order to house a local writer's unique collection of items relating to the life and work of sci-fi author Jules Verne (1828–1905). Exhibits include 19th-century posters advertising books like Twenty Thousand Leagues Under the Sea or, Journey to the Center of the Earth.

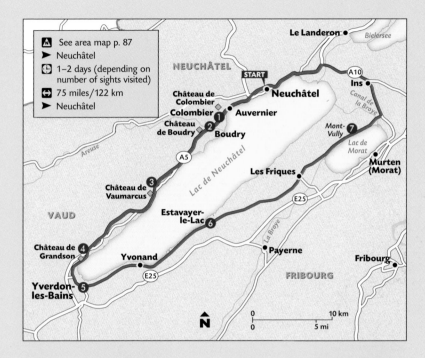

NOT TO BE MISSED:

Château de Colombier • Wine museum Château de Boudry • Baths Centre Thermal

century **Château de Grandson** ❹ *(Grandson, tel 024/445 29 26, closed late Dec.)* one of the nation's largest fortresses, built in Savoyard style with its circular turreted towers, gatehouse and outer defenses. Here during the Battle of Grandson, Swiss troops sided with the Austrians to rout the occupying Burgundian forces. The Burgundians left in such haste that they abandoned the arms now on displayed.

The Return Leg

At the southernmost tip of the lake discover **Yverdon-les-Bains** ❺ founded by the Romans. They named the town Eburodunum, and built thermal baths to exploit the

sulfurous springs. These springs still draw thousands who come to take the waters at **Centre Thermal** *(ave. des Bains 22, Yverdon-les-Bains, tel 024/423 02 32, www.cty.ch, $$$$$).* The town's medieval turreted castle displays six centuries of regional history within the **Musée d'Yverdon et Région** *(The Castle, Yverdon-les-Bains, tel 024/425 93 10, closed Mon., www.musee-yverdon-region.ch, $$),* including two particularly well-preserved Gallo-Roman boats in the vaulted cellar.

Depart Yverdon along the southeastern shore of Lake Neuchâtel via Yvonand to **Estavayer-le-Lac** ❻, with its surprisingly intact medieval walled center, dating to the Savoy rule of 1235 to 1536. Then drive the northern shore of **Lac de Morat,** facing the arcaded medieval town of Murten (Morat). The **themed trails** ❼ through the vineyards of Mont-Vully *(contact Vully Tourisme, route Principale 69, Sugiez, tel 026/673 18 72, www.levully.ch)* afford sweeping views of the Three Lakes region. Proceed to **Ins** and return to Neuchâtel along route A10.

A bohemian waxwing on a rosehip in the Swiss Jura

Dürrenmatt Center

- ✉ chemin du Pertuis-du-Sault 74
- ☎ (032) 720 20 60
- 🕐 Closed Mon. & Tues.
- 💲 $$
- 🚌 Bus 9, 9b (Ermitage)

www.cdn.ch/cdn/index.html?lang=en

Laténium

- ✉ espace Paul Vouga, Hauterive
- ☎ (032) 889 69 17
- 🕐 Closed Mon.
- 💲 $$$
- 🚌 Bus 1 (Musée d'Archéologie)
- 🚢 Ferry (Hauterive)

www.latenium.ch

Center, designed by Mario Botta (see pp. 260–261) and encompassing the home where the Emmentaler author and dramatist Friedrich Dürrenmatt (1921–1990) lived, was created in 2000 to preserve and promote his works. The Fête des Vendanges (Harvest Festival, www.fete-des-vendanges.ch) on the last weekend in September is one of Neuchâtel's annual highlights.

The Suburbs: In the eastern suburb of Hauterive, the **Laténium** archaeological museum and park brings to life 500 centuries of history with its impressive array of local archaeological finds. Be sure to see the **Bevaix Boat,** a 65-foot (20 m) Gallo-Roman shipwreck recovered from Lake Neuchâtel. The lake remains a major base for all kinds of water sport, from canoeing to kite-surfing.

The Jura Area

A little off the usual tourist tracks, the Jura is a well-kept secret. With its sleepy pace of life, and gentle landscapes interspersed with breathtaking geological features, it is perfect country to explore on foot or by bike during the summer and on cross-country skis in winter. The region is also known for its arts and crafts, especially its timepieces and musical boxes.

The Swiss share the Jura Mountains with France. The range dates from the Jurassic period (200–145 million years ago) and occupies about ten per cent of Switzerland's area. The mountains embrace Neuchâtel and Jura cantons, and parts of Vaud and Bern cantons. Jura is the newest of the Confederation's 26 cantons; it was created in 1979 with tiny **Delémont** as its administrative capital.

The scenery throughout the Jura is much gentler than the rugged high Alps. The land rises only to 5,640 feet (1,720 m), at Le Crêt de la Neige in the Chasserel nature reserve, which overlooks Lake Biel. Otherwise, the region's forested and undulating mountainscape is interspersed with lush meadows, pristine lakes, and sleepy villages strung along tranquil valleys. Thanks to a comprehensive network of yellow PostBuses and little red trains, even the remotest towns and villages are easily accessible.

Sainte-Croix: One such remote settlement, tucked away amid verdant landscapes, is Sainte-Croix in the Jura Vaudois, with its chalet-style houses stretched across a sunny hillside. For more than a century, this small town has been revered worldwide for manufacturing musical boxes: A handful of small factories still produce them. The history and art of making these precision instruments over the years is illustrated in the **Musée Cima,** housed in an inconspicuous building in the town center. Its collection includes early musical boxes, automata, and phonographs—all of them made locally. Admission is by guided tour only (in French, with notes available in English). A tour takes about an hour and includes musical demonstrations.

Another museum, **Musée Baud** (Grand Rue 23, L'Auberson, near La Chaux-de-Fonds, tel 024/ 454 2484, closed Mon.–Sat. Oct.–

June, closed a.m., July–Sept., www .museebaud.ch), can be reached by bus a little way west of the town, in the village of L'Auberson. This family run museum displays musical boxes, singing birds, clocks, and musical automata, together with a variety of nickelodeons and gramophones. There is a priceless collection of mechanical musical instruments—the enchanting creations of three generations of the same family. A guided tour lasts about an hour.

The valley is a popular destination for hikers, with the summit of Le Chasseron (5,272 feet/1,607 m; allow two hours from Sainte-Croix) affording grandiose panoramas of the Alps. Its slopes are a popular ski area for families and novices in winter, and it is part of a massive cross-country skiing network. For details of resorts and (continued on p. 102)

Jura Mountains

🅰 87 B3

Visitor Information

✉ Jura Tourisme, place de la Gare 9, Delémont
☎ (032) 420 47 71
🕐 Closed Sun.
www.j3l.ch/en/ portal/bienvenue .html

✉ Tourisme Neuchâtelois-Montagnes, Espacité 1, La Chaux-de-Fonds
☎ (032) 889 68 95
www.neuchatel tourisme.ch/en/ home.html

Musée Cima

✉ rue de l'Industrie 2, Sainte-Croix
☎ (024) 454 44 77
🕐 Closed Mon.
💷 $$$$

Le Corbusier

La Chaux-de-Fonds was the hometown of the famed Swiss architect Le Corbusier (1887–1965). In 1912 he created **La Maison Blanche** (The White House; chemin de Pouillerel 12, La Chaux-de-Fonds, tel 032/910 90 30, closed Mon.–Thurs., www.villa-blanche .ch) for his parents. Within a few years, however, his parents had abandoned the impractical building. The house lay derelict until 1979, when it was granted historic monument status. It is now one of 10 points on a self-guided Le Corbusier walking trail (available from La Chaux-de-Fonds tourist office), together with his Mediterranean-inspired **Villa Turque** (rue du Doubs 167, La Chaux-de-Fonds, tel 032/912 31 23, open first and third Sat.), built in 1917 and now occupied by luxury watchmakers Ebel.

A Brief History of Swiss Timepieces

Switzerland has long been associated with the production of timepieces. Over the centuries, the nation's watchmaking industry has gone from strength to strength, and today the Swiss are the undisputed masters of precision-timing and, perhaps as a by-product, punctuality.

A precision watch engineer at work in La Chaux-de-Fonds

Contrary to popular opinion, the Swiss did not invent the cuckoo clock. That honor is bestowed upon the artisans of the Black Forest, where European clock manufacture started. In the early years, the main pioneers were the Germans, French, and English.

Swiss manufacture of watches and clocks began in Geneva in the mid-16th century, thanks to the austerity measures introduced by the Reformation, when ostentatious shows of wealth were banned. John Calvin forbade the wearing of jewelry, but he acknowledged that watches were useful and therefore acceptable items. That is why the goldsmiths and jewellers of Geneva turned their attention to watch-making, copying the ideas of other nations.

However, it was the French King Charles IX's slaughter of several thousand Huguenot Protestants during the St. Bartholomew's Day Massacre in 1572 (the worst sectarian violence of the Wars of Religion), that ultimately led to Geneva becoming the world capital of luxury watchmaking. Huguenot craftsmen fled France, seeking refuge in the Calvinist bastion of Geneva. The arrival of these artisans, many of whom were already clock and watch manufacturers, spawned the art of watchmaking for which Geneva was to become renowned.

Manufacture gradually spread to other areas, most notably to the Jura region, at the start of the 18th century. Up until this point, only small numbers of extremely expensive watches had been produced in Geneva. In 1709, an anonymous English traveler called into a local blacksmith's shop belonging to Daniel Jean-Richard in the town of Le Locle (see p. 102), because his watch had stopped working. Jean-Richard repaired his watch, made a drawing of its movement, produced a replica, and set up a business producing affordable and reliable timepieces.

Before long, the Jura became the epicenter of watchmaking, with several towns—including Le Locle, La Chaux-de-Fonds (see p. 102), St.-Imier, and Biel becoming particularly important. Their remote locations and austere climate, with long snowbound winters, had already nurtured fine, painstaking handicrafts, including lacemaking. The first Jura watchmakers used the networks already established by lacemakers to spread their watches.

Designer watches in a Zürich store

INSIDER TIP:

To really appreciate the amazing intricacy of Swiss watches, you should visit the Musée International de l'Horlogerie [see p. 102], where you can get a close look at their workings.

—SALLY McFALL
National Geographic contributor

Innovation & Export

Traditionally the men built the watches, while the women adjusted the balance and had the honor of starting each one for the first time. Major technical breakthroughs came in 1770, with Louis Abraham Perrelet's creation of the first self-winding watch in Le Locle; then, in 1801, when Neuchâtelois Abraham-Louis Breguet (arguably the great-est watchmaker of all time) invented the *tourbillon* escapement. This was an accuracy device which, by keeping part of the watch mechanism in constant motion, served to cancel out any body movement.

Swiss watches were exported starting in the 19th century. This was also when the first wristwatches emerged, invented by the Geneva-based company Patek Philippe. Gustav Flaubert, the greatest French novelist of the era, is said to have remarked that a "watch is suitable only if it was made in Geneva."

In the last few decades, Switzerland's watch industry has continued to thrive. Many brands, such as Swatch, Rolex, and Omega, have become household names. And the likes of Tissot, Tag Heuer, Jaeger LeCoultre (with the famous "reverso" sliding watch-face which rotates 180°), and Patek Philippe are at the forefront of innovation. Swatch led the nation's traditional watchmaking industry toward the 21st century with the launch of their trend-setting, colorful mass-market designs in 1983. Six years later, at the luxury end of the market, Patek Philippe created the Calibre 89, the most complex and expensive watch in the world, with a staggering 1,728 parts. The latest development in Swiss horology is the creation of an atomic clock in Neuchâtel in 2010, which is accurate to within one-millionth of a second.

Le Locle

◪ 87 A2

Visitor Information

✉ Le Col 23, Le Locle

☎ (032) 889 68 92

www.neuchatel
tourisme.ch/en/
home.html

Musée de l'Horlogerie

✉ Château des Monts, route des Monts 65, Le Locle

☎ (032) 931 16 80

⊕ Closed Mon.

▦ $$

⑤ Train to Le Locle, then bus 1 (Monts)

www.mhl-monts
.ch/?lang=en

Moulins Souterrains

✉ Le Col 23, Le Locle

☎ (032) 931 89 89

⊕ Closed Mon., Nov.–April

▦ $$$$ (guided tour only)

⑤ Train (Le Locle-Col-des-Roches)

La Chaux-de-Fonds

◪ 87 A3

Musée International d'Horlogerie

✉ 29 rue des Musées, La Chaux-de-Fonds

☎ (032) 967 68 61

⊕ Closed Mon.

▦ $$

⑤ Train (La Chaux-de-Fonds)

routes, including the 100-mile (163 km) Traversee du Jura Suisse trail, contact the Romandie Ski de Fond (www.skidefond.ch).

Le Locle: It was here that Switzerland's celebrated watchmaking industry was born at the start of the 18th century (see pp. 100–101). High above the town, the **Musée de l'Horlogerie** recounts the history of time measurement, and has a collection of locally

INSIDER TIP:

My favorite walk in the entire Jura region has to be the Creux-du-Van. Each time I go there, I'm amazed by the rock formations and the views.

—TOM JACKSON
National Geographic contributor

made clocks, watches, and automata, beautifully displayed within the elegant rooms of an 18th-century castle, Château des Monts. Le Locle still produces watches, with several local factories including the famous Tissot brand. **Musée des Beaux-Arts** (Marie-Anne-Calame 6, Le Locle, tel 032/931 1333, closed Mon., www.mbal .ch, $$), in the middle of town stages temporary exhibitions on printing and contemporary art. And just outside Le Locle is an intriguing museum devoted

to the **Moulins Souterrains** (Underground Mills) of Col-des-Roches, which functioned here in the 18th century, harnessing energy from the Bied River.

La Chaux-de-Fonds: In an upper valley of the Jura, La Chaux-de-Fonds is the nation's highest city (3,281 feet/1,000 m). With a population of 48,000 it is the third largest in French-speaking Switzerland, and its grid-like town plan, implemented after a devastating fire in 1794, is striking. La Chaud-de-Fonds is perhaps best known as the birthplace of Le Corbusier, the pioneer of modern architecture who designed his first building here (see sidebar p. 99). And it is famous as a major center of the Swiss watchmaking industry. If you only visit one watchmaking attraction in the region, make sure it's the largely underground **Musée International d'Horlogerie,** with a remarkable collection of rare clocks, watches, and astronomical instruments illustrating the evolution of timepieces from the sundial to the present day. Next door, La Chaux-de-Fonds' very own **Musée des Beaux-Arts** (rue des Musées 33, La Chaux-de-Fonds, tel 032/967 6077, closed Mon., $$) is also worth a visit to see its collection of artworks and sculpture by 19th- and 20th-century Swiss artists. The collection includes furniture by, and paintings of, Le Corbusier.

EXPERIENCE: Explore Jura's Geological Wonders

The forested mountains of the Jura region conceal a host of natural attractions and opportunities for exciting outdoor activities. Over the millennia, the region's powerful rivers have carved the soft limestone bedrock into a unique landscape of dramatic waterfalls, winding rivers, and seemingly endless cave systems.

Located at the southern end of the Swiss Jura, the picturesque town of Vallorbe makes an ideal base from which to explore the area.

There are numerous hiking trails radiating out from Vallorbe, which showcase the diversity of the local landscape. Information on these hikes, as well as detailed maps, can be obtained from the local **tourist office** (Grandes-Forges 11, Vallorbe, 021/ 843 25 83, www.vallorbe-tourisme.ch).

Stalactites hang from the roof of the Grottes de Vallorbe.

Valleys & Summits

Hiking routes include a 6.8-mile (11 km) hike up the valley to the 4,862-foot (1,482 m) summit of the Dent du Vaulion, from where you can see as far as the Lac de Neuchâtel and Mont Blanc. Alternatively you can take a more relaxed 45-minute stroll southwest along the banks of the Orbe River to the point where it emerges, fully formed, from the bottom of a cliff face.

Caves & Waterfalls

Between the point where the Orbe gushes out of the ground near Vallorbe and its source in the Lac de Joux (about two miles to the southeast), the river runs through a vast complex of caves known as the **Grottes de Vallorbe** (tel 021/843 25 83, www.grottesdevallorbe. ch). This cave complex was first explored in the late 19th century, but was not opened to the public until 1974. Intrepid cavers are still finding new passageways and chambers deep beneath the ground. Non-splunkers can view the river as it roars through its underground course and admire the massive, 98-foot-high (30 m) "cathedral" chamber.

Farther afield, not far from the town of **Le Locle** (about an hour's drive to the northeast), the Doubs River runs through a similarly dramatic landscape between Lac des Brenets and the dramatic 88-foot-high (27 m) **Saut-du-Doubs** waterfall.

Forests & Meadows

If the idea of spending the day under several thousand tons of limestone fills you with terror, you can continue your hike farther south along the Tour du Mont d'Orzeires trail, which takes you another 7.4 miles (12 km) south to the **Juraparc** (Le Pont-Vallorbe, tel 021/843 17 35, www .juraparc.ch), where a variety of once-native animals—from buffalo and wild horses to wolves and a small family of brown bears—live in huge enclosures that stretch through the surrounding forests and meadows.

Fribourg

▲ 87 B2

Visitor Information

✉ Fribourg
   Tourisme,
   avenue de la
   Gare 1

☎ (026) 350 11 11

**www.fribourg
tourisme.ch/en**

Fribourg

Although Fribourg is not on the main tourist trail, its scenic old town represents one of the finest examples of medieval architecture in Europe. The sleepy charm of its cobbled squares, fountains, bridges, and pavement cafés provides a relaxed and easygoing atmosphere. At the same time, it is a cosmopolitan, forward-looking place, whose large student population takes particular pride in the region's contemporary arts as well as its local traditions and festivals.

Officially French-speaking, Fribourg (Freiburg in German) is actually bilingual. The city is situated on a forested peninsula in a loop of the Saane (Sarine) River, which effectively acts as a language boundary. Those living on the west bank (about 70 percent of the population) are mostly French-speakers, while the German-speaking community (the other 30 percent) lives east of the river. Many streets have two names, and even the town's radio station has two separate channels. Some of the older members of the population speak an ancient *Bolze* dialect, which combines both French and German.

Fribourg University is one of the most prestigious in Switzerland. It is also the nation's only Catholic university and Europe's only bilingual one. As a result, it draws students from all regions, further enhancing the city's engaging, cosmopolitan atmosphere.

Just 21 miles (34 km) southwest of Bern, Fribourg has some historic similarities with its more illustrious neighbor. Fribourg was founded in 1157 by Berchtold IV of Zähringen, the father of the founder of Bern. Both cities are sited on a river meander, selected for defense purposes, and both have managed to preserve their

The Fribourg funicular is powered by waste water.

medieval core. Since it is very hilly, Fribourg is tougher than Bern to explore. However, all bus routes serve the main rail station and the helpful tourist office (beside the station) can provide comprehensive street maps and bus plans. A tour by mini-train *(departing from place Georges-Python Tues.–Sun., May–Sept., and weekends only in Oct.)* is a relaxing way to get your bearings, see the more far-flung corners of the city, and experience some of its impressive vistas.

Ride the Fribourg Funicular

The **Fribourg Funicular** *(rue de la Sarine, Fribourg, tel 026/ 351 02 00, $)* is one of the city's curiosities. Built in 1899 and listed as a historic monument, the funicular links the upper and lower parts of town. It is the last of its kind in Europe to run solely on waste water, thanks to a clever system of clanking counterweights, and so is very environmentally friendly. It operates daily with departures (according to demand) every six minutes. The views the funicular affords over the city are very impressive.

Altstadt: The Altstadt is best explored on foot. This allows you to soak up the atmosphere of the ancient cobbled streets, admire the many medieval houses and elegant Renaissance fountains. The town is remarkably well-preserved, with around 1.25 miles (2 km) of its defensive wall and 14 watchtowers still pretty much intact.

From the station, avenue de la Gare leads downhill to rue de Lausanne (a cobbled road lined with intriguing shops and cozy cafés) to the **Bourg district** at the heart of the Altstadt. At the end of rue de Lausanne, the late-Gothic **Hôtel de Ville** (City Hall; *place de l'Hôtel de Ville, closed to visitors)* dominates a spacious square—the venue of a popular Saturday morning market. The square has a fine Renaissance **fountain** showing St. George spearing a dragon. The linden tree here is said to have been planted in 1476 to mark the Swiss victory over Charles the Bold at Morat/ Murten. The south side of the square offers a great view over the Basse Ville (Lower Town) below.

Churches & Museums: The main focus of the Bourg district is the Gothic **Cathédrale St. Nicolas** with its soaring lacy spire, a little farther down the hill *(just off place Notre-Dame).* The cathedral was built in 1283 on the site of an older church, although it remained incomplete until 1490. Fribourg has long been a conservative city and it adhered to Roman Catholicism even during the Reformation, when it became a place of refuge for the exiled bishops of Geneva and Lausanne.

The Catholic university was founded in 1889, and the city remains staunchly Catholic to this day. The cathedral's interior is a fine example of Swiss Gothic style, rich in statues and reliefs. A plaque near the doorway commemorates a mass celebrated here by Pope John Paul II in 1984. Also of note are its 15th-century wooden choir stalls and its art nouveau stained-glass windows. Its highly regarded organ has been played by both the Hungarian composer Franz Liszt (1811–1886) and the Austrian

Cathédrale St. Nicolas

- ✉ rue des Chanoines
- ☎ (026) 347 10 40
- 🕐 Tower closed Oct.–mid June
- 💲 $ (tower only)
- 🚌 Bus 1, 2, 6 (Tilleul)

Église des Cordeliers
- ✉ rue de Morat 6
- ☎ (026) 347 11 60
- 🚍 Bus 1, 2, 6 (Tilleul)

Espace Jean Tinguely & Niki de Saint Phalle
- ✉ rue de Morat 2
- ☎ (026) 305 51 40
- 🕐 Closed Mon. & Tues.
- 💲 $$
- 🚍 Bus 1,2, 6 (Tilleul)

Musée d'Art et d'Histoire
- ✉ rue de Morat 12
- ☎ (026) 305 51 40
- 🕐 Closed Mon.
- 💲 $$
- 🚍 Bus 1, 2, 6 (Tilleul)

composer Anton Bruckner (1824–1896). Climb the 243-foot (73 m) tower for memorable bird's-eye views of the city below.

Just up from the cathedral, the Franciscan **Église des Cordeliers** is part of a friary founded in 1256 and rebuilt in the 18th century. It retains its medieval decor, including some of the oldest wooden choir stalls in Switzerland (dating from 1280) and a beautiful 15th-century high altar painting illustrating the Adoration of the Magi and the Crucifixion.

In contrast, in a former tram depot next door, the ultra-modern **Espace Jean Tinguely & Niki de Saint Phalle** (part of the **Musée d'Art et d'Histoire**) is dedicated to the city's two best-known

artists, and their light-hearted machines and sculptures. This gallery is great fun. A **Sculpture Trail** through the city center, with over 40 works by Tinguely (1925–1991), de Saint Phalle (1930–2002), and other well-known Swiss and international artists, makes a stroll through Fribourg all the more enjoyable (ask at the tourist office for the free guide). One of just three of Jean Tinguely's amusing waterworks, the **Jo Siffert Fountain** (a memorial to the Fribourgeois racing driver, 1936–1971) can be seen near the railway station in a grassy park off Grand-Places. It was once described as "a firework in iron and water."

Farther up the road, the **Musée d'Art et d'Histoire** presents an overview of Fribourgeois art, military, social, and religious history from the Middle Ages to the present day in the Mansion Ratzé. The building it is housed in was built for the commander of the Swiss guards in the 16th century. Canvases by Hodler, Courbet, and Delacroix are displayed in a former slaughterhouse.

From the Bourg, steep cobbled lanes (leading off place de l'Hôtel de Ville), with wrought-iron lamps, fountains, and ornate inn signs tumble down the hillside to the district of **Neuveville,** while Grand'Rue (beside the cathedral) leads downhill past attractive 17th- and 18th-century facades to **Auge,** the oldest part of the Altstadt with its fine medieval artisan's houses, and the meandering river.

Six bridges span the Sarine

EXPERIENCE:
Taste Local Beer

In recent years Fribourg has acquired a reputation as the home of good beer and small breweries in Switzerland.

These breweries include **Freiburger Biermanufaktur** *(rue de Morat 8, Fribourg, tel 076/241 81 25, www.freiburger-bier manufaktur.ch, tours Sat. a.m.),* which was founded a few years ago in an old convent; the eccentric **Brasserie Artisanale de Fribourg** *(rue de la Samaritaine 19, Fribourg, tel 026/322 80 88),* which offers an acclaimed range of beers from its tiny one-room brewery; and the recently-opened **Brasserie du Chauve** *(chemin des Roches 1, Fribourg, tel 079/737 36 78, www.labras serieduchauve.ch, tours Thurs. & Fri, p.m., & Sat. a.m.).* If you're not able to get to any of the brewery tours, the **Café l'Ancienne Gare** *(Gare 3, Fribourg, tel 026/322 57 72, www.cafeanciennegare.ch)* has a good selection of locally brewed bottled beers.

Choosing fruit and vegetables in Fribourg's popular street market

River within the city boundaries. They range from lofty modern iron-and-steel constructions to the oldest—the wooden covered **Bern Bridge,** dating originally from the 12th century. Across the Bern Bridge are five of the towers that once protected the city. And close to the bridge is the charming **Musée Suisse de la Marionnette** (Swiss Puppet Museum), with its large collection of puppets from theaters around the world, a café, and a puppet theater (with shows from Oct.–April). This isn't the only quirky museum in Fribourg. Others include the **Musée de la Bière Cardinal** (Cardinal Beer Museum, *passage du Cardinal, tel 058/123 42 58, open Tues. & Thurs., 2–8 p.m. only, $$*), which promotes the local brew; the **Musée Suisse de la Machine à Coudre** (Swiss Sewing Machine Museum); and the **Chemins de Fer du Kaeserberg** (*Impasse*

des Ecureuils 9, Granges Paccot, tel 026/467 70 40, $$$$, www .kaeserberg.ch), a fascinating fully operational miniature railway in the outskirts of town. In the Neuveville district of the Basse Ville, near the foot of the funicular, the temporary exhibitions at **Fri-Art** *(Petites-Rames 22, tel 026/323 23 51, closed Mon. & Tues., $$, www .fri-art.ch)* feature some of the most avant-garde contemporary artforms imaginable. From here, it is just a stone's throw to the famous funicular (see sidebar, p. 105), which transports its passengers up to the city center in just two minutes.

Gruyères & Around

Standing high on a knoll surrounded by verdant pre-Alpine pastures and cows with clanging cowbells is Gruyères. This picture-postcard medieval town is dominated by its ancient

Musée Suisse de la Marionnette

- ✉ Derrière-les-Jardins 2
- ☎ (026) 322 85 13
- 🕐 Closed Mon. & Tues.
- 💲 $$
- 🚌 Bus 4 (Place du Petit-Saint-Jean)

Musée Suisse de la Machine à Coudre

- ✉ Grand-Rue 58
- ☎ (026) 475 24 33
- 🕐 phone
- 💲 $$ (guided visit)
- 🚌 Bus 1, 2, 6 (Tilleul)

Gruyères

- 🅰 87 B1

Visitor Information

- ✉ Les Gruyères Tourisme, place des Alps 26
- ☎ (084) 842 44 24
- **www.la-gruyere.ch/ en/welcome.cfm**

EXPERIENCE: Walk the Dairy Path

The bucolic, hilly countryside of the Pays de Gruyère, with its lush pastures and bell-ringing cattle, is where the world-famous Gruyère AOC cheese is made. In its honor the 2-mile (3.2 km) **Sentier des Fromageries** (Cheese Dairy Path) leads from Pringy's modern Show Dairy (La Maison du Gruyère; see p. 110) to Moléson-sur-Gruyères' cozy 17th-century chalet, the **Fromagerie d'Alpage**

(place de l'aigle, Moléson-sur-Gruyères, tel 026/921 10 44, closed Oct.–March, reservations recommended), where cheese is made in the traditional way—in a huge cauldron over a wood fire—at 10 a.m., 2 p.m., and 3 p.m. from mid-May through mid-Oct. Choose from two routes, both of which take around two hours. Maps are available from the Gruyères and Moléson tourist offices.

Château de Gruyères

- ✉ Gruyères
- ☎ (026) 921 21 02
- 💲 $$$ (Château & HR Giger Museum combined ticket)
- 🚆 Train (Gruyères)

www.chateau-gruyeres.ch/e/index.html

turreted castle. Gruyères gave its name to the region—the Pays de Gruyère—and to its delicious holey cheese. What's more, following the opening of chocolate-giant Nestlé's La Maison Cailler (see pp. 110–111) in nearby Broc in 2010, the region is now also a magnet for chocoholics.

INSIDER TIP:

The best photo opportunity in Gruyères is through Chavonne Gate up the cobblestone street toward the castle, which is framed by Dent-du-Broc mountain.

—CLIVE CARPENTER
National Geographic contributor

There's no denying that the handsome, fortified town of Gruyères is one of Switzerland's most photogenic treasures and a veritable honeypot for visitors. For this reason it is probably best avoided

in high season when it is swarming with tourists. Thankfully the town is car-free, with a number of car lots just outside the walls (or a ten-minute uphill walk from the train station). Ideally, it is best to stay the night in one of Gruyère's hotels (though they are pricey), to soak up the atmosphere once the crowds have departed.

The town was founded in the 11th century by Peter II of Savoy, and remains surprisingly well preserved within its 15th-century walls. There is only one main street, the cobbled **rue du Marché,** which is lined with beautiful Gothic and Renaissance houses (each one a protected national monument). Several of these contain hotels, restaurants, and craft shops.

Château de Gruyères:

Rue du Marché leads through a chunky gatehouse to the imposing Château de Gruyères, designed in the typical Savoyard-style square plan, with walls up to 12 feet (3.6 m) thick in places. At the start of your visit, an 18-minute "Gruyères" multimedia show reveals the history of the castle and the Counts of Gruyères. The crest of these noble counts contained a white *grue* (French for "crane," the bird), hence the name Gruyères. The subsequent self-guided tour of the castle takes you through the history, architecture, and culture of eight centuries. Highlights include the **Hall of Burgundy** (room 5), which features weapons, armor, embroidered capes, and silk banners, all of which are relics of the Battle of Murat (1470). **Corot's Room** (room 8) contains four medallion landscapes painted by the famous French artist of the same name who stayed here in 1851. **Furets' Room** (room 13) is smothered in decorative panels portraying birds, flowers,

and other nature scenes, painted by Francis Furet (1842–1919) and Jules Crosnier (1843–1917) around 1900. The mural in the **Knight's Room** (room 16) depicts the arrival of the first Count of Gruyères, together with his crane (supposedly the first creature he encountered on arrival). You will see the crane emblem throughout the castle, often in the tapestries and heraldic stained glass. Be sure to walk the ramparts, for views over the geometrical French-style gardens to sparkling Lake Gruyère beyond.

Also located in the castle, and somewhat anachronistic but nonetheless intriguing, the **HR Giger Museum** contains an impressive collection of other-worldly works by Swiss surrealist artist, sculptor,

HR Giger Museum

✉ Château St. Germain, Gruyères
☎ (026) 921 22 00
💲 $$$ (Museum & Château combined ticket)
🕐 Closed Mon. Nov.–March
🚌 Bus (Gruyères)

Rich grazing near Gruyères, a world-famous cheese-making center

**La Maison du
Gruyère**
 87 B1
✉ Pringy-Gruyères
☎ (026) 921 84 00
💲 $$
🚆 Train (Gruyères)
**www.lamaison
dugruyere.ch**

Broc
🗺 87 B1

La Maison Cailler
✉ rue Jules Bellet
7, Broc
☎ (026) 921 59 60
💲 $$
🚆 Train (Broc-
Fabrique)
www.cailler.ch

and set designer, Hans Rudolf Giger (b. 1940), who won an Academy Award for visual effects in Ridley Scott's groundbreaking 1979 science-fiction horror film *Alien*. Across the street, the **Giger Museum Bar** *(Château St. Germain, closed Mon.)* contains floor-to-ceiling representations of Giger's weird and wonderful (and

using modern techniques. The cellars alone have the capacity to store 7,000 wheels of Gruyère AOC. There are cheese-making demonstrations (visible through large glass windows) three or four times a day between 9 a.m. and 2:30 p.m., depending on the season. Also on site, the restaurant offers cheese dishes galore, while

A church near Gruyères

often highly disturbing) artworks, many of which he claims are inspired by night terrors.

The miniature **Train Touristique de Gruyères** *(www.petit-train.info/English.htm, $$)* runs between the town and **La Maison du Gruyère** dairy in the village of Pringy at the foot of the hill, one mile (1.6 km) away. This modern dairy produces a large quantity of Gruyères' renowned cheese,

a multisensory exhibition (with polyglot audio-guides included in the entrance price) reveals the complexity of production, taste, and fragrance of the cheese in its various stages of maturity. A host of entertaining cheesy facts and figures are provided.

Maison Cailler: The other must-see sight in the region—and another treat for gourmands—is Nestlé's Maison Cailler *(rue Jules Bellet 7, Broc, tel 026/921 59 60, $$$, www.cailler .ch),* near the village of Broc. The museum is named for one of the 19th-century pioneers of chocolate-making (see pp. 78–79). This is definitely not a place for the weak-willed or for anyone on a diet. Even as you approach, the sweet aroma of chocolate coming from the neighboring factory is overwhelming. This state-of-the-art museum starts by tracing the history of chocolate from secret Aztec cocoa ceremonies through to Cailler company's history in a multisensory tour. A more hands-on section is devoted to chocolate manufacture from the cocoa bean through production of exquisite chocolates, and climaxes in the all-you-can-eat tasting room. There is even a cinema showing chocolate-themed movies (in French) and an *atelier du chocolat* (chocolate workshop) where you can try your hand at making pralines (reservation necessary).

Visitors on a tight schedule may wish to consider visiting the region on the GoldenPass Chocolate Train *(Rail Center GoldenPass, CP 1426, Montreux, 090/024 52 45, reservations essential, www .goldenpass.ch/goldenpass_choco late_train),* combining a visit to the cheese factory and chateau at Gruyères with a tour of the Cailler factory-museum at Broc. ∎

Moléson-sur-Gruyères

 87 B1

Visitor Information

✉ Moléson Tourisme, place de l'Aigle 6, Moléson-sur-Gruyères

☎ (026) 921 85 00

www.moleson .ch/?lang=en

Getting Active at Moléson-sur-Gruyères

Combining a visit to Gruyères with a visit to the holiday resort of Moléson-sur-Gruyères is a must for all nature lovers and sports fans. The mountain peak of Le Moléson (6,568 feet/2,002 m), dominates the Fribourg Pre-Alps, and is a popular hiking destination. The summit can also be reached by funicular and cable car from the village. Those with a head for heights stop at the middle station (Plan-Francey; 4,986 feet/1,520 m) to tackle the fixed ropes and rungs of the 1,312-foot (400 m) *via ferrata* route up the northern face. At the top, an observatory claims the world's largest binoculars and offers extensive views of the Alps, Jura, and Mittelland. Nighttime visibility is amazing, and the observatory staff hold occasional star-gazing evenings *(tel 026/921 29 96 to make a reservation).*

There are plenty of well-marked hiking trails including a gentle, one-and-a-half-hour botanic path on the eastern slopes. This is comprehensively labeled, enabling walkers to identify an amazing wealth of pre-Alpine flowers. Down in the village itself you can choose from a wide range of activities, including a summer bobsled track *(open weekends May–Nov., and daily June–Oct., in dry weather only).* Additionally there is go-carting and grass-scooting (careering down the hillside on scooters with fat, rubber tires, June–Aug. & weekends in Sept.); mini-golf; basketball; volleyball; and badminton.

During the winter months, Moléson becomes the main ski resort in Fribourg canton, with 21 miles (35 km) of downhill skiing, a snowpark, and boardercross track. If that isn't enough, there are more than 30 miles (50 km) of designated snowshoe trails, and a 2-mile (4 km) sledging track linking Plan-Francey with the village.

The nation's capital and cultural center, the dairies that produce
classic Swiss cheeses, and some of the best mountain sports

Bern &
the Bernese
Oberland

The Schützenbrunnen (Marksman Fountain) and the Zytgloggeturm clock tower in Bern

Bern & the Bernese Oberland

"This is the most beautiful place we have ever seen," wrote German playwright Johann Wolfgang von Goethe (1749–1832) in a letter to a friend during his stay in Bern in 1779. Indeed, few capital cities are as picturesque—or as tiny—as Bern. Encircled by the Aare River and surrounded by wooded hills, it feels more like a village than a capital. However, with a population of nearly 130,000, it is the nation's fourth largest city and has been the Swiss capital since 1848.

5▷

Bern, located in the heart of Switzerland, has excellent road and rail connections to every corner of the country, as well as links farther afield. Indeed, Bern is the only European capital city visited by all three European high-speed train networks: the French TGV, the German ICE, and the Italian Cisalpino. It is easily accessible by plane, with frequent flights into Bern-Belp International Airport from numerous European cities. This makes it an excellent base for touring many of the country's big attractions such as Luzern and the Vierwaldsee; Montreux and the Lake Geneva region; and even the high Alps of Valais. Zürich is one hour away by train, while Geneva can be reached in under two hours.

Bern itself is remarkably small and unassuming for the capital of a European country, and a substantial part of the city center hasn't changed much in the last few hundred years. Nonetheless, it does have all the bustle, official pomp, and excitement you'd expect from a national capital.

NOT TO BE MISSED:

Strolling around Bern's
Altstadt 120–121

Zentrum Paul Klee on the outskirts
of Bern 122

Walking, cycling, or tasting cheese in
the Emmental region 124–125

Attempting wood-carving in
Bönigen 132

Admiring Swiss architecture at
Ballenberg 133

A hike in the Jungfrau region from
Schynige Platte to First 134–135

The waterfalls in Lauterbrunnen
valley 135

Switzerland's top train ride, up the
famous Jungfraujoch 136–137

Skiing in one of the Bernese
Oberland's chic resorts 141

The Mittelland & Oberland

The city is surrounded by the bilingual canton of Bern, which is the second largest in Switzerland—both in terms of population and area. The canton spans two distinct geographical regions: the fertile Bernese Mittelland—where the capital lies—and, to the south, the jagged mountains of the Bernese Oberland (Bernese Highland). The Bernese Mittelland is an

BASEL & NORTHWEST
SWITZERLAND

p. 85

Biel-Bienne

Bielersee

E27

4▷

Aarberg

E25

Lac de Morat

Laupen

E27

3▷

2▷

1▷

Gstaad

A

archetypally Swiss landscape of fertile pastures and picturesque villages that stretches from the rolling hills of the Emmental to the Three Lakes region and the Jura Mountains.

It is the Mittelland's mountainous southern neighbor, however, that draws the most visitors. The awe-inspiring natural scenery of the Bernese Oberland—which includes some of the nation's most majestic peaks—has been a firm favorite with sightseers since the early 19th century. With hundreds of miles of walking and biking trails, countless clear mountain lakes, icy glacier gorges, dramatic waterfalls, and some world-class ski resorts—including Wengen, Mürren, and Gstaad—it is a popular destination for summer and winter sports enthusiasts.

In addition, the region attracts a steady steam of world-class mountaineers, determined to climb one of its famous and formidable mountains. This region also boasts an impressive network of cable cars, funiculars, and mountain trains, including the remarkable railroad line that ascends in a tunnel through the Eiger to reach the summit of the Jungfraujoch. Its final stop is the highest train station in Europe at 11,332 feet (3,454 m). ■

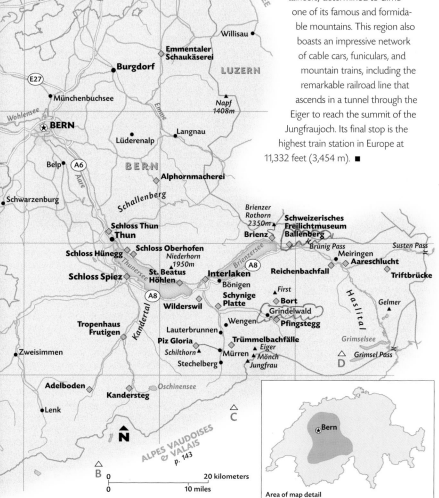

Bern & Around

There's more to the Swiss capital city of Bern than meets the eye. At its heart is the Altstadt (old town), which is located on a narrow peninsula formed by a bend in the Aare River. Here you'll see the cobbled streets and immaculately preserved medieval arcaded buildings that earned the city its UNESCO World Heritage site status in 1983. Yet Bern's old-world charm is infused with a modern vitality, thanks to a handful of examples of contemporary architecture, state-of-the-art museums, and a lively and diverse cultural scene.

The Bundeshaus dominates the Bundesplatz, Bern's focal point.

Bern

🅰 115 B3

Visitor Information

✉ Bern Tourismus, (at the railroad station) Bahnhofplatz

☎ (031) 328 12 12

www.berninfo.com/en/index.cfm

Bern was founded around 1191 by Duke Berchtold V of Zähringen on a fortified crossing of the Aare River. The rocky outcrop here provided a natural fortress, protected by the river on three sides and surrounded by steep wooded hills. It only needed to be strengthened with ramparts on its western side. Legend maintains that the duke named the town *Bern* after the first animal he killed—a bear—while hunting in the surrounding woodlands. This marked the

start of a centuries-long tradition of keeping bears in the city. Indeed, the black bear remains the city's emblem to this day— seen on flags, crests, confectionery, and countless souvenirs around the city.

Bern enjoyed its heyday in the late Middle Ages, when it was the largest and most powerful city state north of the Alps. Its influence extended east to Austria, south to Milan, and west to the French-speaking region of Vaud. In 1353 it joined the *Confoederatio*

INSIDER TIP:
I love shopping in Bern. There are so many tiny one-off boutiques to browse in, and the arcades keep you dry, even when it's pouring rain.

—DANIELA ZEHR
Bern Tourist Officer

Helvetica (Swiss Confederation; see p. 35), which was emerging in central Switzerland. In 1405 the city was devastated by fire, but the original wooden buildings were replaced almost immediately—initially by half-timbered houses and later by the ornate sandstone buildings that are still a defining characteristic of the Altstadt today.

Around Bundesplatz

The 19th century marked a time of significant change for Bern. In 1848 it became the federal capital of the Swiss Confederation and the seat of government. As Bern expanded, most of the long-redundant fortifications were demolished and new public buildings changed the townscape. Elevated bridges were constructed to connect the city center with the burgeoning residential areas on the other side of the river.

The Swiss government resides at the palatial 1902 **Bundeshaus,** an extensive edifice built in the Italian Renaissance style and easily recognizable by its distinctive copper domes. In addition, it contains a stained-glass dome lit by an enormous chandelier and decorated with various emblems of Bern. Guided tours are offered when Parliament is in recess. During parliamentary sessions the public gallery is open to visitors.

Outside the parliament buildings, the expansive **Bundesplatz** (Parliament Square) features a wittily choreographed fountain display with 26 water jets (representing the 26 cantons of Switzerland). The jets spurt unexpectedly out of the pavement every half-hour from 11 a.m.–11 p.m. April through October *(2 p.m. on Tues. & Sat.).* The square is also the venue for a farmers' market on Tuesdays and Saturdays *(8 a.m.–12 p.m.).*

The Altstadt

The 19th-century pomp of the Bundesplatz is surrounded by the lovely buildings of Bern's medieval Altstadt. A short walk east from the Bundesplatz leads

Bundeshaus
- ✉ Bundesplatz 3
- ☎ (031) 322 85 22
- 🕐 Tours Mon.–Wed., Fri., & Sat., 9 a.m., 10 a.m., 2 p.m., 3 p.m., & 4 p.m.
- 🚌 Bus 10/19 (Bundesplatz)

www.parlament.ch

EXPERIENCE:
Celebrating the Onion

Be sure to arrive early at Bern's Bundesplatz market for one of the nation's oldest fairs—the Zibelemärit (Onion Market), held annually on the fourth Monday in November. Trading starts at 4 a.m. with more than 600 ornately decorated market stalls selling braided strings of onions, onion wreaths, onion figurines, and such onion delicacies as *zwiebelkuchen* (onion quiche), onion soup, and even onion sausages. A massive confetti battle officially ends the market at 4 p.m.

Zytgloggeturm

✉ Kramgasse

🕐 Tours May–Oct.
2:30 p.m. & 3:15
p.m.

💲 $$$

🚌 Bus 3, 5, 9,
10, 12, 19
(Zytglogge)

to the iconic **Zytgloggeturm**
(clock tower). The tower was
built in the 13th century as part
of the city's western gate, and
was sometimes used as a prison.
Today it houses an intricate
astronomical calendar clock.

Added to the tower after the
Great Fire of 1405, the clock is a
tour de force of medieval horology.
Several mechanical figures—a
crowing rooster, a bear-parade,
dancing jesters, and the figure
of Chronos (the Roman god of
time)—appear and perform a
clockwork-powered dance four
minutes before each hour. Today's
clock dates from 1527, although
its pendulum—a 329-pound (149
kg) cannon—dates from the Battle
of Murten in 1712. The largest
functioning clockwork system
in Europe, it has to be manually
wound for 20 minutes every day.
In summer tours of the tower

are organized daily by the
tourist center.

Bern boasts the longest
covered shopping promenade
in Europe—3.7 miles (6 km) of
flower- and flag-adorned arcades.
The arcades contain dozens of
cozy bars, cafés, and restaurants,
as well as a host of tempting
boutiques. Additional retail space
is provided by the vaulted cel-
lars of the medieval sandstone
houses that flank the cobbled
streets. Thanks to the arcades
(known as *lauben* by the Bernese),
shopping is pleasurable whatever
the weather. The main shop-
ping streets run east-west and
include **Marktgasse, Kramgasse,**
and **Gerechtigkeitsgasse.** On
Thursdays, many of the shops
stay open until 9 p.m. Take time
out from shopping to admire
the many Renaissance fountains
in the streets, some of which are

A brown bear mother leads her cub in the BärenPark.

ornately gilded and painted (see Churches and Fountains of the Altstadt walk, pp. 120–121). Prior to the 20th century, washing was carried out communally in these various fountains and in the stream that runs through the center of town.

The **Berner Münster** (Cathedral of St. Vincent) is just a short walk east from the Zytgloggeturm. With its lofty triple-naved interior

The Riverside

Continue east along tranquil Junkerngasse and cross the Nydeggbrücke (Nydegg Bridge) to visit one of the city's main tourist attractions—the **BärenPark** (Bear Park). The tradition of keeping Bern's heraldic animal dates back to the foundation of the city. Over the centuries, the city's bears have been kept in various bear

Berner Münster

☒ Münsterplatz 1
☎ (031) 312 04 62
$ $ (tower only)
🚍 Bus 12, 30 (Rathaus)

When Fairy Tales Come to Life

When the curtain rises in Bern's tiny vaulted puppet theater, the stage could be set for anything from *Beauty and the Beast* to *Carmina Burana*, or *Faust*. The **Berner Puppentheater** is housed in a former wine cellar at the heart of the Altstadt. Its charming performances provide a unique theatrical experience

for adults and children alike. Don't worry if you don't speak the language! With its vast array of marionettes, masks, shadow figures, and hand puppets, the stories seem to transcend linguistic barriers *(Gerechtigkeitsgasse 31, tel 031/311 95 85, closed mid-Oct.–end April, www.berner-pup pentheater.ch).*

---

and 331-foot-high (101 m) tower, Berner Münster is Switzerland's tallest sacred building and a magnificent example of late-Gothic architecture. Its construction began as early as 1421, but the tower as it appears today was completed in 1893. Before entering the building, note the depiction of the Last Judgement over the main portal, with 234 intricately carved and colored figures. Just inside the door, a narrow spiral staircase leads up the tower for stupendous views over Bern to the Alps beyond. Outside the cathedral, the cobbled **Münsterplatz** square is the venue for an annual Christmas market and the *Granium-märit* (Geranium Market) in May.

pits around the town. Their current landscaped and spacious location on the banks of the Aare River opened in October 2009. The park is home to two adult bears, Björk and Finn, and their twin cubs, Berna and Urs. Terraced riverside paths, viewing platforms, and infrared cameras enable visitors to view the bears wherever they are in the park. Nearby, the **Rosengarten** (Rose Garden) provides a beautiful and fragrant viewpoint for admiring the old town.

Heading back across the bridge, walk south into the **Mattenquartier** *(www.matte.ch),* a district that once housed the city's artisans and workshops. The river *(continued on p. 122)*

BärenPark

☒ Grosser Muristalden
☎ (031) 357 15 25
🚍 Bus 12 (Bärengraben)
www.baerenpark -bern.ch

Rosengarten

☒ Alter Aargauerstalden 31b
☎ (031) 331 32 06 (restaurant)
🕐 Restaurant closed Dec.–Feb.
🚍 Bus 10 (Rosengarten)

Churches & Fountains of the Altstadt Walk

Bern's atmospheric Altstadt (old town) counts among Europe's best-preserved medieval towns, and is easily explored on foot. With its network of ancient cobbled streets, 250 ornamental fountains, historic churches, and arcaded sandstone houses, the cityscape has barely changed since the Middle Ages.

The ornate spouts of the Mosesbrunnen

Start beside the train station in Bahnhofplatz. Here the imposing facade of the **Heiliggeistkirche ❶** (Church of the Holy Ghost; *Spitalgasse 44, tel 031/300 33 40, www.heiliggeistkirche.ch*) perfectly juxtaposes with the modern glass architecture of the square. Built as a Protestant church in the 18th century (unlike many Swiss churches which were converted from their previous Catholic usage during the Reformation), today it is considered to be one of the finest Protestant churches in Switzerland.

On leaving the church, set off eastward along Spitalgasse. The first fountain of note is the medieval **Pfeiferbrunnen ❷** (Piper Fountain) with the piper, dressed in red and blue, playing his bagpipes.

Farther on, the square of Bärenplatz is dominated by the massive bulk of the 13th-century **Käfigturm** (Prison Tower), which served as a prison until 1897. Pass through the tower into Marktgasse, the main shopping precinct of the old town. Here the **Anna-Seiler-Brunnen ❸** (Anna Seiler Fountain) is devoted to the founder of Bern's first hospital in 1354. She is depicted in a blue dress, pouring water into a small dish. Continue past the armor-clad musketeer of the **Schützenbrunnen ❹** (Musketeer Fountain) to Kornhausplatz. This broad street is named for the **Kornhaus,** a grand 18th-century structure that originally served as the city's main granary. The building—a jewel of late Baroque architecture—today houses the exclusive Kornhauskeller restaurant (see p. 286). Just outside, the grotesque 16th-century **Kindlifresserbrunnen ❺** (Child-eater Fountain) portrays a red and green ogre—based on a local carnival figure—who is eating a naked child, with other children in a bag at his side. It is thought the fountain was constructed to keep children away from the deep city moat which was once located here. Also on Kornhausplatz is the landmark **Zytgloggeturm** (Clock Tower; see p. 118). Pass through the tower into picturesque **Kramgasse,** in order to admire the astronomical calendar clock (1530).

Continue east along Kramgasse, noting the various fine oriel windows, spires, and turrets of its ancient houses, until you reach the **Zähringer Brunnen ❻** (Zähringer Fountain), commemorating the city founder Duke Berchtold von Zähringen, with its emblematic, armored "Bern bear" and Zähringer coat of

NOT TO BE MISSED:

Kindlifresserbrunnen
• Zytgloggeturm • Zähringer
Brunnen • Gerechtigkeits-
brunnen • Berner Münster

arms. Farther down the street, **Einsteinhaus** *(Kramgasse 49, tel 031/312 00 91, www.einstein -bern.ch)* is the former home of scientist and Nobel Prize winner Albert Einstein, who developed his Theory of Relativity here in 1905. His apartment, on the second floor, has changed little in the past hundred years. Just beyond, beside the Konservatorium für Musik (Music Conservatory), the colorful **Simsonbrunnen** ⑦ (Samson Fountain) depicts the biblical story of Samson killing a lion.

Continue down Gerechtigkeitsgasse, with its tempting shops, bars, and restaurants to the famous **Gerechtigkeitsbrunnen** ⑧ (Justice Fountain). Erected in 1543, it personifies Justice with her scales and sword of truth, and with worshipping subjects at her feet.

At the end of the street, pause to visit the **Nydeggkirche** ⑨ (Nydegg Church; *Nydegghof 2, tel 031/352 58 29*) to the left of the bridge. Situated on the site of the former 12th-century Nydegg Castle, it was constructed as part of the city defenses by Duke Berchtold V von Zähringen. As Bern expanded, the castle was destroyed in 1268, and a church was built on its ruins in the mid 14th century.

From here, it's a stone's throw across the Nydeggbrücke (Nydegg Bridge) to visit Bern's most celebrated attraction, the **BärenPark** ⑩ (see p. 119). Alternatively, head up Junkerngasse to visit Bern's impressive Gothic **Berner Münster** (see p. 119) ⑪ and to admire one final fountain, the 16th-century **Mosesbrunnen.** This fountain is topped by a colorful statue of Moses bringing the Ten Commandments down from Mount Sinai.

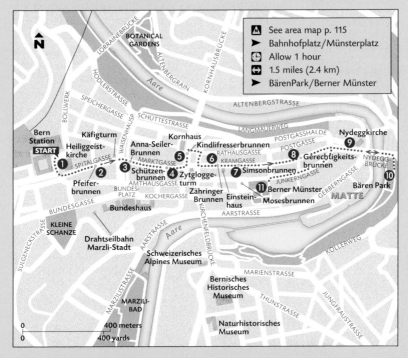

Zentrum Paul Klee

✉ Monument im Fruchtland 3

☎ (031) 359 01 01

🕐 Closed Mon.

💲 $$$$$

🚌 Bus 12 (Zentrum Paul Klee)

www.zpk.org

Kunstmuseum

✉ Hodlerstrasse 8–12

☎ (031) 328 09 44

🕐 Closed Mon.

💲 $$

🚌 Bus 11/20/21 (Bollwerk)

www.kunstmuseum bern.ch

Bernisches Historisches Museum/ Einstein Museum

✉ Helvetiaplatz 5

☎ (031) 350 77 11

🕐 Closed Mon.

💲 $$$$

🚌 Tram 3/5 (Helvetiaplatz)

www.bhm.ch

is still channeled into an open canal here. For centuries, this area of craftspeople and dockworkers had its own dialect—dubbed *Mattenenglisch* by the uncomprehending townsfolk. Today, it remains a close-knit artisan community, and although many of the old warehouses have since been converted into trendy office space, plenty of characterful half-timbered houses and locals' bars remain.

Continue your riverside stroll, under the lofty **Kirchenfeldbrücke,** and you'll find yourself in Marzili, a tranquil residential district best known for the **Marzilibad** *(Marzilistrasse 29, tel 031/311 00 46, www.aaremarzili .ch).* Open during summer months, the complex of open-air swimming pools attracts city dwellers and visitors alike to swim and sunbathe here. The real appeal, however, especially at the height of summer, is to take a dip and be carried along by the strong current of the

---

Mount Gurten

Fancy a quick break from the city? In under 30 minutes from the city center (via tram 9 to Gurtenbahn, then the funicular to Gurten-Kulm), you can be atop Bern's local mountain—Mount Gurten—for a leisurely hike through flowery meadows or to enjoy a romantic sunset. Also here are ski and toboggan runs in winter; mini-golf, a mini train, and playgrounds; as well as a choice of dining options. On a clear day, the 360° views encompass the rooftops of Bern, the Jura Mountains, Emmental, and the eternally snow-capped mountains of the high Alps *(www.gurtenpark.ch/index/ welcome.htm).*

INSIDER TIP:

Swimming in the slow-flowing Aare is a great way to cool down on a hot summer's day. Even at the height of summer, however, you'll find the water is surprisingly cold.

—SALLY McFALL
National Geographic contributor

ice-cold Aare River. While relaxing with the locals, you should take a moment to admire the skyline of the old city center, dominated by the Parliament buildings and the Cathedral. For a less energetic way back to the Altstadt, try the mini-funicular from Bundesterrace (just off Marzilistrasse). The **Drahtseilbahn Marzili-Stadt Bern** *(www.marzilibahn.ch)* prides itself on being Europe's shortest public funicular—with an ascent of just 101 feet (31 m). It takes two minutes to reach the top.

Bern's Museums

As you'd expect from a European capital city, Bern is home to several fine museums and art galleries. The most significant of these institutions, both in terms of cultural importance and popularity, is the **Zentrum Paul Klee** (Paul Klee Center)—a futuristic, wave-shaped building on the outskirts of the city. Inaugurated in 2005, it was designed by Italian architect Renzo Piano (b. 1937, see pp. 260–261). The museum contains an unparalleled collection of works by Bern's most celebrated artist, including 4,000 paintings and drawings donated by private collectors.

Born to a German father and a Swiss mother in Münchenbuch-see (just north of Bern), Paul Klee (1879–1940) grew up in Bern and played the violin in the city orchestra. His work was first exhibited at a local gallery in 1910. The works on display at the Zentrum Paul Klee demonstrate Klee's innovative and varied techniques, which embraced ideas from movements like expression-ism, cubism, and surrealism.

Art lovers should also check out the **Kunstmuseum** (Museum of Fine Arts), located in the northwest corner of the Altstadt. The museum's collection spans eight centuries but has a special emphasis on art created in the last 150 years, including several more pieces by Klee.

Around Helvetiaplatz: Many of Bern's museums are located on or near Helvetiaplatz, which is just across the Kirchen-feldbrücke from the old town. One to see is the **Bernisches Historisches Museum** (Bern Historical Museum). Housed in a turreted neo-Gothic building, it hosts a fascinating account of Swiss and Bernese history. The famous *Millefleurs* (Thousand Flowers) tapestry of Charles the Bold, 15th-century Duke of Burgundy, is also found here.

Under the same roof, the **Einstein Museum** is well worth a visit. Its collection includes memorabilia, documentaries, and

The futuristic curves of Bern's Zentrum Paul Klee, on the outskirts of the city

newsreel footage illustrating the life and ideas of the celebrated scientist and Swiss émigré Albert Einstein (1879–1955). Einstein devised his famous formula $E=mc^2$, as well as many other revolution-ary ideas, while working at the patent office in Bern.

Other less noteworthy museums on or near Helvetiaplatz include the hands-on **Museum für Kommunikation.** It covers various modes of communication from postage stamps and early telephones to the digital culture of the 21st century. The **Schweizeri-sches Alpines Museum** focuses on all aspects of life in the Swiss mountains, their ecology, their history, and the development of tourism in the region. The **Naturhistorisches Museum** (Natural History Museum) houses extensive displays of birds and exotic mammals, has a Hall of Skeletons, and boasts a fine collec-tion of minerals.

Museum für Kommunikation
- ⊠ Helvetiastrasse 16
- ☎ (031) 357 55 55
- 🕐 Closed Mon.
- 💲 $$$
- 🚊 Tram 3/5 (Helvetiaplatz)
- www.mfk.ch/index .html?&L=2

Schweizerisches Alpines Museum
- ⊠ Helvetiaplatz 4
- ☎ (031) 350 04 40
- 💲 $$$
- 🚊 Tram 3/5 (Helvetiaplatz)
- www.alpines museum.ch

Natur historisches Museum der Burgergemeinde Bern
- ⊠ Bernastrasse 18
- ☎ (031) 350 71 11
- 💲 $$
- 🚊 Tram 3/5 (Helvetiaplatz)

Emmentaler Schaukäserei

🅰 115 B4

✉ Schaukäserei-
strasse 6,
Affoltern

☎ (034) 435 16 11

Bernese Mittelland

The city of Bern is surrounded by a quintessentially Swiss landscape of fertile farmland dotted with wooden chalets, verdant hills, sleepy villages, and shimmering lakes. The Emmental, located along the Emme River and a few miles east of Bern, is best known for its eponymous cheese, but additionally it offers visitors a glimpse of a country life rich in traditions and customs.

It is often said that the charming, hardworking locals of the Emmental are the most Swiss of anyone in Switzerland—reliable, conservative, and deeply patriotic. With its gentle pace of life, rural landscape, and distinctive architecture, the region seems somehow timeless. The Emmental's numerous dairies and farmhouses still have distinctively Swiss carved wooden balconies and massive steeply sloping roofs. Emmentaler cuisine, leaning heavily on cheese and cream, is famed throughout the country. Many restaurants offer an *ämmitaler ruschtig menü*, featuring local delicacies. The finest can be found at the **Emmentaler Schaukäserei** (Emmental show dairy) at Affoltern.

The people of the Emmental have preserved many customs and handicrafts, including traditional games such as *hornussen* or *platzgen* and a *schwingen* festival (see p. 228). The **Alphornmacherei** *(Fam. Bachmann, Knubel, Eggiwil, tel 034/491 20 23, www.alphorn macherei.ch)* in the tranquil hamlet of **Knubel** is Switzerland's oldest alphorn workshop. The Bachmann family, who run the place, offer tours demonstrating the ancient crafts of alphorn-making and playing. A beautiful walking trail is the 9-mile (15 km) **Emmentaler ridge walk** from Lüderenalp through fields and forests on a path up to the Napf—the highest point in the region at 4,619 feet (1,408 m)—offering dazzling views over the Alps, the plateau of the Bernese Mittelland, and the Jura.

Cyclists riding their mountain bikes on a section of the *Herz* cycle route, which runs through the center of the Emmental

Biel-Bienne & Solothurn:

The picturesque town of Biel-Bienne lies at the northeastern end of the beautiful Bielersee (Lac de Bienne). The town's dual name is a result of its location on the *Röstigraben,* the nation's French-German divide (see p. 19). It is considered to be Switzerland's most bilingual town, with locals switching tongue even in mid-conversation. A center of watchmaking, Biel is home to such manufacturers as Rolex, Swatch, Tissot, and Omega. Its tiny old district wraps around a plaza called the **Ring.** The area's ancient past is explored in the **Musée Schwab** *(Faubourg du Lac 50, tel 032/322 76 03, closed Mon., $$),* which exhibits local prehistoric finds.

In the north of the Bernese Mittelland lies the small canton of Solothurn. Its capital, also called Solothurn, is a picturesque historic town located about 19 miles (30 km) northeast of Biel-Bienne. The town is known for its beautifully preserved baroque Altstadt, which was built between the 16th and 18th centuries. This period was a kind of golden age for the town, when its predominantly Catholic population led to it being chosen as the residence of the powerful French ambassador to Switzerland. While the ambassador's residence has long since shifted to Bern, Solothurn is still known as the "Ambassador's Town."

Solothurn was the 11th canton to join the Swiss Confederation, and this number is a recurring motif in the town today: The walls have 11 towers and enclose an old town with 11 painted fountains and 11 beautiful churches. The finest of these are the lavish baroque **Jesuitenkirche** *(Jesuit Church, Hauptgasse)* and, a stone's throw away, the **Kathedrale St. Ursen** (Cathedral of Saint Ursus) with its 11 bells, 11 clocks, and 11 altars.

Solothurn's museums include the **Altes Zeughaus** (Old Arsenal Museum), which contains Switzerland's finest collection of armor and weaponry. The **Kunstmuseum** (Fine Arts Museum) features paintings from many Swiss and French artists. ∎

Biel-Bienne
🅰 114 A4

Solothurn
🅰 115 B4
Visitor Information
✉ Region Solothurn Tourismus, Hauptgasse 69, Solothurn
☎ (032) 626 46 46
🕐 Closed Sun.
www.solothurn-city .ch/topic2477.html

Kathedrale St. Ursen
✉ Hauptgasse, Solothurn
☎ (032) 622 87 71

Altes Zeughaus
✉ Zeughausplatz 1, Solothurn
☎ (032) 627 60 70
🕐 Closed Mon.
💲 $$

Kunstmuseum
✉ Werkhofstrasse 30, Solothurn
☎ (032) 624 40 00
🕐 Closed Mon.
💲 $$$

EXPERIENCE: Travel Around on an E-bike

The latest craze in Switzerland is the "flyer," or "e-bike." These bikes (which have pedals and a small electric motor) are available for rent throughout the region through **Rent-a-bike** *(www.rent-a-bike .ch).* They are ideal for traversing the extremely hilly countryside without getting too exhausted. Keen cyclists will enjoy the long-distance *Herz* (heart) route. It is divided into four clearly signed stages (each detailed in a free pamphlet available from local tourist offices, together with bike rental details and suggestions for sightseeing, restaurants, and accommodation). The four stages are: Laupen to Thun (40 miles/64 km); Thun to Langnau (45 miles/72 km); Langnau to Burgdorf (28 miles/45 km) through the heart of the Emmental; and Burgdorf to Willisau (39 miles/63 km). With its exceptional views, the fourth stage counts among the most popular e-bike cycle tours in Switzerland.

Interlaken & the Bernese Oberland

The town of Interlaken stands between the verdant pastures of the Mittelland and the snow-capped mountains of the Oberland. The surrounding area—which includes the lakes of Thunersee and Brienzersee—is one of the most beautiful in the country. It is the perfect base for those who want to experience all that the Bernese Oberland has to offer.

The fairy-tale towers of Schloss Oberhofen on the banks of Thunersee

Deep in the heart of Switzerland, the Bernese Oberland is a popular all-year destination, thanks to its spectacular Alpine landscape. The area has a comprehensive network of paddle-wheelers, cable cars, and cogwheel railways that provide access to hundreds of miles of varied walking trails.

Gateway to the Oberland

The clear mountain lakes of Thunersee (Lake Thun) and Brienzersee (Lake Brienz) form a gateway from the pastures of central Switzerland to the high Alps of the south. The best way to see the sights around these lakes is by boat. Scheduled services are operated by **Schiffahrt Berner Oberland** *(www.bls.ch/ schiff),* and run from April to mid-October. The steamship company offers a number of themed itineraries, including Sunday brunch outings and summer jazz cruises on Thunersee or sunset barbecue tours and Swiss dinner cruises on Brienzersee.

Public transportation (primarily mountain train and PostBus) in this region is reliable and frequent, with a total of 44 railroad lines, cable cars, and ski lifts. From Interlaken Ost rail station, mountain trains full of skiers, snowboarders, hikers, and sightseers snake up from the valley floor to the Jungfrau region's celebrated ski areas—Grindelwald, Mürren, and Wengen (see pp. 134–135). These three resorts showcase a sparkling panorama of peaks that range from 10,000 to 13,000 feet (3,000–4,000 m), and include over 125 miles (201 km) of ski runs and 60 miles (96 km) of winter footpaths and toboggan runs.

If you plan to explore the region extensively, it could be worth purchasing a Berner Oberland travel pass (*www.regiopass -berneroberland.ch/home-en*), valid for 7 or 15 days and available in tourist offices, train stations, and ferry ports. The pass covers the more distant valleys of the East and West Bernese Oberland, going as far as the tumbling waterfalls of the Haslital (see pp. 138–139); the glamorous mountain resorts of Adelboden and Gstaad (see pp. 140–141); and the impressive glaciers and snow-clad peaks of Switzerland's celebrated passes.

Thun & Thunersee

Several castles line the shores of the Thunersee. They can be reached by road, but the most atmospheric way to see them is to take the "Lake & Castle Cruise" (*West Boat Pier, Interlaken, tel 058/327 48 10, www.bls.ch, $$$$$*) that leaves from Interlaken twice a day between April and October. This tour provides

visitors with a one-day pass on the lake cruisers, as well as free admission to any two of the four dramatic castles that line the shores of the lake.

Departing from Interlaken, the first castle the cruise stops at is **Schloss Spiez,** a 17th-century aristocratic residence housed in a converted medieval fortress. About 25 minutes later, the boat puffs its way over to **Schloss Oberhofen,** which contains the **Bernese History Museum.** The next stop is Hilterfingen, from where it is just a short walk to **Schloss Hünegg.** This eccentric building, with its neo-Renaissance

INSIDER TIP:

The steps up the tower in Schloss Spiez seem to go on forever, but the climb is worth the effort. You'll be rewarded by views of the vineyards and the Thunersee.

—CLIVE CARPENTER
National Geographic contributor

exterior and art-nouveau interior, was built for a German aristocrat in the late 19th century. The last stop on the cruise is **Schloss Thun,** a large medieval castle built by the Dukes of Zähringen that towers over the town.

Another local attraction is the **St. Beatus Höhlen** (St. Beatus' Caves)—a maze of caves and *(continued on p. 130)*

Schloss Oberhofen

- ☒ Oberhofen
- ☎ (033) 243 12 35
- ⏱ Closed mid-Oct.–early May
- 💲 $$$

www.schloss oberhofen.ch/en/ home

Schloss Spiez

- ☒ Schloss-Museum, Schlosstrasse 16, Spiez
- ☎ (033) 654 15 60
- ⏱ Closed mid Oct.–March
- 💲 $$

Schloss Hünegg

- ☒ Staatsstrasse 52, Hilterfingen
- ☎ (033) 243 19 82
- ⏱ Closed Oct.–May
- 💲 $$

Schloss Thun

- ☒ Schlossberg 1, Thun
- ☎ (033) 223 20 01
- ⏱ Closed Sun.& Nov.–Jan.
- 💲 $$

www.schlossthun. ch/we-welcome-you .html

St. Beatus Höhlen

- ☒ Beatushöhlen-Genossenschaft, Sundlauenen bei Interlaken
- ☎ (033) 841 16 43
- ⏱ Closed Mon. & late Oct.–March
- 💲 $$$$

www.beatus hoehlen.ch

Cheese & Cheese Dishes

From delicious mountain goats' cheeses to holey Emmental, Swiss cheese is the finest in the world, and—together with their chocolate, mountains, and railroads—the nation's greatest pride. The 450-plus different varieties of cheese, which include the well-known Gruyère, Emmental, Vacherin, and Tilsiter, are a staple of Swiss cuisine, savored by locals like whiskies in Scotland or wines in France.

Testing cheese in the Emmental factory east of Bern

Great Swiss Cheeses

Gruyère is probably the most famous of the Swiss cheeses, made according to an age-old recipe passed down through the generations. There are various types: It takes five months to form Gruyère AOC *doux* (mild); eight months for *mi-salé* (semi-salty, the most popular variety); around 10 months for

salé (salty); and over 12 months for *surchoix* (premium). You can watch it being made into massive rounds, each weighing around 100 pounds (45 kg) at **La Maison du Gruyère** dairy (The Cheese House; see p. 110) at Pringy, near Gruyères.

Another big Swiss cheese is the smooth, mild Emmentaler (*www.emmentaler.ch*), the

INSIDER TIP:

To release its delicate flavors, a Tête de Moine should be eaten using a special knife on an axle called a *girolle*, to scrape the cheese into little rosettes resembling girolle (chanterelle) mushrooms.

—ERIC DORTHE
Cheese-maker, Massonens

archetypal Swiss cheese, with its distinctive holes. Its complicated fermentation process requires the blending of three different types of bacteria, one of which *(Propionibacter shermani)* produces bubbles of carbon dioxide when added to the cheese mixture—hence the holes in the cheese. You can learn more about the process at the **Emmentaler Schaukäserei** (Emmental Show Dairy; see p. 124) in the Emme valley east of Bern.

Although most Swiss cheese is produced in the valleys, some alpine cheeses are still lovingly produced by hand in the high pastures during summer months, in keeping with centuries of cheese-making tradition. These individual artisanal cheeses—made from raw unprocessed cow's and goat's milk heated over a wood fire in tiny mountain chalets—are well worth trying. Each Alpine cheese has its own distinctive aroma and taste, due to the variety of herbs growing in each region.

Other more widely available cheeses to look out for include the extra-hard Sbrinz *(www.sbrinz.ch)*. This Parmesan-type cheese from Brienz is sometimes claimed to be the oldest cheese in Europe: It may be one and the same as the *caseus helveticus* referred to by the Romans and was more certainly made as long ago as 1530 in Bern.

Other varieties to choose from include creamy, semi-hard Tilsiter *(www.tilsiter.ch)* from the Bodensee region; herby, green Schabziger

(www.schabziger.ch) from Glarus; Tête de Moine ("Monk's Head"), which originates from the Bellelay monastery in the Jura, where it was first made in the 12th century; and spicy Appenzeller *(www.appenzeller.ch)*, the richest in fat content of all Swiss cheeses—and reputedly one of the smelliest cheeses in the world.

Raclette & Fondue

Cheese dishes reign supreme in Swiss fare. Two cheese dishes are especially common-place on menus nationwide: the Valaisan *raclette (www. raclette-suisse.ch)* and the fondue. *Raclette* (from the French verb *racler* meaning "to scrape") is a fun, hands-on meal, made by melting slabs of tangy Raclette cheese. Traditionally done over a wood fire, nowadays it is done more often with a special machine that's brought to your table. You scrape the runny cheese onto a pile of potatoes, gherkins, and pickled onions—and give your taste buds a treat.

The fondue (from the French verb *fonder* meaning "to melt") is a veritable Swiss institution. It consists of a large pot of melted cheese, kirsch, and white wine gently bubbling over a flame, into which morsels of crusty bread are dipped on the end of long forks and then eaten smothered in gooey hot cheese. There's even a retro-style Fondue Train *(Transports Publics Fribourgeois, Gare de Bulle, tel 026/913 05 12, runs Nov.–April, Fri. & Sat. evenings, Sat. & Sun. midday; booking essential, www.tpf.ch/index, $$$$)* that runs between Bulle and Montbovon near Fribourg (see p. 104), serving fondues followed by meringues with double Gruyère cream.

Gruyère cheese *(www.gruyere.com)* is one of the main ingredients in a cheese fondue. The most common fondue mix is *motié-motié* (half Gruyère and half Vacherin Fribourgeois). Other regional variations include Fondue Fribourgeois (Vacherin cheese only); Neuchâteloise (a mixture of Gruyère, Vacherin, and Emmentaler); Valaisanne (Raclette and plum brandy); and Appenzell (Appenzell cheese, cider, and apple brandy).

Paragliding and other high-adrenaline sports are popular in Interlaken in the summer months.

Interlaken

⚊ 115 C2

Visitor Information

✉ Interlaken
Tourismus,
Höheweg 37,
Interlaken

☎ (033) 826 53 00

🕐 Closed Sat. p.m.
& Sun. mid-
Sept.–April

**www.interlaken
tourism.ch**

underground lakes that extend beneath the Niederhorn massif. They are located just past Unterseen on the east bank of Lake Thun. Legend has it that St. Beatus slayed a dragon in the caves before choosing to live there himself. Today, they're celebrated for their spectacular chambers of stalactites and stalagmites, but can be visited by guided tour only. Expect to walk 1.2 miles (2 km) and wrap up warm as the caves rarely get warmer than 48°F (9°C).

Interlaken Town

Located on a narrow strip of land between Thunersee and Brienzersee and surrounded by mountains, the attractive resort

of Interlaken—"between the lakes"—has been a popular destination for travelers for more than 300 years. Its excellent transport links make it an ideal base for exploring the Bernese Oberland. Interlaken is one of Switzerland's top adventure-sports destinations, with the surrounding mountains offering opportunities to try your hand at everything from ice-climbing to zorbing (see sidebar, facing page). The picturesque villages surrounding the crystal-blue lakes offer visitors a more tranquil retreat.

Surprisingly for such a small town, Interlaken also offers superb shopping and world-class hospitality, thanks to its long history as a hangout of the jet-set. In summer it hosts a series of traditional open-air concerts that demonstrate such typically Swiss art forms as yodeling, alphorn-playing, and flag waving. In winter, the resort offers easy access to the massive Jungfrau ski region. Year-round, the scenery around Interlaken is breathtaking, with pre-alpine foothills to the north and the mighty 13,000-feet (4,000 m) peaks to the south, most notably the imposing trio of the Eiger, Mönch, and Jungfrau.

Interlaken is easy to explore on foot, by horse-and-carriage, or by mini-train (*from outside Hotel Vic-*

toria-Jungfrau, Höheweg 14), and it is the starting point for numerous excursions in the area, including the ride up to Europe's highest railroad station (see p. 136).

Tourism first began in Interlaken in 1690 when Margrave Frederic Albert of Brandenberg visited the Jungfrau massif. Such luminaries as Goethe, Mark Twain, Mendelssohn, and Richard Wagner followed in his footsteps, and the first large-scale tourism followed in the early 19th century. The nation's first museum of tourism—the **Touristik-Museum der Jungfrau-Region**—traces the development of the industry in the Bernese Oberland. The

Touristik-Museum der Jungfrau-Region

- ✉ Obere Gasse 28, Interlaken
- ☎ (033) 822 98 39
- 🕐 Closed Mon. & mid-Oct.–April
- 💲 $$

www.touristik museum.ch

EXPERIENCE: Extreme Sports in the Mountains

The lakes and mountains surrounding Interlaken are renowned worldwide for their adventure sports. Some of the most thrilling options include:

Bungee-jumping: Outdoor Interlaken *(Hauptstrasse 15, Interlaken, tel 033/826 77 19, www.outdoor-interlaken.ch/en)* offers the opportunity to bungee-jump out of a cable car at Titlis for the ultimate head rush.

Canyoning & river rafting: Contact Alpin Raft *(Hauptstrasse 7, Interlaken/Matten, tel 033/823 41 00, www.alpinraft .com)* for some of the best river-rafting and canyoning in the region, or Outdoor Interlaken (see above) for their scenic "Aare Float Trip" from Thun to Bern on Switzerland's longest river, the Aare.

Ice climbing & glacier trekking: No experience is required for the day courses at Swiss Alpine Guides *(Bergsportschule Interlaken, Matten, Interlaken, tel 033/822 60 00, www.swissalpineguides.ch/english/ english.htm)* for ice-climbing (May–Nov.);

rock climbing; or *Via Ferrata*. They also offer daily glacier tours (May–Nov.) and, for experienced climbers, mountaineering expeditions to such summits as the giant Mönch, Jungfrau, and Eiger.

Kite-surfing: Hang Loose Wassersportcentre *(Seestrasse, Neuhaus, Interlaken, tel 079/233 52 28)* offers all types of adrenaline-packed water action from waterskiing and wakeboarding to wind- and kite-surfing on Lake Thun.

Paragliding & sky diving: Skywings *(meet outside Hotel Metropole, Interlaken, tel 079/266 82 28, www.skywings.ch)* provides tandem paragliding flights that land in the middle of Interlaken and tandem sky-dives in Reichenbach and Lauterbrunnen.

Zorbing: Contact the Alpin Center *(beside the train station, Wilderswil, tel 033/823 55 23, www.alpincenter.ch)* if you fancy Zorbing—rolling downhill at terrifying speed in an air-cushioned clear plastic ball in the mountains high above Interlaken.

Schloss Interlaken/ Zinnfiguren-Austellung

✉ Propstei, Schloss 9, Interlaken

☎ (033) 823 13 32

🕒 Closed Mon., & mid-Oct.–late April

💲 $$$

www.zinnworld .ch/xs_cms/index_ en.php

Brienz

🅰 115 C3

Visitor Information

✉ Brienz Tourismus, Haupstrasse 143, Brienz

☎ (033) 952 80 80

🕒 Closed Sat. & Sun.

exhibitions trace the development of the area from the time when it hosted the occasional solitary adventurer to the glorious era of the *belle époque,* when the mountain railways were loaded with wealthy tourists from all over Europe. It is situated in the old district of Unterseen, across the Aare River. The parish church nearby is one of the region's most photographed sights, with its late-Gothic tower framed by the peaks of the Jungfrau and Mönch.

Just off Höheweg, Interlaken's main street, stands **Schloss Interlaken.** Originally founded as a monastery in the 12th century, today its beautifully restored rooms contain the **Zinnfiguren-Austellung** (Tin Figure Exhibition). Over 50,000 tin figures illustrate scenes of Swiss life. Other exhibitions focus on fairy tales and early Swiss history—ranging from Hannibal crossing the

mountains with his elephants to the legend of William Tell (see pp. 182–183).

Friedrich Schiller's famous version of this story can be seen during summer months at the **Tell-Freilichtspiele** (William Tell open-air theater), located in a woodland clearing at Matten, near Interlaken. It is staged with an impressive cast of more than 200 actors and actresses, as well as 20 horses, cows, and goats. Tickets are available from the Interlaken tourist office or online at *www .tellspiele.ch* (German-language site).

Before exploring farther afield, be sure to take the 10-minute funicular ride (from Interlaken Ost) up to Interlaken's own mountain—Harder Kulm, with its pleasant panoramic restaurant, **Bergrestaurant Harder Kulm** *(Postfach 627, Interlaken, tel 033/828 73 11, www.harderkulm .ch).* The two-hour circular woodland trail at the summit affords awe-inspiring lake and mountain vistas. The hike back to Interlaken Ost takes around 2.5 hours.

Brienz & Brienzersee

Several picturesque settlements nestle along the banks of Brienzersee (Lake Brienz), including the friendly fishing village of Iseltwald and the quaint village of Brienz. The latter is a major woodcarving center—a trade reflected in the ornate wooden chalet-style houses, with their elaborate carved decoration.

The **Museum Holzbildhauerei** (Swiss Museum of Woodcarving, *Hauptstrasse 111, Brienz, tel 033/952 13 17),* located on the

---

EXPERIENCE:
Carving Cows

Cows are an important part of traditional life in this part of Switzerland. One of the more unusual examples of this love of all things bovine can be found in the peaceful lakeside village of Bönigen, near Interlaken. Here, on Wednesday afternoons in July and August, you can spend a relaxing afternoon carving your very own miniature wooden Swiss cow under the expert instruction of a local woodcarver. Children under 10 have the chance to paint their wooden cow. Reserve your place through the local tourist office, Tourismus Information Bönigen *(Seestrasse 6, Bönigen, tel 033/822 29 58).*

INSIDER TIP:

Everywhere you look in the Jungfrau region there is a cable car or a mountain railway— even the most remote parts seem easily accessible.

—TIM HARRIS
National Geographic contributor

Wooden chalets in Brienz

premises of the world-famous music box manufacturer Jobin, is the nation's first museum on the subject. It opened in 2009 and exhibits ancient and modern wood sculptures, musical boxes, and pieces produced in the village's celebrated wood-carving school. Nearby is the 2.5-mile-long (4 km) "Life Trail" *(www.schwander-lebensweg .ch)*, created in conjunction with the wood carving school. This woodland path features 13 carved wooden figures illustrating the theme of life. It is located just above the village of Schwanden, easily reachable by PostBus (from Schwanden to Derfliplatz bus stop).

No trip to Brienz is complete without a ride on the **Brienz Rothorn Bahn** *(tel 033/952 22 22, www.brienz-rothorn-bahn .ch/en.html)*, the oldest steam cogwheel system in Switzerland. Its old-fashioned steam locomotives puff their way up the steep track to the top of the Brienzer Rothorn mountain (7,708 feet/2,350 m). The sweeping views over the lake and the Bernese Alps beyond

are well worth the expense of the ticket. If you want to save money and get some fresh air, however, just buy a single ticket and head back down to Brienz on foot (which takes about four hours).

East of Brienz, in the heart of the Bernese Oberland, over a hundred ancient buildings from all over Switzerland have been carefully preserved at the **Schweizerisches Freilichtmuseum Ballenberg** (Ballenberg Open Air Museum). In addition to the historic structures, there are more than 250 farmyard animals (including the rare *rätische* gray cow) in the surrounding fields, as well as demonstrations and displays of regional crafts, folk music, cookery, and traditional costumes. It creates a vivid impression of rural Swiss life in past times.

Schweizerisches Freilichtmuseum Ballenberg

⊠ Museum Ballenberg, Museumsstrasse 131, Hofstetten bei Brienz

☎ (033) 952 10 30

🕐 Closed Nov.–April

💲 $$$$$

ballenberg.ch

Grindelwald

⛰ 115 C2

Visitor Information

✉ Grindelwald
Tourismus,
Sportzentrum,
Grindelwald

☎ (033) 854 12 12

**www.grindelwald
.travel/en/welcome
.cfm?**

Wilderswil

⛰ 115 C2

Grindelwald & Jungfrau

With such impressive mountains as the Eiger, Mönch, and Jungfrau, it is easy to see why the Jungfrau region is also the birthplace of modern tourism. No other alpine area offers such a diverse range of natural wonders with its emerald lakes, verdant valleys, rugged gorges, thundering waterfalls, and gigantic, snow-capped peaks.

The region's major attractions are clustered along two valleys—the Lauterbrunnental and the Lütschental, which branch off to the south and east from Interlaken.

At the top of the Lütschental valley, 11 miles southeast (and about 1,500 feet up) from Interlaken, lies the family-oriented resort of **Grindelwald.** This small town stands in the shadow of the ice-capped summits of the Wetterhorn, Schreckhorn, and Eiger mountains. Grindelwald is a popular year-round adventure sports resort (for mountaineering, ice-climbing, and Europe's longest toboggan run), world-class skiing in winter, and exceptional summer hiking.

Hiking around Jungfrau:

Visitors will need good footwear and a reasonable level of physical fitness for these hikes. The easiest trail is the **Upper Grindelwald Glacier Route,** which runs from the top of the Pfingstegg cable car route down to Grindelwald. A more challenging route is the **Eiger Trail,** which runs from the Alpiglen station of the Wengen-Alp railroad up to the Eigergletscher. This hike takes walkers directly beneath the Eiger's awe-inspiring, near-vertical North Wall. It takes around three hours and requires a little more fitness.

The area's greatest hike is along the **Schynige Platte Trail,** which runs from the Schynige Platte (a high mountain plateau) to the summit of First (a minor peak near Grindelwald). The trail typically takes around six hours for fit hikers, and ascends to a height of 8,793 feet (2,680 m). To reach

Skiers gather at a restaurant near the Wetterhorn.

the start point, you'll need to take a 50-minute cogwheel train ride from Wilderswil (just south of Interlaken). Before you start it's worth stopping off at the **Alpengarten Schynige Platte,** which contains around 600 species of alpine blooms.

The Lauterbrunnental

Grindelwald's neighboring valley, the craggy, steep-sided Lauterbrunnental, is famous for its 72 waterfalls, including the **Staubbach Fall,** which cascades in free fall for 984 feet (300 m) and the **Trümmelbachfälle** (Trummelbach Falls), a massive, illuminated network of ten glacial waterfalls inside the mountain, reached by tunnel lift. The Trummelbachfälle drains the enormous glaciers around the Eiger, Mönch, and Jungfrau; up to 5,200 gallons (20,000 liters) of water pour over the falls every second. They are the only accessible glacier-waterfalls in Europe inside a mountain, and a UNESCO World Natural Heritage site.

The intimate, traffic-free villages of Wengen and Mürren lie on sunny terraces high above the valley. **Wengen** (4,179 feet/1,274 m) is most easily reached by cogwheel railway from the valley town of Lauterbrunnen. It has been welcoming guests for over a century thanks to the superb skiing and hiking in the nearby Männlichen-Kleine Schiedegg and Eiger Glacier areas. Wengen is also the home of the famous Lauberhorn World Cup; initiated in 1905, it remains one

---

EXPERIENCE:
A Moonlit Walk

What could be more romantic than enjoying a moonlit Alpine walk with a loved one? These guided walks under the stars, from Schynigge Platte to First, run on selected summer nights *(tel 033/828 73 51 for details)*. Alternatively, share a candlelit dinner inside the Pfingstegg cable car *(tel 033/853 26 26)*, for that very special occasion, or join a charming "flowers and healing herbs" walk *(tel 033/828 77 11)*.

---

of the world's fastest, longest, and most famous ski races.

On the other side of the valley at 5,413 feet (1,650m) stands **Mürren,** a lovely village dotted with wooden chalets and cozy restaurants. As the highest ski resort in the Bernese Oberland, the only practical way to get there is by cable car from Stechelberg. The main mountaintop excursion here (for summer hiking and winter skiing) is the Schilthorn (9,744 feet/2,970 m). The journey up there takes around half an hour, traveling on the longest aerial cableway in the Alps. At its summit, the **Piz Gloria** solar-powered revolving restaurant *(tel 033/826 00 07, www.schilthorn.ch)* has views of over 200 peaks. This dramatic location featured in the James Bond movie *On Her Majesty's Secret Service* (1969); clips of the film can be viewed at the **Touristorama** at the summit. There is even a Bond Bar serving the glamorous secret agent's favorite tipple—"Martini... shaken not stirred."

(continued on p. 138)

Alpengarten Schynige Platte

🏔 115 C2
☎ (033) 822 28 35
🕐 Closed Sept.–May
www.alpengarten.ch /homeenglish

Trümmelbachfälle

🏔 115 C2
☎ (033) 855 32 32
🕐 Closed Oct.–March
www.truemmel bach.ch/enmain2/ main2.php

Wengen

🏔 115 C2

Visitor Information

✉ Wengen Tourismus, Dorfstrasse, Wengen
☎ (033) 855 14 14
www.mywengen.ch/ en/welcome.cfm?

Mürren

🏔 115 C2

Visitor Information

☎ (033) 856 86 86
www.mymuerren .ch/de/welcome.cfm

Jungfraujoch Tour

If those on whirlwind tours of Europe do only one thing in Switzerland, it should be a journey up to Jungfraujoch. The experience of reaching Europe's highest railway station, at 11,332 feet (3,454 m), is alone worth the trip, but there is also the panorama down Europe's longest glacier from the mountain's restaurants and spectacular viewing platforms.

The Jungfraubahn train climbs toward the Eiger Glacier, with Mönch and the Eiger itself looming.

The journey begins at **Interlaken** ❶. Here the main lines from Bern and Luzern connect with the network of narrow-gauge lines that run into the Bernese Oberland. From Interlaken it takes less than two hours to reach the summit, making it an easy day trip by train from Zürich, Bern, or Luzern.

From Interlaken, the train races across flat ground before beginning its climb as it passes through the narrow defile of the Lütschine. When it reaches the town of Wilderswil those with time can take the cogwheel train to **Schynige Platte** ❷ (see p. 135) for stupendous views over the lakes of Thun and Brienz. The train divides at Zweilütschinen, with the rear section turning east to Grindelwald and the front section (carrying those heading for Jung-

fraujoch) heading south to Lauterbrunnen. The valley here is so deep and steep-sided that sunlight hardly ever shines on the train as it works its way up alongside the tumbling Lütschine River.

In a rare instance of poor planning in Switzerland, the section of railroad between Lauterbrunnen and Kleine Scheidegg was built to a different gauge from the railroads on either side, necessitating a quick change of train at both places. Leaving Lauterbrunnen the railway twists its way up to the sunny slope on which the car-free resort of **Wengen** ❸ (see p. 135) is laid out, with a glorious view along the Lauterbrunnen valley with its 72 waterfalls. Look out for one of the most famous–the Staubbach Falls–that can look like threads of spun sugar arcing from

NOT TO BE MISSED:

**Lauterbrunnen • The Staub-
bach Falls • Sphinx Observatory
• The Ice Palace**

the top of the rock face hundreds of yards high. After the peaceful year-round resort of Wengen, the railway heaves itself up to the saddle of rock upon which Kleine Scheidegg sits. Every curve of the track opens up a dramatic new panorama over the mountains.

Kleine Scheidegg ④ is a good place to pause before catching a later train, perhaps having a hot drink on the terrace to take in the stupendous sight of the Eiger, Mönch, and Jungfrau. Another short section of railway brings you to **Eigergletscher station ⑤**, where for many years the Greenland dogs that gave sledge rides to the summit were kennelled. These husky-like dogs were descended from six dogs imported from Greenland in 1913 with the help of the polar explorer Roald Amundsen. Just beyond is the portal to the 4.4-mile (7 km) tunnel, much of

it hewn through solid rock. It passes through the mighty Mönch and terminates inside the **Jungfrau ⑥**. This is one of the most remarkable railroad tunnels in the world and a staggering feat of engineering, taking 16 years to bore before finally opening in 1912.

From the unlined rock cavern at the end of the train journey, lifts take passengers up to the various facilities on the mountain. Be sure to visit the **Sphinx Observatory,** which has a glazed observation hall to give views in all directions—most notably down the gently curving 14-mile (22 km) Aletsch Glacier. One of the mountain's most popular attractions is the **Ice Palace**—a vast cavern begun in 1934 by two local mountain guides who carved out a vaulted hall supported by pillars of ice, with sculptures of wildlife and other exhibits. Return the same way to Interlaken.

▲ See area map p. 115
► Interlaken station
🕓 2 hours 20 minutes
⟷ 20 miles (32 km)
► Interlaken station

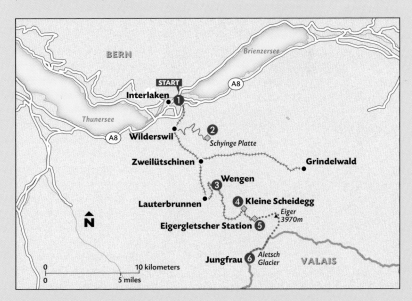

**Meiringen–
Haslital Region**
🅰 115 D2

Visitor Information

✉ Haslital
Tourismus,
Bahnhofplatz
12, Meiringen

☎ (033) 972 50 50

**www.meiringen
-hasliberg.ch/en/
page.cfm/Welcome**

Reichenbachfall
🅰 115 D2

Haslital & the East Bernese Oberland

The Eastern Bernese Oberland lies to the east of Lake Brienz, and its main draw is the little-known Haslital region (Hasli valley). With 316 mountain peaks, 19 waterfalls, 37 glaciers, 158 lakes, and only about 8,000 residents, not only is it one of Switzerland's best-kept secrets, but it is also an excellent base for touring—located midway between Luzern and Interlaken.

Haslital (*www.haslital.ch/en*) has a few scattered clusters of traditional chocolate-box villages on and around the Hasliberg

The statue of Arthur Conan Doyle's famous detective, Sherlock Holmes, outside Meiringen's Anglican Church

mountain. Its two largest towns are the mountain resort of Hasliberg, located on a sunny terrace overlooking the valley, and the picturesque town of Meiringen.

Meiringen: This small mountain village has two main claims to fame. The first is its status as the home (and namesake) of the meringue, which is said to have been cooked up here by an Italian baker called Gasparini in the 18th century. The people of Meiringen are especially proud of these delicious creations, which are sold in the town's ubiquitous tea rooms and cake shops. In 1985, Meiringen set a world record, baking the world's largest meringue. They used 2,500 eggs and 265 pounds (120 kg) of sugar. Drop in at **Frutal** (*Bahnhofstrasse 18, Meiringen, tel 033/971 10 62, www .frutal.ch*) and taste homemade meringues or delicious raspberry or lemon cakes in the tea room.

Meiringen's other claim to fame is that it was the setting for an event that never actually happened. A funicular just ten minutes' walk from the town (at Willigen) leads to the **Reichenbachfall** (*Reichenback-Willigen, tel 033/972 90 10, open mid-May–Sept., www.reichenbachfall.ch*), a series of dramatic waterfalls where the rivers of the Rosenlaui valley meet. The location so impressed one frequent visitor—the British novelist Sir Arthur Conan Doyle (1859–1930)—that he made it the setting for the scene in "The Final Problem," in which the famous fictitious detective

Sherlock Holmes has his deadly final encounter with his nemesis, Professor Moriarty. There is a memorial plaque at the funicular, and a small but intriguing **Sherlock Holmes Museum** beneath the old Anglican Church in town. Every May 4th, Holmes fans dressed in deerstalkers gather here to mark the anniversary of his death, following clues along Holmes' path to the falls.

The Grimsel Massif: Meiringen makes an excellent base for exploring the rugged, upper reaches of the Aare River. There are over 186 miles (300 km) of marked hiking trails and a comprehensive network of cable cars in the region. Those looking for a little excitement can test their nerves crossing the dizzying **Triftbrücke** (Trift Bridge), Europe's highest and longest rope bridge. This narrow wood-and-cable affair is suspended high above the Trift Glacier in the Grimsel region.

Alternatively visitors can explore the cliff-clinging paths and roughly cut tunnels of the rugged **Aareschlucht** (Aare Gorge), or take the **Gelmer Funicular—** which is the world's steepest, climbing the mountain at as much as a 46-degree angle. The latter affords extensive vistas of the high peaks of the Grimsel massif.

Meiringen is strategically located between three alpine passes—Grimsel, Brunig, and Susten—and each August, it is the start-point of the **Alpenbrevet cycle race.** Depending on your level of fitness, this event covers three, four, or five mountain passes. The "easy" Silver route covers 80 miles (131 km), while the 170-mile (276 km) Platinum course takes in all five passes in one day. Most visitors, however, choose to witness the breathtaking scenery of these passes from a PostBus.

As the weather cools, Meiringen's mountainous location makes it a perfect base for skiers and snowboarders. It is not as glamorous as neighboring Wengen or Mürren, but significantly more affordable. The Meiringen-Hasliberg ski area is ideal for intermediates or families, with around 40 miles (60 km) of mainly blue and red runs. Sledging, cross-country skiing, and ice skating are also on offer. The resort is part of the Ski Cross World Cup circuit—a sport which has become increasingly popular since it became an Olympic event in 2010.

West Bernese Oberland

The two principal valleys of the West Bernese Oberland are the

Sherlock Holmes Museum
✉ Bahnhofstrasse 26, Meiringen
☎ (033) 972 18 80
🕐 Closed Mon. May–Sept.; Mon., Tues., Thurs., & Sat. Oct.–April
💲 $$

Triftbrücke
🅰 115 D2

Aareschlucht
🅰 115 D2
✉ Aareschlucht, Meiringen
☎ (033) 971 40 48
🕐 Closed Nov.–Feb.
💲 $$
www.aareschlucht .ch/english/will kommen_e.php

Gelmer Funicular
✉ Grimselwelt, Innertkirchen
☎ (033) 982 26 26
🕐 Closed winter
💲 $$$$
www.grimselwelt.ch

Dwarves of the Haslital

The Haslital area is famous for its long tradition of folk tales about ghosts and friendly dwarves. The best known is Mug-gestutz *(tel 033/972 50 10)*, the oldest of the Hasli dwarfs, and his 3-mile (5 km) **Adventure Trail** *(open mid-June–Oct.)—* runs from the top of the Mägisalp cable car down to Bidmi through meadows, moors, and pine woodlands. It is a fun, easy walk (allow two hours) with such attractions as dwarf-houses, a crystal cave, a swing bridge, and a maze, together with barbecue spots along the route.

Spiez
M 115 B2

Tropenhaus Frutigen
✉ Tropenhausweg 1, Frutigen
☎ (033) 672 11 44
💲 $$$$$
🚆 Train (Frutigen)
www.tropenhaus -frutigen.ch

Adelboden
M 115 B1
Visitor Information
✉ Adelboden Tourismus, Dorfstrasse 23, Adelboden
☎ (033) 673 80 80
www.adelboden .ch/en/index.cfm

Kandersteg
M 115 B1
Visitor Information
✉ Kandersteg Tourismus, Hauptstrasse, Kandersteg
☎ (033) 675 80 80
www.kandertal .travel/en/index.cfm

Simmental and the Kandertal. Their main visitor attractions are the celebrated resorts of Kandersteg, Adelboden, Lenk, and Gstaad. The region also offers visitors who are pressed for time a shortcut through the mountains to Valais and the Rhône valley, via the 21.5-mile (34.6 km) Lötschberg Base Tunnel, the longest land tunnel in the world.

Both valley roads lead south from the town of **Spiez,** on the southern shore of the Thunersee. In contrast to the neighboring rugged Lauterbrunnen valley, the Kander valley is broad and verdant, and punctuated by picturesque villages. The road splits at Frutigen: turn left to Kandersteg or right, along the Englisten valley, to Adelboden.

Near the intersection, the **Tropenhaus Frutigen** (Frutigen Tropical House) provides fascinating insight into sustainable power sources. Its tropical greenhouses are heated by geothermal energy generated from the 1,500 gallons (5,678 l) of warm mountain water that flows from the Lötschberg Base Tunnel every minute.

Adelboden: Against a backdrop of snow-capped mountains, glaciers, and crystal-clear lakes, the homely farming village of Adelboden (4,430 feet/1,350 m) is a paradise for lovers of outdoor pursuits. In summer it has access to 100 miles (160 km) of well-maintained hiking and biking trails—and facilities for many other activities—while in winter it is a popular ski resort, with a relaxed and friendly atmosphere.

Kandersteg: At the top of the Kander valley lies the picture-postcard village of Kandersteg (3,937 feet/1200 m): a huddle of attractive chalets, ancient farm buildings, and charming hotels. The village is at its most spectacular in the spring, when it is surrounded by lush, flower-strewn countryside overlooked by a spectacular jagged alpine skyline. It is best known as a winter resort offering superb cross-country and downhill skiing, as well as snowshoeing, curling, ice-skating, and winter walking trails.

INSIDER TIP:

On the way to Kandersteg from Frutigen, be sure to stop at the Blausee—a tiny crystal-clear blue lake in the forest just a short walk off the main road. It's the perfect spot for a picnic.

—SALLY McFALL
National Geographic contributor

In summer too, Kandersteg's breathtaking scenery makes it a top destination for walkers and nature-lovers. Don't miss the popular excursion to Lake Oeschinensee—a crystal-clear lake, enclosed by spectacular snow-capped mountains. It is accessible via the Kandersteg-Oeschinensee

Gondelbahn. For children, there is a summer toboggan run at the top of the lift. Many people choose to walk back down to Kandersteg—it is a straightforward one-hour hike, but steep in places so wear suitable footwear.

The resort of Kandersteg is served by the Bern-Lotschberg-Simplon (BLS) railway, which also provides a shortcut through the mountains to the Rhône valley and Valais via the Lötschberg Base Tunnel. Trains operate every 30 minutes and booking is not required to drive your car onto the train at Kandersteg. Stay in the car as it rushes through the dark tunnel, emerging 15 minutes later at Goppenstein. While the tunnel is undeniably quick and convenient, the more picturesque route to the Valais is on the **Lötschberger RegioExpress** *(www.bls.ch/e/bahn/linie-express.php)*, which runs every hour between Spiez and Brig.

Engstligen Falls near Adelboden

Mountain Resorts: Across the mountains to the west, the Simmental leads from Spiez to the resorts of **Zweisimmen, Gstaad,** and **Lenk** *(Visitor information: Lenk-Simmental Tourismus, Rawlstrasse 3, Lenk, tel 033/736 35 35)*. With their exclusive hotels, chic boutiques, and sophisticated restaurants, these are the most fashionable mountain resorts in Europe, drawing the jet set year-round for summer hiking and climbing, as well as such winter snow sports as snow-golf, snowshoeing, and curling.

Beyond the bright lights and inflated price tags, the resort of Gstaad retains much of the old-world charm of a simple farming town. It is also the Bernese Oberland's only glacier ski area—with skiing and snowboarding from mid-October to early May—and one of the top cross-country ski areas in Switzerland. For two months every summer, the **Menuhin Festival Gstaad** *(www.menuhinfestivalgstaad.ch/pages/en.html)*, founded in 1957 by American violin virtuoso Yehudi Menuhin (1916–1999), counts among one of the most important classical music events in Switzerland. ∎

Zweisimmen
* 115 A2

Gstaad
* 115 A1
Visitor Information
✉ Gstaad Saanenland Tourismus, Haus des Gastes, Promenade 41, Gstaad
☎ (033) 748 81 81
www.gstaad.ch/en/index.cfm

Lenk
* 115 B1

A region of jagged mountains, Alpine sports, hot-air balloons, and spectacular mountaintop restaurants

Alpes Vaudoises & Valais

Fall colors in the upper reaches of the Rhône Valley

Alpes Vaudoises & Valais

The hugely varied landscape of these two regions, tucked in the southwest corner of Switzerland, ranges from the rolling pre-Alpine countryside of the Alpes Vaudoises (Vaudois Alps) to the splendid mountain scenery of Valais. The latter has glistening blue glaciers, fragrant forests, and the nation's most recognizable mountain—the Matterhorn. The region is a year-round magnet for skiers, hikers, and nature lovers.

The Igloo Village near the Matterhorn in Valais

Alpes Vaudoises

Northeast of the Rhône River, the villages of the Alpes Vaudoises (*www.alpes.ch/en/index.cfm*) hide in the valleys amid lush, vine-clad hills and picturesque peaks. They have all the qualities of "chocolate-box" Switzerland—their timber chalets, friendly bars, and craft boutiques are a world away from the sprawling, purpose-built ski centers that appeared all over Europe in the latter part of the 20th century. Here tourism and sport coexist with rural traditions and a gentle pace of life. The four main resorts—Leysin, Château d'Oex, Les Diablerets, and Villars—have each been awarded Switzerland Tourism's "Families Welcome" seal of approval for their high-quality activity programs, family-friendly accommodation, and excellent amenities.

During the winter they play host to skiers and snowboarders, while in summer they are popular with walkers, cyclists, and climbers.

Valais

Valais (*www.valais.ch/en*) is named for the *Walsers,* people of German origin who came here during the Middle Ages and settled in the highest habitable areas of the Alps. This region is home to around one-third of all the Alpine peaks taller than 13,120 feet (4,000 m), with the imposing Matterhorn (14,691 feet/4,478 m) at its heart. The

Rhône River forms the backbone of Valais canton; its broad and fertile valley is dotted with attractive and welcoming towns, each rich in art and history.

Valais is one of the sunniest regions in Switzerland with an average 300 days of sunshine each year. In the picture-postcard side valleys are small Valaisan villages of dark brown, weatherworn wooden barns and chalets, where time seems to have stood still. The rustic settlements are interspersed with such glamorous and exclusive mountain resorts as Verbier, Zermatt, and Crans-Montana. These towns contain some of the world's most luxurious mountain hotels and restaurants, as well as impressive programs of traditional entertainments and cultural events. With over 120 winter resorts, Valais offers the widest choice of ski experiences in Switzerland. As soon as the first snow begins to fall, people flock from all over Europe to its legendary resorts. ■

NOT TO BE MISSED:

Hiking in some of Switzerland's finest Alpine landscapes **146**

Dinner with a view of the Matterhorn at sunset **147**

Watching an Alpine cow procession **147–148**

Partying with the après-ski crowd in trendy Verbier **153**

Wine-tasting in Sierre **155**

Driving around the picturesque countryside of the Val d'Anniviers **156–157**

Spending a night in the surprisingly cozy Igloo Village near Zermatt **159**

Alpes Vaudoises

Situated on the beautiful route between the resorts of Montreux and Gstaad, the pictur-esque traditional villages of the Alpes Vaudoises offer visitors a wide range of activities and experiences. In addition to enjoying the year-round outdoor sport facilities, visitors can sample the area's fine wines and cheeses, watch a traditional Alpine cow procession, or admire the natural beauty of the region from a hot-air balloon.

A hot-air balloon rises over the houses of Chateau d'Oex during the annual ballooning festival.

Around Montreux

The gateway to the Alpes Vaudoises is the resort of Aigle, which lies in the Rhône valley south of Montreux. Aigle is an ancient town centered on a medieval castle that is set on a rocky outcrop and surrounded by vineyards. Within its fairy-tale turreted ramparts the **Musée du Château** *(place du Château 1, tel 024/466 21 30, www.museedu vin.ch, closed Mon., $$$)* charts the castle's history while the **Musée de la Vigne et du Vin** (Museum of Vines and Wine) traces the history of viticulture in the region. The latter holds one of the world's finest collec-tions of historic wine labels. The Chablais wines that have been produced here since Roman times are considered to be among Switzerland's finest.

The local train service contin-ues upward through picturesque vineyards, pastures, and woodland to **Leysin,** a popular resort on a sunny plateau with superb views over the Rhône plain. In summer, Leysin offers canyoning, rafting, *via ferrata* (walking and climbing difficult mountain routes with the aid of fixed cables and ladders), and rock-climbing, as well as 186 miles (300 km) of clearly marked paths in La Pierreuse Nature

Park. In winter, visitors can enjoy skating, curling, ice-karting, and 155 miles (250 km) of ski slopes that extend up to an altitude of 9,840 feet (3,000 m). Leysin is one of Switzerland's snowboarding capitals and it has successfully kept up with all the latest innovations in snow sports. At the **Toboggan Park,** visitors can try snow-tubing—riding inflated inner tubes down bobsled-style toboggan tracks at exhilarating speeds.

A gondola lift sweeps you from the resort up La Berneuse mountain, where the glittering **Kuklos** restaurant (see p. 290) at the summit (6,719 feet/2,048 m) counts among the most famous buildings in Switzerland. This striking glass and steel building gets almost all its power from a set of wind turbines and solar panels located nearby on the slopes of the mountain. The restaurant rotates, turning a full 360 degrees in around 90 minutes. As it turns it rewards diners with sensations and ever-changing views of Mont Blanc, the Matterhorn, and the jagged peaks of the Bernese Oberland. Leysin's neighbor, **Les Mosses** (*www.lesmosses .ch*), is a world-famous center

for cross-country skiing, with 26 miles (42 km) of trails including a 2,624-foot (800 m) floodlit track (*www.espacenordique.ch*). It is also renowned for its annual dog-sledding race, which draws around 700 purebred dogs and their mushers from as far afield as the Canadian Arctic to cover the 84.5-mile (136 km) course across the Alpes Vaudoises.

L'Evitaz: En route to Château d'Oex, it is worth stopping at **l'Etivaz**—a village renowned for its delicious eponymous cheese. At the **Maison de l'Evitaz** visitors can discover how this aromatic hard cheese is made in the dairy, visit the cheese cellars, and, of course, taste the final product. L'Etivaz is also known for its traditional **Désalpe Festival,** which takes place in early October. This event marks the end of the summer and the transfer of the town's livestock from high Alpine meadows to their winter pastures in the valleys below. All day long, local herders parade their well-groomed cows, goats, and pigs through the town. Often they

Aigle
🅜 144 A2
Visitor Information
✉ Office du Tourisme d'Aigle, rue Colomb 5, Aigle
☎ (024) 466 30 00
www.aigle-tourisme .ch/en/index.cfm

Leysin
🅜 145 A2
Visitor Information
✉ Office du Tourisme, place Large, Leysin
☎ (024) 493 33 00
www.leysin.ch/en/ index.cfm

Leysin Toboggan Park
✉ place des Feuilles, Leysin
☎ (024) 494 28 88
💲 $$$$
www.tobogganing.ch

La Maison de l'Etivaz
✉ l'Evitaz
☎ (026) 924 70 60
💲 $$$
www.etivaz.ch/ index.php

Up, Up, and Away in Château d'Oex

Château d'Oex is a world-famous center for hot-air ballooning. It was from here that the *Breitling Orbiter III*—the first non-powered flight to circumnavigate the world without stopping—was launched in 1999. For one week in January, ballooning experts and enthusiasts from around the world take to the skies over the village for **Le Festival International** de Ballons (International Hot-Air Balloon Festival; *La Place, Château d'Oex, tel 026/924 25 33, www.ballonchateaudoex .ch/en/index.cfm*). Visitors are treated to air shows, balloon flights, and competitions. The festival usually attracts around 80 brightly colored hot-air balloons, which create an unparalleled spectacle as they drift gracefully over the rooftops.

Château d'Oex
145 A3

Visitor Information

Office du Tourisme, 6 La Place, Château d'Oex

(026) 924 25 25

Train (Château d'Oex)

www.chateau -doex.ch/en/index .cfm

Rougemont
145 B3

Visitor Information

Office du Tourisme, Bâtiment communal, Rougemont

(026) 925 11 66

Closed Sun., except in skiing season

Train (Rougemont)

www.chateau-doex .ch/en/rougemont_ en

Les Diablerets
145 A2

Visitor Information

Office du Tourisme, rue de la Gare, Les Diablerets

(024) 492 00 10

Train (Les Diablerets)

www.diablerets.ch

decorate their animals with garlands of flowers and huge ornate bells. There is also a large craft market and a selection of traditional entertainments.

The Saâne Valley: The region's main settlement—and Europe's hot-air ballooning capital (see p. 147)—is **Château d'Oex.** This village is set in an idyllic location encircled by mountains and is named for a castle that was destroyed by fire in the 19th century. In the winter, the village is handy for the Braye ski region, whose gentle pistes are ideal for novices. The area also includes the Highland Park, a snow park equipped with kickers, jumps, and rails for snowboard free-stylers to perfect their tricks.

The ski zone links up with the adjacent ski areas of Rougemont and Gstaad, making a vast skiable domain with 155 miles (250 km) of piste linked by bus, rail, and cable-car. During summer months it is a popular cycling area, with routes ranging from easy family outings to steep and exhausting hillclimbs.

The peaceful village of **Rougemont** grew up around an 11th-century Cluniac abbey, which was destroyed at the time of the Reformation. All that remains of the abbey is the Romanesque church of St. Nicholas. Rougemont is now an elegant, tranquil resort that maintains its rural traditions even though it is just a stone's throw from the glitzy resort of Gstaad. Its 18th-century houses are especially fine,

with their ornately sculpted and painted wooden facades. The town is famed for its soft creamy cheese called *Tomme Fleurette.*

The Diablerets Range:
From Gstaad (see p. 141), the mountain road continues south to Gsteig and on over the Col du Pillon mountain pass to **Les Diablerets,** one of the principal ski resorts of the Alpes Vaudoises. Les Diablerets manages to reconcile traditional village

INSIDER TIP:

Keen walkers should consider Le Grand Tour *(www.legrand tour.ch),* which is a long-distance walk through the Alpes Vaudoises. Each of the 10 sections is manageable in a day.

—AGNÈS BERTSCHY
National Geographic contributor

life with its existence as a thoroughly modern resort, giving it a more welcoming atmosphere than some of its neighbors. It is dominated by the Diablerets range—whose name is derived from the local legend that the devil (*le diable*) once lived among its craggy peaks. The resort offers the highest runs in the Alpes Vaudoises and some of the most challenging freeride terrain. For those who prefer cross-country skiing, the resort

The peaks of Tour d'Ai and Tour de Mayen near the ski slopes of Leysin

has 28 miles (45 km) of track, several stretches of which are floodlit by night.

Atop the Les Diablerets glacier, the futuristic **Botta 3000** restaurant (see p. 289) combines superb cuisine with breathtaking views of Mont Blanc, Jungfrau, and the Matterhorn. The restaurant itself is a masterpiece of modern mountain architecture, designed by Swiss architect Mario Botta (see pp. 260–261). The glacier marks the start of the exhilarating **Alpine Coaster,** the world's highest summer toboggan track *(open April–Nov.).* Other activities include hiking, mountain-biking, climbing, *via ferrata,* and, in winter, dog-sledding, tobogganing, and tours on the Snow Bus—a 17-seat vehicle that crawls up the mountain on caterpillar tracks.

The picturesque village of **Villars** and nearby **Gryon** share a ski pass with Les Diablerets. The twin villages are traditional yet trendy, and especially well suited to families with children. They are located on a sunny south-facing mountain shelf with great views of the jagged Dents du Midi, Mont Blanc, and the Rhône valley. Popular for skiing in winter, the area also appeals to sports enthusiasts in summer, with 186 miles (300 km) of paths; 93 miles (150 km) of mountain-bike trails; and **Golf Club Villars** *(route de Col-de-la-Croix, tel 024/495 42 14, www.golf-villars.ch/E/welcome.php),* one of the highest in Switzerland at 5,905 feet (1,800 m).

Nearby, the small spa resort of **Bex** (pronounced "bay") is famed for its **Mines de Sel,** the nation's only operational salt mines—a huge labyrinth of narrow tunnels and vast mine rooms, which are open to the public in summer. ∎

Villars-Gryon
- 145 A2

Visitor Information
- ✉ Office du Tourisme, rue Centrale, Villars
- ☎ (024) 495 32 32
- 🚏 Bus or BVB train (Villars)
- www.villars.ch/en

Mines de Sel de Bex
- ✉ route des Mines de Sel 55, Bex
- ☎ (024) 463 03 30
- 🕐 Closed weekdays, Jan.–March & Nov.–Dec; closed Mon. April–June & Sept.–Oct.
- 💲 $$$$ (booking essential)
- www.mines.ch

The Great St. Bernard Pass

The Col du Grand-Saint-Bernard (Great St. Bernard Pass) is the oldest mountain pass in the Alps, having been used since Roman times at least. It is also one of the highest Alpine frontier passes, running between Switzerland's Valaisan Alps and Italy's Aosta valley at a height of up to 8,100 feet (2,469 m). The pass is only open between June and September, so most traffic goes through the Great St. Bernard road tunnel, which cuts through the mountains 1,817 feet (554 m) below the pass.

The Great St. Bernard Pass was for centuries the most important transalpine route, providing the fastest way to go between Italy and northern Europe. It was allegedly first used in the Bronze Age (around 800 B.C.). The Carthaginian military commander Hannibal (247–183 B.C.) is said to have brought 25,000 troops, hundreds of pack animals, and scores of elephants over the pass in 217 B.C. in an audacious attempt to surprise the Romans. He certainly crossed the Alps although it is not certain that he used this particular pass. Hannibal got his forces through the mountains successfully but only 37 of the elephants survived.

In 57 B.C. Julius Caesar (100–44 B.C.) took this route—although in the opposite direction—on his failed expedition to conquer Martigny. Under Caesar's successor, Augustus (63 B.C.–A.D. 17), the pass was brought under Roman control and made into a reliable summer trade route. Augustus ordered the construction of a road over the pass and had a temple erected near its summit, which he dedicated to the god Jupiter Poeninus.

The St. Bernard Hospice

The next important chapter in the history of the pass came in 962, when the Archdeacon of Aosta, Bernard of Menthon (923–1008), decided to create a hospice on the site of the old Roman temple as a safe haven for exhausted travelers on these desolate heights. Over the centuries, the pass grew in importance, and the hospice grew in size.

In 1800 the French emperor Napoleon

The Napoleonic crossing post commemorated at the Great St. Bernard Pass

INSIDER TIP:

The traditional mountain route over the Great St. Bernard Pass has lost none of its scenic appeal, so leave the tunnel route to those in a hurry and enjoy the drive over the top.

—PASCAL COLLAUD
National Geographic contributor

Bonaparte (1769–1821) led his Reserve Army through the pass and thence into Italy, stopping off at the hospice on the way (see sidebar below). Most of the time, however, the pass has been used by civilians, not soldiers. By 1817 around 20,000 travelers passed through every year. Nowadays, a better road and helicopter rescue services have considerably diminished the hospice's role, but it still offers a place of rest to weary travelers, with dormitory-style rooms and communal dining, as well as a beautiful chapel and small museum (open between June and September). Bernard of Menthon was beatified soon after his death in the 1080s, and in 1923 Pope Pius IX declared him the Patron Saint of the Alps.

The Dogs of the Pass

The Great St. Bernard Pass enjoys a long association with "St. Bernard" dogs, bred here in the early 18th century from the hunting and herding dogs of local farmers. Large and powerful enough to move through deep snow, these enormous animals were trained by the monks of the hospice as rescue dogs. When the pass was hit by storms or blizzards, the dogs were sent out in packs of two or three to search for lost travelers. Having dug the missing person out of the snow, one dog would then lie on the victim to keep them warm while the other dog returned to alert the monks at the hospice. Contrary to popular belief, the dogs never carried barrels of brandy

on their collars. The most famous of these gentle giants was Barry (1800–1814), who saved between 40 and 100 lives. Perhaps his most famous rescue concerns a small boy he found in a hollow in the ice. The dog licked the boy to warm his body and carried him back to the hospice where he was later reunited with his parents. Barry's stuffed body now resides in the Natural History Museum of Bern (see p. 123), while one dog at the hospice is always named for him. The heaviest dog that ever lived on the pass, "Benedictine," weighed in at over 353 pounds (160 kg).

Some St. Bernards now live in kennels adjoining the **Musée et Chiens du Saint-Bernard** (St. Bernard Dog Museum; see p. 152), in Martigny. The museum recalls the legacy of St. Bernard, his hospice, and the legendary rescue dogs. You can see them being fed and groomed. Nearby, the kennels of the **Barry Foundation** (*www.fondation-barry.ch*) ensure the preservation of the breed. In keeping with tradition, some of these dogs are taken up to the hospice during summer months where, for a fee, visitors are encouraged to walk them.

Napoleon's Debts

When Napoleon Bonaparte crossed the Great St. Bernard Pass from Switzerland to Italy in May 1800 with a staggering 40,000 troops, the spectacle must have been met with amazement among the villagers in the valleys. However, they were less impressed with the emperor's massive debts. During his time at the hospice, he and his army ran up a bill of CHF40,000 and then left without paying. Fifty years later, the monks received a partial payment of CHF18,000 ($22,000), but it wasn't until May 1984 that the French president, François Mitterand, finally settled Napoleon's debts.

Valais

The western half of the canton of Valais is predominantly French speaking. Its deep valleys are rich in art and history, and boast some of the finest ski resorts in the country. In summer the Valaisan landscape is straight out of a picture book—with lush meadows filled with flowers, icy blue lakes, fragrant forests, and giant, snow-capped peaks.

The abstract bronze sculpture *Le Grand Double* at the Pierre Gianadda Foundation in Martigny

However, its strategic location—near to where the borders of Switzerland, France, and Italy converge—has left a fascinating historical legacy since Roman Emperor Julius Caesar's army was defeated here in 57 B.C.

Martigny's most important cultural institution is the **Pierre Gianadda Foundation** *(rue du Forum 18, tel 027/722 39 78, www.gianadda.ch, $$$$),* a cluster of museums and galleries on the southern edge of the town. The core of the complex is the **Musée Gallo-Romain** (Gallo-Roman Museum), built around the excavated remains of an ancient temple. An adjacent building houses the **Musée de l'Automobile,** Switzerland's largest automobile museum. The grounds of the Gianadda Foundation buildings are home to the **Parc de Sculptures** (Sculpture Park), which contains fine artworks by Brancusi, Calder, Moore, Rodin, and others; and the **Cour Chagall** (Chagall Court) which features a mosaic by the Russian-born French artist Marc Chagall (1887–1985).

Also in Martigny, the **Musée et Chiens du Saint Bernard** (St. Bernard Dog Museum; *rue du Levant 34, 027/720 49 20, www.museesaintbernard.ch, $$$),* recounts the history of the Great St. Bernard Pass (see pp. 150–151),

Martigny

145 A1

Visitor Information

✉ Office d'Tourisme, avenue de la Gare 6

☎ (027) 720 49 49

www.martigny.com

Martigny

Approaching Valais from Lake Geneva, Martigny is the first town of note, situated beside the Rhône River and dominated by **Château de la Bâtiaz** (La Bâtiaz Castle; *www.batiaz.ch*).

On first glimpse, it is not an especially impressive town.

its hospice, and its celebrated rescue dogs.

From Martigny, two main roads head south. One goes over the Col des Montets before crossing the French border to Chamonix and Mont Blanc; the other goes through the Great St. Bernard Pass to the Aosta valley in Italy.

Verbier

The route to the Great St. Bernard Pass splits at Sembrancher. To the right, the road continues to the pass, while the left-hand road climbs steeply through the Val de Bagnes to a sun-soaked plateau and the town of Verbier.

Verbier is linked to the neighboring resorts of Thyon, Veysonnaz, Nendaz, and La Tzoumaz to form **Les Quatre Vallées,** one of the largest and most highly-regarded ski areas in the world. It boasts a cutting-edge infrastructure of cable cars and gondolas that provide quick and easy access to all 255 miles (410 km) of runs, as well as Europe's best lift-served, off-piste skiing.

Verbier is as well known for its partying as for its challenging skiing, however, thanks to its lively *après-ski* scene. There are countless restaurants, bars, and clubs that open late into the night, including such famous Alpine institutions as **Mont Fort Pub** and **The Farm Club.** In summer, the resort thrives on extreme sports like rock climbing, mountain-biking, and paragliding.

Les Portes du Soleil

West of Martigny, on the

Best Local Ski Resorts

You are truly spoiled when it comes to ski resorts in Valais (*www.valais.ch.en*). For families, it's hard to beat Portes du Soleil, Grimentz (*http://grimentz-lesalpes.co.uk*), Nendaz (*www.nendaz.ch*), and Anzère (*www .anzere.ch*). Snowboarders and freeriders find Thyon (*www.thyon-region.ch*) especially popular, while die-hard ski fanatics in search of the most challenging, exhilarating descents in the Alps, should head to the vertiginous mogul fields of the Pas de Chavanette in Portes du Soleil, the Montfort and Chassoure runs in Verbier, or the notoriously steep couloirs and powder bowls of Verbier's Tortin and Mont Gélé.

Franco-Swiss border, lies another extensive ski region: Les Portes du Soleil (Gateway to the Sun). This network of lifts and ski runs was created in the 1960s by a group of friends living in 14 local villages (seven in France and seven in Switzerland) who felt that everyone should be able to go from one valley to another on skis, irrespective of international borders.

Situated at the foot of the Dents du Midi and Dents Blanches mountains, Les Portes du Soleil now includes 404 miles (650 km) of marked runs, making it the largest international ski region in the world. There are runs to suit all levels, and seemingly limitless off-piste skiing. Competent skiers can ski the full circuit in a day, with just one short section by bus (from Linga to the lifts at Super-Châtel). Don't forget to take your passport, however, as the border within the park is still actively monitored.

Verbier & Les Quatre Vallées

⚑ 145 B1

Visitor Information

✉ Office d'Tourisme, place Centrale, Verbier

☎ (027) 775 38 38

🚆 Train (Le Châble) then bus (Verbier)

www2.verbier .ch/en/index.php

Les Portes du Soleil

⚑ 145 A2

en.portesdusoleil .com/winter.html

Lac Souterrain de St-Léonard

✉ rue du Lac, 1958 St-Léonard

☎ (027) 203 22 66

🕐 Closed Nov.– mid-March

$ $$$

www.lac-souterrain
.com/173/EN/Home
.html

Sion

🔼 145 B2

Visitor Information

✉ Office d'Tourisme, place de la Planta, Sion

☎ (027) 327 77 27

🚆 Train (Sion)

www.siontourisme
.ch/index.php/en

Musée d'Histoire

✉ Château de Valère, Sion

☎ (027) 606 47 15

🕐 Closed Mon. Oct.–May

$ $$

Musée d'Art

✉ place de la Majorie 15, Sion

☎ (027) 606 46 90

🕐 Closed Mon.

$ $$

Sierre

🔼 145 B2

Visitor Information

✉ Office d'Tourisme, place de la Gare 10, Sierre

☎ (027) 455 85 35

🚆 Train (Sierre)

www.sierre-salgesch
.ch/en/Place

The seven founding Swiss villages are now the thriving resorts of Champéry, Planachaux, Les Crosets, Champoussin, Val d'Illiez, Morgins, and Torgon. Despite their success, they have retained their traditional architecture and hospitable village atmosphere. These villages appeal to sports fanatics, hikers, and nature lovers year-round, with a gamut of activities on offer. In summer you can go paragliding, horse-riding, mountaineering, and mountain-biking; while winter brings chances to go dog-sledding, skating, snow-shoeing, and ice-diving.

The Rhône Valley

The two main towns of the Lower Valais region are Sion and Sierre. Located in the broad, verdant valley that surrounds the Rhône River, Sion and Sierre are ideal bases from which to explore the picturesque valleys that cut southward into the Alps from the Rhône plain. Valais is the county's largest wine-producing region, and the towns of Sion and Sierre are important centers for this traditional industry. The rolling landscape around the towns is character-ized by neatly tended vineyards and small, rustic wineries. Just northeast of Sion, the **Lac Souterrain St-Léonard** is the largest subterranean lake open to visitors in Europe. Tours here include an eerie guided barge tour of the lake and the beauti-fully illuminated cave.

Sion is the region's cultural center, capital of the canton, and arguably Switzerland's oldest

town. It is located at the foot of two isolated, rocky hills—Valère and Tourbillon. Atop the Tourbillon hill stand the ruins of a medieval Episcopal castle, Château de Tourbillon, destroyed by fire in 1788. On the opposite hill, the fortified medieval church of **Notre-Dame-de-Valère** contains one of the world's oldest still-functioning organs (built in 1435). The restored medieval castle contains the fascinating **Musée d'Histoire,** tracing the colorful past of the town and the canton from the first prehistoric traces of man to the present day.

INSIDER TIP:

Visit Sion's city hall (Hôtel de Ville), where you will see the earliest Christian inscription in Switzerland, dating from 377.

—CLIVE CARPENTER
National Geographic contributor

At the foot of the hill, a well-preserved medieval old town con-tains an attractive **Musée d'Art,** devoted to local and national art from the 17th century to the pres-ent day. From May to September, you can take a miniature train—the **P'tit Sédunois**—through the narrow streets of the historic center. Further attractions in Sion include the late-Gothic cathedral in the town center, and the weekly market (which operates every Friday) showcasing the wines and gastronomy of the region.

The town of **Sierre** is the wine capital of Valais, set in the broad, sunny Rhône valley. You can taste and purchase the local wines (predominantly Fendant and Dôle) at the Renaissance Château de Villa, which also houses the informative **Musée Valaisan de la Vigne et du Vin** (Valaisan Vine and Wine Museum). A signposted route through the vineyards, with information boards covering all aspects of the local viticulture, links the castle with the Zumofenhaus at Salgesch, which contains another wine-producing museum (*www.museevalaisanduvin.ch*). Sierre is also the venue for **Vinea**—the largest wine festival in the region—which takes place every September. You can find a list of Valais wine cellars that offer tastings at *www.vinsduvalais.ch*.

North of Sierre, the prestigious twin resorts of Crans and Montana draw moneyed Swiss and international visitors to their sun-drenched, south-facing ski slopes. Perched on a plateau about 4,920 feet (1,500 m) above sea level, in a setting of great beauty overlooking the Rhône valley and the nation's highest peaks, Crans-Montana has been renowned as a curative resort since the 19th century. Today it is best known for its exclusive skiing, sophisticated and cultured *après-ski* scene, and its world-class golf. Several of Switzerland's top courses are here, including the **Golf Club Crans-sur-Sierre.** (*Crans-sur-Sierre, tel 027/483 44 97, www.golfcrans.ch*). The finest of its four courses—the acclaimed **Severiano**

(continued on p. 158)

Château de Villa–Musée Valaisan de la Vigne et du Vin
- rue Ste.-Catherine 4, Sierre
- (027) 456 35 25
- Closed Mon. & Dec.–Feb.
- Train (Sierre)

Crans-Montana
- 145 B2
Visitor Information
- Crans-Montana Tourisme, avenue de la Gare, Montana
- (027) 485 04 04
- Bus or funicular (Crans-Montana)
www.tourism-crans-montana.co.uk

An apple orchard in Valais

Drive: Val d'Anniviers

Val d'Anniviers is undoubtedly one of the most beautiful Valaisan valleys, yet its many wonderful attractions remain largely undiscovered. It is a region of charming villages, exceptional mountain trails, and little-known ski resorts. The twisting, narrow mountain roads, however, are not for the fainthearted.

The medieval town of St. Jean in the Val d'Anniviers

The road winds steeply uphill from Sierre in the Rhône basin, passing into the valley through the hamlets of Niouc and Fang, before reaching the attractive village of Vissoie with its 14th-century tower. Turn right here and head down the sharply decending road, through the hamlet of Mayoux, and on toward St. Jean and Grimentz. **St. Jean ❶** is a typical Annivard village, with sun-bleached wooden barns and sturdy chalets strewn across a verdant, flower-filled landscape.

Continue on to **Grimentz ❷,** a village so quaint and filled with historic buildings that it could pass for an open-air museum. The streets are lined with dark-wood chalets, barns, and grain stores balanced atop mushroom-shaped

NOT TO BE MISSED:

Grimentz • Barrage de Moiry • Glacier view at Zinal • Route des Planetes observatory

stones (to keep rodents at bay). Once an important center of rye farming and milling, many of the houses date from the 16th century, although there has been a spate of recent construction. Investigate the 15th-century **Burgher House** in the center of the village. In winter Grimentz is a popular family ski destination and there are several year-round restaurants.

INSIDER TIP:

You can buy local wines directly from the vintner's caves around Sierre. If you get a chance, try some Vin du Glacier, a white wine blend aged in larch.

—JACKY MICHEL
National Geographic contributor

From Grimentz, follow the signs to the massive 485-foot (148 m) **Barrage de Moiry** (Moiry Dam) ❸. The narrow, challenging road (often impassible in winter) heads 5 miles (8 km) up the Val de Moiry, famed for its edelweiss and Alpine flowers. From the azure blue **Lac de Moiry,** a spectacular walk (allow 2.5 hours) up the valley leads to the **Cabane de Moiry** (*tel 027/475 45 34, www.cabane-de-moiry .ch*) at the base of the Moiry Glacier—one of the most accessible glaciers in the Alps. Stop here for a meal or settle in for an overnight stay.

The Valley Head

Backtrack to Grimentz, then take a sharp right turn at the fork in the road. Continue 5 miles (8 km) through dense forest and the hamlet of Mottec until you reach **Zinal** ❹ at the head of the valley. In winter it is part of the Val d'Anniviers ski area. Spectacular summer hikes into the surrounding mountains include **Lac d'Arpitetaz** (3–4 hours) and the **Cabane de Petit Mountet** (5 hours; *tel 027/476 1380, www.petitmountet.ch*), high above Zinal's glacier. This area is dominated by 14,777 foot (4,506 m the Weisshorn, Europe's fourth highest mountain.

Return through Mottec. After 2.7 miles (4.3 km), take the sharp hairpin to the right (signed Ayer and Sierre) and cross to the valley's eastern side. Continue toward St. Luc, through a string of hamlets characterized by their vernacular wooden architecture, including **Cuimey**—which appears to be hanging off the mountain.

At Vissoie, the road climbs up to **St. Luc** ❺, a cluster of traditional buildings and flower-festooned chalets perched on a hilly slope beneath the Bella Tola peak. While in winter a popular ski resort, summer brings sensational hiking, including the **Route des Planetes**—a 3.7 mile (6 km) path illustrating the positions of the planets in the solar system. The **observatory** (*www.ofxb.ch*) welcomes star-gazers.

The road continues up to the picturesque village of **Chandolin** ❻ (6,561 feet/2,000 m), with sweeping views of lofty Vercorin opposite, the Rhône valley, and distant Crans-Montana. **Le Grand Hotel,** here, has an interesting history. During its construction, building materials had to be carried to the site by donkey, but its completion in 1897 opened up the valley for tourism. From here head back to St. Luc, Vissoie, and back down to Sierre, taking great care on the winding roads.

🅰 See area map p. 145
▶ Sierre
🕒 Allow a full day
↔ 37 miles (60 km)
▶ Sierre

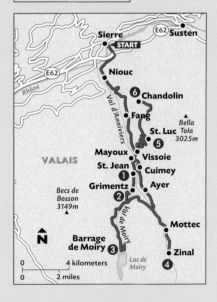

Bathing in hot spring water in the popular thermal spa resort at Leukerbad

Leukerbad
⛰ 145 B2

Visitor Information

✉ Leukerbad Tourismus, Rathaus, Leukerbad

☎ (027) 472 71 71

www.leukerbad.ch/ en/welcome.cfm?

Leuk
⛰ 145 C2

Visitor Information

✉ Leuk Tourismus, Bahnhof 5, Susten, Leuk

☎ (027) 473 10 94

tourismus.leuk .ch/en/tourismus

Ballesteros 18-hole course—stages the annual European Golf Masters Tournament.

Upper Valais

The Upper Valais boasts Switzerland's highest peaks, longest glacier, and highest vineyards. It is a region of rugged mountain scenery, dominated by the most awe-inspiring summit of them all—the Matterhorn. Its picturesque villages, which range from ritzy Zermatt and Saas-Fee to the smaller resorts of the Goms, are a year-round magnet for skiers and hikers.

Leukerbad: Leukerbad is the largest spa and wellness resort in the Alps, and the highest in Europe at 4,629 feet (1,411 m). The town is surrounded by a dramatic rocky amphitheater formed by the Wildstrubel and

Balmhorn mountains, which offer some good ski runs in the winter. Its thermal baths are popular year-round, but particularly in winter when the local ski slopes are in use. There are few things better, after a day on the slopes, than a soothing soak in a hot-water pool surrounded by a carpet of snow and moonlit mountains. The two main complexes are the **Burgerbad** (tel 027/472 20 20, www.burgerbad .ch/en/welcome.cfm?) and the **Lindner Alpentherme** (tel 027/472 10 10, www.lindner.de/ en/LHAT).

Down in the Rhône valley below, the ancient village of **Leuk** dates back to Roman times. It is worth a stop to admire its varied architecture, from its medieval **Bishop's Castle** (recently renovated by Ticinese architect Mario Botta) to the **Ringackerkapelle** (Ringacker Chapel), probably one of the finest baroque buildings in Valais.

The Lötschental

Heading east, the rustic, wild Lötschental (Lötschen valley) is squeezed between the Bernese and Valais Alps. The opening of the 21.5-mile (34.6 km) Lötschberg base tunnel in 2007 (see p. 141) has provided a swift and convenient shortcut to the Bernese Oberland, and has also increased tourism in the valley. At the eastern end of the valley, the village of **Visp** is home to the highest vineyards in Europe (5,492 feet/1,400 m). It is worth stopping off here to sample some of its dry, fragrant

Visperterminen wines, including the famous Heida whites.

Zermatt & the Matterhorn

The exclusive picture-postcard village of Zermatt counts among Europe's most celebrated holiday centers, situated below the unmistakable peak of Switzerland's most iconic mountain, the Matterhorn. This resort is easily reached in just 15 minutes on the Matterhorn–Gotthard train from Täsch. Transport within the village is by horse-drawn carriage or electric taxi only—cars are not permitted. The romantic, chalet-lined streets are brimming with bars, restaurants, galleries, shops, and nightclubs worthy of a capital city. The town is also home to some of the most glamorous hotels in the Alps. As it is now packed with tourists throughout the year, Zermatt has lost some of its old-fashioned charm. It is not hard, however, to see what made this town a favorite destination of the international jet set and international mountaineering community.

Ever since the dramatic first ascent of the Matterhorn by Edward Whymper (1840–1911) in 1865, Zermatt has been the mecca of mountaineers. In addition to the 14,692-foot (4,478 m) peak of the Matterhorn, one-third of all the 4,000-meter peaks in the Alps are grouped around the village. Alongside the village church, the **Matterhorn Museum** reveals the story of Switzerland's most famous mountain; how a small farming community became an interna-

tionally famous resort; and why more than 3,000 alpinists climb the world's most photographed mountain every year.

Zermatt is consistently ranked as one of the world's top five ski resorts, with skiing 365 days a year on the Theodule Glacier, making it Europe's largest summer ski zone. The ski area links up with Cervinia in Italy, though the best skiing is on the slopes of the Gornergrat *(www.zermatt.ch/en/ page.cfm/pp_gornergrat),* reached after a spectacular cog-wheel train ride on Europe's highest open-air railway. Summer activities include walking trails (with stunning views), mountain-biking, and mountaineering.

Saas Valley

One valley along to the east, the Saastal (Saas valley) is the

Zermatt
- 145 C1

Visitor Information
- Zermatt Tourismus Bahnhofplatz 5
- ☎ (027) 966 81 00
- 🚆 Train (from Täsch)

www.zermatt.ch/en

Matterhorn Museum
- Kirchplatz, Zermatt
- ☎ (027) 967 41 00
- ⏱ Closed Nov.– mid-Dec
- 💲 $$$
- 🚆 Train (from Täsch)

EXPERIENCE:
Spend the Night in an Igloo

For the ultimate in romance, book a night at the **Igloo Village** *(www.iglu-dorf.com)* right by Switzerland's iconic Matterhorn mountain at Zermatt. The experience includes mulled wine, cheese fondue, night-time snowshoeing, an ice bar, and a whirlpool for your perfect evening under the stars. If that sounds too chilly, consider Les Cernier's **Whitepods** *(www.whitepod .com)*—unique geodesic domes designed to provide luxurious accommodation in total harmony with its surroundings. With just 15 pods, log-burning stoves, spa, sauna, and a central chalet for meals, this also promises to be an intimate and memorable experience.

EXPERIENCE: Spot Mountain Wildlife

There is little as relaxing as sitting patiently in the cool, clear mountain air on a sun-soaked summer morning for an animal or bird to reveal itself. If you are very quiet and still, a foraging mammal will often give away its presence by rustling the Alpine vegetation. Similarly, if you hear a high-pitched call or snatch of song, stop, try to identify where it is coming from—and stay alert. Any wildlife seen at high altitude in the Alps will be out-of-the-ordinary.

Mammal-watching

Hardly any other region of Switzerland offers as much natural beauty to hikers as Valais. There are 5,000 miles (8,000 km) of marked pathways in the area that wind their way through some of the wildest, least-populated regions of the country.

Keen-eyed walkers may spot red deer, mountain hares, weasels, ibex (mountain goats with huge scimitar-shaped horns), or chamois (a goat-antelope species with smaller hook-tipped horns).

Some areas have specially designed trails for animal-spotting, with information panels at intervals en route (contact the local tourist offices for details). Among the best are the two-hour **Wolf Trail** from Eischoll (near Visp) to Ergisch; the three-hour **Bears' Trail** from Unterems to Oberems (near Visp); Arolla's four-hour **Marmot Trail** in the Val d'Hérens; and the four-hour **Alpine Ibex Trail,** at the top of the Grand Dixence Dam in the Val des Dix. Verbier's **Chamois Trail** (allow five to six hours) leads into the Upper Val de Bagnes nature reserve—one of the Alps's finest protected wildlife areas, and the second largest in Switzerland—where it is not uncommon to see such species as ibex and the elusive chamois on the steep, rocky terrain.

Birding

For the birder, the real lure of the Alps is the chance to see genuine high-altitude species. For these it is best to access areas above about 7,200 feet (2,200 m) in spring and summer. Mountain trails around **Gornergrat** (see p. 159) can be good for ptarmigan, golden eagle, Alpine accentor, Alpine chough, snowfinch, rock thrush, and dotterel in summer, and the elusive wallcreeper is a possibility. Gornergrat can be accessed via the spectacular rack railroad from Zermatt *(www .swisstravelsystem.com).* In winter some of these species may be seen lower down the valley, near Zermatt itself. In summer, birders should keep a look out for redstarts along any forest margins.

Chamois are goat-like animals that live on the upper slopes of the Swiss Alps.

INSIDER TIP:

The best thing to do in Saas-Fee is to get a guide from the village and go off for a full day hiking, or ski-touring, to Zermatt. There are so many amazing routes and there's nobody else around.

—NICK HARRISON
National Geographic contributor

birthplace of Johann Imseng (1806–1869), the man who, in 1849, traveled from Saas-Fee to Saas-Grund on wooden planks—an exploit that earned him recognition as the first Swiss skier. Its most popular resort is the pretty, pedestrianized village of **Saas-Fee,** known as the "Pearl of the Alps."

The village is located on a high plateau encircled by the 13 peaks of the Mischabel mountain range. All of the nearby peaks are over 13,000 feet (3,962 m) high and include the Dom, which, at 14,812 feet (4,545 m), is Switzerland's tallest mountain. Saas-Fee offers world-class, snow-sure skiing year-round, together with more unusual winter sports like husky-sledding; tobogganing; and snowshoeing.

Saas-Fee has numerous excellent restaurants including the highest revolving restaurant in the world, the **Drehrestaurant Allalin,** located on the 11,482-foot (3,500 m) Allalin peak. The Allalin Glacier houses Switzerland's largest

ice grotto, the **Eispavillon** *(tel 027/957 35 60, www.eispavillon.ch/ eispavillon_welcome.htm, $$).*

The valley town of **Brig** has for centuries been a major trading center and railway junction at the start of the Simplon Pass. The 40-mile (64 km) pass is usually closed between December and May, and cars are diverted onto flatbed trains through the Simplon Tunnel instead.

Goms Valley

Beyond Brig, the **Gomstal** (Goms valley)—an upper section of the Rhône valley—links to the cantons of Bern, Uri, and Ticino via the tortuous hairpin turns and breathtaking mountain scenery of the Grimsel (see p. 139), Furka (see p. 180), and Nufenen passes. The Goms contains 23 picturesque settlements. These include the sporting center of **Fiesch** and **Niederwald,** famed as the birthplace of César Ritz (1850–1918)—the "hotelier of kings and king of hoteliers"—who founded the famous Ritz Hotels of London and Paris.

Gletsch is the easternmost town in Valais, named for the Rhônegletscher (Rhône Glacier) which looms over the town. The main attraction of the area is undoubtedly the Aletschgletscher (Aletsch Glacier), the largest glacier in the Alps. At 16 miles (24 km), it resembles a gigantic icy highway as it descends from the Jungfrau to form the *pièce de resistance* of the Jungfrau-Aletsch-Bietschhorn UNESCO World Nature Heritage site. ∎

Matterhorn Museum

- ✉ Kirchplatz 11, Zermatt
- ☎ (027) 967 41 00
- ⊕ Closed Nov.–Dec.
- $ $$$

Saas-Fee

- ▲ 145 C1

Visitor Information

- ✉ Saas-Fee/Saastal Tourismus, Postfach, near Saas-Fee
- ☎ (027) 958 18 58
- www.saas-fee.ch/ en/welcome.cfm

Drehrestaurant Allalin

- ✉ Mittel-Allalin, near Saas-Fee
- ☎ (027) 957 17 71

The cobbled streets of Luzern's Altstadt, the shimmering waters of Vierwaldstättersee, and the fabled homeland of William Tell

Luzern &
Central
Switzerland

Visitors enjoying the summer sunshine on the Vierwaldstättersee with the twin spires of Luzern's Hofkirche in the background

Luzern & Central Switzerland

This region of Switzerland is defined by towering mountains and plunging gorges. It is a rugged landscape where the route between two towns is never a straight line. The large and oddly shaped Vierwaldstättersee, or Lake Luzern, lies at its heart. And since the surrounding mountains prevent easy passage around its shores, the lake itself has long been a major trade artery for the region. This has in turn fueled the growth of the city of Luzern.

As the closest major settlement to the majestic scenery of the Alps, Luzern was one of the first Swiss cities to be "discovered" by travelers. The first to visit the area were the poets, philosophers, and painters of the 19th-century Romantic movement, who saw the region's combination of stunning beauty and deadly danger as the purest embodiment of what they called "the sublime."

In their subsequent works, these poets and painters portrayed the Swiss Alps as a landscape of transcendent, almost spiritual beauty. Thousands of people were entranced by these artistic depictions and many decided to see the mountains for themselves. By the mid-19th century, every cultured person in Europe wanted to go and watch the sunrise from the summit of Mount Rigi.

The first small hotel near the peak of Rigi opened in 1816; by 1875 the Hotel Schreiber had lavish accommodation for 300 guests. The opening of a rack railroad to the summit in 1873 brought even more visitors. The atmosphere of Rigi during this boom period is memorably described by Mark Twain (1835–1910) in his travel memoir *A Tramp Abroad* (1880).

While the sunset from Rigi is still an impressive sight, today the area has far more to offer than scenic mountain vistas. The historic city of Luzern, with its medieval Altstadt and lively cultural scene, is one of the highlights of any trip to Switzerland. Like Zürich and Geneva, Luzern is located at the point where the waters of a great lake (in this case the Vierwaldstättersee) drain into a fast-flowing river, providing it with historic trade links to the towns downstream, and those around the lakeshore.

NOT TO BE MISSED:

Transportation Crossroads

While it is not an important trade route anymore, the Vierwaldstättersee remains the focal point of the region. A large fleet of ships provides links between the many small lakeside communities, some of which are still more easily reached by boat than by any other means. It is hard to imagine a more delightful commute than, say, Weggis to Luzern, enjoying a coffee and morning paper on the boat as you glide between the mountains. Smaller lakes to the north—the Sempachersee, Baldeggersee, and Hallwilersee—are attractive, but lack the majestic scale of the mountains that ring Lake Luzern.

The region retains its role as a vital transport link between north and south. To the east are the Gotthard rail and road tunnels that connect northern and southern Europe. For years locals have been concerned over the environmental damage done by the constant stream of tractor-trailers that pass through the area. In 1992 plans for a new longer tunnel that would allow freight traffic to largely bypass the region were approved in a national referendum. As a result the twin 35.4-mile-long (57 km) Gotthard Base Tunnel was bored in 2010 and will open in 2017. The northern portal is at Erstfeld and the southern at Bodio in Ticino. ■

Luzern & Around

Switzerland's most magnificently situated city is clustered around the inlet where the Reuss River leaves the northern end of the Vierwaldstättersee ("lake of the four forest states"). Most visitors know it more simply as Lake Luzern.

Diners seated on a terrace overlooking the 14th-century Wasserturm

Luzern

 166 A3

Visitor Information

 Luzern
Tourismus,
Zentralstrasse 5

☎ (041) 227 17 27

🕐 Closed Sun. p.m.
in winter

www.luzern.com/en

Luzern

For centuries the city of Luzern has attracted visitors seeking to experience the breathtaking views and dramatic landscapes for which the region is known. The Vierwaldstättersee is considered by many to be the most beautiful lake in Switzerland, and few visitors to the area return home without climbing one of the nearby mountains to see it at its finest.

Luzern is far more, however, than just a gateway to the Alps:

It is a charming lakeside city with a rich and fascinating history, remarkable architecture, and several top-class museums. All of these visitors appreciate on the not infrequent days when rain and cloud obscure the mountain vistas.

Situated on one of the many arms of the Vierwaldstättersee, Luzern's origins lie with the establishment of a Benedictine convent (ca 750). It was granted parish status in 1178, but the catalyst for its expansion was the opening of the road through the Gotthard Pass

INSIDER TIP:

The one-, two-, or three-day Luzern Card, obtainable from Luzern Tourismus, gives unlimited use of public transportation and discounts on museum charges.

—NICOLE KAUFMANN
National Geographic contributor

early in the 13th century. Because no road could be built along the precipitous eastern shore of Urner See (Lake Uri), goods and passengers traveling between Italy and northern Europe had to be carried by boat between Luzern and Fluelen, at the southern end of the lake. By 1450 more than 400 inns had been opened in Luzern to serve these travelers.

The City Center: Today, most visitors to Luzern arrive by train rather than by boat. Stepping out of the main railroad station, they only have to walk a short distance north to be treated to an outstanding view of the city's medieval heart.

Luzern's most famous landmark is the covered wooden bridge across the Reuss River, the **Kapellbrücke** (Chapel Bridge), which was built in around 1350. Visible as soon as you leave the railway station, it is dominated by the even older **Wasserturm** (Water Tower) which dates from around 1300. Over the years this solitary tower has been used as

a treasury, prison, and torture chamber.

Most of the Kapellbrücke that stands today, however, is a modern reconstruction, built after the original burned down in 1993. While the destruction of the bridge was a blow to the city, the greater tragedy was the loss of the 110 medieval paintings that were built into the original roof. Of these, only 25 survived the flames. The paintings depicted scenes from the history of Luzern and Switzerland, as well as from the lives of the city's two patron saints, St. Leodegar and St. Maurice. The lost paintings have been replaced with good replicas, however, and the rebuilt bridge has quickly weathered to match its former appearance.

The bridge leads into the most appealing part of Luzern, the **Altstadt.** This warren of pedestrianized streets on the north bank of the river contains many of the city's more interesting, smaller shops, as well as numerous restaurants and cafés. Near the bridge's north end is the 12th-century **St. Peterskapelle** (St. Peter's Chapel), for which the nearby bridge was named. If you turn left and head west along the riverbank toward Kornmarkt, you will find yourself in front of the Italian Renaissance-style **Rathaus.** The arcades underneath the building are used for the Tuesday and Saturday morning markets. Built between 1602 and 1606, it has a medieval tower on Kornmarkt and a hipped saddleback roof in the style of a Bernese farmhouse.

A few steps farther downstream

St. Peterskapelle
✉ Kapellplatz 1, Luzern
☎ (041) 410 57 00

Richard Wagner in Luzern

The German composer came to live near Luzern at Haus Tribschen in April 1866, accompanied by Franz Liszt's daughter, Cosima von Bülow, whom he married in Luzern in 1870. At Tribschen, Wagner composed *Die Meistersinger von Nürnberg* and began work on *Ring of the Nibelung/Götterdämmerung*. The first performance of *Siegfried Idyll* was given here, and a conducted by Arturo Toscanini in 1938 in the park around the house inaugurated the famous Luzern Festival. The city of Luzern bought the property in 1931 and converted it into the **Richard Wagner Museum** *(Richard Wagner Weg 27, 041/360 23 70, closed Mon., www.richard-wagner-museum.ch/en/index/index.php, $$).*

Jesuitenkirche
✉ Bahnhofstrasse 11a
☎ (041) 210 07 56

Historisches Museum
✉ Pfistergasse 24
☎ (041) 228 54 24
🕐 Closed Mon.
💲 $$$
🚌 Bus 2, 9, 12, 18 to Kasernenplatz

www.historisches museum.lu.ch (German only)

Museum Sammlung Rosengart Luzern
✉ Pilatusstrasse 10
☎ (041) 220 16 60
💲 $$$$
🚌 Bus stop Bahnhof and Kantonalbank

www.rosengart.ch/ welcome.php5

is the **Spreuerbrücke** (Mill Bridge), built in 1408 and decorated in 1635 with paintings depicting the Dance of Death—a common motif in medieval Christian art that shows death carrying away people from all walks of life. This rather grim expression of medieval Christian thought contrasts vividly with the nearby **Jesuitenkirche** (Jesuit Church of St. Francis Xavier) on the south bank of the Reuss. It has a particularly beautiful interior, with restrained stucco work and delicate colors, while the absence of stained glass gives the church a light, welcoming atmosphere. It was consecrated in 1672 and reflects Luzern's Catholic leanings.

It is worth continuing along the river into Reusssteg to reach the **Historisches Museum** (History Museum). This contains an impressively diverse collection of local artifacts, which can be

"interrogated" by using a barcode-reading hand-held scanner that gives you information about each object (in English).

A short walk beyond the Historisches Museum stands the **Sammlung Rosengart Luzern,** Luzern's finest art gallery. This establishment contains the exceptional collection of modern paintings gathered by Siegfried Rosengart (1894–1985) and his daughter Angela (b. 1932), who gave it to the city. They were close friends of Pablo Picasso—he painted Angela Rosengart five times—and their success as art dealers allowed them to keep their favorite pieces. Opened in 2002, the gallery occupies a cleverly adapted former bank building. The collection includes works by Monet, Cézanne, Bonnard, Matisse, Braque, Miró, and Chagall, as well as several paintings by Picasso himself. The basement gallery contains 125 watercolors, drawings, and paintings by Paul Klee.

Outside the City Center:

Northeast of the Altstadt, on Löwenstrasse, is one of the city's most unusual museums. The **Bourbaki Panorama** *(Löwenplatz 11, tel 041/412 30 30, www .panorama-luzern.ch, $$)* is the largest round mural in the world, covering 11,840 square feet (1,100 sq m). It depicts a low point in French military history, when the bedraggled Eastern Army of General Bourbaki sought asylum in Switzerland after its defeat by the Prussians in 1871. The canvas took seven painters two years to complete and has been in Luzern since 1889. An English-language audio commentary can be requested. It is best to view this painting early in the day when there are few other visitors.

In a park farther up the hill you'll find the **Löwendenkmal** (Lion Monument). The fatally wounded lion was carved out of the wall of a quarry to a design by the Icelandic–Danish sculptor Bertel Thorwaldsen. It commemorates the 796 officers and men of the Swiss guard who were killed at the Tuilleries Palace in Paris during the French Revolution (1789). They were defending the French royal family from an armed mob.

Opposite the Lion Monument is the **Alpineum.** This curious institution was created in 1900 by a father and son, both named Ernst Hodel. Inside, visitors can view a series of 3-D panoramas, made using a mixture of painted backdrops and small-scale models, that reproduce the views from famous mountains around Switzerland. The panoramas, which look a little like old-fashioned movie sets, are supplemented by model houses, ships, and mountain railroads, as well as an exhibition of stereoscopic photography.

Close by is the **Gletschergarten** (Glacier Garden), a unique mix of sights and entertainments to delight children. Its centerpiece is the largest glacial pothole ever found, with a depth of 30 feet (9 m). It contains petrified palm leaves and seashells from 20 million years ago, when the site of Luzern was a subtropical shoreline. The pothole was discovered in

Alpineum
- ✉ Denkmalstrasse 11
- ☎ (041) 410 62 66
- 💲 $$
- 🚌 Bus 1 to Löwenplatz, 2 to Lozernerhof

www.Alpineum.ch

Gletschergarten
- ✉ Denkmalstrasse 4
- ☎ (041) 410 43 40
- 🕐 Closed Nov.–March
- 💲 $$$
- 🚌 Bus 1 to Löwenplatz, 2 to Lozernerhof

www.gletscher garten.ch

The Löwendenkmal is dedicated to the Swiss soldiers who died in the French Revolution.

Museggmauer

✉ Museggstrasse

🕐 Closed
Nov.–April

**www.musegg
mauer.ch (German
only)**

KKL Luzern & Kunstmuseum

✉ Europaplatz 1

☎ (041) 226 78 00

🕐 Closed Mon.

💲 $$$$

🚌 Bus to Bahnhof

**www.kunstmuseum
luzern.ch/index_
en.php**

1872 during excavations for a wine cellar.

The site also contains a maze that has been confusing visitors since 1896 thanks to the fact that it is made entirely from mirrors. (A similar maze, made entirely from glass, can be found at Glasi Hergiswil; see sidebar opposite.) Other unusual attractions include a detailed model of Luzern as it looked in 1792 and an enormous relief of the mountains to the south of the city.

A little to the west, off Museggstrasse, is the eastern end of what remains of the city's 15th-century fortifications, the **Museggmauer** (Museum Wall). On a clear day it is well worth the effort of climbing the worn stone stairs of one of the towers (not all are open and cyclical repairs mean that access arrangements can alter). There are nine towers along the wall, but normally only the Schirmer, Zeit, and Männle towers are open to the public. Another

tower, the Zyturm, is open less frequently but is well worth a visit if you get the chance; it contains a large 16th-century clock that uses crudely carved boulders as weights.

The Waterfront: In the center of town, the waterfront is dominated by the modern structure of the **KKL Luzern** (Luzern Culture & Convention Center), designed by French architect Jean Nouvel (b. 1945). It houses a fine art gallery, but disappointingly there is no permanent exhibition. As a result the institution's historic landscape collection can be seen only during relevant themed events.

For music lovers, however, the center offers one of the great concert halls of the world, hosting many of the performances during the **Luzern Festivals**. The Easter festival focuses on sacred music; the main Luzern Festival from mid-August to mid-September presents both classical and modern music; and the November festival is devoted to the piano.

The acoustics of the hall are exceptional, and the magnificent building—with its cantilevered roof that reflects the water of the adjacent lake—has become a Luzern landmark. For views of the redeveloped waterfront, take a walk along the lakeside promenade, which runs alongside Schweizerhofquai and Nationalquai. The promenade was created as part of a land reclamation project in the late 19th century. This saw the swampy inlet that once separated the Hofkirche from the Altstadt

A glassblower at work at Glasi Hergiswil glassworks

EXPERIENCE: Glassblowing at Glasi Hergiswil

Ever tried glassblowing? Visitors to **Glasi Hergiswil** (*Seestrasse 12, tel 041/632 32 32, closed Sun.*) can find out whether they have the lungs needed to make something from a blob of molten glass. After a little effort you can make a small circular bowl that you can take home, complete with a photograph of you doing it. And it's free! The excellent walk through his-

tory has an English commentary option, and provides a graphic introduction to the history of glass and its manufacture at Hergiswil. Factory visits are so popular that shop sales account for half the factory's output. Visitors are also entertained by an extraordinary maze of mirrors, and a playable collection of glass musical instruments.

filled in. It was along this stretch of reclaimed land that the city's grand Victorian hotels were built, attracting such visitors as Tolstoy, Wagner, and German Kaiser Wilhelm II. Unfortunately the land reclamation entailed destruction of the medieval wooden Hof Bridge, which was once the main route from the Altstadt to the **Hofkirche** (Court Church).

This magnificent building is Luzern's largest church. The 15th-century towers survived a fire in 1633 that destroyed the rest of the earlier Romanesque church. The church's main doors are carved with images of the saints to whom the church is dedicated: St. Leodegar (St. Leger), a French bishop who is shown holding the drill with which he was blinded in 679, and St. Maurice, a Roman soldier who was martyred in Switzerland in around 287. The interior has a fine pulpit and wrought-iron choir screen, elaborate pews (many donated to the church by the wealthy families that for many years occupied them), and an altar carved from black marble.

Beyond the Hofkirche, the promenade between the hotels

and the lake forms a continuous tree-lined walk that goes all the way to the **Verkehrshaus der Schweiz** (Swiss Transport Museum). Europe's largest transport museum has been considerably expanded since it opened in 1959, with the addition of new buildings and an IMAX cinema. The sections devoted to railroads and shipping are almost wholly Swiss-oriented, but those on road, air, and space are more international. There are around 35 vintage aircraft in the collection, as well as numerous racing cars, some dating back to the 1920s, arranged in multilevel racks. You'll find lots of hands-on exhibits and simulators—you can test your skill at driving a train—and a ride shows you the 1875 construction of the Gotthard Tunnel to illustrate the challenges of excavating railroad routes through the Alpine massifs.

Close to the Transport Museum is the city **Lido,** which has been a popular summer destination since 1929. It has a restaurant, children's play area, and beach volleyball, as well as a swimming pool. There is also a (free) sandy beach on the lake. ∎

Hofkirche

- ✉ St. Leodegar-strasse
- ☎ (041) 410 29 89
- 🕐 Closed Sun. & Mon.
- 🚌 Bus 6, 8 to Kursaal

Verkehrshaus der Schweiz

- ✉ Lidostrasse 5
- ☎ (041) 370 44 44
- 💲 $$$$$
- 🚌 Train to Verkehrshaus station; buses 6, 8, 24 to Verkehrshaus

www.verkehrshaus .ch/en

Lido

- ✉ Lidostrasse 6A
- ☎ (041) 370 38 06
- 💲 $$

Touring Vierwaldstättersee

No visitor to Luzern should leave without experiencing a trip on its lake, the Vierwaldstättersee. Apart from the sheer beauty of the surroundings, the lake fleet includes five graceful paddle-wheelers whose immaculately maintained steam engines draw an admiring audience to the viewing gallery. Moreover, the lake's bizarre shape and very long shoreline means that boats are often the fastest way to reach the towns dotted along its banks.

A small fleet of pleasure cruisers and passenger ferries connect Luzern with 33 piers dotted around the edges of the lake, providing enough walking and sightseeing opportunities to keep most people happy for weeks. The highlights are the two famous peaks of Pilatus and Rigi. Pilatus is south of Luzern, high above the Alpnachersee; while Rigi is to the east, close to the charming lakeside town of Weggis. Both can be reached easily by ferry and cogwheel railroad from Luzern.

Pilatus

The cogwheel trains that ascend Pilatus (www.pilatus.ch, $$$) start near the pier at Alpnachstad. This is the steepest rack railway in the world with a gradient of almost 1 in 2, and the vertiginous drops on the higher sections are not for the faint of heart. The 7,000-foot (2,132 m) summit has some of the most far-reaching views in central Switzerland and the usual facilities of mountain hotel, restaurant, and café. Many choose to make a circular trip by descending by cable car to Fräkmüntegg, where visitors with children almost invariably pause to enjoy the suspension rope park, the **Seilpark Pilatus,** with aerial log bridges, cablewalks, and ladders. There is also a 4,429-foot-long (1,350 m) dry toboggan run, the **Fräkigaudi Rodelbahn** (www.rodelbahn.ch, $$$$). This is essentially a steel channel that you ride down on wheeled sled with a handle between your legs to control the speed. In the winter it's a conventional toboggan run. From Fräkmüntegg another cable car descends to Kriens for a short connecting bus ride back to Luzern.

Weggis & Rigi

Mark Twain thought Weggis "the most charming place we have ever lived in for repose and restfulness" and it continues to attract visitors in search of a quieter resort. It has lovely views over the mountains to the south and plenty of good walks. Some footpaths ascend the Rigi, and there is a cable car to the mountain's largest resort at Rigi

Transportation Across the Lake

Traveling around Vierwaldstättersee by train, bus, and boat is made simple by the **Tell Pass** (www.tell-pass.ch). Like other national travel passes, it allows unlimited travel on public transport for two days within seven, and half-fare travel on the other five, or five days' unlimited travel within 15 and half fare on the other 10. Accompanied children under 16 get to travel free.

The Tell Pass is available between April and October from train and boat ticket offices and tourist information centers. It covers most mountain railways, but there is an Alpine surcharge on a few, such as Titlis.

The paddle-wheeler *Unterwalden* arriving at Weggis

Kaltbad. The next town, Vitznau, is the starting point for trains up the roadless Mount Rigi (see p. 175), as well as the location of two five-star hotels.

Other Piers on the Lake

The best-known footpath near Vierwald-stättersee is the **Felsenweg,** reached by taking the funicular from the pier at **Kehrsiten-Bürgenstock.** Those who make it all the way to the end of the path are rewarded with one of the most impressive sights in the region. A long tunnel leads into the core of the mountain, where a man-made cavern houses the entrance to the **Hammetschwand Elevator.** This remarkable feat of engineering, completed in 1905, takes passengers 540 feet (165 m) up to the Bürgenstock Plateau. The first two-thirds of the shaft is carved through solid rock, while the last third rises through a latticed steel structure that is bracketed out from the

sheer cliffs near the summit. After enjoying the spectacular views from the top, you can take one of several scenic paths back to Bürgenstock.

Unquestionably the most picturesque pier on the lake is in the idyllic cove at **Treib,** overlooked by a solitary boatman's house built in 1659 and sheltered by trees. Adjacent to the pier is the lower station of the funicular to **Seelisberg,** a small resort from where there is a path down to the beginning of the Swiss Path at Rütli (see p. 38).

One way to enjoy the lake while traveling to or from Ticino is to take the **Willhelm Tell Express** (*www.wilhelmtellexpress.ch*). Heading south you are served lunch in a belle époque dining room aboard one of the lake's two antique paddle-wheelers before disembarking at Flüelen. Here you transfer to a train, with special panoramic windows, that will take you up through the spirals of the Gotthard Pass to either Lugano or Locarno in the south.

Central Switzerland

If the cantons of Schwyz, Unterwalden, and Uri are geographically in the center of Switzerland, one of them—Schwyz—has a good claim to be called the very heart of the nation. This is because it gave its name to the country following the victory of the League of the Three Forests over the Habsburgs at Morgarten in 1315 (see p. 34).

A chairlift ascent on Mount Rigi

Schwyz Canton

 165 C3

Visitor Information

 Swiss Knife Valley Tourist Board, Rössligasse 2, Brunnen

☎ (041) 820 60 10

www.swissknife valley.ch

Schwyz Canton

Schwyz's historic associations can be better understood by a visit to the canton's main town, also called Schwyz. Here the **Bundesbriefmuseum** (Federal Archives Museum; Bahnhofstrasse 20, tel 041/819 20 64, www .sz.ch, $$) houses all the charters of the Swiss Confederacy from 1291 to 1513. Similar subjects decorate the exterior of the **Rathaus,** built in 1643–1645

with stained glass and decorative woodwork in its main hall. Located in the cobbled **Hauptplatz,** it can be visited by guided tour *(Mon.–Fri. 10 a.m.–3 p.m.).* To the south of the Rathaus is the oldest building in Schwyz, the **Archivturm** (Archive Tower), built around 1200.

A marvellous insight into the town's economic and social history is given by the **Ital Reding House** and its estate. Now owned by a foundation, it includes the 17th-century manor house, as well as a baroque garden with pavilions, a mercenary recruitment building, and the wooden Bethlehem House—parts of which were built as early as 1287.

The most visited resort in Schwyz canton is **Brunnen,** which stands down the valley from Schwyz. Brunnen offers unsurpassed views of the Urner See and the surrounding mountains, but there isn't much to see in the town itself. It is, however, a convenient base for those who want to explore Schwyz canton.

The most popular destination for daytrips from Brunnen and Schwyz is the magnificent **Einsiedeln Abbey** (Kloster Eisiedeln, tel 055/418 61 11, www.klostereinsiedeln.ch). There has been a monastic community here since 867, but the present-day abbey

INSIDER TIP:

Take the train to the summit of Mount Rigi for its extensive views of the Alps. Pioneering travel writer Karl Baedeker described them as "unsurpassed for beauty in Switzerland."

—ANDRES CALVO
National Geographic contributor

complex dates from the early 18th century. The grand baroque facade of the abbey church stands in jarring contrast to the austere simplicity of the surrounding abbey buildings. Inside, the church is even more ornate, with lavish rococo ornamentation and lots of gold leaf. Cherubs and angels gaze down on the congregation from pediments and archways, while great crowds of biblical figures are arrayed in the frescoes above.

For more than a millennium the abbey has been a pilgrimage destination, with people coming from all over Europe to pray before the Black Madonna, a statue that is associated with numerous miracles. In the 16th century the monastic community included the religious reformer Huldrych Zwingli (see p. 195), who railed against the practice of pilgrimage during his time there.

Mount Rigi: A short distance west of Schwyz and Brunnen lies Mount Rigi (5,896 feet/1,797 m), a mountain renowned for the views from its summit. During the 19th century it was an important part of any European travel itinerary, famously visited by Queen Victoria in 1861. By 1873, its popularity was such that a special rack railroad (the first in Europe) was built to ferry tourists to the summit. The **Rigi Railway** *(www.rigi .ch, $$$$),* as it is known, still operates today, running to the peak from the lakeside towns of Weggis and Vitznau.

From the top of the mountain it is easy to see why it became so popular; no other spot in the Alps boasts such a varied and unobstructed viewpoint. Just down from the summit, the **Rigi Kulm Hotel** *(Goldau, tel 041/880 18 88, www.rigikulm.ch)* offers rooms with stunning views. There is another rack railroad to the summit from Arth-Goldau to the north of Rigi.

(continued on p. 178)

Ital Reding House
✉ Rickenbach strasse 24, Schwyz
☎ (041) 811 45 05
🕐 Closed Mon.
💲 $$
www.irh.ch/english .html

Brunnen
🄰 165 B3

Einsiedeln
🄰 165 C3
Visitor Information
✉ Einsiedeln Tourismus, Hauptstrasse 85, Einsiedeln
☎ (055) 418 44 88
www.swissknife valley.ch (German only)

Swiss Army Knives

Appropriately enough, the Swiss Army Knife had its beginning in Ibach-Schwyz, where a cutler and entrepreneur, Karl Elsener, formed the company in 1884. It was named Victorinox for his mother, Victoria, plus *inox,* French for stainless steel. The first knives were supplied to the Swiss Army in 1891, but the spring-loaded knife was perfected in 1897. Since then, the company's products have become a byword for compact utility, and they are exported to more than 100 countries. The **Victorinox factory** *(Schmiedgasse 57, tel 041/818 12 11, closed Sat. & Sun.)* welcomes visitors to an exhibition about the Swiss Army Knife's history, as well as a shop selling its full range of products.

Drive: The Lakes of Zentralschweiz

This circuit takes you through a variety of landscapes and some small towns and farming villages. The early section between Brunnen and Weggis is the most scenic part of the circuit but it also demands total concentration from the driver, as the road twists and turns for most of the way. It can be enjoyed in a more relaxed fashion by taking the bus (Line 2) between Schwyz and Küssnacht railroad station, from where you can catch a train to Luzern.

The hard-to-beat view from Mount Rigi, looking out over Viewaldstättersee. Pilatus mountain is in the distance.

From the center of Schwyz, take road 2/8 to **Brunnen** ❶ where you choose road 2b, which is signposted Vitznau and Weggis. Once out of the town, this joins the eastern end of Vierwaldstättersee and provides glorious views of the forest and mountains lining the southern shore. The water looks turquoise in bright sunlight, and you are almost certain to see a steamer sending its wake to both shores.

If you are making a full day of the excursion, stop at Vitznau for a ride on the rack railway up **Mount Rigi** ❷ (see p. 175). A diversion from the main road is necessary to see Weggis. The principal attraction of this charming lakeside resort—at least for nonresidents—is its waterside

promenade. At Küssnacht take road 2 signed for Meggen and Luzern. On the left of the long straight out of the town stands a tiny stone chapel set in a pretty garden. The **Astrid Chapel** ❸ was built as a memorial to Queen Astrid of Belgium who was killed in 1935 when the car driven by King Leopold crashed into a pear tree. There are parking lots on both sides of the road.

The road brings you into Luzern alongside the **Transport Museum** ❹ (see p. 171). Follow signs for Emmenbrücke and Basel by road 2. Be careful not to take motorway 2 heading in the same direction. The road winds over lush hills past farms of cattle and corn, with some huge wooden barns testifying to healthy crops. To the east are views over the small Sempacher See. The outskirts of **Sursee** ❺ are unremarkable, but the lovely old town is known as the "golden village." It's worth pausing to appreciate two surviving medieval towers, several fine houses from the 16th–18th centuries, and a magnificent late-Gothic town hall dating from 1539–1545. *Ramseier,* the delicious nonalcoholic drink made from more than 30 different varieties of apple, is made in the town.

Turn right briefly along road 24 (signposted for Aarau) and look out for signs to **Beromünster** ❻, reached by a steep hill. At the top of the village's main street is the collegiate **Church of St. Michael,** which was built as a monastery in 981. The tower was constructed in the 13th century, but it was rebuilt in the baroque

NOT TO BE MISSED:

Stunning lakeside views
- **The "golden village" of Sursee**
- **The church of Saint Michael**

style at the end of the 17th century and again in 1773–1775. The church's Romanesque origins can clearly be seen in the crypt. The interior has striking peppermint-colored stucco decoration, elaborate pulpit, and exquisitely carved choir-stalls. Note the three sets of organ pipes and the decorative door handles. A small cloister with numerous painted heraldic arms on the white walls lies to the west, enclosing a garden.

The church stands in a square of handsome 17th- and 18th-century houses, and the crow-step gabled **Hotel Hirschen,** formerly the college administrative building, dates from 1536. Off Hauptgasse stands the so-called Schloss (castle) which was once a residential

tower. It was in this building that Switzerland's first printed matter is thought to have been produced in 1470 by Ulrich Gering, who went on to found the first printing press in France, at the Sorbonne.

At the T-junction beyond Beromünster, turn right toward Hildisrieden, after which a left turn at the roundabout takes you toward Hochdorf. Follow the railway to Ballwil where you turn left to across to Ottenhausen and then Sins—look out for the Madison County-style **covered bridge 7** across the River Reuss—to join road 25 around north and east shores of the Zuger See. Imposing mountains rise up to the east. At **Goldau 8** you rejoin road 2 to return to Schwyz.

⚊	See area map p. 165
►	Schwyz
🕐	3–4 hours
↔	93 miles (150 km)
►	Schwyz

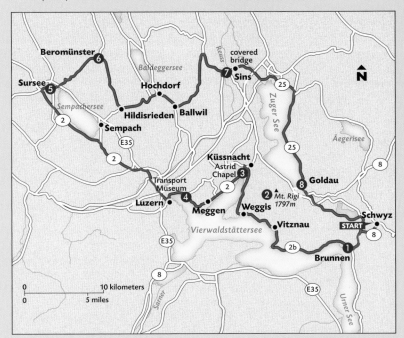

Inside the Benediktinerkloster at Engelberg

Engelberg

⚑ 165 B2

Visitor Information

✉ Engelberg-Titlis
Tourismus,
Klosterstrasse 3,
Engelberg

☎ (041) 639 77 77

**www.engelberg
.ch**

**Benediktiner-
kloster
Engelberg**

✉ Klosterstrasse 3

☎ (041) 639 61 61

🕐 Closed
Sun.–Tues.

Unterwalden Canton

Located in the very center of
the country, Unterwalden became
a founding canton of what is
now Switzerland when it joined
Uri and Schwyz in the alliance of
1291. It embraces the mountains of Pilatus and Titlis and is
heavily wooded, making forestry,
agriculture, and tourism its main
industries.

Engelberg: The principal
resort in the half-canton of
Obwalden ("upper forest") is
Engelberg, which means "angel
mountain." Engelberg is reached
by a scenic railroad from Luzern,
which stops at several stations
along the way where you can
catch cable-car rides up nearby
mountains. Engelberg is at its
busiest in winter when the
skiers and snowboarders are in
town, but in summer it offers

marvelous walking. The best
walks are reached by a network
of cable cars and chairlifts that
begins with a funicular to Gerschnialp, just ten minutes' walk
from the railroad station.

Though outdoor activities are
Engelberg's forte, the village has
one of Switzerland's finest monasteries, **Benediktinerkloster
Engelberg,** founded in 1120.
The magnificent white buildings
that dominate the upper end of
the valley date from 1730–1737.
What you encounter as you
enter the monastery church is
breathtaking. Facing you are a
matching pair of exquisitely inlaid
marble side altars, and beyond
them seven ceiling frescoes
depicting scenes from the life of
Mary lead the eye straight to the
main altar.

Tours of the monastery enable
visitors to see the Great Hall,

INSIDER TIP:

Being at the end of the valley and the railroad line, Engelberg is a wonderfully peaceful resort, perfect for those who enjoy walking and the quiet of the mountains.

—JANINE HESS
Engelberg resident

Library, and the guests' refectory. The monastery still has a small cheese factory *(www.schaukaeserei-engelberg.ch)*, which can be visited; a shop and café serving light meals have been cleverly built around the glass-walled factory.

Titlis: The most popular destination in the area is **Titlis Glacier Park,** which covers a vast area on the upper slopes of Titlis (10,623 feet/3,238 m), the highest mountain in the region. Part of the attraction is the final cable car to the summit, which revolves to give passengers panoramic views of the icy landscape below. The last cable-car stop is at about 10,000 feet (3,020 m), meaning that visitors only have to manage a 45-minute climb up the last 623 feet (189 m) to reach the top. The really adventurous can experience a roped descent into a glacier crevasse.

Summer adventure focuses on the five *via ferrata*—"iron paths"—of varying difficulty that appeal to inexperienced as well as seasoned climbers. Mountain-bikers will find plenty of challenging routes, but if that seems too much like hard work you can rent *Devil* bikes (which have large low-pressure tires that absorb the bumps) for the descent from Jochpass to Trübsee, or ride the gentler *Trotti* bikes (small-wheeled scooters) from Gerschnialp to Engelberg and free-wheel down quiet mountain paths and roads.

On the way back, visitors can walk down the Gerschnialp and Trübsee mountain flower trails, which have notes in English that identify the flowers and explain their uses. At the base of the mountain visitors can take a soothing whey bath at nearby **Gerschnialp** *(Alpkäserei Gerschnialp, tel 079/431 52 45)*–a uniquely Swiss combination of cheese dairy and beauty spa.

Titlis Rotair & Glacier Park

🅰 165 B2
☎ (041) 639 50 50
🄢 $$$$
www.titlis.ch

EXPERIENCE:
Exhilaration on Ice at the Titlis Glacier Park

Snow-tubing down a specially prepared run is the main adrenaline rush at the Glacier Park. The tirelike tubes whip you down the slopes at a hair-raising speed. Other exhilarating sliding options on snow include the Balancer, Snow-Scoot, Airboard, and Snake Gliss. To cut out the boring ascent, there's a moving walkway to get you back up to the top after each run. The best way to reach it from the glacier station is by the **Ice Flyer** chairlift, a bench chairlift that takes you over crevasses with stupendous views. These facilities are open from May to October but depend upon the weather; make sure to always check before leaving Engelberg.

Uri Canton

△ 165 B2, C2

Visitor Information

✉ Tourist
Information,
Tellspielhaus,
Schützengasse
11, Altdorf

☎ (041) 874 80 00

🕐 Closed Sun. &
Mon.

www.uri.info/en/
welcome.cfm?

Uri Canton

Canton Uri, another of the four founding cantons of Switzerland in the Alliance of 1291, lies on the northern approach to the Alps. As the supposed birthplace of William Tell, it has enjoyed a unique opportunity to build a tourist industry on his life story.

The most visited part of the canton is the Urner See, or Lake Uri, known for its natural beauty and its associations with Swiss history. The pier at Flüelen remains the busiest, since this is where ships terminate before returning to Luzern and where passengers on the William Tell Express transfer between boat and train.

A PostBus from Flüelen station which passses through Altdorf offers magnificent views over the lake as it climbs through forests and meadows to Isenthal St. Jacob. From there catch a cable car to Gitschenen to see its striking conical mountains. Another PostBus, the Historic Route Express (www.postbus.ch), heads east over the desolate Klausen Pass to Linthal.

To mark Switzerland's 700th birthday in 1991, the Swiss Path (see p. 38) was created around the southern part of the Urnersee. This area was chosen because of a meadow where, on 1 August 1291, three men met and made an oath that is regarded as the first step in the country's formation. The 22-mile (35 km) path begins in the Rütli meadow and extends to Brunnen, where the Urner See becomes Vierwaldstättersee.

While it is possible to hike it in one day, many walkers choose to enjoy a night in Flüelen or Altdorf midway through their journey. It is easy to divide the walk into sections thanks to boats serving piers at Rütli, Bauen, Isleten, Flüelen, Sisikon, and Brunnen, as well as railway stations at Flüelen, Sisikon, and Brunnen. It is a delightful route through fields and woods, but it does require a fair amount of climbing, both from Rütli to Bauen and Sisikon to Brunnen. Stone markers identify the canton represented by each section of path, the lengths of which are proportional to their current populations.

EXPERIENCE: Steam Over the Furka Pass

If you like steam trains, you'll love the 11-mile (18 km) narrow-gauge line between Realp and Oberwald. Enjoy the sight and sound of steam belching from the engine as it pulls you up the steep gradient to the Furka Pass. Once a main route, it was so vulnerable to snow that it had to close during the winter months. Today, the old line has been restored by volunteers and offers one of the most spectacular railway journeys in Europe. Eight lovingly restored steam engines work the line, including two locomotives that spent many decades climbing the mountains of Vietnam. They pull historic carriages through wild mountain landscapes with an impressive view over the Rhône Glacier near Gletsch.

Passengers on the deck of a paddle-wheel steamer on Lake Urner See

Altdorf: Links with William Tell attract visitors to Altdorf where, since 1895, a huge statue of the crossbowman and his son has stood in the main square. To learn more about Tell, a 1-mile (1.6 km) walk to the southeast brings you to his supposed birthplace of Bürglen and the **Tell Museum**. Altdorf's patrician mansions are a reminder of the wealth that trade through the Gotthard Pass once brought to places on the route. Altdorf is on the Alpine Pass walking route, and there are some fine walks to the northeast into the heavily forested valley of the Muotathal.

Toward the Gotthard Pass: The canton is also renowned for the Gotthard Pass and the Gotthard railway—including its tunnels—that links Zürich with Ticino and Milan. The rail route, opened in 1882, is an engineer-ing masterpiece, employing numerous bridges and a series of spiral tunnels to lift the line up to the 9-mile (15 km) Gotthard Tunnel. This connects Göschenen and Airolo. Before the tunnel opened it took all day to travel between these two places; it now takes less than 10 minutes. The scenery on the approach to the Gotthard Tunnel—from either side—is so spectacular that some trains offer coaches with windows that extend to the roof line.

To illustrate the steepness of the climb, and the circuitous route the train has to take to accommo-date it, look out for the Catholic church of St. Gallus in Wassen. Trains going toward the Gotthard Tunnel pass this prominent landmark three times—at different heights—as the line twists and loops around.

(continued on p. 184)

Tell Museum

✉ Postplatz

☎ (041) 870 41 55

⌚ Closed mid-Oct.–mid-May

💲 $$

www.tellmuseum.ch

The Story of William Tell

Ask someone to name a Swiss and the chances are that William Tell will be the first name to come up (unless they are tennis fans, of course). Yet there is no certainty that this heroic figure ever actually existed. As with the stories of John Henry or Robin Hood, however, the lack of historical evidence has been no barrier to this legend's enduring popularity.

The famous statue of William Tell (Wilhelm Tell) in Altdorf town center

The story with which Tell is indelibly associated—the shooting of an apple placed on his son's head—has its roots in the events that led up to the first alliances between Swiss cantons. When Rudolf of Habsburg was crowned as Rudolf I of Germany in 1273, he set about gobbling up Swiss land by conquest and coercion. He fueled resentment by imposing venal agents to carry out his local business and raise taxes.

One of the most hated bailiffs was Herman Gessler, who was in charge of tax collection in the canton of Uri. According to the legend Gessler placed his hat on a pole in the marketplace at Altdorf and ordered everyone to bow to it. When William Tell was seen to ignore the instruction, he was arrested. The ensuing altercation between Gessler and Tell resulted in the famous ultimatum, that Tell should shoot an apple off his son's head or both he and his son would be executed.

Tell successfully pierced the apple, and both he and his son were released by Gessler's men. Before he allowed him to leave, however, Gessler asked Tell why he had taken two crossbow bolts from his quiver. Tell replied that he had drawn the second so that, if he missed and hit his son, he would be able to turn his weapon on Gessler. Gessler immediately had Tell tied up and and put on a boat heading for his castle at Küssnacht.

On the way a storm blew in and Tell's captors untied him so that he, a local man with knowledge of the hazards in the lake, could steer them to safety. He edged the boat close to the shore to the south of Sisikon, grabbed his crossbow, and leapt out of the boat and into the forest. A chapel was erected on this spot in 1879 and decorated by Ernst Stückelberger of Basel with murals of the Gessler story. (An earlier monument to Tell on this site, from either the 14th or 16th century, is the subject of a painting by J. M. W. Turner currently in the Yale Center for British Art in New Haven, Connecticut.) Tell made his way around the lake on foot and later ambushed Gessler, shooting him with his crossbow as he walked down a sunken lane.

INSIDER TIP:

For many people of a certain age Rossini's *William Tell Overture* conjures up images of the Lone Ranger and Tonto rather than a historic Swiss freedom fighter.

—TIM HARRIS
National Geographic contributor

Fact or Fiction?

All this is supposed to have happened in 1307. Tell purportedly went on to fight at the Battle of Morgarten in 1315, when the Swiss overwhelmed an Austrian army, and died in 1354 trying to save a child from drowning in the Schächenbach River in Uri. Oral history was then much more important in keeping alive the story of events, so it is unsurprising that it is not until 1475 that the first written reference to William Tell can be found, in the famous *White Book of Sarnen*. A play about Tell is thought to have been performed in Altdorf in either 1512 or 1513, and a book written by Aegidius Tschudi (c. 1550) entitled *Swiss Chronicle* is credited with merging various previous accounts into the story known today. Yet a Swiss historian writing in 1607 expressed the view that the whole story had been invented to foment hatred for the Austrians. More recently, other academics have pointed out the striking similarity between the William Tell story and much older tales from Norse and Germanic mythology.

Tell's Influence

Whatever the veracity of the story, Tschudi's writings formed the basis of its most influential rendering, Friedrich Schiller's 1804 play *William Tell*. The idea was suggested to Schiller by Johann Goethe after he visited the place where Gessler is supposed to have

met his end. Schiller's play, in turn, provided the basis for the libretto in Rossini's opera of the same name, first performed in 1829 in Paris. Play and opera joined other cultural references to Switzerland, such as Byron's *The Prisoner of Chillon, Childe Harold's Pilgrimage,* and *Manfred,* to address the very people—most from England—with the requisite leisure and money to visit the country.

The Swiss have an ambivalent relationship with William Tell: According to a 2004 survey most Swiss people believe he existed, and for some nationalists denial of his existence is tantamount to treason. Nonetheless, a substantial minority recognize the lack of irrefutable evidence that he was a real person. However, just as the legend of Robin Hood permeates English culture and fosters atavistic notions of an Anglo-Saxon quest for a just society, the idea of William Tell is inseparably entwined with the Swiss sense of identity and nationalism. He also developed into a European-wide symbol of resistance to tyranny as a wider audience learned of him through Schiller and Rossini.

Initially Adolf Hitler admired Schiller's play and approved of a production in which Goering's mistress Emmy Sonnemann played Tell's wife. For reasons unknown he banned the play in June 1941, though this may have had something to do with an attempt on his life by a young Swiss three years earlier. Or perhaps he was late in discovering that Gessler was, like Hitler himself, an Austrian.

Commercially, William Tell is a useful character. Innumerable products feature his hirsute and commanding physique, and his story has spawned many screen adaptations. The first film about him was made by French director Charles Pathé in 1900.

Today, Schiller's play can be seen every summer in an open-air theater in Interlaken (see pp. 130–132), a town that has no connection with Tell but plenty of tourists happy to watch local actors (and cows) enliven the evening to the stirring sound of Rossini's *Overture.*

Andermatt

▲ 165 B1

Visitor Information

✉ Andermatt-
Gotthard
Tourismus,
Gotthardstrasse
2, Andermatt

☎ (041) 888 71 00

www.andermatt
.ch/de/info-m456

From the railroad station at the northern portal of the Gotthard Tunnel, Göschenen, there is a short but scenic rack railway to Andermatt across the infamous Schöllenen Gorge. It affords a fine view of the single-arch **Devil's Bridge,** which was the only practical way across the gorge until the 20th century. Local legend states that the devil agreed to help with its construction on the condition that he could claim the first soul to cross it. The builder tricked the devil by sending a goat across first!

Andermatt: Andermatt is located in an unusually broad flat valley and is busy with skiers in winter and hikers and mountain bikers in summer. The main town of the Urseren valley, it has an attractive white-rendered **Rathaus** (built in 1767) and a main street of attractive houses and hotels. The town's landmark is the baroque pilgrimage chapel of Maria-Hilf,

INSIDER TIP:

The hotel on the Gotthard Pass (see sidebar below) has been renovated and must be one of the most atmospheric places to stay in Switzerland. The museum is full of fascinating things.

—ROBERT BROOKES
National Geographic contributor

on account of its elevated position. It commands a fine view, and a path from it leads to the Gurschenbach Falls. A cable car to the 9,761-foot (2,961 m) summit of Gemsstock provides exceptional panoramic views of the Alps, with about 600 peaks visible on a clear day.

Andermatt is the startpoint for possibly the most romantic excursion across the Gotthard Pass—in a replica mid-19th century

Gotthard Pass

In the national museum in Zürich (see p. 205) you will find gold bracelets and necklaces dating from the fourth century B.C., which were made as offerings for safe transit over the Alps. Some early travelers were so terrified of the dangers that they asked to be blindfolded. However, ever since the first road opened through the Gotthard Pass in the first or second quarter of the 13th century, it has been one of the principal arteries between northern and southern Europe. The **National St. Gotthard Museum** (*Gotthard Pass, tel 091/869 15 25, open*

daily June–Oct., www.museen-uri.ch) demonstrates the importance of the pass in a cluster of buildings at the 6,912-foot (2,108 m) summit. They originally formed a hospice build by Capuchin monks, part of which still serves as a hotel. Basic rooms are still available at the Albergo San Gottardo (*Gotthard Pass, tel 091/869 12 35*). The best way to cross the pass is by PostBus between Airolo and Andermatt or, in historic fashion, by horse-drawn coach. The road ceased to be important when the railway opened in 1882 but its historical interest remains.

horse-drawn mail coach, operated by the **Gotthard Post** *(www .gotthardpost.ch)*. Once it would have been seen as an exhausting journey; today it is an unforgettable experience. The period-costumed driver calls at a former coaching inn en route for the passengers to take refreshments. The coach also stops at the summit hospice for lunch and a visit to them pausing to look for the source of the Vorderrhein River, which joins the Hinterrhein River just to the west of Chur (see pp. 238–239) to become the early stages of the mighty Rhine.

The station at Andermatt is the terminus of one of the great PostBus circuits of Switzerland, the Romantic Route Express to Meiringen. The journey begins

A historic five-horse stagecoach approaching the Gotthard Pass

the museum. The journey ends in Airolo for tea.

Andermatt station is also an interchange on the route of the **Glacier Express** (see pp. 240–241) between Zermatt and St. Moritz. Waiting passengers watch in wonder as eastbound trains snake their way up a series of hairpin bends to reach the summit of the Matterhorn Gotthardbahn at Oberalppasshöhe.

Walkers disembark here for hikes in wild country, some of with a sinuous climb to the Furka Pass before dropping down to Gletsch, affording the best views of the Rhône Glacier and the steam railway over the pass. The bus then climbs again, over the Grimsel Pass—with a stop for coffee at the summit café—to Meiringen. From there another bus returns to Andermatt via the valley up to the Susten Pass, followed by views of the Gotthard railroad between Wassen and Göschenen. ■

World famous shopping, varied nightlife, and a stunning
lakeside location—Switzerland's most exciting city

Zürich &
Zürichsee

Cafe Sprüngli: great for coffee, cakes, and chocolate

Zürich & Zürichsee

Framed between the shimmering waters of the Zürichsee (Lake Zürich) and the jagged peaks of the Alps, Zürich is a uniquely beautiful city. Its bustling streets and vibrant, cosmopolitan atmosphere stand in striking contrast to the dour city of banks and businessmen that many visitors expect. The area around the city—with its scenic towns, unspoiled shoreline, and natural woodland—offers a host of great daytrip options.

The City

For many years, Zürich was known as an upstanding example of the Protestant work ethic: a sober, hardworking city that had little time for fun. It was the country's first industrial hub, and later the home of its most important financial institutions. For most of the last century it has been one of the world's major commercial centers (up there with New York, London, and Tokyo) and the famed home of Switzerland's secretive international banks.

In the last few decades, however, Zürich has reinvented itself as the cultural hub of German-speaking Switzerland. It is home to over a hundred museums and art galleries; a glut of fine restaurants; a world-class music scene; and the most glamorous shopping district in Switzerland. It is little wonder Zürich is often voted the world's number one place to live.

Zürich is by far the largest city in Switzerland. Around 370,000 people live in the inner city, while over a million more regularly commute in from the suburbs and surrounding towns. The city's historic core, known as the Altstadt (Old Town), occupies both banks of the Limmat River as it emerges from the Zürichsee. The western half, known as the Lindenhof Quarter, is a maze of narrow streets located between the Limmat River and the Bahnhofstrasse (which follows the route of the medieval city wall). On the opposite bank stands the Rathaus Quarter, which stretches along the riverfront from the Bahnhofbrücke to the lake shore.

To the northwest of the Altstadt, on the other side of the Hauptbahnhof (central station), lies the up-and-coming neighborhood of Zürich West. Here the abandoned hulks of the city's industrial past are being converted into a trendy bohemian district with a burgeoning arts scene and exciting nightlife.

You don't have to go far from the city center to find a relaxing park, ornamental garden, or lakeside lido. In the summer months the people of Zürich flock to the waterfront to swim in the cool waters of the lake, or just to merrily float down the Limmat.

These scattered sights are linked by one of the densest public transport networks in the world, where, true to Swiss form, everything runs like clockwork. There is no subway network, but the city's streetcars and buses are very efficient. The Zürich Card (valid for 24 or 72 hours and available from hotels, transport offices, and the tourist office) provides unlimited access to public transport, together with free admission to 39 museums around the city.

Away from Zürich

Just a few miles to the northeast of Zurich lies Winterthur, Switzerland's sixth largest city. This former industrial town is now, like its southern neighbor, a thriving financial center. While it lacks the vibrant atmosphere of Zürich, Winterthur is worth visiting for its crop of excellent museums and galleries.

Long, narrow Zürichsee—the fourth largest lake in Switzerland—stretches southeast from downtown Zürich to the causeway bridge at Rapperswil. The lake offers an enormous variety of short excursions from Zürich, with daily cruises to the picturesque villages punctuating its shoreline. Flanked by lush, hilly countryside clad in forests and vineyards, this region is a veritable walker's paradise. There are historic villages and towns to visit, fine restaurants to dine in, and trails to walk or cycle. Even if you have no interest in hiking, it's worth making your way to the Stäfa district for its fine wines. ■

Area of map detail

Zürich & Around

With its idyllic lakeside setting and extensive parks and gardens, this compact, picturesque city combines a village-like atmosphere with a newfound cosmopolitan image. Alongside the beautiful and historic buildings of its medieval heart, Zürich offers its visitors a world-class contemporary art and music scene, the most luxurious shopping district in Switzerland, and the most sophisticated nightlife too.

Zürich's history begins in 15 B.C. when a Roman fortified settlement was established on the banks of the Limmat. The settlement, called Turicum, was located roughly where the Lindenhof stands today. It had a harbor, vineyards, and public baths—the remains of which can still be seen through a metal grating in Thermengasse. The Romans left the area in A.D. 401, making way for the Franks and the Alemans to settle here.

For most of the Middle Ages, Zürich was ruled by a city council headed by the abbess of the Fraumünster's Benedictine convent. The abbess' rule lasted until 1336, when a group of local tradesmen seized control of the city. They made Zürich part of the Swiss Confederation and established the 13 *zünfte* (guilds) that steered the city for the next few hundred years. Under the *zünfte*, Zürich's castle was dismantled and its stones used to create the Altstadt as it appears today.

The Lindenhof Quarter

This historic neighborhood in the heart of Zürich's Altstadt is named for the steep hill that stands at its northern end. In Roman times there was a small fort here, while during the Middle Ages it was the site of a large stone castle. Today, the summit of this hill is occupied by a small public square that offers stunning views over the Limmat River to the Rathaus Quarter.

One of several landmark churches in the city: Grossmünster

Just off the Lindenhof, the **Zürcherspielzeugmuseum** (Zürich Toy Museum) is a must-see for young families. It houses a delightful collection of dolls, teddy bears, train sets, toys, and books dating from the 18th century to the 20th century.

The southern slopes of Lindenhof Hill are home to some of Zürich's oldest streets and churches, with parts of its surviving relatively unchanged since the 14th century. On your left as you leave the park is the tiny neighborhood of **Schipfe,** where a tangle of narrow medieval streets zigzags down to the river. The area is filled with brightly colored 16th- and 17th-century houses, which come in an infinite variety of shapes and sizes thanks to the irregularly-shaped sloping plots they were built on.

A few hundred yards away, on the southwestern side of Lindenhof Hill, stands one of Zürich's oldest churches, the plain but elegant **Augustinerkirche** *(Münzplatz, closed Sun.).* This church was built in the 13th century by an Augustinian monastic community,

but abandoned during the reformation. In the mid-16th century it was turned into the city's mint and not returned to its original use until 1841.

A little farther down the hill is the gently curving cobbled street of **Augustinergasse.** The houses along here are distinguished by their attractive little enclosed balconies. These are always found on the second floor in an off-center position, as they were built to allow the residents to easily see who was knocking on their door. This street is home to the **Zürich James Joyce Foundation,** a literary institution with a comprehensive library of the author's manuscripts. While he is usually associated with his home town of Dublin—where he set most of his stories—Joyce actually spent most of his life traveling around Europe. He lived in Zürich from 1915 to 1920, while he was working on his novel *Ulysses* (1922), and returned to the city shortly before his death in 1941. The foundation organizes readings and exhibitions of works by Joyce, together with works by other contemporary writers.

Zürich

 189 A2

Visitor Information

✉ Zürich Tourismus, Hauptbahnhof, Zürich

☎ (044) 215 40 00

www.zuerich.com/ en/Visitor.html

Zürcher Spielzeugmuseum

✉ Sammlung Franze Carl Webber, Fortunagasse 15

☎ (044) 211 93 05

🕑 Closed Sun.

🚊 Tram 6, 7, 11, 13 (Rennweg)

Zürich James Joyce Foundation

✉ Augustinergasse 9

☎ (044) 211 83 01

🕑 Closed Sat. & Sun.

🚊 Tram 6, 7, 11, 13 (Rennweg)

www.joyce foundation.ch

Shop Till You Drop

There is nowhere quite like Bahnhofstrasse when it comes to shopping. Its prestigious boutiques, chic designer stores, glitzy jewelers, and watchmakers simply ooze affluence and elegance. Look out for such noteworthy Swiss brands as Rolex, Cartier, and Breitling at **Bucherer** *(Bahnhofstrasse 50)* or **Beyer** *(Bahnhofstrasse 31).* Bahnhofstrasse is also home to a more affordable **Swatch** outlet

(Bahnhofstrasse 94). **Franz Carl Weber** *(Bahnhofstrasse 62)* is one of Europe's largest toy shops, while **Bally Capitol** *(Bahnhofstrasse 66)* is the world's largest outlet of this famous Swiss shoe manufacturer. Be sure to end your shopping spree at **Confiserie Sprüngli** *(Bahnhofstrasse 21),* where you can treat yourself to the finest cakes and pastries in town in the coffee shop upstairs.

Fraumünster
- ✉ Münsterhof 2
- ☎ (044) 211 41 00
- 🕐 Closed during services
- 🚊 Tram 2, 6, 7, 8, 9, 11, 13 (Paradeplatz)

Zunfthaus zur Meisen
- ✉ Münsterhof 20
- ☎ (044) 221 28 07
- 🕐 Closed Mon.
- 💲 $
- 🚊 Tram 2, 6, 7, 8, 9, 11, 13 (Paradeplatz)

www.musee -suisse.ch/e/meisen/ index.php

INSIDER TIP:

Watch Zürich's guilds in action at the Procession of the Guilds in the Sechseläuten spring festival. Thousands of uniformed guild members parade through the city in their various uniforms.

—CATHERINE RICCUCCI
National Geographic contributor

At the far end of Augustinergasse stands what is arguably the city's oldest church, **St. Peterskirche.** Although the building that stands today was erected in the 16th century, archaeologists have found evidence to suggest there has been a church on the site since the eighth century. It may have even been built over a ruined

Roman temple. Wherever you are in Zürich, it's hard to miss this landmark building, as its tower has the largest clock face in Europe, at a diameter of 38.5 feet (8.7 m).

Münsterhofplatz: At the bottom of the hill, the narrow streets of the Lindenhof Quarter open out into the medieval square known as Münsterhofplatz. On the southern side of the square stands the elegant **Fraumünster.** This church was built on the site of an early Benedictine abbey, whose crypt has been preserved beneath the current 13th-century edifice. The church contains some impressive stained-glass windows by Swiss sculptor Augusto Giacometti (1901–1966), but its crowning glory is a series of five chancel windows created by Russian-born French artist Marc Chagall (1887–1985) in 1970.

During the Middle Ages, when the abbess of the Fraumünster was the effective ruler of the city, Münsterhofplatz became Zürich's most prestigious address. This continued after the guilds took over the city, with many of the more powerful groups building their grand *Zunfthauser* (guildhalls) here. The finest surviving examples are the pale blue **Zunfthaus der Waage** (Weavers' Guildhall), which houses a popular restaurant (see p. 296), and the **Zunfthaus zur Meisen** (Wine-growers' Guildhall). The latter building is today home to the porcelain and faience collection of the Schweizerisches Landesmuseum (see p. 205). Most

---

EXPERIENCE:
Learn to Cook Regional Delicacies

The **Laughing Lemon cookery school** *(Tezet Quatierzentrum, Gubelstrasse 10, 8050 Zürich-Oerlikon, tel. 044/312 4025, or book online at www.laughinglemon.ch)* is run by an American-Swiss couple in the suburb of Zürich-Oerlikon. The school offers courses on such themes as handmade pasta; pumpkin delicacies; cooking with potatoes; and chocolate specialties—each focusing on traditional Swiss recipes and also the development of new regional traditions. The Laughing Lemon also offers a hugely popular introductory course to Swiss wines.

The Barfuss Bar with floodlit Grossmünster church in the distance

of the delicate tableware and painted figurines on show were made at the Kilchberg-Schooren factory (on the western shore of the Zürichsee) between the 17th and 18th centuries.

This part of the Lindenhof Quarter isn't all cobbled streets and historic buildings, however. Just around the corner from the Fraumünster is the **Frauenbadi** *(Stadthausquai, tel 044/211 95 92, open May–Sept., $$)*, the only surviving example of the 19th-century floating lidos that once lined both banks of the Limmat River. As no one in Zürich needs to come down to the river for a bath anymore, the Frauenbadi now offers massages, spa treatments, and yoga classes. Although it is open only to women during the day, in the evening it reopens as the **Barfussbar** *(www.barfussbar .ch)*, a relaxed poolside bar and club where everyone has to be *barfuss* (barefoot).

Bahnhofstrasse: When construction started on the Hauptbahnhof—Switzerland's largest train station—in 1865, it was decided that Zürich's crumbling medieval defenses were not really in keeping with its image as a modern industrial city. The western walls were knocked down and the moat was filled in, freeing up space for a broad avenue—the Bahnhofstrasse—that could showcase the city's modern charms. Today there are few more powerful symbols of Zürich's wealth than this pedestrianized shopping mile. Here traditional boutiques vie with international brands for some of the most expensive retail space in the world.

Bahnhofstrasse begins outside the Hauptbahnhof. This grand neo-Renaissance edifice was built between 1865 and 1871 by the local industrialist Alfred Escher (see p. 202). A bronze statue of

Bahnhofstrasse

🅰 197

✉ Bahnhofstrasse

🚊 Tram 6, 7, 11, 13 (Bahnhof-strasse); Tram 2, 6, 7, 8, 9, 11, 13 (Paradeplatz); Tram 2, 8, 9, 11 (Bürkliplatz)

www.bahnhofstrasse -zuerich.ch

Zürich's Own Mountain, the Uetliberg

The Uetliberg is the highest point in the city at 2,857 feet (871 m), and is affectionately dubbed "the top of Zürich" by the Zürichers below. It takes just 20 minutes to reach the panoramic sun terrace of **Hotel-Restaurant Uto Kulm** (www.utokulm.ch/en/hotel) at its tranquil summit, far removed from the jet-set glamour of the city's bustling boulevards. (Catch the S-Bahn S10 to Uetliberg station from the Hauptbanhof. Trains run every 30 minutes.) From here, a leisurely two-hour hiking route along a forested ridge and through lush flower-filled meadows to Felsenneg affords sweeping vistas of Zürich, the lake, and the snow-capped mountains beyond. The trail is punctuated by models of the planets (on a scale of 1:1,000,000,000), which are especially appealing to older children.

At Felsenneg, take the cable car down to Adliswil and complete your roundtrip by catching the S-Bahn S4 back to Zürich's Hauptbahnhof.

Escher, who is widely regarded as the architect of modern Zürich, stands outside the main entrance.

Approximately halfway along Bahnhofstrasse, the street widens to form **Paradeplatz.** This busy streetcar intersection was a medieval marketplace until the 19th century, when it became the main venue for military processions. It is now lined with bars and restaurants including the main branch of **Confiserie Sprüngli** (Bahnhofstrasse 21, closed Sun., www.spruengli.ch), the city's finest confectioner. On the ground floor you will find lavish displays of pralines, truffles, Luxembourgerli (tiny, cream-filled meringues), and other specialties, all handmade daily according to traditional recipes.

Paradeplatz is most notable, however, as the home of the Swiss banking industry. Almost every major Swiss bank has its headquarters on or near the square. These banks are the reason why Zürich is the economic capital of Switzerland, and how this one city is able to generate more than half the nation's income. One of the ways in which the city's banks generate so much money is through the international gold market. Not far under the flagstones of Paradeplatz and the sidewalks of Bahnhofstrasse, the banks have built enormous steel vaults that contain hundreds of tons of gold bullion.

Near Paradeplatz, in the basement of the celebrated Beyer chronometry store on Bahnhofstrasse, the tiny **Uhrenmuseum Beyer Zürich** (Beyer Zürich Clock and Watch Museum) displays over 500 items ranging from ancient sundials and wooden-wheel clocks through traditional cuckoo clocks to state-of-the-art contemporary timepieces.

The Rathaus Quarter

The eastern half of the Altstadt covers a slightly smaller area than its neighbor across the river, but has just as many historic landmarks. These include the neighborhood's namesake, the Rathaus, as well as the Grossmünster and the Cabaret Voltaire. With its cobbled lanes, sunny courtyards, quirky boutiques, and pavement cafés the neighborhood has a special village-like charm; indeed, it is affectionately known to locals as the "Dörfli" (little village).

The neighborhood's social center is **Niederdorfstrasse,** a broad pedestrianized avenue just up the hill from the Rathaus. Here there are many bars, cafés, and restaurants that spill out onto sidewalk terraces during the summer months.

Along the Limmatquai: The

Limmatquai, along the east bank of the river, has recently been pedestrianized. With its elegant guild-houses and smart shops, it is now a popular place to stroll.

Heading south from the Bahnhofbrücke, the first major landmark is the 17th-century **Rathaus** (Town Hall). This fine baroque building is built on columns sunk into the riverbed, so from some angles it almost appears to be floating. The Rathaus is still home to the city's council, and so it is not open to the public.

Down on the riverbank stands the late-Gothic **Wasserkirche** (Water Church). The church is reputed to have been built on the spot where Zürich's two patron saints, Felix and Regula, were martyred in A.D. 286. The extant building dates from the 15th century and was sacked of all its treasures during the Reformation. The neighboring **Helmhaus,** formerly a court of justice and a market hall, is today used as an exhibition space to show the works of contemporary Swiss artists.

The Grossmünster &
Around: A flight of stone steps

lead up to the city cathedral, the **Grossmünster,** from the Limmatquai. According to local legend, the first church on this site was constructed by the first Holy Roman Emperor, Charlemagne (ca 742–814). He chose the site because a sign from God told him it was the location of Felix and Regula's graves. Today's church was built between 1170 and 1230. It is best known for its connection with Huldrych Zwingli (1484–1531), the priest who initiated the Swiss-German Reformation from here in 1519.

(continued on p. 198)

**Wasserkirche &
Helmhaus**

✉ Limmatquai 31
☎ (044) 251 61 77
🕐 Closed Mon.
🚋 Tram 4, 15 (Helmhaus)

www.helmhaus.org

Grossmünster

✉ Grossmünster-platz
☎ (044) 252 59 49
💲 Cathedral free; $$ for tower
🚋 Tram 4, 15 (Helmhaus)

www.grossmuenster
.ch

A selection of confectionery in Sprüngli

Walk: Zürich's Altstadt

This walk shows off the best of Zürich, with its beautiful lake, elegant boulevards, graceful spires, and labyrinth of cobbled alleyways fringing the river. On it you will find some of the finest views and landmarks in the welcoming pedestrianized districts of Altstadt and Niederdorf.

The water in Zürich's fountains is drinkable.

Zürich's tranquil medieval Altstadt is the city's most charming district. With its beautiful mansions, historic guildhalls, steep cobbled lanes, and shady squares, it is a delight to explore. Start your walk at the west end of **Rudolf-Brun-Brücke ❶**, one of the bridges over the Limmat River. Head south along the west bank of the river, through the neighborhood known as **Schipfe**. This is one of the oldest parts of the city. In the Middle Ages it was where the fishing boats that plied the lake were made, and during the 16th and 17th centuries it was the home of the city's weavers and tailors. Today, Schipfe is known for its tiny cafés, craft workshops, and independent boutiques.

From here, climb the steep cobbled street of Wohllebgasse, then turn right up Pfalzgasse. This will take you to the peaceful, leafy **Lindenhof**

NOT TO BE MISSED:

Lindenhof Square • The view from the tower of the Grossmünster • Zürichhorn Park

Square **❷**, where you will be rewarded with impressive views over the roofs of the Altstadt. This peaceful, tree-shaded square is popular with locals on their lunch breaks and chess-playing pensioners.

Walk back down Pfalzgasse and continue straight on when you reach the junction with Rennweg. As you head downhill you'll pass **St. Peterskirche ❸** (see p. 191), with its distinctive clock tower. Next to the church, a stepped alley named Thermengasse leads down to a small section of excavated Roman baths.

A few hundred yards farther south the road reaches **Münsterhofplatz ❹**, the grandest square in the Altstadt. Once the venue of a medieval pig market, today it is flanked by grand Baroque guildhalls, and watched over by the imposing **Fraumünster ❺** (see p. 192).

Walk over the Münsterbrücke to the other side of the Limmat, pausing to admire the impressive **Helmhaus** and **Wasserkirche ❻** on the right-hand side of the bridge. Just a short climb from the bridge is the **Grossmünster ❼** (see p. 195), whose towers provide the best views in town.

After admiring the Grossmünster, head a little farther uphill and then turn left onto Münstergasse. This long curving street takes you past the **Cabaret Voltaire ❽** (see p. 198) and onto **Niederdorfstrasse ❾**, where you'll find numerous sidewalk cafés to stop for coffee.

Take one of the narrow, steeply sloping streets back down to the river and head south along the Limmatquai. This will take you past the fine baroque **Rathaus** ⑩ to the open spaces of Utoquai, where you can stop off at the **Odeon Bar** ⑪ (*Limmatquai 2, tel 044/251 1650*). This plush *Jugendstil* bar, first opened in 1911, has an eyecatching interior bedecked with mirrors and chandeliers. During the 20th century it drew such luminaries as the authors

Somerset Maugham and James Joyce; musicians Arturo Toscanini and Alban Berg; and the politicians Vladimir Lenin and Leon Trotsky. Today it is a popular gay bar.

From here, a pleasant 20-minute stroll along the shores of the lake leads to **Zürichhorn Park** ⑫ Here there are swimming areas, cafés, and shady gardens. Buses and trams on nearby Bellerivestrasse will return you to the city center.

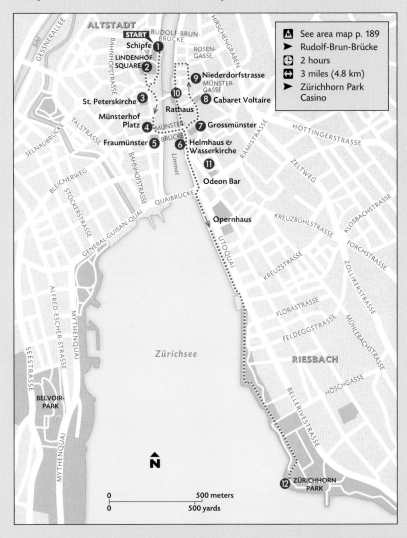

Diners at one of the outdoor terraces on Niederdorfstrasse

Cabaret Voltaire

✉ Spiegelgasse 1
☎ (043) 268 57 20
🕐 Closed Mon.
🚊 Tram 4, 15 (Rathaus)

www.cabaret
voltaire.ch

Kunsthaus

✉ Heimplatz 1
☎ (044) 253 84 84
🕐 Closed Mon.
💲 $$$$$
🚊 Tram 3, 5, 8, 9 (Kunsthaus)

www.kunsthaus
.ch/en

His motto "pray and work" was to have a profound effect on the Zürichers, who gladly adopted the more sober Protestant ways. As a consequence, by the 19th century Zürich had become the country's commercial and financial center.

In accordance with Zwingli's beliefs, the interior of the Grossmünster is largely unadorned; however, the choir does have some striking stained-glass windows by the Swiss artist Augusto Giacometti (1877–1947). The twin towers of the Grossmünster are one of the city's most recognized landmarks. For a small fee visitors can go up the spiral staircase to the top for a bird's-eye view of the Altstadt.

Just north of the Grossmünster, on Spiegelgasse stands the **Cabaret Voltaire,** an institution Zwingli would have thoroughly disliked. During the First World War this eccentric, café-cum-cabaret venue attracted a diverse clientele of writers, painters, musicians, and intellectuals. In the midst of the political and moral crisis that had gripped Europe, they formulated an outlandish and rebellious anti-art movement that they called Dadaism (see sidebar, facing page).

Soon after the war ended most of the Zürich Dadaists returned to their home countries. After a few years of artistic prominence, however, the movement dwindled and Cabaret Voltaire fell into disrepair. In 2002 the then-abandoned building was occupied by a group calling themselves neo-Dadaists. They organized a series of artistic events at the venue that continued the anarchic tradition of Dadaism and called for its rebirth. After their eviction, the space reopened in 2004 as a small museum, café, and cabaret venue, dedicated to the history of Dada in Zürich.

Switzerland's premier art gallery, the **Kunsthaus** (Museum of Fine Arts) is located about five minutes' walk uphill from the Grossmünster. Swiss artists are well represented here, with a large collection of works by Alberto Giacometti, Ferdinand Hodler (1853–1918), and Paul Klee; there is also a small exhibition devoted to the city's contribution to art

INSIDER TIP:

For a breathtaking view across the city, take the elevator in Brasserie Lipp (Uraniastrasse 9) to the Jules Verne Panorama Bar.

—CLIVE CARPENTER
National Geographic contributor

history, Dada. The big draw, however, is the museum's collection of works by the late-19th-century impressionists, including paintings by Monet, Cézanne, van Gogh, Gauguin, and Bonnard.

The Lake Shore

As Zürich has grown, its city boundaries have extended outward to envelop around four miles (6.4 km) of Zürichsee shoreline. The districts that line the shore are more open than the nearby Altstadt, with parks and promenades that are cooled by the breeze off the lake. Here you'll find a number of cultural institutions that benefit greatly from their relaxed setting. It is the Zürichsee itself, however, that draws most visitors to these neighborhoods. Whether it's a bracing winter hike or a refreshing swim to avoid the summer heat, the Zürichsee is a great place to go and unwind.

The Western Shore: Bahnhofstrasse ends by the water's edge at Bürkliplatz, the main departure point for boat trips on Zürichsee (Lake Zürich; see p. 208). Here there is a fruit and vegetable market every Tuesday and Friday morning, and the location of the annual Expovina wine festival (see p. 210).

From Bürkliplatz it is a short lakeside stroll to the **Rieterpark,** a former country estate filled with lush formal gardens and shady woodland. At the heart of the park is the 19th-century Villa Wesendonck Villa, now the main building of the **Museum Rietberg.** Founded by the banker and art collector Eduard von der Heydt (1882–1964) in 1952, this is Switzerland's only gallery devoted to non-European art and culture.

The museum's exhibits are shared between several buildings around the park. The Villa Wesendonck houses displays of Buddhist art, together with cultural treasures from Polynesia and the Americas. The Smaragd

Museum Rietberg

⊠ Gablerstrasse 15
☎ (044) 206 31 31
🕐 Closed Mon.
💲 $$$
🚊 Tram 7 (Museum Rietberg)

www.stadt-zuerich.ch/content/kultur/en/

Dadaism

In 1916 a group of Zürich-based intellectuals devised a radical artistic movement as a response to the destruction of the First World War. They decided that since reason and logic had failed to stop the war, they should embrace chaos and irrationality. They created art that was deliberately nonsensical, confusing, and offensive in the hope that it would shake people from the apathy that had allowed the war to take place.

Opernhaus

- ✉ Falkenstrasse 1
- ☎ (044) 268 64 00;
  (044) 268 66 66
  (box office)
- 🕐 Box office closed
  Sun.
- 🚋 Tram 2, 4
  (Opernhaus)

www.opernhaus.
ch/en/index.php

Chinagarten Zürich

- ✉ Bellerivestrasse
  144
- ☎ (044) 380 31 51
- 🕐 Closed
  Nov.–Feb.
- 💲 $$
- 🚌 Bus 912, 916
  (Chinagarten)

www.chinagarten.ch

(emerald) underground extension was built in 2007 to house exhibits of Chinese and Japanese art, as well as the striking sculptures, bronzes, and masks of the African collection. The Park-Villa Rieter focuses on Indian and Iranian art, as well as ancient Oriental and Middle Eastern textiles.

The Eastern Shore: The eastern shore begins at broad, leafy Utoquai, just across the Quaibrücke from Bürkliplatz. This lakeside square is the location of several lakeside lidos, and a popular summer hangout. In the spring it is the venue for the *Sechseläuten* (Six O'Clock Chimes) festival, during which a giant effigy of a snowman is burned to symbolize the end of winter. On the southern side of the square stands the neo-

baroque **Opernhaus** (Opera House), one of Europe's leading opera and ballet stages.

Farther along the lakeshore are a number of attractions including two small museums. The fragrant **Johann Jacobs Museum** *(Seefeldquai 17, www.johann-jacobs -museum.ch, closed until mid 2012 for refurbishment),* housed in a charming baroque villa, is devoted to the history of coffee; while **Museum Bellerive** *(Höschgasse 3, tel 043/446 44 69, closed Mon., www.museum-bellerive.ch, $$)* contains changing exhibitions of applied arts.

The minimalist glass-and-steel edifice of the **Heidi-Weber-Haus —Centre Le Corbusier** *(Höschgasse 8, tel 044/383 64 70, www .centrelecorbusier.com, $$),* with its eccentric colored enamel blocks and free-floating roof, was the

"Circular Shapes" by the French artist Robert Delaunay in the Kunsthaus Museum

last building designed by the influential Swiss-born architect Le Corbusier (1887–1965). Created as a *Gesamtkunstwerk* (a total work of art), it represents the culmination of his achievements in architecture, interior design, and visual arts. Sadly, the interior is only open occasionally. Next door, the **Chinagarten**—a traditional southern Chinese garden that was a gift from Zürich's twin town Kunming—is an oasis of calm at Zürichhorn Park.

A few minutes walk from Zürichhorn there is another, very different garden, the **Botanischer Garten der Universität Zürich** (Zürich University Botanical Garden). It breaks with the traditions of many botanical gardens by having no formal beds and wild species of flowers. The water garden and a "useful plants" garden are of particular appeal.

The nearby **E.G. Bührle Collection,** housed in an elegant 19th-century villa, is one of the world's most important private art collections. It was amassed by the German-born Zürich industrialist Emil Georg Bührle (1890–1956). The collection includes several major paintings by European Old Masters, but the main focus is a dazzling exhibition of impressionist works. In 2008 the museum was the victim of the largest art robbery in Switzerland's history; thieves escaped with paintings by Cézanne, Degas, Van Gogh, and Monet collectively valued at $163.2 million. Since then its opening hours have been extremely restricted, so phone in advance to avoid disappointment.

A short distance farther from the lake is **Zoo Zürich,** which houses over 360 different species. It is world-renowned for its work with endangered animals and for its attempts to provide authentic habitats, including a remarkable recreation of a Masoala rain forest.

Zürich West

In the past 15 years the former industrial quarter of Zürich West has undergone radical change as old warehouses and factories have been put to new use. This once seedy district—wedged between the Limmat River and the railroad tracks—is now a focal point for Zürich's artistic community, as well as the heart of the city's nightlife.

In the second half of the 19th century Zürich was the country's main industrial center and railroad hub. This was thanks to the efforts of local politician

---

EXPERIENCE:
Zürich's Most Unusual Dining

The **Blinde Kuh** (Blind Man's Bluff; *Mühlebachstrasse 148, tel 044 421 50 50, www.blindekuh.ch/en, $$$$*)—the world's first "dark restaurant"—offers diners the unique experience of losing your sight for the duration of your meal. No lights are allowed inside the dining area—you even have to place your watch and mobile phone in a locker to ensure total darkness—then the waiters, who are blind or partially sighted, lead you to your table by hand. With the loss of sight, it is surprising how sensitive your tastebuds become. Reservations strongly recommended.

Botanischer Garten der Universität Zürich

- ✉ Zollikerstrasse 107
- ☎ (044) 634 84 61
- 🚌 Bus 33 (Botanischer Garten)

E.G. Bührle Collection

- ✉ Zollikerstrasse 172
- ☎ (044) 422 00 86
- 🕐 Open first Sun. of every month
- 💲 $$$$$
- 🚊 Tram 2, 4 (Wildbachstrasse)

www.buehrle .ch?lang=en

Zoo Zürich

- ✉ Zürichbergstrasse 221
- ☎ (044) 254 2505
- 💲 $$$$$
- 🚊 Tram 6 (Zoo)

Polybahn crossing the street from Central Square to the University, Zurich

Puls 5

⊠ Giessereistrasse 18

☎ (043) 444 48 88

Migros Museum für Gegenwartskunst

⊠ Limmatstrasse 270

☎ (044) 277 20 50

🕐 Closed Mon.

💲 $$$

🚊 Tram 4, 13 (Dammweg)

www.migros museum.ch/en

and business tycoon Alfred Escher (1819–1882). He brought Zürich gas and hydroelectric power, and made sure it was at the center of the nation's railroad network. In Zürich West, his company—Escher Wyss & Co.—built the largest engineering works in Switzerland, making everything from boats to railroad cars. It was the first of many factories built in the area over the ensuing decades.

During the 1980s, the Swiss industrial sector began to decline and many factory buildings in Zürich West fell vacant. Before long, small businesses and artists began to move into the area. They turned the abandoned factories into nightclubs, galleries, and live music venues. Today these creative entrepreneurs share their district with the big-budget architectural projects that have transformed the huge old factories along the riverfront into an area known as

the Technopark. One foundry became a private television studio; another is now **Puls 5**—a trendy lifestyle complex in the Technopark, with shops, restaurants, and apartments.

Although extensively redeveloped, Zürich West has retained the earthiness of its industrial background. The district is not exactly easy on the eye, yet it is fast becoming one of the most dynamic and fashionable quarters of the city. This is a part of town where one innovative project follows another, turning the hollow hulks of the area's abandoned factories into exciting cultural institutions, commercial districts, and even homes.

Around Hardbrücke: Hardbrücke is a major throughfare that runs across Zürich West from the river to the railroad tracks. It cuts through the center

INSIDER TIP:

My favorite Swiss shop is Einzigart– "unique art"– at Josefstrasse 36. It's a showcase for local designers to present their latest quirky gadgets and gizmos.

—EMMANUEL VERMOT
National Geographic contributor

of what was the home of Zürich West's biggest factories and industrial buildings. The properties in this area were simply too big for the kind of small-scale regeneration that had transformed the district to work.

Its rebirth didn't begin until 1996, when the **Löwenbräu Areal** cultural complex was opened in the old Löwenbräu brewery on Limmatstrasse. The lofty spaces of this sturdy red-brick brewery were converted into an arts complex with two major modern art museums (see below) as well as a clutch of smaller galleries, a bookshop, a bar, and a club. Today the main attraction

is the **Migros Museum für Gegenwartskunst** (Migros Museum for Contemporary Art). Its permanent collection contains around 1,300 artworks by 700 internationally renowned artists. This collection is shown alongside temporary exhibitions and installations. In an adjoining building, the **Kunsthalle Zürich** focuses on the cutting edge of the contemporary art scene. Exciting temporary exhibitions showcase the work of up-and-coming artists.

The next major building project around Hardbrücke took place in 2000 when the Schiffbau, where ships and lake cruisers were once made, was converted into a cultural center for the critically acclaimed Schauspielhaus Theater. Known as the **Schiffbau Schausspielhaus,** this avant-garde venue attracts leading international stars. The cavernous halls where the ships were once built are also home to a classy restaurant, bar, and the sophisticated jazz club, **Moods.** The nearby **Hürlimann Brewery** has recently been converted into a boutique hotel and thermal spa, tapping into the city's natural hot springs. Near Hardbrücke railway

Kunsthalle Zürich
- ⊠ Limmatstrasse 270
- ☎ (044) 272 15 15
- 🕐 Closed Mon
- 💲 $$$
- 🚊 Tram 4, 13 (Dammweg)

www.kunsthalle zurich.ch

Schiffbau Schausspielhaus
- ⊠ Giessereistrasse 5
- ☎ (044) 258 7777
- 🚊 Tram 4, 13 (Escher-Wyss-Platz)

Moods
- ⊠ Schiffbaustrasse 6
- ☎ (044) 276 80 00
- 🚊 Tram 4, 13 (Escher-Wyss-Platz)

www.moods.ch/en/ concerts-parties/ program

A Classic Trolley Tour

A two-hour tour aboard a unique old-fashioned trolley-bus is a great way to get your bearings of the city, and to learn a little about the history and lifestyle of the Zürichers as it rolls through various neighborhoods of interest, starting in Zürich West and taking in the Altstadt, the shopping and financial center, historic Limmatquai, the University district, and the stately villas of the Zürichberg. State-of-the-art headsets provide a polyglot commentary as you go and there are two photo stops en route. Tours run daily from the bus station *(Sihlquai, tel 044/215 40 00, www.zuerich.com/en/Visitor/tours/ city-tours.html, $$$$$).*

Im Viadukt

⊠ Viaduktstrasse

🕐 Closed Sun.

🚆 S-Bahn (Hardbrücke)

Sommerbad Oberer Letten

⊠ Lettensteg

☎ (044) 361 07 37

🕐 Closed mid Sept.–April

🚆 Tram 4, 13 (Limmatplatz)

www.pierwest.ch

Museum für Gestaltung Zürich

⊠ Austellungstrasse 60

☎ (043) 446 67 67

🕐 Closed Mon.

💲 $$$

🚆 Tram 4, 13 (Museum für Gestaltung)

www.museumgestaltung.ch

station is the area's newest landmark, the **Prime Tower.** At 414 feet (126 m) tall, it will be the tallest building in Switzerland when it is completed in late 2011. The first shops and offices have already moved in, and there are plans for restaurants on the upper floors with panoramic views over the city.

A few streets away stands another iconic, if rather less elegant, tower belonging to the cult **Freitag Shop** *(Geroldstrasse 17, tel 044/366 95 20, closed Sun., www.freitag.ch)*. This countercultural Zürich institution is constructed from 17 rusty shipping containers stacked on top of each other. The shop contains a variety of unique purses, wallets, and accessories made from recycled materials in all colors, shapes, and sizes. They are crafted from discarded tractor-trailer tarpaulins, old seatbelts, and even worn-out bicycle tire inner tubes.

Just a stone's throw away lies the smart shopping precinct known as **Im Viadukt.** Opened in 2010 under the arches of the 19th-century railway viaduct, it houses a variety of trendy boutiques, delicatessens, craft studios, coffee shops, and restaurants.

Along the Riverside:
Nearer the Hauptbahnhof, the **Sommerbad Oberer Letten** (Oberer Letten Summer Baths) is one of the trendiest lidos in town, where locals come to swim in the canal or float down the river. Those who don't feel like swimming can relax on the sundecks, or make use of the skate park and beach volleyball courts. On summer evenings, there is an open-air cinema *(www.filmfluss.ch)* here, and the relaxed Pierwest club alongside the canal plays music late into the night.

A short walk from the park stands the **Museum für Gestaltung Zürich** (Zürich Design Museum), which presents temporary exhibitions of graphic design and applied arts. It is also home to the **Plakat-raum** (Poster

---

Zürich's Hottest Nightlife Venues

Zürich offers the liveliest nightlife with the highest density of clubs in Switzerland. Recent changes in legislation permitting some all-night opening have given the city's club scene a newfound energy, with over 500 bars and clubs open after midnight, some until 6 a.m. or later on weekends.

There is everything from the alternative scene at the **Rote Fabrik** *(Seestrasse 295)* and **Exil** *(Hardstrasse 245);* and the cutting-edge beats at **Rohstofflager** *(Josefstrasse 224)* and **Oxa** *(Andreasstrasse*

70), the premier venues for techno and house; to the best of the 1980s at **Mascotte** *(Theaterstrasse 10),* the city's oldest club. Partygoers can also go for funky disco beats at **X-tra** *(Limmatstrasse 118),* or salsa and funk at **El Cubanito** *(Bleicherweg 5).*

Despite the emergence of numerous dance venues in Zürich West, however, the legendary **Kaufleuten Club** *(Pelikanstrasse 18)* near the Altstadt remains Zürich's ultimate party Mecca and the place to see and be seen.

Crowds gather at one of Zürich West's popular clubs

Collection) where the curators assemble temporary exhibitions from the museum's huge archive of over 300,000 posters.

From here it is a short stroll to **Platzspitz Park,** which is squeezed between the rivers Limmat and Sihl. This island of greenery is a pleasant place to relax, picnic, or play by the water's edge. River cruises—operated by the **Zürichsee-Schifffahrtsgesellschaft** (*www.zsg.ch*)—run from here to the lake, passing under seven bridges on the way and providing a unique perspective on Altstadt.

On the same narrow plot of land is the **Schweizerisches Landesmuseum** (Swiss National Museum of Art and Culture). This is one of the most important museums in Switzerland, housed in an immense neo-Gothic building beside the Hauptbahnhof.

The museum provides a fascinating insight into the development of Swiss national identity, politics, and culture from prehistory to the present day. It is best tackled in small chunks as there is simply too much to see in one visit. An ideal starting point is the state-of-the-art **Geschichte Schweiz** (History of Switzerland) exhibition, opened in 2009. Highlights here include a vast model of the Battle of Morgarten (see p. 34) which involves over 6,000 tin soldiers; the amusing Wheel of Myths (featuring the likes of William Tell and Heidi); and a collection of medieval reliquaries stripped from the city's churches after the Reformation. Permanent collections are periodically enhanced by temporary exhibitions of artifacts and documents loaned from regional museums.

Schweizerisches Landesmuseum Zürich

✉ Museumstrasse 2, 8001 Zürich

☎ (044) 218 65 11

🕐 Mon.

💲 $$$

💲 Tram 4, 11, 13, 14 (Bahnhofquai)

www.national museum.ch/e/ zuerich/index.php

Winterthur

Winterthur—or "Winti" as the locals call it—lies in the Töss valley some 16 miles (26 km) northeast of Zürich.

The city was founded some time in the 7th century A.D. as a

Portrait of Ottilia Giacometti by Giovanni Giacometti, on display at the Museum Oskar Reinhart "am Stadtgarten"

Winterthur

🅰 189 B3

Visitor Information

✉ Winterthur Tourismus, Im Hauptbahnhof

☎ (052) 267 67 00

www.winterthur-tourismus.ch

began to take shape, and its first churches, including the Stadtkirche and the church of St. Laurenz, were built. Winterthur eventually received its town charter in 1264 under the Habsburgs. They sold the city to Zürich in 1467, from where it was controlled for over three centuries. It remained subject to the larger city for the next 331 years. The Industrial Revolution powered massive growth in the late 19th century, and Winterthur remained an important industrial center until the 1970s, when the collapse of several local manufacturers sent the city into a decade-long slump.

This period has left few scars on the city today, however, which recently reached 100,000 residents. It is both a distant suburb of Zürich and a minor financial center in its own right. While it's not first on the list for many visitors to Switzerland, its attractive Altstadt and numerous impressive museums are drawing an increasing number of curious travelers from its larger neighbor.

Galleries & Museums: The city's most popular attraction is the **Sammlung Reinhart "am Römerholz"** *(Haldenstrasse 95, tel 052/269 27 40, closed Mon., www.roemerholz.ch, $$$).* This large art gallery was the life's work of local industrialist Oskar Reinhart (1885–1965), who channeled a large proportion of his vast wealth into acquiring fine works of art. On his death, he bequeathed his home, Villa Romerholz, together with the more than 200 paintings and

small farming town. It didn't really begin to grow, however, until the late 12th century when the local ruler, Count Ulrich of Kyburg, decided to make Winterthur the administrative capital of his domains. It was during this period that Winterthur's Altstadt

INSIDER TIP:

Below the slopes of Schloss Kyburg are some picnic places beside the Töss River. Under linden trees in front of the castle, benches invite visitors to rest in the shade.

—MARIELAURE KÜTTEL
National Geographic contributor

sculptures on display inside, to the nation. The collection ranges from German, Spanish, and Flemish Old Masters to a magnificent collection of French impressionist art.

Reinhart also bequeathed to the city around 600 paintings and drawings by 18th–20th-century Swiss, German, and Austrian artists, which can be seen at the **Museum Oskar Reinhart "am Stadtgarten"** *(Stadthausstrasse 6, tel 052/267 51 72, closed Mon., www.museumoskarreinhart.ch, $$$)* in the city center. If time is limited, be sure to see the collection of Swiss landscape paintings on the first floor.

Just across the Stadtgarten (City Garden), another gallery—the **Kunstmuseum** (Museum of Fine Arts)—contains a spectacular collection that includes art from every major movement of the last century. A few minutes' walk to the southeast brings another crop of galleries. The closest to the city center is the **Villa Flora** *(Tösstalstrasse 44, tel 052/212 99 66, closed Mon., www.villaflora.ch,*

$$$), which has a small collection of French post-impressionist and Fauvist works. Nearby stands the **Fotomuseum Winterthur** *(Grüzenstrasse 44, tel 052/233 60 86, closed Mon., www.fotomuseum .ch, $$$)*, an appropriately minimalist and modern museum with a collection that includes some of the 20th century's best-known photographers.

Just northeast of the city center, **Technorama** is the only Science Center in Switzerland—a fun and fascinating hands-on experience with over 500 interactive exhibits.

Beyond the City: Around four miles (6 km) to the south stands **Schloss Kyburg,** the largest medieval castle in eastern Switzerland. This imposing fortress houses an interesting museum that traces the rise and fall of the Kyburg, Habsburg, and Zürich dynasties. ■

Kunstmuseum
🖂 Museumstrasse 52
☎ (052) 267 51 62
🕐 Closed Mon.
💲 $$$$
🚌 Bus 1, 3, 6 (Stadthaus)
www.kmw.ch

Technorama
🖂 Technorama-strasse 1
☎ (052) 243 05 05
🕐 Closed Mon.
💲 $$$$$
🚌 Bus 5 (Technorama)
www.technorama.ch

Schloss Kyburg
🖂 Kyburg
☎ (052) 232 46 64
🕐 Closed Mon.
💲 $$$
🚌 Train to Effretikon then bus to Kyburg.
www.schloss kyburg.ch/e

The Museum Pass & Museumsbus

The **Winterthur Museum Pass** (available from museums or the tourist office) is the best way to visit the city's 16 museums, providing free admission for one day (excluding Technorama and Kyburg) or two days (excluding Kyburg). Use of the Museumsbus is also included in the pass. It departs from Stadtbus stop G at the train station (Tues.–Sun., hourly from 9:45 a.m. to 4:45 p.m.), and serves the following museums: Museum Oskar Reinhart am Stadtgarten, Kunstmuseum, Sammlung Oskar Reinhart am Römerholz, and the Museum of Nature; plus the Museum of Photography and Villa Flora on Sundays.

Zürichsee

Extending more than 17 miles (28 km) to the southeast of Zürich, Zürichsee (Lake Zürich) provides much needed breathing space for the bustling city. Its surprisingly clean, warm, and perfectly clear waters are essential to the enjoyment of summer in Zürich. At other times of year, the picturesque villages and scenic countryside that line its shores offer a host of enjoyable excursions from the city.

The pretty village of Küsnacht on Zürichsee's eastern shore

Zürichsee
189 A1–2, B1, C1

Visitor Information

✉ Zürichsee Tourismus, Hintergasse 16, Rapperswil

☎ (084) 881 15 00

www.zuerichsee.ch

Technically, the name *Zürichsee* only applies to the area between the city of Zürich and the bridge at Rapperswil; the stretch of water upstream of this point is known as the Obersee (upper lake). Between Zürich and Rapperswil, the lake is crossed by no other bridges, nor overlooked by any large towns. The only way to quickly get from one side of the lake to the other is to take a ferry (see p. 210).

The water that fills the Zürichsee is carried down from the mountains by the Linth River, which runs through man-made channels for most of its route. As a result, the waters of Zürichsee are exceptionally clean and clear, enticing swimmers, sailors, and all manner of other watersports enthusiasts to its shores.

The region around the lake has seen surprisingly little development, and remains open to hikers and cyclists. You can find marked trails, picnic areas, and campgrounds in many places around the lake. For the energetic, there is the Zürich Lake Trail, a 77-mile (124 km) network of footpaths that winds all the way around the lake. It is organized into 10 stages

INSIDER TIP:

A cheese fondue cruise at sunset on Zürichsee is an unforgettable experience (www.zsg.ch/index .php?en_specialcruises).

—CLIVE CARPENTER
National Geographic contributor

(each ideal for a day excursion) with routes carefully chosen to show off the historical, natural, and cultural diversity of the region.

The Northeastern Shore

Zürich's most exclusive suburbs line the northeastern and south-western shores of Zürichsee. The northeastern shore, in particular, is one of Switzerland's (and the world's) most glamorous addresses. For several decades wealthy Swiss nationals and super-rich expats have been building their dream homes on the northeastern shore of the lake. Locals call this stretch of shoreline the *Goldküste* (gold coast) for its private estates and luxury villas.

At the heart of this exclusive region is the hamlet of **Küsnacht,** best-known as the location of **Ricos' Kunststuben** *(Seestrasse 160, Küsnacht, tel 044/910 07 15, closed Mon., kunststuben.com/ wp, booking essential, $$$$$).* This restaurant is considered by many

Küsnacht
🄼 189 A2

EXPERIENCE: Swimming in the Zürichsee

Be sure to bring your bathing suit when visiting the Zürich area! You can swim in the Zürichsee, which is exceptionally clean and, in summer, pleasantly warm. Popular beaches include **See-Badanstadt** *(Bühleralle, Rapperswil)* on the north shore, and **Strandbad Seefeld** *(Seestrasse, Lachen)* on the south.

Also on the southern shore, near Hurden, the town of Pfäffikon (see p. 215) is home to **Alpamare** *(Gwattstrasse 12, Pfäffikon, tel 055/415 15 15, www.alpamare .ch, $$$$)*, Europe's largest indoor water park with thrilling waterslides and indoor and outdoor pools providing fun for young and old alike. Those in search of relaxation will enjoy the thermal baths, whirlpools, saunas, and 96.8°F (36°C) iodine brine pool.

Alternatively, visit one of the public swimming areas in Zürich and its environs. It provides more public swimming areas per capita than any other city in the world, with no fewer than 40 swimming facilities, including 18 lakeside and riverside bathing areas. Some of them are at the very heart of the city (pp. 193, 204) while others are a little farther away. To the south of the city, on the western shore of Zürichsee, is **Seebad Enge** *(Mythenquai 9, near Hafen Enge, tel 044/201 3889, www.seebadenge.ch)* where the in-crowd hang out and indulge the body and soul with yoga, exotic massages, and, in winter, a lakeside sauna.

The most family-friendly lido is the **Tiefenbrunnen** at Zürichhorn *(Bellerivestrasse 200, tel 044/422 3200, www .badi-info.ch/Tiefenbrunnen.html)* on the eastern lakeside. With its sandy shore, paddling pools, pontoons, and waterslides, restaurants, barbecue areas, grassy sunbathing areas, and playgrounds, it offers hours of fun and relaxation.

Stäfa

🗺 189 B1

🚆 S-Bahn S7 (Stäfa)

Rapperswil

🗺 189 B1

Visitor Information

✉ Zürichsee Tourismus, Fischmarktplatz 1, Rapperswil

☎ (055) 220 57 57

🚆 Hourly boat from Bürkliplatz (duration 2 hours); S-Bahn S5, S7 (Rapperswil)

www.zuerichsee.ch

to be one of the country's finest, thanks to the inventive and sophisticated Swiss cuisine created by its Michelin-starred chef and owner, Horst Petermann. Walk off your meal afterward on the Küsnachter Tobel Trek, an easygoing 4.5-mile (7 km) pathway that climbs from Küsnacht pier, through picturesque woodland, to the hilltop town of Forch.

Farther down the northern shore is the waterside town of **Stäfa.** Stäfa is situated at the foot of the Pfannenstiel (Panhandle)—the main vine-growing area of the canton—and is the region's largest wine-producing community.

Ever since the Romans introduced grapevines to the area from southern Europe, wine has been an integral part of the region's

economy. With more than 1,483 acres (600 hectares) of vineyards, Zürich is the most productive wine-growing canton in German-speaking Switzerland. Its vineyards offer 40 different varieties of red and white wine, including Räuschling, Schiterberger, and Gamaret.

There are plenty of well-stocked wine cellars around Stäfa for those who want to get their wines direct from the vineyards. Visitors who want to sample the full range of Zürich's wines, however, should attend **Expovina** (www.expovina.ch), the world's largest public wine-tasting exposition. This event, which involves more than 4,000 wines from 24 countries, is held aboard 12 boats anchored at Bürkliplatz in Zürich each November.

Getting Around the Lake by Bike, S-Bahn, & Boat

The Zürichsee region is easy to explore by boat, train, on foot, or on wheels. The area is ideal for cyclists: You can either pedal around the lake along the Seestrasse or ride a section of the Route des Lacs. One of nine national bike routes, the latter takes keen bikers from Lake Geneva across the nation to Bodensee (see www.schweizmobil.ch for route details and maps). Bikes are available for rental at the rail stations at Zürich Hauptbahnhof, Ziegelbrücke, and Rapperswil (tel 090/030 03 00, www.rentabike.ch).

S-Bahn urban train lines run the length of both shores of the lake, offering an easy, scenic journey to such destinations as Küsnacht and Rapperswil. Depending on the time you intend to travel, consider purchasing a 9-Uhr Tagespass (9 o'clock Daypass), which is valid after 9 a.m. weekdays, and all day Saturday and Sunday.

No trip to Zürich is complete without a boat trip on the lake, whether aboard the sedate Stadt Zürich paddle-steamer or a more futuristic vessel, such as the sleek Panta Rhei. Boats are operated by **Zürichsee Schifffahrtsgesellschaft** (Lake Zürich Navigation Company, tel 044/487 13 33, www.zsg.ch). They depart from the Boat Station in Bürkliplatz, at the southern end of Bahnhofstrasse and, during summer months, the ferries stop at every lakeside town. They also offer a variety of lake cruises, lasting between one and seven hours, which operate year round.

If you prefer a themed outing, you'll find a wealth of special tours to choose from, ranging from brunch outings to sunset barbecue tours and, in winter months, fondue cruises. Or you can spend a Saturday night in summer learning to dance aboard the Salsa-Ship.

Having fun with the elephants at Knies Kinderzoo in Rapperswil

Stäfa is also the starting point for two hiking trails though the Pfannenstiel region. The shorter one runs through nearby vineyards, and features multilingual information boards that explain the techniques and traditions of the area's wineries. The longer of the two trails is the 17-mile (27.6 km) **Pfannenstiel Panoramaweg** (Panhandle Panoramic Footpath), which runs from Zollikon to Hombrechtikon. This path connects a number of hilltop lookouts that boast panoramic views over the lake to the Alps beyond.

Pfäffikersee

A few miles north of Stäfa lies the beautiful, reed-fringed lake of Pfäffikersee. On its northern shore lies the small town of Pfäffikon, which is easily reached by railroad from Zürich. Close to the lake is **Irgenhausen Castrum,** one of Switzerland's most important Roman sites. This

is an unusually well-preserved frontier fortress, with walls 5 feet (1.4 m) thick and massive stone towers on each corner. It was probably built some time in the fourth century A.D., and originally included baths, barracks, and a temple within its walls. As late as the 19th century, the ruins were thought to be a medieval castle. When archaeologists demonstrated their early origin, the federal authorities stepped in to protect the site. A red ribbon in the wall marks where restoration has taken place.

Rapperswil

The medieval town of Rapperswil is located on a peninsula at the southwestern end of Zürichsee. In the Middle Ages it was one of Zürich's great political rivals, but it wasn't able to match its neighbor's industrial

Irgenhausen Castrum

🏔 189 B2

✉ Irgenhausen, Pfäffikon

(continued on p. 214)

Sports New & Old

High-energy outdoor sports attract millions of visitors to Switzerland every year. While most come for the skiing, the country's varied landscape offers opportunities for a wide range of activities. The Zürich region, which includes the open waters of the Zürichsee, the mountains to the south, and the fast-flowing waters of the Linth River, has more than its fair share of options for active outdoor types.

The extreme sport of ice-climbing originated in the Alps in the 19th century. There are good sites within an hour's drive of Zürich.

The Mountains

In the summer months, both the high Alps and the lower, undulating Jura range (see pp. 98–103) are popular for mountaineering and ice-climbing. For less-adventurous climbers, there are also plenty of *via ferrata* ("iron routes") in the area. These routes guide climbers over the mountains using fixed cables, steel ladders, and zip lines. They don't require as high a level of physical fitness as other forms of climbing, but can still be pretty daunting to beginners.

Just about any part of the country, including the Zürich region, is good for hiking and biking. There are more than 37,000 miles (60,000 km) of hiking trails in Switzerland,

all color-coded according to difficulty. The easiest are the yellow-signed *Wanderwege*, which include footpaths in valleys, beside lakes, and between towns. Next up are the more demanding white-signed *Bergwege* mountain paths. Last are the challenging white-and-blue marked *Alpinerouten* (Alpine Routes). These are only for experienced, well-equipped mountain hikers. Zürich canton has about 1,700 miles (2,700 km) of *Wanderwege* routes and several of the more challenging *Bergwege* routes.

As well as short hikes, the Alps offer some spectacular long-distance walks. For example, from Rapperswil, which is particularly well connected, long-distance routes go to St. Gallen, Konstanz, Luzern, and Altdorf. Contact

SwitzerlandMobility *(www.switzerlandmobility .ch)* and the Swiss Hiking Federation *(www .swisshiking.ch)* for routes, maps, and guided walking tours. Nordic-walking is all the rage and, in winter months, snowshoe hiking is popular too.

In Swiss valleys the skies are frequently colored with the canvases of paragliders, and there's a popular location not far away, at Schwammeg *(10 miles/16 km northeast of Rapperswil)*. The area around **Atzmännig** (see sidebar below) is good for skiing, tobogganing, snowshoe hiking, and snowboarding.

Watersports

Mountain lakes are perfect for boating, fishing, and swimming, while faster-flowing mountain rivers are ideal for rafting and canyoning. The Linth River, which flows into the Zurichsee near **Uznach,** is a great place to test your skills in a canoe, kayak, or raft boat. Rental is available at **Kuster Sport** *(St. Gallerstrasse 72, Schmerikon, tel 055/286 13 73, www.kustersport.ch, $$$$$).*

Farther west, the wide-open waters of the Zurichsee provide ideal conditions for a number of watersports. The **Thomas Zwick Sailing School** *(Tödistrasse 30, Hombrechtikon, tel 079/630 84 78, www.segelschulezwick.ch, $$$$$)* operates out of marinas in Küsnacht, Kilchberg, and Rapperswil. At these locations you can take part in single- or multiday sailing courses that are tailored to all ages and levels.

On the northern shore of the Zurichsee, in the picturesque lakeside town of Stäfa, **Cec- cotorenas Stäfa** *(Bahnhofstrasse, 2A, Stäfa, tel 076/383 66 58, www.ceccotorenas.ch)* provides instruction and equipment rental for those who would like to try wakeboarding. Those who feel this is a little too fast-paced can always rent one of their brightly colored pedal boats instead.

New Games

As a nation of sporting fanatics, it is not surprising that the Swiss have invented some games of their own. These include snow polo; *velogemel* (snow-bike) racing; and *skijöring,* which involves skiers being pulled along by racehorses. *Schwingen* is the Swiss equivalent of sumo wrestling; *steinstossen* involves tossing massive rocks as far as pos- sible; and the new sport of *hornussen* involves one person throwing a *hornuss* (disk) into the air while someone else tries to hit it with a large wooden bat. These activities can be seen in local fêtes and at Interlaken's **Unspunnen-Schwinget Festival** *(www .unspunnen-schwinget.ch)* each September.

Some other quirky Swiss "sporting" events involve animals, and include summer cow wrestling in Valais; Riederalp's *Chüefladefäscht* (cow-pat throwing festival) in August; and the Hotschrennen pig race at Klosters on New Year's Day. The winner of this event is given the title of *glücksschwein* (lucky pig) and made the town's mascot.

EXPERIENCE: Sportbahnen Atzmännig

An excursion to Alp Atzmännig *(Atzmän- nig, northeast of Rapperswil, tel 055/ 284 64 34 www.atzmaennig.ch)* makes a fun day out for families, even in sum- mer. This sports center is home to one of Switzerland's most exciting summer toboggan runs. It descends 413 feet (126 m) through a hair-raising series of sharp bends, steep gradients, and tunnels.

There is also a boating lake, petting zoo, and a series of high-wire courses—which guarantee an adrenaline rush as you climb through the trees and fly along zip wires. During winter months, the snowy slopes are popular with skiers and snow- shoe hikers. From Zürich it takes one hour by car. Alternatively, take the S-Bahn to Rütli, then bus to Atzmännig Schutt.

INSIDER TIP:

When you visit Rapperswil, there might be a different museum in the castle. The locals have been trying to evict the rather out-of-place Polish museum for years.

—BEN HOLLINGUM
National Geographic contributor

growth. Today, this picturesque town is a popular destination for boat trips from Zürich. At the center of the town stands the 14th century Rapperswil Castle, a neat triangular fortress that offers commanding views over the lake. Since the 1870s, when it was leased to a Polish aristocrat, Wladyslaw Plater (1808–1889), the castle has been home to a small museum that traces the history of Switzerland's Polish community.

Beside the castle, the 15th-century **church of St. Johannes** was almost entirely rebuilt following a fire in 1882, but it retains two bell towers from the original edifice. A flight of steps leads from the Schlossberg (Castle Hill) to **Hintergasse,** which is flanked by ancient colonnaded houses.

Rapperswil is sometimes called the "City of Roses," for its numerous rose gardens. One of these gardens is unique for having been designed for the blind, with highly fragranced specimens and information in braille. Another is contained within the grounds

of the lovely 16th-century Cappuchin monastery at the foot of the Schlossberg. Visit during June and July to see the blooms at their best.

Families will enjoy the **Circus Museum** *(Fischmarktplatz 1, Rapperswil, tel 055/220 57 57, $$)*, which provides a fascinating glimpse into the history of Rapperswil's famous Knie family and its National Circus (founded here in 1919). There are exhibitions of magnificent old costumes and archive footage of performance highlights. On the same site is the **Knies Kinderzoo** (Knies Children's Zoo), where children can pet and feed many of the animals; ride the elephants, camels, and ponies; and marvel at the performing sea lions.

At the southern end of the Rapperswil peninsula is Switzerland's longest wooden bridge. Originally built by pilgrims en route to Santiago de Compostela in Spain, it stretches across the narrowest point of the lake between Rapperswil and Hurden. The bridge has been rebuilt many times over the centuries, and the current incarnation is only ten years old. This low wooden bridge gives the impression that you are walking on water.

Boat trips run from Rapperswil and Zürich to the tiny, peaceful island of **Ufenau** *(www.ufenau.ch)*, which is owned by the monastery at Einsiedeln. As it is a protected as part of the Frauenwinkel nature reserve, visitors are not permitted to camp here, go swimming, or enter certain sensitive areas. Even so, it still provides a peaceful

Ice-skating at Wädenswil, on the southern shore of Zürichsee

retreat: take a stroll around the scenic perimeter; visit the St. Peter & Paul church with its second-century Gallo-Romanic temple; or enjoy a meal at the restaurant. Bird-watching here can be very productive, and it is the last breeding area in Switzerland for Eurasian curlews.

The Southern Shore

On the southern shore of Zürichsee, near Hurden, another town called Pfäffikon is home to **Alpamare waterpark** (see sidebar p. 209). Farther along the shore, Wollerau has two claims to fame: It boasts Switzerland's lowest tax rates; and it is the home of Basel-born world tennis ace, Roger Federer (b. 1981). (These two facts may or may not be related.) Winter is the best time to visit nearby Wädenswil, when the open-air **eisbahnwädi** (ice rink) on the edge of the lake is open for ice-skating.

En route back toward Zürich, explore several museums on the southern coast. The **Weinbau-museum** (Viticulture Museum) at Au-Wädenswil offers a tour through Zürich's wine history, along with special exhibitions and wine tastings.

A few miles to the north, in the town of Kilchberg, the air is filled with the smell of chocolate. This is thanks to the vast **Lindt & Sprüngli Chocolate Factory** located here. Although the factory is closed to the public, there is a very tempting shop. Kilchberg also has some interesting literary associations. It was the home of the Swiss poet Conrad Ferdinand Meyer (1825–1898), and also of the German author Thomas Mann (1875–1955), who spent the last years of his life here and is buried in the village churchyard. ∎

The quietest regions of Switzerland, immersed in traditional customs and crafts

Northeast Switzerland

Traditional *Schönen Kläuse* masked singer in Appenzell

Northeast Switzerland

The rural northeast, known as Ostschweiz, lacks the show-stopping natural beauty of the Alps and is often bypassed by tourists en route to the glamorous resorts of southern and central Switzerland. However, the scenery is picture-perfect: chocolate-box villages, stunning lake vistas, and verdant hilly landscapes. The region also offers an astonishing array of historical, cultural, and culinary attractions.

The lighthouse of Lindau by the Bodensee

Northeastern Switzerland comprises the cantons of Schaffhausen, Thurgau, St. Gallen, Appenzell, and Glarus. All can be visited as daytrips from Zürich, thanks to the efficient and comprehensive transport network.

The remarkably unspoiled Bodensee (Lake Constance), on the northeastern border, is divided between Switzerland, Austria, and Germany. The Swiss shore is a haven for watersports enthusiasts and nature lovers. Fish restaurants abound, serving such delicacies as the blue *felchen*, a fish found only in the Bodensee.

The Bodensee is fed and drained by the Rhine River en route to the impressive Rheinfall (Rhine Falls), the largest waterfalls in Europe. The stretch of the Rhine between the lake and Schaffhausen is among the country's most beautiful cruises. Its lush, gentle landscapes are further enhanced by fairy-tale villages and countless castles and monasteries, all bearing witness to the cultural and historical importance of the mighty river over the centuries. This area is an important wine-growing region, thanks to its mild climate. Grape production is helped by the warm southerly *föhn* wind—peculiar to this part of the Alps. Most of the vineyards grow the Blauburgunder and Mueller Thurgau grapes, and local wines can be tasted at cellars and wineries throughout the region.

Farther down the Rhine valley lie Schaffhausen and Stein am Rhein, which are among Switzerland's best-preserved medieval towns. Schaffhausen has the dubious distinction of being the only part of neutral Switzerland to be bombed during World War II. Surrounded on three sides by Germany, the Allied forces mistook the town for enemy territory.

St. Gallen & Glarus

St. Gallen, the main city of Ostschweiz, nestles between the Bodensee and the rolling Appenzell region. It is famous for its Benedictine Abbey Library and Cathedral, both listed as UNESCO World Heritage sites, and for its textile and lace production. Its modern outskirts stand in stark contrast with the pastoral landscapes of neighboring

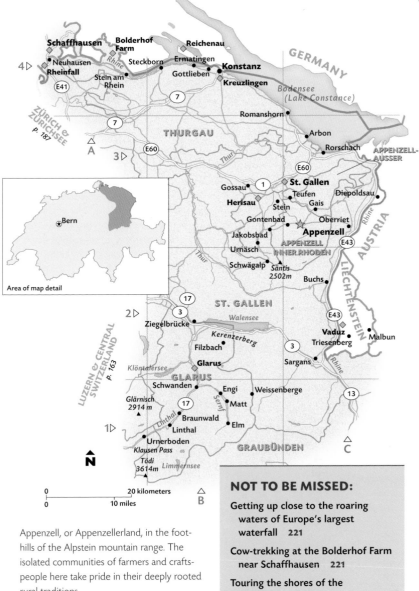

4 ▷
3 ▷
2 ▷
1 ▷

Schaffhausen Bolderhof Farm Reichenau
Neuhausen Steckborn Ermatingen Konstanz
Rheinfall Stein am Rhein Gottlieben Kreuzlingen
GERMANY
E41
Bodensee (Lake Constance)
7
ZÜRICH & ZÜRICHSEE P. 187
7
THURGAU
Romanshorn
A
E60
Arbon
Rorschach
APPENZELL-AUSSER
Thur
E60
Gossau 1 St. Gallen
Teufen Gais Diepoldsau
Herisau Stein
Bern
Gontenbad Oberriet
Jakobsbad Appenzell
Urnäsch APPENZELL INNER RHODEN
E43
AUSTRIA
Area of map detail
Schwägalp Säntis 2502m Buchs
LIECHTENSTEIN
17
ST. GALLEN
3 Walensee
E43
Ziegelbrücke
Kerenzerberg
Vaduz Malbun
Filzbach
Triesenberg
3
LUZERN & CENTRAL SWITZERLAND P. 163
Klöntalersee Glarus Sargans
GLARUS
Schwanden Engi Weissenberge
Glärnisch 2914 m 17 Matt
Braunwald Elm
13
Linthal
Urnerboden
Klausen Pass
GRAUBÜNDEN
Tödi 3614m Limmernsee
C

N↑

0 ——— 20 kilometers
0 ——— 10 miles
B

Appenzell, or Appenzellerland, in the foot-hills of the Alpstein mountain range. The isolated communities of farmers and crafts-people here take pride in their deeply rooted rural traditions.

Ostschweiz, the nation's lowest Alpine region, has just two main mountain ranges: the Alpstein massif on the southern fringes of Appenzell, which rises to 8,208 feet (2,502 m) at the summit of Säntis; and the Glarner Alpen (Glarus Alps), which encircle the wild and beautiful canton of Glarus, with its little-known year-round mountain resorts. ■

NOT TO BE MISSED:

Getting up close to the roaring waters of Europe's largest waterfall 221

Cow-trekking at the Bolderhof Farm near Schaffhausen 221

Touring the shores of the Bodensee 222–223

A trip to the miniscule Principality of Liechtenstein 224–225

Hiking barefoot through the rolling hills of Appenzellerland 229

Soaking in a whey bath high in the Glarus Alps 232

Schaffhausen & Bodensee

The quaint towns and villages of Schaffhausen canton are so picturesque they seem to have come straight out of a Hans Christian Andersen fairy tale. They owe their existence to the mighty Rheinfall (Rhine Falls), which impeded the progress of the medieval river merchants and gave the site great strategic importance.

Schaffhausen

◭ 219 A4

Visitor Information

✉ Schaffhauserland Tourismus, Herrenacker 15, Schaffhausen

☎ (052) 632 40 20

www.schaffhauser land.ch/en

Schaffhausen Town

On the northern bank of the Rhine, just north of the falls, the small town of Schaffhausen is a maze of cobbled alleyways, fountain-splashed squares, and picture-postcard houses.

The town was founded in the 11th century at the point on the river where trading ships had to set anchor because the Rheinfall made it impossible to travel farther. The name *Schaffhausen* is thought to originate from the "ship houses" where cargo was stored before being transported past the falls by road.

Over the centuries, Schaffhausen prospered from river trade. Many of the houses visible today—with their intricately carved ornamentation and brightly painted facades—were built during the town's Renaissance heyday. Many of the town's merchants added *erker* (oriel windows) to their homes, which were often embellished with ostentatious decorative carvings. Schaffhausen gets its nickname of *Erkerstadt* (Oriel Town) from these distinctive windows.

On the southern side of Schaffhausen, the circular **Munot Fortress** looms over the town from the top of a vine-clad hill. For centuries the tower that rises out of the southern side of the fortress has been the home of the Munot Guard, a watchman charged with keeping the peace in Schaffhausen. The current Munot Guard has few duties other than to ring the famous Munot Bell at 9 p.m. (this was once a signal for the town's inns to close their doors). The fortress is a popular

Getting close to the thunderous Rheinfall spray

venue for open-air concerts, and its battlements offer sweeping views over the town and the vineyards beyond.

You can sample the local wines at the **Vinorama** *(Branchenverband Schaffhauser Wein, Herrenacker 15, Schaffhausen, tel 052/620 40 82, closed Sun., reservation required, www.blaubergunderland.sh)* at the heart of the Altstadt.

The Rheinfall: At Neuhausen, around 2 miles (3.2 km) downstream from Schaffhausen, the Rhine River plunges over a massive waterfall known as the Rheinfall. Around 11 million gallons of water pour over the falls every minute, making it the biggest waterfall in Europe.

Two castles overlook the falls: **Schlössli Worth** on the north bank, and the larger **Schloss Laufen** to the south. A footpath leads from various car lots to the falls. Get closer by boarding one of the small cruise boats. The best trip—the **FelsenfahrtPanorama Sicht** *(departing from the pier at Schlössli Worth)*—enables you to climb the rock in the middle of the cascade.

If climbing a rock in the middle of a raging waterfall doesn't provide enough excitement, the nearby **Adventure Park** *(www.rheinfall.ch/Attraktionen/Adventure-Park)* has a range of dizzying treetop rope courses. For a more sedate day out, take a ferry downriver to **Klosterinsel Rheinau**, a Benedictine monastery that stands on a river island. Its church has one of Switzerland's finest baroque interiors.

EXPERIENCE:
Cow-trekking

Get close to nature by riding a cow through the beautiful countryside of Schaffhausen canton. Saddle-up and take a three-hour cow-trek across the meadows surrounding Bolderhof Farm at Hemishofen village, near Stein am Rhein. The farm also offers cheese-making and rustic *schlaf im stroh* **(sleep in straw) farm vacations (Bolderhof 1, 8261 Hemishofen, tel 052/742 40 48, www.bolderhof.ch).**

Stein am Rhein

The riverfront town of Stein am Rhein, nestled beside the Rhine 12.5 miles (20 km) east of Schaffhausen, is among Switzerland's most beautiful medieval towns. Take a stroll though its quaint cobbled streets, admiring the half-timbered houses and their fanciful exterior frescoes.

The town's Benedictine monastery has had very few alterations since the 15th century. In the 1920s, when its monastic community left, the uniquely preserved monastery became the **Klostermuseum St. Georgen** *(Fischmarkt, Stein am Rhein, tel 052/741 21 42, closed Mon. and Nov.–March, $$)*, allowing visitors to look around this fascinating old building. Other historic buildings in the town include the **Museum Zum Lindwurm,** whose interior is an exact re-creation of a typical 19th-century family home, and, high above the town, the 13th-century **Hohenklingen Castle** *(Hohenklingenstrasse 1, Stein am Rhein, closed Mon.)*, which offers fine views and an excellent restaurant.

Munot
✉ Munotwächter, Munotstieg 17, Schaffhausen
☎ (052) 625 42 25
🚆 Train (Schaffhausen)

Rheinfall
✉ Rheinfallstrasse, Neuhausen am Rheinfall
🚆 Train (Schloss Laufen am Rheinfall)
www.rheinfall.ch/home

Museum Zum Lindwurm
✉ Unterstadt 18, Stein am Rhein
☎ (052) 741 25 12
🕐 Closed Tues. & Nov.–Feb.
💲 $$
🚆 Train (Stein am Rhein)
www.museum-lindwurm.ch

Kreuzlingen

 219 B4

Visitor Information

 Kreuzlingen Tourismus, Haus zum Hammer, Sonnenstrasse 4, Kreuzlingen

☎ (071) 672 38 40

🕐 Closed Sat. p.m. & Sun., May–Sept.; Sat. & Sun., Oct.–April

Kirche St. Ulrich

✉ Hauptstrasse 96, Kreuzlingen

☎ (071) 672 22 18

Bodensee

The Bodensee, also known as Lake Constance, is the second largest lake in Switzerland after Lake Geneva (see pp. 70–71). The shores of the Bodensee are considerably less developed than those of Lake Geneva. A carpet of green pastures and vineyards, punctuated by quaint medieval towns, fairy-tale castles, and ancient monasteries, surrounds the Bodensee. The lake itself offers sandy beaches, boat trips, and watersports.

The main part of the lake, the Obersee (Upper Lake), acts as a natural frontier between Switzerland, Germany, and Austria. Its 162-mile (261 km) shoreline is shared by the three countries: Austria in the southeast, at the head of the lake; Germany along the northern shore; and Switzerland on the southern shore. At its western end, the Bodensee splits into

two narrower, shallower branches: the Überlingersee and the picturesque, marshy Untersee (Lower Lake). The latter stretches west to Stein am Rhein (see p. 221).

Summer months bring many lake cruises—some in nostalgic paddle-steamers—and there are two year-round car ferry services (Romanshorn–Friedrichshafen and Konstanz–Meersburg). The relatively flat countryside around the lake is a paradise for hikers and cyclists, with dozens of well-signed trails, including the 186-mile (300 km) **Bodensee Radweg** (Lake Constance Cycle Route; *www .bodensee-radweg.com*), which can be shortened by using ferries.

Kreuzlingen

The major town on the Swiss shore of the lake is Kreuzlingen. This town is located on the narrow strait between the Obersee and the Untersee. Only a few signs and a bit of parkland separate it from the genteel German city of Konstanz.

Kreuzlingen contains some fine buildings, including the rococo **Kirche St. Ulrich,** part of a 17th-century former **monastery.** The town's 18th-century castle houses Switzerland's oldest toy museum, the **Puppenmuseum** *(Schloss Girsberg, Kreuzlingen, tel 071/672 46 55, open only on first Sun. of every month, www.schloss-girsberg.ch/puppenmuseum.html, $$$).* Elsewhere in the town there is a fascinating maritime museum, the **Seemuseum.**

As well as providing plentiful opportunities for swimming, windsurfing, waterskiing, sailing,

---

Bodensee Erlebniskarte

Lake Constance Experience Cards *(www .bodensee-erlebniskarte.info, available from tourist offices April through October)* offer superb savings for anyone touring the Bodensee and Appenzellerland regions. Choose from three packages: Landratten *("landlubbers," $$$$$)* provides free entry to more than 180 destinations, excluding Mainau Island; Sparfüchse *("smart spenders," $$$$$),* gives free access to over 170 attractions, with a 30 percent discount for Mainau Island; or, the best value, Seebären *("sea dogs," $$$$$),* which includes free boat transport on the lake and the Rhine, free admission to Insel Mainau and the St. Gallen Abbey Library, the Säntis cable-car, and numerous other attractions.

A display of traditional fishing at the Seemuseum in Kreuzlingen

and diving, Kreuzlingen also serves as a departure point for cruises on the Untersee, the Rhine, and to the German islands of Mainau and Reichenau.

The Untersee

Connected to the German mainland by a causeway, but only 1 mile (1.6 km) from the Swiss coast of Untersee, Insel Reichenau (Rich Pasture Island) is famed for its historic Benedictine abbey, a UNESCO World Heritage site. Founded in 724, it was the artistic and literary center of southwest Germany from the 9th to 11th century.

Facing it across the waters of the Untersee, the Swiss villages of **Steckborn, Ermatingen,** and **Gottlieben** each have attractive medieval old towns on the waterfront. Above Ermatingen, **Arenenberg Palace** is known for its association with the French Emperor Napoleon III (1808–1873), who spent his formative years here, recalled in the palace's **Napoleon Museum** (*Schloss und Park Arenenberg, Salenstein, tel 071/663 32 60, closed Mon. a.m., www.napoleonmuseum.ch, $$$*).

The Obersee

The Swiss shore of the Obersee is dotted with picturesque villages and resorts, such as Romanshorn, Arbon, and Rorschach. Each has its own lakeside promenades, sandy beaches, and jetties for lake cruisers. From Romanshorn, it is just one hour by ferry to Friedrichshafen in Germany. **Arbon** is sited on a promontory jutting into the lake, with fine views of Konstanz. The picturesque medieval harbor town of **Rorschach** was once the lake's main port. It is now an excellent watersports center, with an intriguing 1920s wooden bathing hut built on stilts over the lake. ∎

Seemuseum
- ✉ Seeweg 3, Kreuzlingen
- ☎ (071) 688 52 42
- 🕐 Closed Thurs. & Fri. summer, Mon.–Sat. winter
- 💲 $$

Arbon
- 🅰 219 C3

Visitor Information
- ✉ Schmiedgasse 5, Arbon
- ☎ (071) 440 13 80
- 🕐 Closed Sun.

Rorschach
- 🅰 219 C3

Visitor Information
- ✉ Hauptstrasse 56, Rorschach
- ☎ (071) 841 70 34
- 🕐 Closed Sat. & Sun., Sept.–April

Liechtenstein

Squeezed onto a tiny sliver of land between Switzerland and Austria, the Principality of Liechtenstein is one of the strangest features of the political map of Europe. Although it looks like another part of northeast Switzerland it is in fact an independent nation state, ruled by the Prince of Liechtenstein. To visit Liechtenstein you'll need to bring your passport, but crossing the border is usually hassle-free.

Schloss Vaduz is not open to the public, but visitors can view the grounds on August 15 every year.

Liechtenstein has a population of around 36,000 and covers an area of about 62 square miles (160 sq. km)—which makes it a bit less than three times the size of Manhattan. It is the only country located entirely within the Alps, with most of its territory occupied by mountains. Most of the population live in the towns and cities along the state's western border, which lies in the fertile Rhine valley.

The origins of this European micro-state lie in the ambitions of an Austrian aristocratic fam-ily, the Princes of Liechtenstein. They rose to prominence during the Renaissance, and soon became one of the wealthiest families in the Habsburg Empire. However, while they were staggeringly rich, they weren't rulers of any territories or states, so they were denied a voice in the highest levels of Habsburg politics. In the early 18th century, the Prince of Liechtenstein decided to remedy this situation by purchasing the obscure mountain regions of Vaduz and Schellenberg, making them into a single state, and naming that state Liechtenstein.

For most of its history, the country only really existed on paper, with life in the rural regions of Vaduz and Schellenberg carrying on exactly as before. The Liechtenstein family didn't live in their eponymous state, nor did they even visit until 1866. It was only after World War I, when conditions in Vienna deteriorated severely, that the family actually moved to Liechtenstein, gradually transforming it into the lucrative tax haven that it is today.

INSIDER TIP:

Discover the beautiful Liechtenstein countryside on a relaxed Flyer e-bike. The electric bike does all the hard work for you, and there are numerous hire and battery-exchange stations around.

—PATRIK SCHÄDLER
Liechtenstein Tourist Officer

With no international airport and no rail network, access to Liechtenstein is by bus or car. There are rail connections from Swiss cities to the towns of Buchs and Sargans, near the principality's western border. Buses run from there to Vaduz.

Liechtenstein is a peaceful, law-abiding nation. It has no army, a token police force, and its jail has space for just 22 people. It started to form close ties with Switzerland in 1919 and adopted the Swiss currency in 1924. The close relations between the two countries have endured to this day, even after the Swiss military accidentally invaded the country in 2007.

Vaduz

The capital of Liechtenstein, Vaduz, sits on the right bank of the Rhine. Don't expect a metropolis: The town has a population of just 5,000. It is dominated by a medieval castle, **Schloss Vaduz,** which is the private residence of the royal family. The castle is not open to visitors, but it is worth climbing up the hill behind the town center to admire the castle's exterior and its immaculately tended gardens.

Another important attraction in the town is the stylish, modern Kunstmuseum **Kunstmuseum** (*Städtle 32, Vaduz, tel 235 03 00, closed Mon., www.kunstmuseum.li, $$$$*). This museum is home to a large portion of the Liechtenstein family's massive collection of fine art (the rest is exhibited at the family's ancestral home in Vienna). Nearby, the **Landesmuseum** (*Liechtensteinisches Landesmuseum, Städtle 43, Vaduz, tel 239 68 20, closed Mon., $$$*) contains artifacts relating to the history of the region, as well as items from the Liechtenstein family treasury. The postage-stamp-sized **Postmuseum des Fürstentums Liechtenstein** (*Städle, Vaduz, tel 239 68 45, www.landesmuseum.li*), boasts a world-famous philatelic collection.

While in Vaduz take the opportunity to walk around **Mitteldorf** and the surrounding streets; their traditional houses give a hint of what the town was like 50 years ago.

The East

The eastern two-thirds of the country is composed of the forested foothills of the Rhätikon Massif, which forms part of the central Alps. The region is dotted with pretty villages. **Triesenberg** is especially worth a visit to see the **Walsermuseum** (*Jonaboda 2, Dorfcentrum, Triesenberg, tel 262 19 26, closed Sun., $*), a small museum devoted to the Walser community, who moved here from Valais in the 13th century. **Malbun** (5,250 ft/1,600 m), the last town on the border before Austria, is a tiny, exclusive ski resort, frequented by members of the Liechtenstein and British royal families. With a total of 11 Olympic medals (all in Alpine skiing), Liechtenstein has won more Olympic medals per capita than any other nation, and is the only country to have won medals in the Winter Games, but not the Summer Games.

St. Gallen

Situated between the Bodensee and the rolling hills of Appenzellerland, the city of St. Gallen is world famous for its textile industry and its monastery district. The latter, which includes the renowned Stiftsbibliothek (Abbey Library) and Stiftskirche (Cathedral), made the city one of the most important religious and cultural centers in medieval Europe.

The incredibly ornate 18th-century interior of the Stiftskirche, St. Gallen's cathedral

St. Gallen-Bodensee

⚑ 219 C3

Visitor Information

✉ Bahnhofplatz 1a, St. Gallen

☎ (071) 227 37 37

🕐 Closed Sat. p.m. & Sun.

🚆 Train (St. Gallen)

St. Gallen is brimming with history and fine architecture, and nowhere is this more apparent than in the pedestrianized **Altstadt,** or old town. The narrow lanes here remain in more or less the same condition as when they were laid out after the Great Fire of 1418. Many of the fine buildings in the Altstadt feature brightly painted oriel windows dating from the 16th century, built by merchants as a display of their wealth.

The Altstadt leads to the imposing baroque **Stiftskirche** and Benedictine **Abbey,** together with various other ecclesiastical and administrative buildings (including the **Neue Pfalz,** seat of the cantonal government). All are clustered around the **Klosterhof,** a spacious square that was once the monastery courtyard. The entire abbey complex was added to the UNESCO World Heritage list in 1983.

Stiftskirche: Located on the pilgrimage trail to Santiago de Compostela in Spain, the twin-towered baroque cathedral was built in the 18th century. Its lofty white interior is surprisingly light, adorned with gilt and malachite-green stucco work. The painted ceiling represents paradise, and relief works on the chancel walls portray scenes from the life of St. Benedict. The east crypt contains the grave and part of the skull of St. Gallus.

Stiftsbibliothek: The south side of the square leads to the *pièce de resistance* of the monastic complex, the grandiose baroque Stiftsbibliothek (Abbey Library). Dubbed the "writing room of Europe," the abbey was a major medieval cultural center. After the monastery closed in the early 19th century, its library was preserved and is today regarded as one of the finest in the Western world. Some of its priceless books and manuscripts date from the eighth century. The interior is an extravaganza of rococo decoration, with ceiling frescoes, stucco work, cherubs, parquetry, and ornate wood paneling. Only 30,000 of the total 160,000 volumes are on display at any one time, with the most beautiful treasures displayed in glass cases. A wall to the northeast of the abbey complex was erected during the Reformation to separate the Catholic and Protestant areas of town. The monks tried to lure Catholics back by offering free beer after the services in the neighboring Protestant neo-Gothic **St. Laurenzen Kirche.**

Other attractions: St. Gallen has long been an important hub of the Swiss textile industry, known especially for high-quality embroidery and lace, which is known throughout the world. Around 1910, the production of lace and embroidery was Switzerland's largest export industry, and St. Gallen supplied more than half of global demand. The fascinating **Textilmuseum** displays some of the earliest mechanical looms and hand-embroidery machines; some delicate examples of St. Gallen lace; a sample of Michelle Obama's mustard-yellow inauguration dress (embroidered in St. Gallen); and a selection of the latest fabrics.

Nearby, St. Gallen's **Stadtlounge** (City Lounge) in the Bleichele district is billed as "the world's largest open-air living room." A red carpet is spread over roads, benches, sofas, and even a car, all designed by local multimedia artist Pipilotti Rist and Carlos Martinez. ∎

Stiftskirche (Cathedral)
- ✉ Klosterhof 6a, St. Gallen
- ☎ (071) 227 34 16
- 🚆 Train (St. Gallen)

Stiftsbibliothek (Abbey Library)
- ✉ Klosterhof 6d, St. Gallen
- ☎ (071) 227 34 16
- 💲 $$$
- 🚆 Train (St. Gallen)
- **www.stifts bibliothek.ch**

Textilmuseum
- ✉ Vadianstrasse 2, St. Gallen
- ☎ (071) 222 17 44
- 🕐 Closed Feb.– March
- 💲 $$$
- 🚆 Train (St. Gallen)

The Legend of St. Gallen

St. Gallen owes its existence and its name to Gallus, a wandering Irish monk who came to the wild, high valley of Steinach in 612 in search of a suitable place for his hermit's cell. According to legend, he stumbled and fell into a bush of thorns. Soon after, he had a close encounter with a bear. He considered these two incidents to be signs from God and so he decided to settle there. The bear was commanded to help build the hermitage, and together they laid the foundations for what was to become the famous Benedictine monastery.

Appenzellerland & Glarus

No area of Switzerland is as steeped in its cultural heritage and time-honored customs as Appenzellerland, a predominantly rural region located between the Bodensee and the high mountains of southeast Switzerland. Off-the-tourist trail Glarus (or Glarnerland) has mountains, lush, broad valleys, and just a scattering of small settlements.

A traditional schwingfest *wrestling bout in Frauenfeld*

Appenzellerland

🅰 219 C3

Visitor Information

✉ Appenzellerland Tourismus, Hauptgasse 4, Appenzell

☎ (071) 788 96 40

🚆 Train (Appenzell)

Appenzellerland's small, homely villages seem virtually untouched by the 21st century, and life moves along at an enviably leisurely pace. The few visitors who visit this off-the-beaten-track region are charmed by the locals' devotion to its traditions, not to mention its unique, picture-perfect scenery.

The people of the region—known as Appenzellers—are renowned for their conservatism, their adherence to tradition, and, of course, their eponymous cheese.

The landscape of Appenzellerland is not as dramatic as that of the Alps to the south, with no jagged peaks or deep ravines. Instead Appenzellerand offers a mesmerizing landscape that resembles a child's painting. The meadows are an impossibly rich shade of green, the sky clear blue (in the summer at least), and the countryside dotted with traditional cottages. To the south this landscape gives way to the mountains of the Alpstein range, with Säntis at their summit. This is a unique area for hikers with a network of marked valley and mountain footpaths stretching no less than 745 miles (1,200 km), with a further 87 miles (140 km) of cross-country ski routes in winter.

The region is easily accessed by car, PostBus *(www.postauto.ch/ost schweiz),* or by the narrow-gauge Appenzell Railway. The latter runs trains from St. Gallen every half an hour. There are two routes: a direct train via Gais (which takes a little under an hour) and another that involves changing trains in Herisau, so you can return a different way.

Appenzellerland is split into two half-cantons: Inner Rhoden and Ausser, their main centers

INSIDER TIP:

If you are visiting Herisau, try Restaurant Schafräti *(Schützenstrasse 11)* for the chef's recommended *cordon bleu* menu.

—CLIVE CARPENTER
National Geographic contributor

being the towns of Appenzell and Herisau, respectively. Both places make excellent bases for exploring the region.

Herisau & Appenzell

Picturesque Herisau is dominated by the 16th-century **Church of St. Laurentius,** a stop on the Rorschach (see p. 223) to Einsiedeln leg of the pilgrims' way to Santiago de Compostela, in Spain. The small **Museum Herisau** examines cantonal life over the centuries.

The main focus of quaint Appenzell is the **Landsgemeinde-platz,** the main square where an open-air parliament takes place on the last Sunday in April. There, locals in traditional dress vote on cantonal policies by the raising of a dagger. The square is framed by traditional houses, hotels, and restaurants, many with elaborately-painted facades.

The fascinating **Appenzell Museum** showcases the history, lifestyle, and traditional customs of the region. You'll encounter prehistoric finds, old musical instruments, and an impressive embroidery collection. Appenzeller embroidery was greatly

influenced by St. Gallen's thriving textile industry (see p. 227) and has long been held in high esteem. Local crafts are showcased by the elaborate traditional costumes and masks, known as *kläuse,* that locals don for holidays. These include New Year's Eve, Ascension Day, and the drives when the cattle are led up to their Alpine pastures.

Throughout the canton, skilled craftsmen are still occupied in trades that have long since died out elsewhere, including bell-saddling, hand-spinning, and the making of cowbells and dulcimers. The mountain inns resound with Appenzeller folk music: a string quintet or yodelling, accompanied by *talerschwingen* (coin-spinning in a pottery bowl to create a "humming" accompaniment), and *schölleschötte* (the rhythmical swinging of cowbells).

(continued on p. 232)

Museum Herisau

- ⊠ Am Platz, Herisau
- ☎ (071) 352 40 10
- 🕘 Closed Mon.–Tues., & Jan.–April
- 💲 $$
- 🚆 Train (Appenzell)

Museum Appenzell

- ⊠ Hauptgasse 4, Appenzell
- ☎ (071) 788 96 31
- 🕘 Closed Mon. (Nov.–March)
- 💲 $$
- 🚆 Train (Appenzell)

EXPERIENCE:
Shoes Off!

Gonten's Barfussweg (Barefoot Path) is exactly what its name would suggest: a walk without shoes. Start in the car park at Jakobsbad *(4 miles/6 km west of Appelzell)* **and head east along a clearly-signed track, experiencing the various sensations of walking barefoot on timber, bark, mulch, pebbles, and grass, as well as through stretches of marsh and bog. As you walk you will be improving your health according to the ideas of Bavarian Pastor Sebastian Kneipp (1821–1897). Allow 90 minutes to cover the 3 miles (5 km) to Gontenbad, where there is a hose to rinse your feet near the train station. A train will take you back to your car at Jakobsbad.**

Drive: Appenzellerland

This circular drive gives you a chance to experience the picturesque countryside at the rural heart of Appenzell, with its gentle hills enfolding characterful towns and villages, as well as a detour to Säntis mountain. Though relatively low by Swiss standards, at 8,208 feet (2,502 m) it is the highest peak in the area and, on a clear day, its vistas embrace six nations.

Cowbell souvenirs from Appenzell

NOT TO BE MISSED:

Natur-Moorbad spa • Museum of Traditions Cow-bell ringing • Schwagalp mountain views

Start in **Appenzell** ❶, with its gaily painted houses and absorbing shops. Discover the culture, customs, and handicrafts of the people at the **Appenzell Museum** (see p. 229). Head west from Appenzell, following signs to Urnäsch. After 1 mile (1.6 km), you pass through the tiny hamlet of **Gontenbad** ❷ where mineral water springs have been rejuvenating body and mind for centuries. If time permits, enjoy a therapeutic moor-bath, a stimulating hay and herbal soak, or luxuriate in a soothing rose-bath at the **Natur-Moorbad spa** (Gontenbad, tel 071/695 31 21, www.moorbad.ch, $$$$$) before continuing another mile (1.6 km) to the village of **Gonten** ❸. Here you'll find the region's most famous restaurant, the **Bären** (or Bear, see Travelwise, p. 298), which champions original Appenzell cuisine.

Drive west through **Jakobsbad** to the lovely old village of **Urnäsch** ❹, with its charming half-timbered village square. At the **Museum of Traditions** (Appenzeller Brauchtumsmuseum, Am Dorfplatz, Urnäsch, tel 071/364 23 22, closed a.m., Sun., & Nov.–March, $$) test your hand at cowbell ringing and talerschwingen (coin-spinning), and try on some of the eccentric masks of the kläusen—figures who parade during the colorful Silvesterkläusen festivities on New Year's Eve and also again for a second new year (according to the ancient Julian calendar) on January 13.

From Urnäsch, it's a 7-mile (11.2 km) climb to **Schwägalp** ❺ and the start of the **Säntis cable car** (Schwägalp, closed mid-Jan.–mid-Feb., www .saentisbahn.ch/en/home.html). The rugged peaks of Säntis, Kronberg, Hohe Kasten, and Ebenalp stand in sharp contrast to the gently rolling hills as their feet, and provide some fantastic easy-to-moderate mountain tours, with skiing in winter.

Back in Urnäsch continue straight past a scenic waterfall (on the right) to **Waldstatt,** following signs for Herisau (see p. 229). On the northern edge of the town you'll come to a T-junction. If you're hungry it's worth turning left here and then continuing toward Herisau. Just before the town center, take a right-hand turn signed Rechberg and climb the winding lane until you reach a cozy hilltop restaurant, the

Wirtschaft zum Rechberg ❻. Alternatively turn right as you leave Waldstatt and continue east to **Hundwil ❼**. After Hundwil, turn left (signed Stein, Teufen, and St. Gallen). After 2 miles (3.2 km) you will arrive at Stein.

Stein ❽ is about as touristy as Appenzell gets. However, both its **Folklore Museum** *(Volkskunde Museum, Dorf, Stein, tel 071/368 50 56, closed Mon., www.appenzeller-museum-stein.ch/ pages/en/home_en, $$$)*, portrays the region's traditional life, and the neighboring **Showcase Cheese Dairy** *(Appenzeller Schaukäserei, Dorf 711, Stein, tel 071/368 50 70)* are worth a visit. From Stein, the scenic route back to Appenzell is via the sleepy village of **Teufen ❾**, whose small **museum** *(Hätschen, Teufen)* covers the history of local architecture. From Teufen, it is around five miles (8 km) back to Appenzell.

EXPERIENCE:
Bibber & Bitters

Appenzellerland's regional food specialties include *mostbröckli* (dried, smoked meat), *chäshappech* (pancakes made with cheese), and *häselbei-zonne* (warm blueberries). Most famous of all is *bibber*, a kind of spiced gingerbread made with honey and nuts. Join the **Bibber & Bitters Experience** *(contact tourist office, Hauptgasse 4, Appenzell, tel 071/788 96 40)*, where you make your very own *bibber*, followed by a visit to the producers of the distinctive Appenzeller Alpenbitter, a digestif liqueur entirely made from natural herbs.

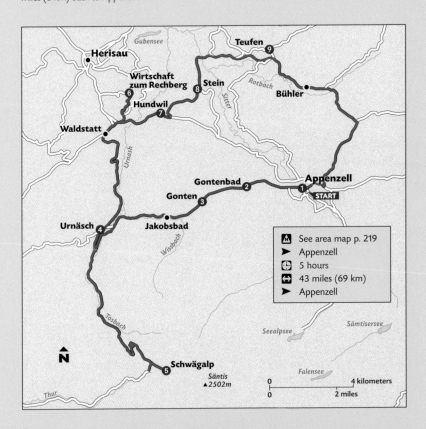

See area map p. 219
► Appenzell
🕐 5 hours
↔ 43 miles (69 km)
► Appenzell

Glarnerland

📖 219 B2

Visitor Information

✉ Glarner Tourismus, Raststätte A3, Niederurnen

☎ (055) 610 21 25

www.glarusnet
.ch/tourismus

Glarus

The tiny canton of Glarus, also known as Glarnerland, is one of Switzerland's least-known and least-visited regions. The landscape of Glarus is characterized by the striking contrast between its fertile lowland valleys and the icy heights of the Glarus Alps. These mountains rise to a height of 11,857 feet (3,614 m). Most visitors to Glarus are hikers and skiiers who want to get away from the crowds and high prices of Switzerland's better-known resorts. Its reputation as an isolated, secret spot is surprising considering the fact that it's only 44 miles (70 km) from Zürich and well connected by road and rail.

Glarus is one of Switzerland's oldest cantons, squeezed between St. Gallen, Schwyz, Uri, and Graubünden and fringed by the slender Walensee (Lake Walen). The town of **Ziegelbrücke,** at the lake's western tip, marks the start of routes heading to the heart of the canton.

Glarus Town

The quaint town of Glarus, the capital of the canton, is located amid the splendid Alpine scenery of the Linth Valley, at the foot of the sheer Glärnish massif. By train, the town is about an hour from Zürich and 90 minutes from St. Gallen.

Its main square is the setting for the *Landsgemeinde* on the first Sunday in May. During this centuries-old democratic open-air assembly, cantonal affairs are decided by public voting. The citizens then tuck into a traditional dish of veal sausages and mashed

---

EXPERIENCE: Sporting Pursuits in Glarnerland

Contact the tourist office (*www.glarus net.ch*) for details of the region's wide selection of local sporting activities, including pony trekking, mountain-biking, and climbing, as well as more eccentric pursuits such as trekking with llamas, rappeling down the wall of Limmern Dam, or zip-wiring above Diesbach waterfall.

In the north, there's swimming, fishing, sailing, and windsurfing on the Walensee. Farther south, the Glarus Alps offer fine skiing, snowboarding, tobogganing, and snowshoeing in Elm, Braunwald, Weissenberge, and Filzbach. There are more than 186 miles (300 km) of well-marked footpaths, from simple hikes in the Alpine pastures above Braunwald, Elm, Kerenzerberg, and

Schwanden to high-altitude treks on the peaks of Glärnisch or Tödi, the region's highest mountain. Keen cyclists will enjoy the 25-mile (40 km) virtually traffic-free cyclepath which runs alongside the river from Linthal to Rapperswil on Zürichsee (see p. 211).

After exerting yourself, why not end your day soothing your aching limbs in a therapeutic whey bath, a honey bath, or a bath of Alpine herbal infusions at Berglialp Matt (tel 055/642 14 92, www .molkenbad.ch). This rustic open-air spa experience is idyllically located in the meadows high above Matt (allow three hours to hike here from the top of Berg-station Mettmenalp at Kies) and con-cludes with a restorative *schlaf im stroh* (sleeping on straw) night at the farm.

A spring vista from Braunwald: wildflower meadows and snow-covered peaks

potatoes—a local specialty. Other local delicacies to try include the *glarner pastete* (an airy pastry filled with dried plums and almonds) and *schabziger* (a hard cheese made with herbs).

Farther Afield

From Glarus, the narrow Klöntal valley heads west to the village of Richisau and the beautiful fjord-like Klöntalersee lake, while the main road continues southward to Schwanden and on to the deep valley town of **Linthal.** There, a short funicular ride climbs 1,991 feet (607 m) to the relatively undiscovered, car-free mountain resort of **Braun-wald,** perched on a sun-soaked plateau with breathtaking views, including of Tödi mountain (11,857 feet/3,614 m). Its host of year-round mountain sports, include climbing, mountain-biking, angling, and skiing.

Beyond Linthal, the road climbs west over the stunning **Klausen Pass** (open only from June to October), which links Glarus with central Switzerland. This narrow, twisting road is not for the fainthearted, but its numerous switchbacks and clifftop sections provide breathtaking views of the Urnerboden valley, Switzerland's largest Alpine pasture. Allow at least 90 minutes to reach Altdorf (see p. 180), 29 miles (47 km) away in the canton of Uri.

Southeast of Schwanden, the picturesque holiday region of the Sernftal (Sernf valley) leads to the traditional, remote resorts of Engi, Matt, and Elm. The valley is of particular geological note, being the site of the **Glarner Über-schiebung** (Glarus Overthrust). At this major Alpine fault enormous tectonic forces have forced dark older rock above paler, young rock strata. ■

Braunwald
Ⓜ 219 B1
Visitor Information
✉ Braunwald-Klausenpass Tourismus, Braunwald
☎ (055) 653 65 65
www.braunwald.ch

Glarner Überschiebung
Ⓜ 219 B1
Visitor Information
✉ East of Matt village
whc.unesco.org/en/list/1179

Fantastic snow sports and one of the world's most enthralling mountain rail journeys

Graubünden

St. Moritz, with the snow-covered Alps beyond

Graubünden

Switzerland's largest canton is also the country's most sparsely populated and, for many, its most scenic. Best-known for the playground-of-the-rich resort of St. Moritz, Graubünden is favored for its varied outdoor activities, a remarkably sunny climate, and bracing, clean air.

Edelweiss, the national flower of Switzerland, grows on rocky limestone slopes in the Alps.

Sometimes called the "land of 150 valleys and 615 lakes," Graubünden (or Grison) has thousands of miles of well-signed and mapped routes for hiking, cycling, mountain biking, and rafting. Accommodations range from some of the country's finest five-star hotels to mountain huts with impeccable environmental credentials.

There are some world-class restaurants, but a meal of veal stew and polenta cooked on an open fire in a mountain restaurant can be every bit as memorable as the region's *haute cuisine*. The canton is known for a dried-beef delicacy called *Bündnerfleisch* and for a nut and honey pie known as *Bündner Nusstorte*. Another specialty, eaten mostly in the western part of the canon, is *Capuns*, a filling meal of meat, cheese, and salad leaves.

Every railroad line—most of them operated by the bright red narrow-gauge trains of the Rhaetian Railway—passes through scenery that makes reading impossible. They are also such remarkable feats of engineering that a large part of the Rhaetian Railway's main route between Thusis and Tirano has been made a World Heritage site by UNESCO. It also has many of the classic PostBus routes over the high passes, such as the San Bernardino, Septimer, Flüela, Bernina, Julier, and Maloja—some over roads built and used by the Romans. The reliable yellow PostBuses also reach deep into remote valleys. One of them reaches the hamlet of Juf, at 6,975 feet (2,126 m) the highest settlement in Europe. It has been continuously inhabited for nearly 800 years.

Graubünden became a canton in 1803. About one-seventh of its inhabitants speak Romansch, derived from vernacular Latin. The canton has a strong claim to having instigated many of today's winter sports. Until the 1860s the mostly British tourists came for the summer only. The enterprising St. Moritz hotelier Johannes Badrutt (who later switched on the first electric light bulb in Switzerland) made an offer to a group of his summer regulars that he would pay their travel costs if they came in winter and didn't enjoy it. He proved how agreeable the season can be, the fortunate guests concurred, and thousands followed, developing the winter pastimes that are now Olympic sports.

Graubünden has long been a conservative canton: It was the last canton to resist the motor car, only allowing the "precarious vehicle" on to its roads in 1925. Tourism is the Graubünden's most important industry, with over 30 percent of the population relying on it. The canton benefits from its glorious scenery and some of the most unspoilt villages in Switzerland, where prizes have been awarded for their sensitive conservation. ∎

NOT TO BE MISSED:

Gasping at the exhilarating view down into the Rhine gorge from the Il Spir viewing platform   **239**

Riding on the Glacier Express **240–241**

The panorama from the open-air section of Scuol's spa   **244**

An organ concert at Tarasp Castle   **244**

Enjoying the tranquility of the Benedictine convent at Müstair, a World Heritage site   **244**

The view from Piz Nair or Diavolezza   **248–249**

Hiking through the Via Mala Gorge   **251**

⊛Bern

Area of map detail

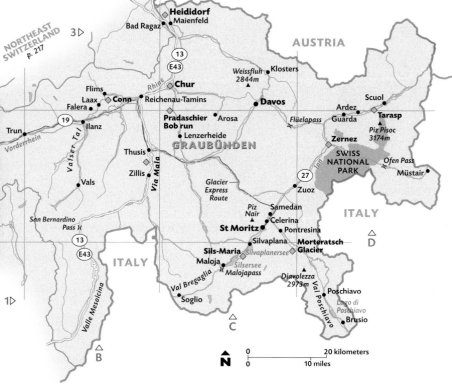

Heididorf
Maienfeld
Bad Ragaz

NORTHEAST SWITZERLAND p. 217   3▷

AUSTRIA

13
E43

Weissfluh 2844m   Klosters

Flims   Chur
Laax ◇ Conn   Reichenau-Tamins   Davos
Falera

Rhine

Scuol
Ardez
Flüelapass   Guarda   Tarasp

19

Trun
Vorderrhein

Ilanz

Pradaschier Bob run   Arosa
Lenzerheide

GRAUBÜNDEN

Zernez   Piz Pisoc 3174m

Valser Tal

Thusis

Via Mala

SWISS NATIONAL PARK   Ofen Pass

Zillis

Vals

Glacier Express Route

27

Zuoz

Müstair

San Bernardino Pass

13
E43

Piz Nair   Samedan
Celerina
St Moritz ● Pontresina

ITALY

D

ITALY

Silvaplana
Sils-Maria   Silvaplanersee
Maloja   Silsersee
Malojapass

Morteratsch Glacier

Diavolezza 2973m

Val Poschiavo

Poschiavo
Lago di Poschiavo

Val Bregaglia

Soglio

Valle Mesolcina

1▷

C

Brusio

B

N

0   20 kilometers
0   10 miles

Chur & Around

The northern half of Graubünden contains some of the best ski resorts in Switzerland, some associated with royal and celebrity visitors. Best known for skiing is Klosters, while Davos features in the news every year for its World Economic Forum meetings when world leaders create the usual security nightmare. Most resorts, however, are devoted to pleasure and active holidays, winter and summer.

Inside Chur's 12th- and 13th-century cathedral

The industrial outskirts of Graubünden's capital at Chur conceal a delightful old town that makes a visit worthwhile. The pedestrianized center is clustered around **Martinsplatz,**

and all the attractions are within easy walking distance. Most notable is the largely Gothic **Cathedral** built between 1150 and 1272. The **Rätisches Museum** occupies a lovely house that dates from 1676 and provides a good introduction to the canton's history. Also worth a visit if you have the time are the **Bündner Kunstmuseum** art gallery, which has around 8,000 works of fine art from the 18th century to the present, and the **Bündner Naturmuseum** (Grisons Museum of Natural History). The latter has exhibits of the area's flora, fauna, and geology. A fine flower collection reflects the region's 2,000 or so plant species.

Out of Town

West of Chur, on the route of the **Glacier Express** (see pp. 240–241), lies **Disentis,** which is dominated by a colossal white Benedictine monastery. Built in 1712, this is regarded as the finest baroque building in the canton. Disentis sits in the attractive Vorderrhein valley and is especially proud of its tennis courts, which visitors can use.

The related resorts of **Flims, Laax,** and **Falera** are well connected by bus with Chur and with each other. In winter they form a ski area the size of Liechtenstein with 138 miles (220 km) of slopes. Laax has become the resort of choice for snowboarders. In summer these resorts offer excellent walking; cable cars and chairlifts carry walkers to the higher areas. Flims specializes in mountain biking and was one of the first resorts to offer Flyer electric bikes. They make it easy to reach the unmissable **Il Spir viewing platform** over the Rhine gorge near Conn, which projects out over a fearsome drop. The gorge here has been called, with pardonable exaggeration, "Switzerland's Grand Canyon."

The resort of **Arosa** is at the end of a railroad from Chur. It is best known for its skiing but attracts more summer visitors for the beauty of its location—in a huge elongated bowl—and for its walking and mountain biking. Arosa is popular with snowshoers, and there is a half-mile (0.8 km) track for skijoring (see p. 250).

Lenzerheide has become a favorite with families for its child-friendly hotels and facilities, including a pirate ship beside a sandy beach on a shallow lake. Close by is the Pradaschier railed bob—a bobsled on rails—in which you can hurtle down a 2-mile (3.2 km) track. Lenzerheide also hosts major mountain biking events thanks to over 190 miles (305 km) of trails.

Though not contiguous, **Davos** and **Klosters** are close enough to come together to jointly promote the area for skiing. Davos is the highest town in Europe and stretches for 2.5 miles (4 km) along the Landwasser valley. Among the mountain cableways to whisk visitors to the higher reaches of the 280 miles (450 km) of paths is the unique double-deck, 140-seater Parsennbahn. This serves **Weissfluhjoch** at 8,737 feet (2,663 m), from where one can climb even higher by cablecar, to the top of the **Weissfluh.** This barren peak stands 9,331 feet (2,844 m) above sea level. **Klosters** is more like an Alpine village and offers equally good hiking. ∎

Chur
🅰 237 C3
Visitor Information
✉ Chur Tourismus, Bahnhof 3, Chur
☎ (081) 252 18 18
www.churtouris
mus.ch/Home.4164
.0.html?&L=4

Rätisches Museum
✉ Hofstrasse 1, Chur
☎ (081) 251 16 40
🕐 Closed Mon.
💲 $$

Bündner Kunstmuseum
✉ Postplatz, Chur
☎ (081) 257 28 68
🕐 Closed Mon.
💲 $$$$

Bündner Naturmuseum
✉ Masanserstrasse 31, Chur
☎ (081) 257 28 41
🕐 Closed Mon.
💲 $$

EXPERIENCE: Walk in Heidi's Footsteps

The enduring popularity of the novel *Heidi* by Johanna Spyri (1827–1901) has encouraged claims to a connection. The author was born at Hirzel in Zürich canton, but her novel is set in Steigwald, close to Maienfeld in Graubünden. It was published in 1880 and has been translated into over 50 languages. It describes the childhood of the heroine with her reclusive grandfather, who lives on a mountain, and the way Heidi becomes deeply attached to the landscape and the pastoral way of life.

Locals have capitalized on the link with Maienfeld and named a local village **Heididorf** with a **Heidihotel** *(Falkertsee 2, Patergassen, www.heidi-hotel.at)* and Heidihaus from where you can follow the Heidiweg path on to the Heidialp. There is also a petting zoo for children and a souvenir shop selling all manner of Heidi-related items.

Train Ride: The Glacier Express

The Glacier Express is Europe's most popular long-distance train catering to travelers. It links the two famous resorts of Zermatt and St. Moritz, and arguably offers the finest landscapes of any train journey in Europe.

One of the 291 bridges on the Glacier Express route from Zermatt to St. Moritz

The **Glacier Express** *(tel 031/378 0101, info@railtour.ch, www.glacierexpress.ch/en/ Pages/default.aspx, $$$$$)* has been dubbed the slowest express train in the world: It averages just 22 mph (35 k/hr). While the prospect of more than seven hours on a train may seem daunting, it's astonishing how 180 miles (290 km) of Alpine scenery can be so varied and how quickly it passes. Every twist and turn of the train opens up a new view, and the sheer size of the mountains is awe-inspiring. Carriages have huge panorama windows reaching to the roofline, and the earphone commentary is in six languages.

Eating on trains is one of the great pleasures of travel, and a three-course menu is offered in the dining car, or the dish of the day at your seat (reservation required). All trains have a bar.

As the train leaves car-free Zermatt look up

NOT TO BE MISSED:

Dining on the Glacier Express
- **Filisur's spiraling track**
- **Gringiols viaduct view**

at the peaks thousands of feet above the puny train. At **St. Niklaus** ① the railway rides just above the river before the water plunges through a gorge that leaves the railway perched on a ledge. To cope with the steepness of the gradient at such points, a rack mechanism is used. Cogwheels beneath the train engage a rack between the rails, helping the locomotive claw its way uphill and retard the descents.

As soon as the train leaves **Brig** ②, the railroad follows the Rhône almost to its source. At Morel the route reaches the first spiral of the journey. After crossing Grengiols viaduct, the line curves sharply left inside a tunnel to loop round over itself and emerge high above the lower level.

Climbing through forests of pine, spruce, and birch, the train reaches the upper Goms, a broad valley with villages of chalets and barns. Ahead, mountains crowned with snow signal the approach to the Furka Pass. Lunch is served after **Andermatt** ❸, where the line ascends without rack assistance through a series of U-shaped loops—the closest a railroad can get to a hairpin road. With a final twist the train turns into the long valley of the Vorderrhein and the wildest section of the journey. Near the 6,670-feet (2,033 m) summit of the route at **Oberalppasshohe** ❹, the infant Rhine is so narrow that you could jump across it.

Engineering Masterpiece

Beyond Ilanz a gorge with tree-fringed cliffs the color of dirty chalk towers over the bends in the river. And shortly before **Reichenau-Tamins** ❺ the railway crosses the Vorderrhein River near its confluence with the Hinterrhein to become the Rhine.

Having reversed direction, the train heads south beside the Hinterrhein to reach the valley of the Albula and the tunnel that takes the railroad under the Albula Pass. Shortly before Filisur is the **Landwasser Viaduct** ❻, famous for its graceful curve and the way the final arch springs from a sheer wall of rock where the line enters a tunnel.

Beyond Filisur lies one of the most dramatic and ingeniously engineered sections of railroad in the world and a major reason this line is a World Heritage site. The builders used three horseshoe loops and three spirals, often inside a tunnel, to avoid the use of a rack. From the long **Albula Tunnel** ❼, the train descends through the valley of the Bever River to Samedan and the junction of three valleys. Then passing the foot of the Cresta Run at Celerina, the train climbs through spruce and larch into its final destination, **St. Moritz** station.

🅰	See also map p. 237
▶	Zermatt
🕐	7 hours 30 minutes
↔	105 miles (169 km)
▶	St. Moritz

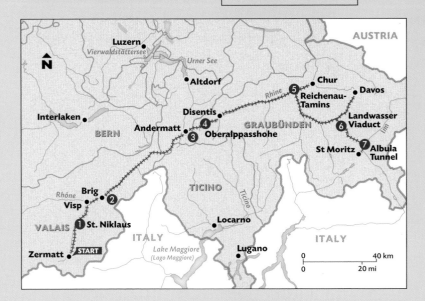

The Engadine Valley

The Lower Engadine (Unterengadin) must rank as one of Switzerland's most beautiful valleys, with villages of white-walled houses decorated with the characteristic *sgraffito* decoration, a complex process that produces colored decoration out of a white background. The Upper Engadine is better known among the traveling community and includes the much-loved and much-visited resort of St. Moritz.

Fall in the Swiss National Park, south of Zernez

Zernez
⚞ 237 D2

Swiss National Park Visitor Center
⚞ 237 D2
✉ Zernez
☎ (081) 851 41 41
🕐 Very variable opening times; check web site

www.nationalpark .ch/go/en

The Lower Engadine

The Lower Engadine is generally thought of as the section of the Inn River valley east of **Zernez.** It is not easy to define what makes a landscape appealing to the eye, but by common consent the Lower Engadine valley has all the necessary qualities. It can be appreciated by taking the train from St. Moritz to Scuol, and there is also a popular—largely off-road—bike route from both towns. The area encompasses Switzerland's only national park and one of the country's seven cultural World Heritage sites.

Zernez is a good starting point to explore. The most striking feature of this attractive village is **Wildenburg Castle** *(closed to the public)*, parts of which date from 1280. The village **church** has a Romanesque tower and elaborate baroque decoration. Most importantly the village houses the **visitor center** of the Swiss

National Park. This provides a good introduction to the park and the options for visitors.

Swiss National Park: The national park covers over 650 square miles (1,700 sq. km). It was established in 1914 in an area that had been a center of iron ore, lead, and silver mining as well as a source of wood for smelters. The park differs from many around the world in that it has adopted a policy of minimal management, so nature is generally allowed to take its course. If a tree falls, it will be left where it is, unless it is blocking a path. A much higher level of protection is enforced: no grazing of animals is permitted; dogs are not allowed into the park, even on a lead; visitors must stick to the paths; no camping or biking is allowed; and the usual country codes of not picking fruit or flowers, or disturbing animals are strictly enforced.

Because of this, it is an unusual environment and offers great rewards for those who love nature and walking in wilderness. There are more than 600 plant species, thanks to the variety of habitats and the great range of altitude—from 4,592 feet (1,400 m) to 10,413 feet (3,174 m) at the summit of **Piz Pisoc.** Larch, spruce, mountain pine, dwarf pine, Alpine alder, Alpine rose bush, and cembra pine are the principal trees. The best months for flowers are June and early July. They include spurred violet, gentian, catch-fly, saxifrage, Alpine rununculus, mountain crowfoot, hawkweed,

---

Lammergeiers in the Swiss National Park

Lammergeiers, or bearded vultures, became extinct as breeding birds in the Alps in the late 19th century. Attempts to reintroduce them to the region had once seemed impossible because of the difficulties of breeding the birds in captivity. Once these problems were overcome, people started to release the captive-bred young. Now, more than 100 lammergeiers are flying in the Alps again, and in April 2007—for the first time in more than a century—a chick was hatched into the wild in the Swiss National Park.

---

yellow rhaetian mountain poppy, bearberry, and primrose.

The national park has 50 miles (80 km) of authorized marked trails, including a three-hour hike from Zernez through Val Cluozza to **Chamanna Cluozza mountain hut.** Built in 1910, this large log building is 6,175 feet (1,882 m) above sea level and accommodates up to 68 people. The hut is open from the end of June to early October for overnight stays with or without half-board. The only accommodation alternative is on the main road through the park, at **Hotel Il Fuorn** (*Swiss National Park, tel 081/856 1226, www.ilfuorn.ch, $$$$$$*).

The most popular walking routes into the park begin near this hotel, served by PostBus from Zernez. A circular path leads off the road into cembra and mountain pine forest, following a stream up Val dal Botsch, through carpets of edelweiss and pansies. It climbs to Margunet, where there is a 360-degree panorama

Piz Pisoc
🄰 237 D2

Chamanna Cluozza mountain hut
✉ Swiss National Park
☎ (081) 856 12 35 or (081) 856 16 89
💲 $$$$–$$$$$
**www.nationalpark
.ch/go/en/visit/
accommodation**

St. John's Convent

✉ Müstair

☎ (081) 851 62 23

www.muestair.ch

Schloss Tarasp

✉ Near Scuol

☎ (081) 861 20 52

🕐 Closed mid-Oct.–mid-May; open for one guided tour on Tues. & Thurs. p.m., May–Oct.

💲 $$

Scuol

🅰 237 D3

Visitor Information

✉ Scuol Tourismus, Busbahnhof, Scuol

☎ (081) 861 22 22

www.scuol.ch/en/welcome.cfm

of many peaks. The return to the road and the PostBus stop is down wild Val da Stabelchod and its rocky riverbed. This is one of the easier walks in the park. On any trek in this area you are almost certain to see marmots; sightings of chamois and ibex are likely. One exception to the park's no-intervention rule has been the reintroduction of lammergeiers (bearded vultures), in collaboration with the Worldwide Fund for Nature (WWF). The first three vultures were transferred to the park in 1991 (see sidebar p. 243).

Toward the Border: Zernez is also the start of a PostBus route over the Ofenpass to the border village of **Müstair,** the most easterly in Switzerland. There, Benedictine nuns still live in the vast **St. John's Convent.** This was made a World Heritage site for its largely medieval buildings, Carolingian

wall-paintings that date from ca 800 and a Romanesque statue of Charlemagne.

Between Zernez and Scuol are the villages of Guarda and Ardez, which have both been commended for their sensitive conservation. Approaching Scuol the magnificent 11th-century **Schloss Tarasp** comes into view, complete with its picture postcard setting. The castle stands on a hill above the flower-filled village and owes its survival to the German inventor of a mouthwash, who saved it from decay in 1900. Today, visitors can have a guided tour of the knights' hall, ballroom, dining room, chapel, and bedrooms.

Scuol: Scuol is the main town of the Lower Engadine. With more than 20 mineral springs, it has long been known for its waters and clement position— with about 300 days of sunshine

EXPERIENCE: Enjoying Local Spas

Graubünden is blessed with many fine natural spas, many of them originally used by the Romans. They have been developed into some of the finest spas anywhere, with distinguished architecture and unrivaled settings. In the razor-sharp light of a clear winter's day, there can be no more beautiful setting than the **Roman-Irish** spa at Scuol (www.bad.scuol.ch/dynamic/design/index.html).

Though most of the spas are part of a hotel, day visits by nonresidents are generally welcomed. The remote village of Vals, reached by PostBus up the Valsertal from Ilanz, has the award-winning **Therme Vals** spa and hotel (www.therme

-vals.ch/en) designed by Graubünden architect Peter Zumthor using 60,000 slabs of quartzite. At the five-star **Tschuggen Grand Hotel** in Arosa (www.tschuggen.ch/en), the internationally renowned architect Mario Botta has created an equally striking spa lit by nine glass sails with tapered spirals of pale Domodossola granite rising above the large pool. Some stunningly attractive spaces have been created in the **Kempinski Grand Hotel des Bains** in St. Moritz (www.kempinski.com/en/stmoritz), and the Grand Resort Bad Ragaz has added stylish **Tamina Therme** (www.resortraga.ch/en/2/tamina-therme).

A marmot at the entrance to its den in the Swiss National Park

INSIDER TIP:

I never tire of the train journey between Samedan and Scuol-Tarasp; it's beautiful in any season but especially in the colors of fall.

—RETO ROSTETTER
National Geographic contributor

every year. The Roman-Irish spa (see sidebar facing page) is in an attractive complex with the usual wide range of baths, treatments, and therapy. A different kind of water therapy—altogether less relaxed—is available on the Inn River: Scuol is a popular center for river rafting (*www.swissraft .ch*). The old center of Scuol is enchanting, with thick-walled

houses lit by deeply recessed splayed windows and decorated with oriel windows and sgraffiti. Other houses have wrought-iron balconies, coats of arms emblazoned on a wall, or ornately carved wooden doors. The **Museum d'Engiadina Bassa** (Museum of Lower Engadine), housed in a beautiful old building with arched loggia, gives insights into the area's past.

Near Scuol is the **Schmelzra Museum** in the renovated former administrative building of the S-charl lead and silver mines. The museum shows how for 300 years the ore was dug out by hand before it was smelted in the valley to obtain silver and lead. The cellar and ground floor contain a mining exhibition while the upper floor in the roof is used by the Swiss National Park.

(continued on p. 248)

Museum d'Engiadina Bassa
- Scuol Sot (Plaz)
- (081) 864 19 63
- June & Oct., open Tues. & Fri. 4 p.m.–6 p.m.; Jul.–Sept. open Tues. Wed., & Fri. 3 p.m.–8 p.m.
- $$

Schmelzra Museum
- Chasa du Parc, near Scuol
- (081) 861 22 22
- June–Oct: Wed., Fri., & Sun., 2 p.m.–5 p.m.
- $$

www.nationalpark .ch/go/en/visit/ schmelzra-museum

A Short History of Skiing

The months of December, January, and February bring heavy snowfalls to the Alps, and skiers, snowboarders, and other winter sports enthusiasts from around the world head to Switzerland, Europe's top winter playground. With more than its fair share of 13,124-foot-plus (4,000 m) peaks and sensational mountain scenery, it undoubtedly offers some of the world's best skiing.

Skiing in the Grisons Alps, Graubünden

There is something very special about skiing in Switzerland, and Graubünden has its own magic. Perhaps it is the cachet of skiing the world's most famous resorts, such as St. Moritz. Or maybe it's the long tradition of excellent hotel service. Perhaps it's the appealing après-ski scene (from cozy fondues in chalet-style restaurants to lively ultra-chic bars and clubs). Then again, simply it's the fact that the Swiss Confederation is the home of winter sports holidays.

Just 75 years ago, Alpine skiing was an elite pastime practiced by a select few in a handful of Swiss mountain resorts. In the short time since then, skiing has developed far beyond the wildest dreams of its pioneers, drawing over 40 million skiers each year to resorts around the world. Switzerland alone boasts a remarkable 2,920 miles (7,400 km) of ski runs.

It is difficult to determine the exact origins of skiing, although the first evidence of propulsion on skis dates from Stone Age rock carvings in the arctic rim. Alpine or "downhill" skiing as we know it, has its origins in the Telemark farmlands of Norway in the late 1800s. The word *ski* originates from the ancient Norse *skíð* (a stick of wood). Switzerland's first skier was Johann Imseng (1806–1869), a pastor from Saas-Fee who used a pair of crude wooden skis to get around his parish in the 1850s.

Competitive Skiing

In 1894 Sir Arthur Conan Doyle (author of the Sherlock Holmes books; see p. 138) took part in the Alps' first ski tour, which took place in Graubünden, between Davos and Arosa. The first Swiss ski lessons were given in Zermatt in 1902, followed the next year by the first packaged ski holidays, to Adelboden. In 1908 the Alpine Ski Club was founded; three years later it organized the Kandahar Cup downhill ski race in Crans-Montana (see p. 155). This race, following an unmarked course over rough snow and against the clock, marked a transition from ski mountaineering to the start of Alpine ski racing. To this day the Kandahar Inferno race—the longest downhill in the world, with around 1,800 competitors—is held annually at Mürren (see p. 135). Mürren staged the first Ski World Championships with downhill and slalom racing in 1931. Rival resorts organized similar fixtures, including the celebrated "Lauberhorn" at Wengen (see p. 135), which still takes place annually on the International Ski Federation (FIS) World Cup circuit. By 1935, Alpine racing had truly made its mark, and downhill and slalom disciplines were incorporated into the third Winter Olympics (in Bavaria).

The increase in skiing tourism in the second half of the 20th century coincided with the construction of more lifts and cable cars, more Alpine hotels remaining open in winter, and innovations in ski equipment—fiberglass skis and all-plastic boots were introduced in the 1960s. The start of competitive mogul skiing led in 1979 to the FIS recognizing free-style—epitomized today in the awe-inspiring acrobatics of the annual Verbier Ride *(www .verbierride.com)*. The Vancouver Winter Olympics of 2010 staged three freestyle events: aerials, moguls and, for the first time, skicross (with four skiers at a time racing through a course of turns, banks, rolls, and ridges). The emergence of snowboarding in the 1980s, with its counterculture fashion, drew a new genera-tion of skiers to the slopes, with their half-pipes (acrobatic jumps and tricks inside a half-cylinder-shaped tube of snow), boardercross, and extreme free-riding skills.

As snow sports continue to develop apace, traditional methods such as Telemark and cross-country have nonetheless always been preserved. In Switzerland, downhill skiing continues to go from strength to strength, and cross-country skiing is as popular as ever, especially in Gräubunden and the Jura.

Henry Lunn, the Skiing Preacher

Skiing didn't catch on early in Switzer-land: A few minutes of fun skiing down a mountain could not justify the strenuous hike required to get to the starting point. All that changed with the first cogwheel railroads and cable cars. The pioneers of Swiss skiing were British and German tourists, who came to the mountains "for their health" from the 1860s onward. The most prominent of these visitors was Henry Lunn (1859–1939), an English sportsman and church minister, whose enthusiastic advocacy of the sport, and Switzerland's suitability for it, greatly boosted the development of Switzer-land's travel industry. In 1922, Henry Lunn's son Arnold organized the first modern slalom competition near Mürren.

"White turf" horse racing in St. Moritz provides a fantastic spectacle.

St. Moritz

⚠ 237 C2

Visitor Information

✉ St. Moritz Tourismus, Via Maistra 1, St. Moritz

☎ (081) 837 33 33

🕑 Sun., mid-April–mid-June and mid-Sept.–mid-Dec.

www.stmoritz.ch

The Upper Engadine

The Upper Engadine (Obereng-adine) is centered on St. Moritz and is much better known to travelers than the lower valley. Settlements became established here on trade routes before the arrival of the railroads. Once travelers could reach it more easily, the combination of a sunny climate—322 days a year on average—and the develop-ment of winter sports, turned St. Moritz into one of Switzerland's best-known areas for winter and summer vacations.

St. Moritz: St. Moritz wears the undisputed crown of the Upper Engadine, though nearby Pontresina has some hotels to rival anything at its more glitzy neighbor. Outdoor activities are at the heart of the Upper Enga-dine, and St. Moritz has cleverly developed some unusual ones (see sidebar, p. 250). Mountain biking and walking are the most common, but there is also sailing on Lake St. Moritz and wind- and kite-surfing on the Silvaplanersee (www.engadinwind .com). The local microclimate makes it one of the most favored spots in Switzerland for these activities.

Near St. Moritz town center is the start of a funicular to Corviglia, where a cable car continues to rise to the 10,026-foot (3,055 m) summit of **Piz Nair.** The route incorporates a Clean Energy Tour to illustrate and promote sources of renewable energy. The summit offers the best views in the area, and a good circular walk leads down through the Survetta Pass and back to St. Moritz.

One of the most famous art-ists working in Graubünden was

INSIDER TIP:

Many people seeing Segantini's paintings for the first time are amazed by the way he captured Graubünden's clear, brilliant light.

—GIERI SPESCHA
National Geographic contributor

Giovanni Segantini, the largest collection of whose evocative landscapes can be seen in St. Moritz at the **Segantini Museum.**

Celerina: This is a busy winter resort with numerous ski lifts. Together with Samedan, it occupies the edge of a large expanse of flat land where three valleys meet, making it excellent for cross-country skiing. Railroads head off in four directions, and each offers spectacular journeys. To the northeast lies **Zuoz,** en route to Zernez and Scuol, where many of the houses bear a bear's claw emblem to denote the Planta family, whose 13th-century three-story **tower** survives off Dorfplatz.

A short distance to the southeast of Celerina is **Pontresina,** an excellent base for excursions toward the Bernina Pass and into various side valleys. South of Pontresina is a graphic illustration of climate change. When the railroad opened in 1908, the glacier was within sight of Morteratsch station; today it's a—very worthwhile—half-hour

walk. A memorable diversion from Bernina Diavolezza station is the cable car journey to the mountain hotel and restaurant **Berghaus Diavolezza 3000m** (*Pontresina, tel 081/839 39 00, www.diavolezza .ch, $$$$$*) at 9,754 feet (2,973 m). The view is so impressive that the hotel does well from people wanting to watch the sunrise over the surrounding jumble of saw-toothed peaks.

Val Poschiavo: South of the Morteratsch Glacier, the Bernina railroad (St. Moritz–Tirano, Italy) passes through the Italian-speaking enclave of Val Poschiavo. This spectacular route rises to make the highest rail crossing of the Alps. Near the summit station of Ospizio Bernina—the start of many walks—the line

Segantini Museum

✉ Via Somplatz 30, St. Moritz
☎ (081) 833 44 54
🕐 Closed Mon.
💲 $$$

www.segantini-museum.ch/htmls/englishch/index2 .htm

EXPERIENCE:
Ride the Cresta Run

The Cresta Run owes its existence to some bored British convalescents in St. Moritz who developed the sport of tobogganing. Gradually more serious competition led to a New Yorker fitting sprung steel runners on a sled. The Cresta Run was built in 1884 near the hamlet of Cresta, close to Celerina, by a certain Major Bulpett and some local people. Bulpett went on to found the St. Moritz Tobogganing Club (SMTC). The track is 3,978 feet (1,212 m) of natural ice and is one of the few runs dedicated primarily to skeleton (head-first) tobogganing. Although the SMTC is a private club, nonmembers may apply for temporary membership, which entitles them to ride in the early mornings on certain days (*www.cresta-run.com/html/sl_mem bership.cfm, $$$$$*).

Palazzo Mengotti Museum

🅰 237 D1

✉ Palazzo Mengotti, Poschiavo

☎ (081) 839 03 22

🕐 Open Tues. & Fri. 2–5, June–Oct.

💲 $$

Lago di Poschiavo

🅰 237 D1

tops out at 7,405 feet (2,257 m). It then drops down past the Palü Glacier and into a great mountain bowl—Val Poschiavo. The town of **Poschiavo** is a jewel of fine 17th- and 18th-century patrician houses with a lovely central piazza—a great place to have morning coffee and watch the world go by. Palazzo Mengotti houses a **museum,** whose working textile section has looms and flying shuttles making linen for sale.

of 5,994 feet (1,827 m) in just under 24 miles (38 km)—from glaciers to palm trees.

Returning to the Upper Engadine, southwest of St. Moritz the valley continues to **Silvaplana,** overlooking the Silvaplanersee (Lake Silvaplana), a great little lake for kite-surfing, kite-sailing, and windsurfing. Sils-Maria is a small resort between the small lakes of Silvaplanersee and the Silsersee. Here, in the **Nietzsche-Haus,** where the philosopher

Unusual Snow Sports

Snow golf is based on an idea that originated in the United States. The first Engadine Winter Golf Tournament was held on frozen Lake St. Moritz in 1979 with 87 players. The competition was so successful that it became a permanent fixture in January's winter sports calendar, moving in 1996 to Silvaplana, a few miles to the southwest. The course comprises nine holes, each of 394–590 feet (120–180 m). St. Moritz has also become the spiritual home of snow polo, hosting the annual St. Moritz Polo World Cup

in January, when four high-goal teams battle for the coveted Cartier Trophy on the frozen lake.

The annual February International Horse Races of St. Moritz began in 1907 for thoroughbreds from all over Europe to fly across the flattest racecourse in the world for the highest race prize money in Switzerland. The event also includes concerts, art exhibitions, and culinary events. Skijoring—where the skier is pulled by a horse or dogs—can be enjoyed at Arosa as well as St. Moritz.

Silviplana

🅰 237 C1

Visitor information

✉ Tourist Info Silviplana, Via dal Farrer 2, Silviplana

☎ (081) 838 60 00

Nietzsche-Haus

✉ Sils-Maria, near Silviplana

☎ (081) 826 52 24

🕐 Closed Mon.

💲 $$

www.nietzschehaus .ch

A little to the south lies beautiful **Lago di Poschiavo** whose rock walls rise sheer out of the water to form a series of peaks on the eastern side of the valley. South of **Brusio**—almost at the Italian border—is the most famous feature of the Bernina railroad. This is a spiral viaduct that allows the railway to drop down so steeply that it loops under one of its own arches. Roads and railroads cross the border into Italy shortly before the town of Tirano, having descended a vertical height

Friedrich Nietzsche spent eight summers in the 1880s, is a collection of his memorabilia. Farther up the valley is the even smaller settlement of Maloja just before the Maloja Pass, the watershed between the Danube and Po rivers. Beyond the pass, the road contorts through a series of hairpin bends as it descends through Val Bregaglia toward the Italian border. This is the route of the Palm Express, the best-known PostBus journey in Switzerland, linking Lugano (in Ticino) and St.

Kite-surfing on Silvaplanersee, between St. Moritz and Maloja

Moritz. Just before the border is **Soglio,** which Segantini (see p. 249) described as "the gateway to paradise." Its historic main hotel, **Palazzo Salis** *(Soglio, tel 081/822 12 08, www.palazzosalis.ch, $$$$$)* dates from 1629 and has an award-winning garden.

Beyond the Engadine: A tongue of Graubünden bordering Ticino to the west and Italy to the east contains the **San Bernardino Pass,** route of the eponymous Route Express PostBus between Bellinzona (in Ticino) and Chur. As it leaves Val Mescolina, the road climbs a series of tortuous hairpins to reach the new road tunnel under the pass before descending through the fabled **Via Mala Gorge.** To appreciate fully this extraordinary slit between limestone cliffs, it should be approached on foot or bike from **Thusis** at its northern end, since the modern road provides only glimpses of it. Pause before Thusis to see the **Church of St. Martin** at **Zillis.** It contains the most complete series of 12th-century ceiling paintings in existence. ∎

San Bernardino Pass
🅰 237 B2

Thusis
🅰 237 B2

Church of St. Martin
🅰 237 B2
✉ Zilllis
☎ (081) 661 22 55

Wonderful locally sourced cuisine in a land of lakes and mountains—and all with a distinctly Italian flavor

Ticino

The mountainside village of Gandria, perched high above Lake Lugano

Ticino

Ticino has been part of the Swiss Confederation since 1803. It is the only Swiss canton lying entirely on the southern side of the Alps and the only Italian-speaking canton. The Gotthard massif often marks a transition between weather systems, usually to the advantage of Ticino, which attracts those in search of early- and late-season sun.

A Lugano chef shows off his fresh mushrooms.

Although Ticino has no shortage of high, snow-capped peaks, few visitors to the canton spend much time among them. Ticino's tourist industry—as well as most of its population—is based in the south of the canton, around the beautiful Lake Lugarno and Lake Maggiore. Here visitors can go on boat trips to picturesque lakeside villages, explore the historic towns of Locarno or Lugarno, or simply enjoy fine al fresco dining in the shade of the ubiquitous chestnut trees.

Ticino has a generally mild climate, which starts to feel decidedly Mediterranean in the southern town of Locarno. Visitors should be aware, however, that its warm microclimate also brings a high number of spectacular thunderstorms, which bombard the mountaintops with lightning in the spring. The region surrounding the lakes is characterized by densely forested hills and verdant river valleys. It is a landscape that offers great hiking trails and mountain biking runs. Road cyclists, too, are a common sight in Ticino, which frequently hosts large sections of the Tour de Suisse cycle race.

Italian Influences

Many travelers are drawn to Ticino by its enviable combination of Swiss efficiency and Italian culture. The region's food and wine, in particular, is renowned throughout Europe for its mixture of Italian and Swiss styles. The best place to sample this unique cuisine is in a *grotto*—a kind of small, rustic restaurant typical of Ticino. These are often small family-run businesses with open-air seating and a limited menu based on fantastically fresh ingredients. Dedicated foodies will travel far from the canton's big towns in search of the best *grotti.*

The dishes and ingredients you can expect to find on the menu are home-cured pork products, especially salami and mortadella, risotto, minestrone, *vitello tonnato* (cold veal in a tuna and mayonnaise sauce), polenta with braised beef, stewed rabbit, wild mushrooms, zabaglione, and peaches in wine. Chestnuts are still used to accompany fall dishes of game and in the production of flour, bread, cakes, jam, and *marrons glacés* (crystallized chestnuts).

Ticino's wines can be sampled by heading straight to the wineries themselves, which are connected by a series of "wine routes" near Lake Lugano. Many of the area's vineyards grow local varieties of the merlot grapes that were imported from Bordeaux in the early 20th century. The area is also known for its grappa, made by distilling americana grapes, which is prized for its aromatic qualities. Local grappa is the key ingredient of nocino, another Ticino specialty. This is a liqueur made by steeping freshly chopped walnuts in grappa, sugar, and spices. ■

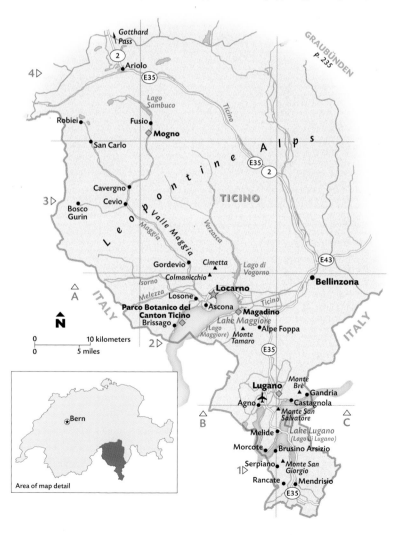

Bellinzona & Lugano

Bellinzona is a charming small town, too often rushed past on the way to Lugano or Locarno. Its largely pedestrianized and tree-lined streets and squares within the old town walls are a pleasure to wander around, and you'll stumble across lots of good cafés and restaurants. Towering over all of this are the city's three castles, whose sturdy walls are a relic of the historic struggles for control of the town.

Vineyards on the slopes below Bellinzona's Castelgrande

Bellinzona

A 255 C2

Visitor Information

✉ Tourist Information, Palazzo Civico, Bellinzona

☎ (091) 825 21 31

🕐 Closed Sun.

www.bellinzona turismo.ch

Castelgrande Museum

✉ Monte San Michele, Bellinzona

☎ (091) 825 81 45

💲 $$ (combined, all three castles)

Bellinzona

Thanks to its strategically vital position on the approach to the St. Gotthard, Lukmanier, and St. Bernard passes, the town of Bellinzona has always been an important regional center. For many centuries it was held by the Dukes of Milan, but in the early 16th century they were forced to cede the town to the cantons of Nidwalden, Schwyz, and Uri. Back then, the cantons, while political allies, weren't on particularly friendly terms. When they took control of the town, each canton's representa-

tive had to have his own castle. Sasso Corbaro was occupied by Nidwalden, Montebello by Schwyz, and Castelgrande by Uri.

Today Bellinzona is the capital of the canton of Ticino and an important transport hub. It serves as the terminus for many of the rail and PostBus routes through the mountains.

Bellinzona's heart is Piazza Nosetto, an attractive public square outside the **Palazzo Civico** (Town Hall). Few would guess that this grand building, with murals of historic scenes decorating the loggias around its courtyard, was built as recently as 1924. The nearby Piazza Colleg-giata is a more authentic square, lined with elegant 18th-century patrician houses and overlooked by the **Church of St. Peter & St. Stephen,** which combines Renais-sance and baroque elements.

The town's finest church, how-ever, is **Santa Maria delle Grazie,** a 15th-century edifice located a few minutes' walk from the town center. This Franciscan church is distinguished by the 16th-century frescoes painted above the rood screen (a partition between the nave and the choir). These depict Christ's crucifixion and 15 scenes from his life. Close by there is an even older church, **San Biagio,** which dates from the 13th cen-tury. Its interior is decorated with frescoes that are thought to date from the 14th century.

Opposite San Biagio is the town's art gallery, **Civica Galleria d'Arte,** housed in the **Villa dei Cedri** (*Piazza S. Biagio, Bellinzona, tel 091/821 85 20, closed Mon., www.villacedri.ch, $$$*). It is home to a collection of 19th- and 20th-century paintings as well as a small section of contemporary works.

The Castles: The oldest and largest of the town's three castles is **Castelgrande.** This fortress has Roman origins, though the oldest parts of the surviving structure date from the 12th century. The castle is accessed through a lift whose shaft cuts straight up through the castle's rocky foundations. Inside there is a restaurant and a small archaeological **museum**

that were added as part of a recent renovation project.

The slightly more recent castle of **Montebello** was begun at the end of the 13th century and progressively enlarged with two surrounding walls and a long wall connecting with the town. On a clear day Lake Maggiore can be seen from the battlements. An **Archaeological and Civic Museum** in the tower contains stone carvings, historic drawings, and engravings, as well as a wide range of glassware, ceramics, and jewelry—some of which dates to around 1500 B.C.—that has been discovered in the local area.

To reach the recently restored third castle of **Sasso Corbaro,** visitors have to ascend a winding road and cross two working drawbridges. Built by the Sforza family in just six months in 1479, the compact castle stands on a

Civica Galleria d'Arte
- Villa dei Cedri, Piazza S. Biagio, Bellinzona
- (091) 821 85 20
- Closed Mon.
- $$$
www.villacedri.ch

Montebello Archaeological & Civic Museum
- Salita ai Castelli, Bellinzona
- (091) 825 13 42
- Open daily in summer
- $$ (all castles)

Sasso Corbaro Castle Museum
- Bellinzona-Artore
- (091) 825 59 06
- Open daily in summer
- $$ (all castles)

EXPERIENCE:
Sample Local Specialties at the Saturday Market

On Saturday mornings a traffic-free market is held in arcaded Piazza Nosetto, the town's main square, where the roads that once led to the city's main gates meet. The colorful market is of medieval origin and full of local produce that changes from season to season and week to week. It is a great place to buy fruit, vegetables, cheeses, breads, and meats from local farmers, but you can also peruse stalls sell-ing local crafts such as pottery and textiles, household items, and leisure goods. Get there soon after it opens at 8 a.m., before it gets really busy. On market days local restaurants have a "dish of the day."

Lugano

⛰ 255 C2

Visitor Information

✉ Lugano
Tourismo,
Riva Albertoli,
Palazzo Civico,
Lugano

☎ (091) 913 32 32

🕐 Closed Sun. &
Nov.–March

www.lugano-
tourism.ch

Museo Cantonale d'Arte

✉ Via Canova 10,
Lugano

☎ (091) 910 47 80

🕐 Closed Mon.

💲 $$$

www.museo-
cantonale-arte.ch

Museo Cantonale di Storia Naturale

✉ Viale C.
Cattaneo 4,
Lugano

☎ (091) 815 47 61

🕐 Closed Sun. &
Mon.

Museo d'Arte

✉ Riva Caccia 5,
Lugano

☎ (058) 866 72 14

🕐 Closed Mon.

💲 $$$$

forested crag that offers commanding views over the area. A **museum of folk art** inside contains a magnificent walnut-paneled room (dating from the 17th century) that was recovered from a house in the Blenio valley.

Lugano

The compact city of Lugano is Ticino's main social, economic, and cultural hub. Some Swiss banks have their headquarters here, and many more have offices around the city center. The presence of these institutions gives Lugano an affluent, cosmopolitan atmosphere that is surprising considering the geographic and cultural gulf between it and Switzerland's other major cities.

The historic core of the town is located on a hill that rises steeply from the lake's northwestern shore. It is bounded on the western side by the city's main railroad station (connected to the old town by a funicular) and to the north and west by the Via Cantonale, which divides the old town from the financial district.

The heart of this neighborhood is the Piazza della Riforma, where the city's wonderful Renaissance **Palazzo Civico** is located. Most days the square is filled by a lively **market** (Tues.–Fri., 8 a.m.–12 p.m; Sat., 8 a.m.–5 p.m.).

Just off the northeast corner of the Piazza della Riforma is the **Museo Cantonal d'Arte.** Inside this attractive 15th-century building visitors will find an impressive art gallery, whose collection focuses on 19th- and 20th-

INSIDER TIP:

An art trail from the village of Brè links paintings, sculptures, and mosaics by local artists, though the frescoes in San Fedele were the work of the émigré Hungarian Josef Birò.

—OMAR GISLER
Ticinese artist

century artists, particularly those from, or connected with, Ticino. Its permanent collection includes works by Turner, Degas, Renoir, Pissarro, Hodler, Arp, and Klee.

A few minutes' walk farther east, in an attractive park beside the lake, stands the **Museo Cantonale di Storia Naturale.** This museum explains the natural history of the canton with dioramas of plants and animals, fossils, and minerals. There is a large exhibition devoted to the wild mushrooms that are a key ingredient of the region's cuisine. Other attractions in the same lakeside park include the **Museo d'Arte,** which puts on exhibitions of primarily modern art, and the **Palazzo dei Congressi.** The latter hosts a variety of open-air concerts in its 1,300-seat amphitheater.

Heading west from the Piazza della Riforma, you'll soon see the romanesque tower of the **Cathedral of San Lorenzo,** located on the hill above the station. Behind its ornate Renaissance facade is a beautiful painted interior, with lavish colorful decoration and

Upscale shops in a Lugano market

many fine frescoes. About ten minutes' walk south down the Via Nassa stands **Chiesa Santa Maria Degli Angioli,** another church noted for its painted interior. Here the focal point is a fresco depicting the passion and crucifixion of Christ, painted by Bernardino Luini (1480–1532)—a student of Leonardo da Vinci—in 1529.

The Funiculars: Few visitors to Lugano leave without making an excursion up **Monte Brè** or **Monte San Salvatore.** The former has the distinction of being the sunniest mountain in Switzerland, and the two-stage funicular to the summit restaurant operates all year. The lower funicular station can be reached by bus route 1 to the Cassarate–Monte Brè stop. A more exciting descent can be made by hiring a mountain bike at the funicular station. There are marked routes

(www.montebre.ch/?locale=en) down the mountain for beginners and experts. There are also paths through woods of chestnut, oak, beech, and birch, and an **Art Trail** leads past outdoor artworks.

(continued on p. 262)

Free Guided Walking Tours

The Lugano tourist office offers four different free walking tours. The "Classic Tour" *(Mon. 9:30 a.m.–noon, late March–mid-Oct.)* **is a tour of the principal cultural sights of the city. "Lugano, yesterday and today"** *(Thurs. 9:30 a.m.–noon, mid-May–mid-Nov.)* **looks at the churches, civic buildings, statues and squares that embellish the city. "Lugano's parks and gardens"** *(Sun. 10 a.m.–12:30 p.m., late March–mid-July, mid-Aug.–mid-Oct.)* **takes you on a circuit of the city's green spaces. "Monte Brè–Lugano"** *(Fri., 2:30 p.m. –6:30 p.m., mid-May–mid-Oct.)* **is a guided visit by cable car up the mountain** *(tel 091/ 913 32 32, www.lugano-tourism.ch).*

Modern Architecture

It is not surprising that the part of Switzerland bordering Italy should have become the region where great architects have been nurtured. During the 16th and 17th centuries the area produced such prominent names as Francesco Borromini, Carlo Maderna (who designed the facade of St. Peter's Basilica in Rome), and Domenico Gilardi. The region still produces fine architects.

One of Mario Botta's finest designs: the church of San Giovanni Battista, Mogno

Today Ticino is known as the home of a thriving community of avant-garde artists and architects including Aurelio Galfetti, Luigi Snozzi, Livio Vacchini and, most notably, Mario Botta. The canton has a remarkable and diverse stock of modern architectural marvels, as well as several of those bold—some might say ugly—buildings that are of interest to architects but disliked by everyone else.

A landmark 20th-century building was the flat-roofed reinforced concrete **Cantonal Library** *(Via Cattaneo 4, Lugano)*, completed in 1941 to a design by Rino Tami (born in Lisora,

INSIDER TIP:

Mario Botta's modern chapel in its lonely position on Monte Tamaro must be one of the most extraordinary and moving memorials to a loved one.

—OMAR GISLER
Ticinese artist

Ticino). However, it was the rapid growth of the canton, and particularly the development undertaken in the area around Lugano, that gave architects of the modern movement the opportunity to make a name for themselves. Many of the buildings have a commercial or civic function—schools, public baths, and libraries, for example—but there are also apartment buildings and private residences.

Not fitting this pattern but probably the most visited and accessible building of the Lugano "new wave" buildings is the **chapel of Santa Maria degli Angeli** on Monte Tamaro (see p. 269), designed by Mario Botta (b. 1943, in Mendrisio, Ticino) and completed in 1996. It combines an unforgettable design with an incomparable position on the mountain. The building was commissioned by the owner of the Monte Tamaro cablecar company in memory of his wife. The stone and concrete chapel combines elements of a church, a bridge, and a tower; a stepped bridge flies over its entrance. The impact is enhanced by its position: on a 4,921-foot-high (1,500 m) ridge just south of Lake Lugarno.

Visitors to Bellinzona will also encounter the Ticinese architects' unusual approach to the revitalization of a historic building. Though **Castelgrande** (see p. 257) is the closest of the town's three castles to the center, by the 1980s it had ceased to play any part in the modern life of the town. In 1986, when a donor offered CHF 5 million to restore the castle, local architect Aurelio Galfetti (b. 1936) decided on a principle of "preservation through transforma-

tion" by adapting a medieval military space into one for relaxation with restaurant, conference hall, and museum. Particular attention was paid to the routes leading to it, reconnecting the building with the urban fabric. This was done most strikingly through the insertion of a lift from Piazza del Sole reached by a long straight tunnel cut into the rock.

In the village of Mogno is another of Mario Botta's structures, the marble and granite church of **San Giovanni Battista** *(Mogno, Vallemaggia, www.vituvio.ch)*. Built between 1986 and 1995, this replaced a 17th-century church that had been swept away by an avalanche.

Away from Ticino

Ticinese architects have designed buildings in other cantons, such as the Dürrenmatt Center near Neuchâtel and the Tinguely Museum (see p. 90) in Basel. Both buildings were designed by Mario Botta.

Ticino is not the only canton to produce great architects, however. The modern skyline of the city of Basel has been strongly influenced by the work of the local Herzog & de Meuron partnership. Their commissions in the city range from bold takes on functional buildings, like the railroad switching box at Basel station (1994), as well as more prestigious projects like the Schaulager (2003) at Münchenstein. Another notable piece of Swiss architecture in the city is Karl Moser's Antoniuskirche, Switzerland's first concrete church.

The most famous Swiss architect of all, however, is the great founding father of modernism: Le Corbusier. Although he spent most his career working outside his home country, Le Corbusier's earliest works can all be found in the region around his hometown of La-Chaux-de-Fonds in Neuchâtel. Many of these buildings are simple commissions that bear none of the hallmarks of his later work, but no one with an interest in the modernist movement should miss his first completed project: the Maison Blanche (see p. 99), which he designed for his parents in 1912.

Lake Lugano
🗺 255 B1, C1–2

Rancate
🗺 255 C1

Museo Doganale Svizzero
✉ Cantine di Gandria
☎ (091) 910 48 11
🕐 Closed mornings & late Oct.–late March
www.musee-suisse .ch/e/gandria/index .php

Morcote
🗺 255 B1

The funicular up Monte San Salvatore operates from mid-March to early November and can be reached by train to Lugano–Paradiso station or buses 9 or 10 from Lugano. The terrace around the summit restaurant is a good place to work out the complex topography of Lake Lugano. The **chapel** near the summit was built in 1705 using materials carried up the mountain by the women of Pazzallo and Carabbia.

Lake Lugano

Two-thirds of Lake Lugano's exceptionally convoluted shape lies in Switzerland, and the remainder in Italy. It was bisected in 1848 when a dam was built on a glacial moraine between Melide and Bissone, later forming the route of the Gotthard railroad to Milan and the A2 motorway.

The best way to experience Lake Lugano is from the deck of one of the motor vessels that ply the waters between the lake's 14 piers. They provide access to splendid walking along shoreline paths or the woods that clothe many of the hills surrounding the lake. For those in search of less energetic diversions, enchanting villages with lakeside restaurants and cafés beckon, as well as some unusual museums.

Among the finest walks is the challenging ascent of the World Heritage site of **Monte San Giorgio,** which rises to a height of 3,599 feet (1,097 m) from the shore of the lake. The walk can be shortened by taking the cable car from the pier at Brusino Arsizio to Serpiano where there are lovely views over the lake from the restaurant terrace.

Much easier are the three circular **Mendrisiotto wine trails,** devised to give an introduction to the region that produces 40 percent of Ticino's grapes. One links the village of **Rancate** with Monte San Giorgio (allow four hours). Another themed walk in the area—the Olive Path—leads from **Castagnola** (near Lugano) across hillsides of ancient and reintroduced trees to picturesque Gandria; both villages are served by boat. The path is dotted with information boards (in English)

A performer at the Lugano Music Festival

explaining the use of olives and the production of olive oil.

Gandria is a jumble of houses with narrow paths meandering between them. There are pots of oleanders, prickly pears, and rosemary covering balconies and lining stone stairways. Vaulted passages burrow under houses and no passageway is wider than the panniered donkeys that once walked through them.

Opposite Gandria is the pier for the **Museo Doganale Svizzero** (Swiss Customs Museum), which

Museo del Manifesto Ticinese (Ticino Poster Museum) in the ancient Casa della Torre displays more than 100 original posters promoting the delights of the canton, some more than a century old. For many the highlight of Morcote is **Parco Scherrer.** This botanical garden is filled with architectural follies like a Greek temple, a Siamese tea house, and an Egyptian temple dotted among the cedars, Mexican pines, camphor trees and Chinese magnolias.

Museo del Manifesto Ticinese

- ⊠ Riveta de la Tor, Morcote
- ☎ (091) 996 30 50
- 🕐 Closed Sat.–Sun. & Nov.–Feb.
- 🚤 Boat to Morcote pier

Parco Scherrer

- ⊠ Morcote
- ☎ (091) 996 21 25
- 🕐 Closed Nov.–Feb.
- 💲 $$
- 🚌 Bus to Morcote

EXPERIENCE: Ticino's Music Festivals

Ticino's music festivals are astonishing in their range and quality, from classical "Camelia Concerts" in Locarno in March or April to **Estival Jazz** in Mendrisio (www.estivaljazz.ch/home) in June or July and **Blues to Bop** in Lugano (www .bluestobop.ch) in August. Italian operatic composer Ruggero Leoncavallo's links with Brissago are marked by an annual

festival in May. Jazz rhythms fill the night air during **JazzAscona** in late June and early July. During July's **Moon and Stars,** Locarno's Piazza Grande hosts international pop-rock performers. The **Classical Music Weeks of Ascona** (August–October) feature symphony concerts, chamber music, and solo instrumental recitals in churches in Ascona.

---

can be reached only by boat or footpath. In the four-story building from which officials once intercepted contraband, there are displays showing the ingenious methods, old and new, used to smuggle illicit goods.

Morcote & Melide

If time is limited, do not miss Morcote, one of the most attractive villages in Ticino, set at the end of the Ceresio peninsula. Its lakeside villas and tree-shaded promenade are overlooked by the tall campanile of its 14th-century church. The

A rack railroad ascends Monte Generoso to offer an unrivalled panorama over the canton and into Italy from its 5,591-foot (1,704 m) summit. The mountain has 32 miles (51 km) of footpaths and 17 miles (27 km) of mountain bike routes. At **Swissminiatur** in Melide, the owners boast that they allow visitors to see all of Switzerland in an hour. They have reproduced the country's most famous buildings in exquisite detail at a scale of 1:25, and connected them with a tiny version of the Swiss railroad network. ∎

Swissminiatur

- ⊠ Via Cantonale, Melide
- ☎ (091) 640 10 60
- 🕐 Closed mid-Oct.–mid-March
- 💲 $$$$$
- 🚤 Melide station (200m) or boat

www.swissminiatur .ch

Locarno & Lake Maggiore

Locarno has a quieter atmosphere than Lugano and relies more on tourism and culture than its larger neighbor. The city became part of Switzerland in 1512 and achieved international fame when it hosted the 1925 Locarno Peace Conference. Today it is best known for jazz and world music festivals, as well as for its International Film Festival—held in August—which sees the main square become the world's largest open-air cinema.

Cyclists enjoying summer sunshine on the waterfront in Ascona, with the Ticino Alps looming behind

Locarno

Locarno is the lowest and sunniest of all Switzerland's cities. With its Mediterranean climate and Italianate architecture, it can be hard to believe that it is really part of Switzerland. It would be wrong to think that the town is somehow isolated or cut off from the Swiss heartland, however. In fact, the centrally located train station provides direct services to Zürich, Basel, and Luzern.

The heart of Locarno is its largely pedestrianized old town, which is centered on the **Piazza Grande.** This broad cobbled square, surrounded by elegant mansions, is the best place to start exploring the city. On the northern side of the square a few narrow streets lead into a warren of alleyways lined with delightful old buildings and independent stores. To the north, these alleyways open out into the beautiful **Piazza San Antonio** with its fine baroque church. Here stands the **Casa Rusca Municipal Gallery** *(Piazza San Antonio, tel 091/756 31 70, closed Mon., $–$$),* which features paintings, woodcuts, and engravings by Swiss artists.

To the southeast of the Piazza Grande is Locarno's oldest and most significant building, the

INSIDER TIP:

The Centovalli is one of the most outstanding railroad journeys in the world, with lots of dramatic drops into the Melezza Gorge, glorious forests, and picturesque villages.

—OWEN HARDY
Writer, International Railway Traveler

Castello Visconteo. The oldest parts of this castle date from the 9th century, but most of what visitors can see today was built between the 13th and 15th centuries, when the castle was occupied by the powerful Visconti family. Some historians have speculated that parts of the castle may have been designed by Leonardo da Vinci (1452–1519). Inside, the castle is a maze of narrow passages, spiral staircases, and gloomy dungeons, with some of the larger interior spaces converted to house the exhibits of a historical museum.

Around Locarno: On the northern edge of the town, in the neighborhood of Orselina, stands the impressive 16th-century church of **Madonna del Sasso.** This church is best reached by taking the funicular from the Via Alla Romogna, just two minutes' walk from the main rail station. The staircase to the church passes several life-sized terracotta figures representing the Last Supper, Pentecost, and

the Birth of Christ.

From Orselina, there is a **cable car** to the 3,100-foot (945 m) peak of Colmanicchio for outstanding views over the lake and north toward the Alps. A chairlift continues on to Cimetta at 5,479 feet (1,670 m) for an even more astonishing panorama.

Bird-watchers may want to take a boat to **Magadino** *(Gestione Governativa Navigazione Laghi, Lago Maggiore, www.navlaghi.it)* where a path from the village takes you to the Bolle di Magadino, a wetland area where over 300 species of birds have been recorded. The crossing takes about 20 minutes. If you prefer a longer, more relaxing cruise, there are excursions to Stresa—three hours away in Italy—from Muralto.

(continued on p. 268)

Locarno
⚜ 255 B2
Visitor Information
✉ Tourist Information, Largo Zorzi 1, Locarno
☎ (091) 791 00 91
🕒 Closed Sun. Nov.–Feb.
www.asconalocarno.com/en

Museo Castello Visconteo
✉ Piazza Castello
☎ (091) 756 31 80
🕒 Tue–Sun, April–Oct.
💲 $$
🚌 Buses 10, 21, 22, 23, 31, 32

EXPERIENCE:
The Centovalli Railroad

This is one of Switzerland's greatest railway journeys. The narrow-gauge railroad links Locarno with the Italian town of Domodossola on the Milan–Luzern/Bern main line. The railroad takes its name from the hundred side valleys that it crosses, many of them spanned with bridges of masonry or a gossamer fretwork of steel. The thick forest that covers most of the hills and mountains along the route makes the route especially beautiful in fall, and there are spectacular views into the gorge cut by the Melezza River, occasionally crossed with lovely stone arches with a shrine at the apex of the parapet. Contact **Ticino Tourism** *(tel 091/825 7056, www .ticino-tourism.ch)* or **Ferrovie Autolinee Regionale Ticinese** *(tel 091/756 0400)* for ticket details.

PostBus Around Valle Maggia

While Ticino lacks the colossal mountains of its northern neighbors, its landscape is far from flat or boring. Even as far south as Locarno, the unimaginable forces that shaped the Alps are still evident in Ticino's landscape of deep, steep-sided valleys, rocky ridges, and mountains that still have snow on their summits well into spring. This landscape is the setting for one of the most remarkable road trips in Switzerland, a PostBus route that winds its way up through the Valle Maggia from Locarno.

Bosco Gurin is one of the most charming mountain villages in Switzerland.

Several beautiful valleys are within easy reach of Locarno, but the longest and most impressive is Valle Maggia *(www.vallemaggia .ch)*, which runs 30 miles (50 km) northwest and north of the city. To enjoy the valley jump on a bus (leaving hourly) from Locarno headed toward Bignasco (line 315).

There are various villages and side valleys en route to the head of the main valley at Fusio. While it isn't possible to explore all these options in one day, decide which you would like to investigate further, then—depending on how long you spend there—get the PostBus back to Locarno or catch the next one climbing farther up the valley. Check the timetable before you travel *(http://fahrplan.sbb.ch)*. The bus ride to Fusio (with a transfer at Bignasco) takes just over an hour and a half. Note that the last bus

NOT TO BE MISSED:

Saddle stones of Cavergno • San Carlo cable car • Village of Fusio • Walser's museum

back from Fusio leaves at 5 p.m.

A short way from Locarno, the road enters the gateway to the valley, **Ponte Brolla ❶**, where the Maggia River has cut a deep, narrow gorge into the rocks. North of Ponte Brolla is **Gordevio ❷**, take note of the 17th-century church of St. Giacomo e Filippo with its interior decorated by local artist Giovanni Antonio Vanoni in the 19th century. This is one spot to break your journey.

Discover Valle Maggia, a rare amalgam of Alpine and warm temperate vegetation, with woods of oak, birch, lime, ash, and chestnut trees. PostBuses run up side valleys. At **Cevio** ❸ you can alight and investigate the 17th-century **Museo di Valmaggia** (tel 091/754 1340, www.museovalmaggia.ch), which provides insights into how the valley residents have lived for hundreds of years. Another bus will take you to the enchanting stone-roofed, white-walled village of **Bosco Gurin** ❹ (www .bosco-gurin.ch), set among larch forests and the highest village in the canton, at 4,941 feet (1,506 m). This ride takes 40 minutes. Visit the **museum** (Walserhaus, Bosco Gurin, tel 091/754 1819), then pop into the **Walser Restaurant**

(Walser Hotel, tel 091/759 0202) for a bite to eat.

Alternatively, stay on the bus to Bignasco where you can investigate neighboring **Cavergno** ❺, a large village of ancient farm buildings (many on staddle stones) and a 1826 communal washing trough. Or you take the small bus west to **San Carlo** ❻ for a cable car to Robiei—which provides views over the Basodino Glacier. The third option is the bus to Fusio, which passes through **Mogno** ❼, where you'll see the most unlikely modern church set among traditional stone buildings (San Giovanni Battista, see p. 261). Finally, **Fusio** ❽, a beautiful village of stone houses and wooden barns, clings to the valley's side. Good walks lead from the village, but take care not to miss the last PostBus back to Locarno.

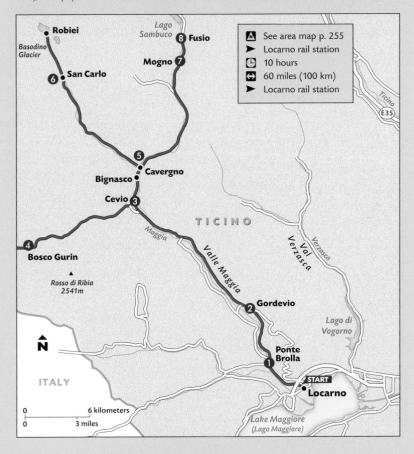

- Robiei
- Basodino Glacier
- Lago Sambuco
- ❽ Fusio
- Mogno ❼
- ❻ San Carlo

See area map p. 255
Locarno rail station
10 hours
60 miles (100 km)
Locarno rail station

- ❺
- Cavergno
- Bignasco
- Cevio ❸
- TICINO
- Maggia
- ❹
- Bosco Gurin
- Rosso di Ribia 2541m
- Valle Maggia
- Val Verzasca
- Verzasca
- ❷ Gordevio
- Lago di Vogorno
- N
- ITALY
- Ponte Brolla
- ❶
- START
- Locarno
- 0   6 kilometers
- 0   3 miles
- Lake Maggiore (Lago Maggiore)
- E35
- Ticino

Monte Tamaro, in the Ticino Alps, with Lake Maggiore in the distance

Ascona

 255 B2

Visitor Information

 Ente Turistico
    Lago Maggiore,
    Casa Serodine,
    Ascona

☎ (091) 791 00 90

🕑 Closed Sun.
    Nov.–Feb.

**www.ascona-
locarno.com/en**

Lake Maggiore

Lake Maggiore is more than four times the size of Lake Lugano, but only about a fifth of its total area is in Switzerland (the rest is in Italy). It is long, sinuous, and relatively narrow. This not only makes it visually interesting but marks a transition from the Swiss Alpine character at its northern end, through gentler hills to end near the plain of Lombardy in Italy.

On the opposite bank of the Maggia River from Locarno stands its smaller, quieter neighbor, **Ascona.** This lakeside resort has been a popular destination for more than a century, and was particularly popular with artists and intellectuals. In the early 20th century it was home to a remarkable community of expatriates that included the writers Hermann Hesse, James

Joyce, and Erich Maria Remarque; the painters Paul Klee and Hans Arp; the famous dancer Isadora Duncan; and the psychoanalyst Karl Jung.

Ascona's waterfront is bright with the blue, orange, and yellow umbrellas outside restaurants and cafés. Plane trees shade the promenade by the small harbor, which is usually filled with fishing boats. The narrow, largely pedestrianized streets and alleyways around the soaring campanile of the **Church of St. Peter & St. Paul** are lined with small boutiques and shops. High-end clothes, galleries, and antique shops rub shoulders with traditional delicatessens that sell an impressive number of different kinds of polenta, pasta, and olive oil.

Few visitors to Ascona leave without an excursion on the lake. The most popular destination in the Swiss part of the lake is the village of **Brissago** and the nearby islands of the same name. The old part of the village is huddled around the Renaissance church of **St. Peter & St. Paul.** Narrow lanes punctuated by small gardens of lemon and orange trees lead down to the water. The village became the home of the composer Leoncavallo, and a baroque villa here contains the **Leoncavallo Museum,** a collection of memorabilia associated with the Italian opera composer Ruggero Leoncavallo (1857–1919), who fell in love with the place after a visit to Lake Maggiore.

Just offshore, on the larger island of San Pancrazio is the **Parco Botanico del Canton Ticino,** the canton's botanical garden, which was created in the late 19th century by a Russian baroness of German origin. The garden contains over 1,700 species from the Mediterranean, subtropical Asia, South Africa, the Americas, and Oceania. Unlike other Swiss botanical gardens, the mild climate obviates the need for greenhouses. There is just one small one, devoted to orchids and carnivorous plants.

The island is accessible by boat from Brissago *(Gestione Governativa Navigazione Laghi, www.navigazio nelaghi.it/eng/mag/loc/isolebris sago.html, $$$$$).* Many garden lovers continue south across the border to Isola Bella, which has an outstanding mansion and 17th-century garden created by the aristocratic Italian renaissance Borromeo family.

Mountain Walks

One of the most famous and spectacular walks in the region is the 8-mile (13 km) ridge walk between **Monte Tamaro** (6,434 feet/1,961 m) and **Monte Lema** (5,318 feet/1,621 m). Monte Tamaro is reached by taking the train between Lugano and Bellinzona to Rivera-Bironico station, which is 450 yards (500 m) from the cable car to Alpe Foppa. From there it is about a 90-minute trek to the start of the walk on Monte Tamaro. Allow four and a half hours from summit to summit and make sure to carry plenty of water. From Monte Lema a cable car takes you down to Miglieglia from where PostBuses run back to Lugano. ∎

Leoncavallo Museum

✉ Palazzo Branca-Baccalà, Brissago
☎ (091) 793 02 42
🕐 Closed Mon. & Nov.–Feb.
💲 $$
🚌 Boat/bus to Brissago

Brissago
🅰 255 B2

Parco Botanico del Canton Ticino

✉ Isole di Brissago
☎ (091) 791 43 61
🕐 Closed Nov.–Feb.
💲 $$$
🚌 Boat from Brissago
www.isolebrissago.ch/welcome.php?l=e

EXPERIENCE: Touring Lake Maggiore

Since most of Lake Maggiore is in Italy, boats on the lake are operated by an Italian company, and the Swiss Pass (see p. 272) is therefore not valid. Services call at 36 places around the lake. One of the best ways to see the lake and take in the outstanding railroad journey between Domodossola and Locarno, especially in fall, is the **Lago Maggiore Express** (*www.lagomaggioreexpress.com*). Starting in Ascona, Brissago, Locarno, or Magadino, the one- or two-day circular excursion by boat and train can be used to stop at 16 places in Italy in addition to the Swiss ports of call. Lunch can be taken on board (reservation required) or at a restaurant.

TRAVELWISE

Hop on a tram to explore the city of Zürich.

PLANNING YOUR TRIP

When to Go

The time of year you choose to visit is naturally determined by the object of your trip. The months of December to early April are dominated by those in search of winter sports—about 40 percent of whom forego skis in favor of activities such as snowshoeing and sledging. Crystal-clear winter days offer some of the most dramatic mountain views, with a visibility that warmer months seldom offer.

The period in spring when the snow is melting and in November are perhaps the only times of year visitors to rural and mountain areas might wish to avoid. As the snow thins, the grass looks pale, paths become muddy, and many hotels close for a break between winter and summer seasons, as they do in November. However, toward the end of snow melt, mountain meadows become a mass of color as spring flowers punch their way through the thinning snow. Most rain falls in the spring and fall. The Jura region is particularly wet in spring and also endures some of the lowest winter temperatures, especially in the Brevine valley.

Summer sunshine is often characterized by haze, but this is the most popular time for family visits and offers the chance to undertake long walks that require the most hours of daylight. Once the schools reopen at the end of the summer vacations, hotels become much quieter that, combined with the onset of fall colors, encourages trekkers and child-free visitors to take advantage of often lower room rates.

Switzerland has a central European climate except for Ticino, which has a Mediterranean climate. The passage of the Gotthard Tunnel often marks a major transition in the weather. Average daytime temperatures in the summer seldom exceed 80°F (27°C), while those in winter hover above freezing, gradually rising to a peak in July.

What to Take

Again, clothing will be dictated by the activities planned, but you won't have any difficulty buying anything forgotten unless you are well off the beaten track. If you are planning to do any walking, comfortable walking shoes—or boots for mountain paths—are essential. Sneakers are not a sensible substitute. Weather conditions and temperatures in the mountains can change very quickly, so it is wise to be prepared. Those undertaking long walks are well advised to take a first-aid kit, energy bars, sunscreen, sunglasses, a hat, a small flashlight, whistle, and water (though there are no shortage of places in the mountains with potable water disgorging from a pipe into a hollowed-out wooden log). Many walkers find telescopic walking sticks helpful, and they are easily found in sports shops (many of the best poles are made in Switzerland). Unless you are planning extensive or remote walks, maps are seldom needed because the signage of walking routes is so good. However, local maps are usually available from tourist offices. Binoculars increase the pleasure of walks, especially in mountains where you may be able to watch ibex, marmots, or eagles.

Entry Formalities
Visas
Visas are not required for citizens of the U.S., Canada, Europe, Australia, New Zealand, or Japan for visits of less than three months. A passport valid for three months past the end travel date is required.

Customs
Medicine may be imported for personal use only. Meat may not be imported, and the allowance on alcohol is 2 liters (0.5 gallon) for beverages up to 15 percent proof or 1 liter (0.25 gallon) for those over 15 percent. Visitors from outside Europe may bring in 400 cigarettes and 100 cigars. Those from European countries may import 200 cigarettes and 50 cigars.

Insurance
There is no state medical service in Switzerland so care has to be paid for and is expensive. It is therefore unwise to travel without insurance coverage against personal accident and sickness. Check your coverage carefully if you are going for winter sports. Residents in the U.S. can obtain advice on health and vaccination for Switzerland at www.cdc.gov/travel. Canadian residents should check online at www.hc-sc.gc.ca.

Coverage for damage to luggage or personal effects, or cancellation charges is also helpful.

Switzerland Embassies
United States
Embassy of Switzerland
2900 Cathedral Ave, NW
Washington, DC 20008
Tel 202/745-7900
Fax 202/387-2564
E-mail: vertretung@was.rep.admin.ch
www.swissemb.org,
www.eda.admin.ch/washington

United Kingdom
Embassy of Switzerland
16-18 Montagu Place
London W1H 2BQ
Tel 020 7616 6000
Fax 020 7724 7001
E-mail: vertretung@lon.rep.admin.ch
www.swissembassy.org.uk,
www.eda.admin.ch/london

Canada
Embassy of Switzerland
5 Marlborough Avenue
Ottawa, ON
K1N 8E6
Canada
Tel 613/235-1837
Fax 613/563-1394
E-mail: switzerland@access wave.ca

FURTHER READING
History
A Short History of Switzerland by E. Bonjour, H.S. Offler, and G.R. Potter (1952)
How the English Made the Alps by Jim Ring (2000)
Switzerland, from Roman Times to the Present by William Martin (1971)
Switzerland: How an Alpine Pass Became a Country by Joëlle Kuntz (2008)
The Swiss and the British by John Wraight (1987)

Culture & Miscellaneous
Swiss Me by Roger Bonner (2008)
Swisswatching by Diccon Bewes (2010)
So Sweet Zerland by Xavier Casile (2008)
Once Upon an Alp by Eugene V. Epstein (1978)
Living Among the Swiss by Michael Wells (2002)
Beyond Chocolate: Understanding Swiss Culture by Margaret Oertig-Davidson (2002)
The Surprising Wines of Switzerland by John C. Sloan (1996)

Outdoors & Nature
The Alpine Flowers of Britain and Europe by Christopher Grey-Wilson and Marjorie Blamey (1979).
The Bernese Alps by Kev Reynolds (2008)
Central Switzerland: A Walker's Guide by Kev Reynolds (1995)
Walking in the Engadine by Kev Reynolds (2005)
The Most Complete Guide to the Birds of Britain and Europe by Lars Svensson, Peter Grant, Killian Mullarney, and Dan Zetterstrom (1999)
Tour of the Jungfrau Region by Kev Reynolds (2009)
Walking in Ticino by Kev Reynolds (1992)
Walking in the Valais by Kev Reynolds (2007)

Travel
Neither Here Nor There by Bill Bryson (1992)
A Tramp Abroad by Mark Twain (1893)

Fiction
Heidi by Johanna Spyri (2000)
The Magic Mountain by Thomas Mann (1928)

HOW TO GET TO SWITZERLAND
By Airplane
Switzerland is well connected to most parts of the world thanks not only to its importance economically and as a major tourist destination but also due to the number of international organizations with headquarters in the country. There are scheduled flights to Zürich Airport from 163 airports worldwide

The national flag carrier of the country, **Swiss International Air Lines** (www.swiss.com), better known as SWISS, serves 48 destinations in Europe and 24 beyond, including North America where SWISS flights land at Boston, Chicago, Los Angeles, Miami, New York (JFK and Newark), and San Francisco in the U.S., and Montreal in Canada. Other North American cities are connected to Switzerland by codeshare partner airlines or different carriers.

SWISS offers more flights from the British Isles than any other airline. Flights from Birmingham, Dublin, Edinburgh, London (City and Heathrow), and Manchester fly to Basel, Geneva, and the principal hub at **Zürich Airport** (ZRH; tel 043 816 3422, www.zurich-airport.com). Zürich Airport is one of the few airports in the world to offer staffed nurseries and playrooms. These are located near Gates A and E. Children should always be accompanied by at least one adult. There are also play areas scattered around the airport with dolls, toys, painting sets, and computer games.

Geneva International Airport (GVA; tel 022 717 7111, www.gva.ch) has connections with about 130 airports worldwide, while almost all services from **Basel EuroAirport** (BSL; tel 161 325 3111, www.euroairport.com) are with European destinations.

A great advantage of Switzerland's three principal airports is that they enjoy excellent connections. They are close to the cities they serve and are linked by quick public transport. At both Zürich and Geneva, main rail stations with fast trains to destinations throughout the country are located directly beneath the terminals, making transfers quick and easy.

There are also smaller airports at **Bern** (www.flughafenbern.ch), **Grenchen** (www.airport-grenchen.ch), **La Chaux-de-Fond** (www.leseplaturesairport.ch), **Lugano** (www.lugano-airport.ch), **St. Gallen** (www.airport-stgallen.com), **Samedan** (www.engadin-airport.ch), and **Sion** (www.sionairport.ch). However, a combination of short distances and long waiting times at airports make internal flights impractical, given the speed and efficiency of alternative modes of transport.

By Train
Switzerland's central location in continental Europe means that it is also easily reached by train, making travel part of the pleasure of the holiday. High-speed or intercity trains reach the country from dozens of cities in neighboring countries. If you are traveling to other countries, it may save money to obtain an InterRail Pass. These are available for first- and second-class travel. They cover either a single country or up to 29 different countries, for either continuous travel or a selected number of days within a time period. For full information about the InterRail Pass, visit www.raileurope.co.uk. For rail travel from the UK, visit www.seat61.com.

GETTING AROUND
By Public Transport
Switzerland has the best national public transport system in the world, leaving first-time visitors astonished at the quality and dependability of the carefully integrated system. It means that connections between trains, and between trains and other modes—whether PostBus, tram, city bus, lake steamer, funicular or cable car—are scheduled for seamless transfers. Many places cannot be reached by road, and mountain roads demand intense concentration so there is little chance of the driver enjoying the landscape. Combine this with some of the most scenic railway journeys in the world and it is no surprise that the proportion of visitors to Switzerland choosing to use the Swiss Travel System is exceptionally high.

Swiss Pass
For visitors one of the great benefits of the Swiss Travel System is the range of good-value passes, starting with the most comprehensive, the **Swiss Pass**. Valid for 4, 8, 15, 22 days or 1 month, it covers unlimited travel on trains, PostBuses, boats, and the public transport systems of 41 Swiss cities, with 50 percent off most mountain summit trains, cable cars, and funiculars. For those who will not need a pass every day, the **Swiss Flexi Pass** covers three, four, five, or six days' travel within a one-month period. On other days, the Flexi Pass offers a 50 percent discount. For young people up to 26 years

old, the **Swiss Youth Pass** confers the same benefits as the Swiss Pass, but under-16s traveling with one or two parents travel free of charge with a **Swiss Travel System Family Card**. If you are visiting only one place, the Swiss Transfer Ticket takes you from a border or airport to your destination. The first three passes are also valid as a **Swiss Museum Pass**, giving free admission to over 400 museums. If two or more people are traveling together, each receives a 15 percent discount on the purchase price of any pass.

It saves time to buy passes before leaving home, through Switzerland Tourism or from a travel agent. On arrival in Switzerland it is very easy to use the system. Everything is designed to make life simple for the traveler. For example, railroad stations are the hub of bus or tram routes. Also, information about the next leg of your journey is explained with extreme clarity, and timetables are displayed at stations and bus stops; the timetable section of *www.rail .ch* is an object lesson in good web design.

By Bus

The distinctive yellow PostBuses which connect with trains at numerous stations have been a feature of Swiss life since the first motorized postal bus was introduced in 1906 (see sidebar, p. 30). They operate routes that are complementary to the rail and tram networks. For the visitor, the principal attraction of PostBus routes is the opportunity to experience some of the most dramatic roads over the high passes. The roads leading to the passes are often a series of tortuous hairpins. When you first see a series of vehicles having to reverse on a hairpin bend, you will be very happy to leave the

driving to someone else, especially when they are as competent and experienced as the PostBus drivers.

The most scenic PostBus routes are usually served by "Route Express" buses with limited stops, and some are even double-deckers offering grandstand views for the upper-level passengers. The most famous is the Palm Express between Lugano and St. Moritz. This passes through Italy and beside long stretches of lakes Lugano and Como as well as the larch forests of the Upper Engadine and the Maloja Pass. Other notable journeys cross the Julier, San Bernardino, Simplon, Nufenen, Klausen, Gotthard, Grimsel, and Furka passes.

By Train

Trains use the same platform every day and are in the same formation, so for long-distance trains a blue information board shows you which sector of the platform to stand for first- and second-class carriages or even a dining car. Nearly all rail routes have at least an hourly service for half the day. The entire network is electrified. Swiss Federal Railways derives all its current from hydroelectricity so one's carbon footprint is very small.

Eating a freshly cooked meal on a train while weaving through lovely countryside is one of life's pleasures, and there are 90 dining cars on the main routes of **Swiss Federal Railways** *(SBB, www.sbb.ch)*. A cooked lunch is also served to first-class passengers on the Glacier Express between Zermatt and Chur.

Passenger Services

If you're arriving via Zürich or Geneva airports, **Fly Rail Baggage** *(www.railaway.com)* allows you to check your baggage through from any airport in the world and by any airline to the rail station

at your destination within the country. See *www.rail.ch/check-in* for more details. If you're moving on to one of 45 different tourist destinations, **Fast Baggage** *(www .rail.ch/baggage)* allows you to send your suitcases ahead so that you can travel unencumbered. If you are traveling with cases and need a trolley, they are designed to go on escalators; it's a little unnerving the first time, but they cannot roll once on. Large stations have various sizes of locker *($$)*.

By Car

Switzerland is connected to Europe's motorway network and has a good road network, though it is naturally limited by topography and environmental considerations. Note: There are a large number of car-free resorts, and many of the country's finest views can be reached only by mountain railroad or cable car.

Driving in winter is not recommended unless the driver is experienced in driving on snow, as many mountain roads require extreme care. For example, snow chains should be carried everywhere in Switzerland during winter; if you do not carry and fit them when conditions demand the police can prevent you from continuing your journey. Roads over Alpine passes are often closed in winter.

Driving Laws

If you bring a car into Switzerland, you have to buy a Motorway Vignette, before entering the country, either through the Switzerland Tourism website or at the border. It saves time and hassle to purchase it in advance. The sticker, or vignette, must be displayed on the windshield or you will be liable for a fine of CHF100 plus the cost of the sticker. You do not need to purchase a Motorway Vignette if you rent a car in Switzerland. RVs and trailers require a separate sticker.

Switzerland has very strict drink-driving laws, allowing only a blood alcohol level of 0.5. Anything over that and you could face penalties as severe as imprisonment.

A full driving licence is required, and the minimum age for driving a car is 18. Seat belts are obligatory in the front and rear. Speed limits are 31 mph (50 kmh), or lower where marked, in built-up areas, 50 mph (80 kmh) on open roads, and 75 mph (120 kmh) on motorways. Speeds are enforced rigorously, and radar traps are frequent. Traffic offences are subject to on-the-spot fines. Fines are linked not only to the offence but the ability to pay.

It is important to carry your driving licence, vehicle registration document, and certificate of motor insurance at all times. If your licence does not incorporate a photograph, be sure and carry your passport to validate the licence. If the vehicle is not registered in your name, carry a letter from the registered owner giving you permission to drive.

Children under the age of 7 are prohibited from traveling in the front of a car unless they use a proper child restraint. Children between 7 and 12 must use seat belts or child restraints which are appropriate to their size and age.

By SwitzerlandMobility

SwitzerlandMobility is the largest national network of nonmotorized routes ever created. Nearly 12,500 miles (20,000 km) of itineraries have been devised for hikers, touring cyclists, mountain bikers, inline skaters, and canoeists. All are marked with standardized signage and services that include accommodation, luggage transfer, equipment rental, and discounted use of public transport.

The routes are marked by over 100,000 discreet, color-coded signposts and 57 printed route guides published in English, German, and French. The network builds on Switzerland's reputation as a paradise for active, environmentally friendly leisure pursuits. It entails the involvement of more than 1,100 establishments along the routes, from hotels and family-run guest houses to bike-rental companies. There is a web-based booking system (www.switzerlandmobility.ch) that offers detailed information on the routes to help choose an appropriate holiday, and all arrangements are then made by SwitzerlandMobility. The routes themselves are accessible through 18,000 stops on the public transport network.

Travel by Bike

The contour lines of Switzerland might suggest that this is the last country one would choose to explore by bike. In fact, there is plenty of gently undulating countryside, countless easily graded river valleys, and numerous lakes to circumnavigate. The popularity of cycling among the Swiss, both for commuting to work and for pleasure, is both cause and effect of the excellent cycling facilities. There are plenty of places to rent bikes, and excellent directional signs everywhere.

Bike rental is possible at more than 80 rail stations. Available are city bikes with seven gears, mountain bikes with 21 gears, children's mountain bikes with seven gears and, at some outlets, electric Flyer bikes which give a welcome boost on hills. It is advisable to book ahead (www.rail.ch/bicycle or www.rentabike.ch), especially in July and August. There is also a network of free bike loan in operation in Bern, Geneva, Zürich, Lausanne, Neuchâtel and various towns in Valais. Simply provide your passport for identification and a

returnable deposit ($$$$$) at one of the appointed booths (see www.suisseroule.ch/www.schweizrollt.ch for locations and details), and the bike is yours for the day. Another small fee ($$$) gives you overnight rental.

Bikes on Trains

Bikes can be taken on most trains and many PostBuses, though there are some date, time, and space restrictions. For example, on fine days trains leaving Zürich for the Graubünden or the Jura between 7 and 9 a.m. are likely to be especially full. At weekends, there are no restrictions on accompanied bikes on S-Bahn trains in Zürich, but from Mondays to Fridays accompanied bikes are allowed only from 8 a.m. to 4 p.m. and from 7 p.m. to 6 a.m. From mid-March through October, passengers wishing to take their bikes with them on intercity tilting trains (train-category ICN) must pay a small reservation fee ($$).

The blue train information board on station platforms shows where carriages with a bike compartment will stop, and a bike symbol on the train door indicates the precise location.

PRACTICAL ADVICE
Communications
Internet Access

The vast majority of hotels have Wi-Fi or cable internet access, in bedrooms and/or public areas. Even the smallest hotel usually has a terminal for guests' use. Surprisingly, use is often free in smaller, cheaper hotels—but can be expensive in grander establishments, where it is evidently assumed that most guests are on expense accounts.

Internet access is available in Internet cafés and phone booths, which are found in most major towns and cities. In the case of phone booths, charges are payable by phonecard or credit card, whereas cafés are mostly independently run. Internet coverage is good throughout most of Switzerland, but don't expect too many options in mountain areas.

Mail
The Swiss postal system, **Swiss Post** *(www.swisspost.ch)* is as efficient as most Swiss public services. Post offices are generally open between 8 a.m. and noon, and 2 p.m. to 6:30 p.m., Monday to Friday and from 8 a.m. to 11 a.m. on Saturday. Post offices in larger towns and cities do not close for lunch.

Any Swiss post office will hold mail for up to one month before collection. where you can collect your mail for one month. In addition to the name of the recipient, this mail must always bear the words "poste restante." If you send letters with proof of delivery to a poste restante address, the name of the recipient must be clearly indicated. In locations with more than one post office, it is essential to indicate clearly at which post office the items should be held for collection. Otherwise, items will be held at the relevant main post office. The service is free of charge. Items which have not been collected after one month are returned to the sender.

Telephones
The national system is excellent with direct dialing for all international calls. The country code for Switzerland is +41. When dialling Swiss numbers while in the country, the full area code including the 0 should be used. A phone card called Taxcard is available from post offices, newsagents, and rail stations (in denominations of CHF5, CHF10,

and CHF20) and is required for most public payphones. As in most countries, hotel telephones should be used with caution because of usually punitive surcharges.

Conversions
The metric system is universally used.

Electricity
Swiss power stations supply voltage at the continental European standard of 220V AC 50Hz. However, the most common plug is peculiar to Switzerland and has three pins, two of which are spaced 19 mm apart as on the continental standard two-pin plug. Less common is the two-pin socket/plug. Adaptors are easily obtained.

Appliances made for 240V will cope with 220V but North American appliances require a step-down transformer; read the instructions to see whether this has been built in.

Etiquette & Local Customs
It is customary to shake hands with everyone and to allow a host to introduce you at a party or meeting. The Swiss do not start using given names on first acquaintance; wait to be invited. If you know someone well enough to greet them with an embrace, it is customary to kiss three times, on alternate cheeks (left, right, left). A gift of roses or carnations implies love, and white chrysanthemums and white lilies should be bought only for funerals. Avoid giving expensive gifts; they cause embarrassment. Though business attire is formal, many diners do not wear ties except at the smartest restaurants. Hands, but not elbows, should be rested on the table

rather than in your lap.

Notwithstanding the differences between the three main language areas, the Swiss value cleanliness, honesty, hard work, and material possessions, though vulgar displays of wealth are frowned upon. They are very proud of their environment, and it is one of the most litter-free countries in the world. The Swiss also value sobriety, thrift, tolerance, punctuality, and a sense of responsibility.

Holidays
Public holidays do vary between cantons so it is advisable to check as these may affect your plans. Some public holidays are confined to a single canton. National holidays are held on the following days:

January 1—New Year's Day
January 2—Berchtold's Day (in 14 cantons; Duke Berchtold V founded Bern)
January 6—Epiphany (in six cantons)
March/April—Good Friday Easter Sunday, and Monday
May/June—Ascension Day
August 1—National Day, Whit Sunday and Monday
December 25—Christmas Day
December 26—Boxing Day

Liquor Laws
The minimum legal age for drinking beer, wine, and cider is either 16 or 18, depending on the canton. For spirits, liquor, and alcopops it is 18 in all cantons. Liquor is widely available in shops and bars.

Media
The main broadcaster in Switzerland is the public **Swiss Broadcasting Corporation** *(www .srg-ssr.ch)*, which operates seven TV networks (three in German, two in Italian, and two in French)

and 18 radio stations. Private TV and radio stations operate in the regions. Multichannel cable and satellite TV stations from France, Germany, and Italy are widely available in hotels, as is CNN and BBC News.

English-language newspapers are readily available in larger towns and cities, and most of the more expensive hotels offer free newspapers on a table at breakfast.

Money Matters
The currency is the Swiss franc. One franc equals 100 centimes. Notes come in denominations of CHF10, CHF20, CHF50, CHF100, CHF200, and CHF1,000 supplemented by CHF5, CHF2, and CHF1 coins. Centime coins come in 5, 10, 20, and 50 centime denominations. Travelers' cheques and Eurocheques may be cashed at banks and large hotels (usually at an inferior rate), and all major credit cards are widely accepted. ATMs can be found throughout the country.

Opening Times
Shops are generally open from 8 a.m. to 6:30 p.m. on weekdays, with a 90-minute to three-hour break for lunch outside of the cities and large towns. Late opening is on Thursday, but only in larger towns and cities. Shops close at 4 p.m. or 5 p.m. on Saturday. Sunday opening is uncommon. Banks are generally open on weekdays from 8:30 a.m. to 4:30 p.m.

Religion
Christianity is the predominant religion of Switzerland (79 percent of the total resident population), with Roman Catholicism being the largest church, followed by the Swiss Reformed Church. However, there are marked variations between cantons. The

larger cities (Bern, Zürich, Basel, and Geneva) are traditionally Protestant, while central Switzerland and Ticino canton are traditionally Catholic. The largest minority religion is Islam.

Rest Rooms
These are widely available and are almost invariably immaculately clean.

Time Difference
The country is on a single time six hours ahead of Eastern Standard Time in the U.S. and one hour ahead of the U.K.

Tipping
A service charge (10–15 percent) is automatically added to all hotel and restaurant bills. For exceptional service, round up the bill. A small gift rather than a tip may be more appropriate for a tour guide.

Travelers with Disabilities
Switzerland is generally welcoming to disabled travellers. Trains can accept wheelchairs as wide as 2.3 feet (70 cm), 3.93 feet (120 cm) long, and 3.6 feet (109 cm) high. There is wheelchair space on virtually all trains, and more than 150 staffed stations (all but small stations) have a lift to raise wheelchairs from the lower continental-style platform height (these are gradually being raised) to the carriage door. Advance notice of at least 1 hour is needed to procure the lift (call the toll-free number 0800 00 71 02; from abroad +41 051 225 71 50). Wheelchair passengers need to be at the station (for boarding the train) at least 10 minutes before departure.

Hotels adapted for wheelchairs are marked with a symbol in brochures, or a check can be made

through www.swisshotels.ch where there is a field listed "suitable for wheelchairs."

Visitor Information
The principal web site for visitor information is www.myswitzer land.com. Outside Switzerland there are major tourism offices at the following places:

Swiss Center
608 Fifth Avenue
New York
New York 10020
Tel 608-527-6565
E-mail: info.us@myswitzerland .com

Switzerland Tourism
30 Bedford Street
London WC2E 9ED
Tel 00800 100 200 30
E-mail: info.uk@myswitzerland .com

Switzerland Tourism
480 University Avenue,
Suite 1500
Toronto
Ontario M5G 1V2
Tel 800-794-7795
E-mail: info.caen@myswitzer land..com

EMERGENCIES
Crime & Police
Crime rates in Switzerland may be very low compared with most other countries, but it is foolish not to take the usual precautions when traveling. Don't leave valuables in railway station lockers, even though they are almost invariably a safe way to store luggage while exploring a place, and beware of anyone offering to help with a locker.

Policing is organized largely on a cantonal basis, and the standard of helpfulness is as high as would be expected of Switzerland.

Embassies
United States Embassy
Sulgeneckstrasse 19
3007 Bern
Tel +41 031 357 70 11
(calling Switzerland)
Tel Emergency (24 hours)
+41 031 357 70 11
(calling Switzerland)
Fax +41 031 357 73 44

Passport Services
Tel +41 031 357 72 34
(calling Switzerland)

American Citizen Services
Tel +41 031 357 72 34
(calling Switzerland)
E-mail: bernPA@state.gov
www.bern.usembassy.gov

British Embassy
Chancellery
Thunstrasse 50
3005 Bern
Tel +41 031 359 77 00
(calling Switzerland)
Fax +41 031 359 77 01

Consular Services
Tel +41 031 359 77 41
Fax +41 031 359 77 65
info@britishembassy.ch
www.britishembassy.ch

Canadian Embassy
Chancery & Consular Services
Kirchenfeldstrasse 88
3005 Bern
Tel +41 031 357 32 00
(calling Switzerland)
Fax +41 031 357 32 10
bern@dfait-maeci.gc.ca
www.dfait-maeci.gc.ca/
switzerland/

Emergency Telephone Numbers
Police   117
Fire   118
Ambulance   144
Rescue by helicopter
    1414/1415
Poisoning emergencies   145
Emergency road service   140
The helping hand   143
Telephone support for
    children   147

Health
Apart from those travelers who have visited a high-risk destination in the two weeks prior to arriving in Switzerland, no vaccinations are required to enter the country.

Switzerland poses very few health risks. Tap water is not one of them—it is safe to drink everywhere.

Two of the most frequently encountered problems are sunstroke and altitude sickness. Sunstroke is relatively common in the Alps where the air is thin and sunshine reflects from snow. Make sure you always have adequate sunscreen protection. Altitude sickness is a problem for some new arrivals in the mountains, but usually only above about 10,000 feet (3,000 m). Symptoms can be unpleasant, including nausea and headaches, but a little bed rest and an aspirin or two usually ease the symptoms. However, if they persist it is wise to move to a lower altitude.

Healthcare in Switzerland is privately funded, so it is important to ensure you carry health insurance before you travel to the country. Lists of local doctors are available at many hotels and at all tourist information offices. Prescription medicines are available in pharmacies, which are indicated by a green cross logo. If the local pharmacy is closed when you visit, details of the nearest open one should be posted in the window. In larger towns and cities there will always be at least one that is open. You will find that pharmacy staff are both helpful and informed. They will certainly be able to offer advice on minor ailments. Most hospitals have an accident and emergency department.

Lost Property
Public transport organizations have lost property offices, and objects found elsewhere are usually handed to the police. Most insurance policies require a police report made within 24 hours of the loss.

Hotels & Restaurants

Switzerland is renowned throughout the world for its first-rate hospitality and tourism industry. It comes as no surprise, therefore, to discover that it offers a huge choice of places to stay and eat, and an unsurpassed excellence of service throughout the Confederation.

Accommodation

There is a wide array of one- to five-star hotels and country inns spanning the country, and suiting the pockets and needs of most travelers. These include a growing number of spa and wellness hotels, which offer a good range of nurturing treatments as well as accommodation. Other options include staying in a chambre d'hote or B&B (bed & breakfast) for a special taste of Swiss domestic life and hospitality (see www .bnb.ch). Families should consider the Swiss KidsHotels collection (www.MySwitzerland.com/kids hotels) or, for an authentic rural experience, treat your children to a night's sleep on a bed of hay at more than 200 farms (www .schlaff-im-stroh.ch; www.aventure-paille.com).

Don't dismiss youth hostels! Some offer quality accommodation at excellent prices and appeal to all ages (www.youthhostel.ch). If you prefer self-catering, there are also countless chalets and holiday apartments to choose from (see the local tourist offices' websites). Finally, for the ultimate Swiss experience, hikers and hardy nature lovers should consider sleeping in mountain hut accommodation (www.sac-cas.ch) to rediscover the simple pleasures in life.

Restaurants

Our selection reflects the huge assortment of eateries in Switzerland, from sausage stands, beer cellars, and simple mountain huts accessible only to walkers and skiers, to chic designer bistros and gourmet temples, not to mention the increasingly multicultural gastronomic scene in the larger cities. Geneva is the nation's culinary capital, with its numerous haute cuisine restaurants, closely followed by Zürich with its trend-setting restaurants of "modern Swiss" fare. Many of the top Swiss restaurants are rated by such organizations as GaultMillau (www.gaultmillau.fr), Les Grandes Tables de Suisse (www.grandes tables.ch) and, for the ultimate accolade, the very best are awarded Michelin stars (www .michelin.ch).

Eating out is popular, so it is advisable to book a table, especially on weekends. Since May 2010 smoking has been banned throughout Switzerland in the workplace and in enclosed spaces that are accessible to the public (bars, restaurants, hotel lounges), with only a few exceptions made in some private establishments (for instance, hotels with devoted cigar lounges).

Our Selection

The accommodation and restaurants listed here are limited to some of the best or most interesting choices in a variety of price ranges. Wherever possible we have chosen venues that are both individual and typical, perhaps with notable local or historic associations. Price categories are given only for guidance.

Always try to book your accommodation in advance (especially in major cities), if possible confirming by fax or e-mail. Understand that the busiest months are usually July and August in summer and the school holidays in winter. Then, accommodation prices are at their highest. In cities, location is relatively unimportant, as the urban areas are relatively small and transport connections are excellent. Most large towns and cities (including Basel, Geneva, and Zürich) offer a complimentary ticket that allows you free travel on public transport in the region for the duration of your stay. Ask for details at your hotel reception.

Organization & Abbreviations

The hotels and restaurants are listed by chapter and location, then arranged alphabetically by price. Hotels are listed first. The number of rooms listed for hotels includes both rooms and suites. Restaurants are listed second. No smoking indicates smoking is not allowed anywhere in the hotel or restaurant. Abbreviations used are AE (American Express), DC (Diner's Club), MC (MasterCard), V (Visa).

■ GENEVA & LAKE GENEVA

CHEXBRES

HOTEL

🏨 **LE BARON TAVERNIER**

🍴 **$$$$**

ROUTE DE LA CORNICHE
1071 CHEXBRES
TEL 021 926 60 00
FAX 021 926 60 01
E-mail: info@barontavernier
.com
www.barontavernier.com

🏨 Hotel 🍴 Restaurant 🛏 No. of Guest Rooms 🪑 No. of Seats 🅿 Parking 🕐 Closed 🛗 Elevator

PRICES

HOTELS
The cost of a double room with private bathroom in peak season is given by $ signs.

$$$$$	Over $550
$$$$	$351–$550
$$$	$251–$350
$$	$125–$250
$	Under $125

RESTAURANTS
The average cost of a two-course meal for one person, excluding tip or drinks, is given by $ signs.

$$$$$	Over $175
$$$$	$126–$175
$$$	$91–$125
$$	$50–$90
$	Under $50

Named for the 17th-century French explorer Jean-Baptiste Tavernier, this small, stylish hotel is at the heart of the Lavaux vineyards just 15 minutes drive from Montreux. It affords exceptional views of Lake Geneva and the mountains. Its open-air lounge bar-cum-restaurant draws Geneva's beautiful people for romantic dinners and lazy Sunday lunches in summer.
⒤ 18 P ⊟ Ⓢ ⓐ All major cards

GENEVA

HOTELS

SOMETHING SPECIAL

🏨 D'ANGLETERRE
🍴 **$$$$$**
QUAI DU MONT-BLANC 17
1201 GENEVA
TEL 022 906 55 55
FAX 022 906 55 56
E-mail: bookan@rchmail.com
www.dangleterrehotel.com
Founded in 1872, this regal family-owned and run five-star hotel has been ranked as one of the world's top 50 hotels. It boasts a relaxed ambiance, impeccable service, and a grandiose lakeside setting opposite Geneva's celebrated Jet d'Eau. Its stylish individually decorated rooms skilfully combine old-world charm with high-tech amenities. Facilities include gourmet dining; sauna and fitness facilities; and the exclusive Leopard Room with an intimate ambiance, cocktails, log fire, and live music six nights a week.
⒤ 45 P ⊟ Ⓢ ⓐ ⓦ ⓐ All major cards

🏨 LA RÉSERVE
$$$$$
ROUTE DE LAUSANNE 301
1293 BELLEVUE
TEL 022 959 59 99
FAX 022 959 59 60
E-mail: infogeneve@lareserve
.ch
www.lareserve.ch/en/home
This extensive hotel and spa complex offers simple, stylish luxury within a tranquil 10-acre lakeside park. Each room has a terrace with views over the gardens and the lake. The acclaimed spa offers a complete program of wellness, beauty therapies, and relaxation. It offers complimentary transfers to the city for shopping and sightseeing in an elegant Venetian water taxi.
⒤ 102 P ⊟ Ⓢ Ⓢ ⓐ ⓐ ⓦ ⓐ All major cards

SOMETHING SPECIAL

🏨 DOMAINE DE
🍴 CHÂTEAUVIEUX
$$$$
CHEMIN DE CHÂTEAUVIEUX 16
1242 PENEY-DESSUS
TEL 022 753 15 11
FAX 022 753 19 24
E-mail: chateauvieux@relaiset
chateau.com
www.chateauvieux.ch/
A beautiful 16th-century stone country house, surrounded by flower-filled gardens, orchards, and vineyards just outside the city center. The country-style rooms have subtle contemporary touches, but the pièce de resistance is the cuisine. Chef Philippe Chevrier creates inventive dishes from the freshest of produce, with herbs and vegetables grown in the garden and his own local wines, all served in a grand, beamed dining room. Geneva's premier address for dining, with two Michelin stars.
⒤ 13 P Ⓢ non-smoking Ⓢ ⓐ All major cards

🏨 TIFFANY
🍴 **$$$$**
RUE DE L'ARQUEBUSE 30
1204 GENEVA
TEL 022 708 16 16
FAX 022 708 16 17
E-mail: info@tiffanyhotel.ch
www.hotel-tiffany.ch
This luxurious belle époque boutique hotel with plush, stylish furnishings and art deco touches is ideally situated at the heart of the cultural and arts district on the fashionable Rive Gauche (Left Bank). There is also a good-value contemporary restaurant and terrace, a cozy wood-paneled bar, and a small basement fitness area.
⒤ 47 P ⊟ Ⓢ ⓐ ⓦ ⓐ All major cards

🏨 EDELWEISS
🍴 **$$**
PLACE DE LA NAVIGATION 2
1201 GENEVA
TEL 022 544 51 51
FAX 022 544 51 99
E-mail: edelweiss@manotel
.com
www.manotel.com

Ⓢ Nonsmoking ⓐ Air-conditioning ⓐ Indoor Pool ⓐ Outdoor Pool ⓦ Health Club ⓐ Credit Cards

If you don't have time to visit the mountains, consider staying here. The snug wood-clad rooms, log fires, hand-painted furniture, and fresh flowers offer all the charm and atmosphere of an authentic alpine chalet, yet the hotel is located at the heart of Geneva and is just a stone's throw from the lake. The eccentric basement restaurant combines authentic local cuisine (fondues, röstis, and raclettes) in a rustic mountain-hut setting, with live folk music and yodeling nightly amid cowbells and other Swiss kitsch.

🛏42 🚪🔄💳💳💳 All major cards

RESTAURANTS

🍴 LE CHAT-BOTTÉ
$$$$$
HÔTEL BEAU-RIVAGE, 13 QUAI DU MONT-BLANC
1201 GENEVA
TEL 022 716 69 20
E-mail: info@beau-rivage.ch
www.beau-rivage.ch
One of Geneva's top restaurants. Expect inventive contemporary French cuisine from Michelin-starred chef Dominique Gaulthier, and an exceptional wine cellar. Located in the elegant Beau-Rivage Hotel, a grandiose belle époque mansion on the Rive Droite, facing the lake. For a unique dining experience, book the Chef's Table (for a maximum of eight people) in the kitchen.

🪑60 🅿💳💳💳 All major cards

🍴 BUFFET DE LA GARE DE CELIGNY
$$$
ROUTE DE FOUNEX 25
1298 CÉLIGNY
TEL 022 776 27 70
FAX 022 776 70 54

E-mail: info@buffet-gare-celigny.ch
www.buffet-gare-celigny.ch
This chic art deco-influenced bistro on the outskirts of Geneva is renowned for its exquisite *filets de perche du Léman* (perch filets), a local specialty fresh from the lake. On Wednesday nights in summer, live jazz in the garden is an added attraction.

🪑65 🅿🕐 Closed Sun. & Mon. 💳💳 AE, MC, V

🍴 AU PIED DE COCHON
$$
PLACE DU BOURG-DU-FOUR 4
1204 GENEVA
TEL 022 310 47 97
FAX 022 310 47 97
E-mail: pieddecochon@switel.ch
www.pied-de-cochon.ch
A Genevois institution at the heart of the Old Town. This lively bar and brasserie, with its traditional interior of mirrors, tiles, and leather banquettes, serves generous portions of Swiss and Lyonnais specialties. These include hearty stews, tripe, and pigs' trotters.

🪑80 🕐 Closed Sun. 💳 All major cards

🍴 CAFÉ DES BAINS
$$
RUE DES BAINS 26
1205 GENEVA
TEL 022 231 57 98
FAX 022 231 58 38
E-mail: info@cafedesbains.com
www.cafedesbains.com
This stylish bar and corner-bistro is situated near the MAMCO in the trendy Plainpalais district, and attracts a loyal, arty Genevois clientele. Its cool, minimalist design is reflected in the light, innovative fusion cuisine.

🪑78 🕐 Closed Sun. & Mon. 💳💳 💳 MC, V

LAUSANNE

HOTELS

🏨 BEAU-RIVAGE PALACE
🍴 $$$$$
PLACE DU PORT 17-19
1006 LAUSANNE
TEL 021 613 33 06
FAX 021 613 33 34
E-mail: info@brp.ch
www.brp.ch
The prestigious, belle époque Beau-Rivage Palace is one of most famous hotels in world, known for its unadulterated luxury, service, and beautiful setting, in a lakeside park. Facilities include three restaurants, including that of French chef Anne Sophie Pic, the only woman to have been awarded three Michelin stars.

🛏168 🅿🔄💳💳💳💳💳 All major cards

SOMETHING SPECIAL

🏨 ANGLETERRE &
🍴 RÉSIDENCE
$$$$
PLACE DU PORT 11
1006 LAUSANNE
TEL 021 613 34 34
FAX 021 613 34 35
E-mail: ar@brp.ch
www.angleterre-residence.ch
Neighboring the Beau-Rivage Palace on Ouchy's attractive tree-lined waterfront, the Angleterre is the hotel's smaller, more affordable option. It is an attractive cluster of six contemporary pavilions, with luxuriously appointed bedrooms and the same exceptional standards of service, but with a more affordable price tag. Guests are entitled to use the spa facilities at the Beau-Rivage.

🛏75 🅿💳💳💳💳💳 💳💳 All major cards

🏨 Hotel 🍴 Restaurant ⓘ No. of Guest Rooms 🪑 No. of Seats 🅿 Parking 🕐 Closed 🔄 Elevator

AULAC
$$$

PLACE DE LA NAVIGATION 4
1006 OUCHY–LAUSANNE
TEL 021 613 15 00
FAX 021 613 15 15
E-mail: aulac@cmdgroup.ch
www.aulac.ch
This comfortable waterside
hotel is near the Olympic
Museum. Ask for a room
overlooking the lake. Its jolly
restaurant—**Le Pirate**—specializes in perch fillets from
the lake, served in a variety
of ways alongside other fish
specialties.
🛏 84 🅿 🔄 🚭 🪑 All major
cards

RESTAURANTS

CAFÉ DU GRÜTLI
$$

RUE MERCERIE 4
1003 LAUSANNE
TEL 021 312 94 93
FAX 021 312 94 93
E-mail: cafedugruetli@
bluewin.ch
www.cafedugruetli.ch
A family-run, old-fashioned
restaurant near the market
square (in the Old Town). It
serves regional home-cooked
fare in a simple wood-paneled
dining room, with a quick,
friendly service. The snails in
garlic and the local specialty
papet vaudois (leek and potato
stew crowned with a fat *saucis-
son vaudois*) are especially tasty,
and there is a good selection
of fondues.
🍽 105 🕐 Closed Sun. 🚭
🪑 MC, V

CAFÉ ROMAND
$–$$

PLACE ST-FRANCOIS 2
1003 LAUSANNE
TEL 021 312 63 75
www.caferomand.com
This authentic café-cum-
brasserie at the heart of town
is a veritable Lausannois

institution. Call in for a coffee
and a croissant or for a more
substantial meal of traditional
dishes from the Vaud region.
The fondues, steaks, and *croûte
au fromage* (melted cheese on
chunky slices of rustic-style
bread) are recommended.
🍽 130 🕐 Closed Sun. 🚭 🪑
MC, V

LUTRY

HOTEL

HOTEL DU RIVAGE
$$

RUE DU RIVAGE 1
1095 LUTRY
TEL 021 796 72 72
FAX 021 796 72 00
E-mail: info@hotelrivage
lutry.ch
www.hotelrivagelutry.
ch/en.html
A charming small hotel, right
on the edge of Lake Geneva.
It is located in the former
Hôtel de Ville (Town Hall),
right by the old port in the
attractive medieval market
town of Lutry. This is an
ideal startpoint for exploring
the prestigious vineyards of
the region. Ask for a room
overlooking the lake with a
backdrop of the Savoy Alps.
🛏 32 🅿 🔄 🚭 🪑 🪑 All
major cards

RESTAURANTS

CAFÉ DE LA POSTE
$$

GRAND RUE 48
1095 LUTRY
TEL 021 791 18 72
Many locals consider this tiny
waterfront restaurant to be
the place in all of Switzerland
to eat *filets de perche* (perch
fillets) served fresh from the
lake with tartar sauce. Early
booking is essential, especially
for a table on the sunny
terrace.

🍽 30 🕐 Closed Sun. & Mon.
🚭 🪑 🪑 AE, V, MC

RESTAURANT DU
LÉMAN
$–$$

GRAND RUE 19
1095 LUTRY
TEL 021 791 33 87
www.restaurant-du-leman.ch
The specialty at this beautiful,
vaulted cellar-restaurant is
fondue Bacchus, made with
local Lavaux white wine and
veal served on wooden skew-
ers and accompanied by an
impressive selection of pickles,
sauces, and potatoes.
🍽 80 🚭 🪑 MC, V

MONTREUX

HOTELS

FAIRMONT LE
MONTREUX PALACE
$$$$$

GRAND-RUE 100
1820 MONTREUX
TEL 021 962 12 12
FAX 021 962 17 17
E-mail: montreux@fairmont
.com
www.fairmont.com/
montreux
This glamorous spa hotel with
floors and glittering chandeliers combines tradition and
innovation to capture all the
style and luxury of the belle
époque. Vladimir Nabokov,
author of *Lolita*, spent 20
years here in its heyday, and
the hotel was also home to
Lord Byron and Leo Tolstoy.
Its illustrious guest list has also
included the Russian composers Tchaikovsky and Stravinsky.
American singer-songwriter
Frank Zappa played a concert
there when someone set the
casino on fire, resulting in the
Deep Purple hit "Smoke on
the Water."
🛏 236 🅿 🔄 🚭 🏊 🏊 🪑
🪑 All major cards

L'ERMITAGE AU LAC
$$$$

RUE DU LAC 75
1820 MONTREUX
TEL 021 964 44 11
www.ermitage-montreux
.com/en/index.php
Expect unadulterated luxury
at this small, chic manor
house on the lakefront near
Montreux. Each of the seven
rooms overlooks the lake and
gardens. Here, too, is one of
the Riviera's finest restaurants.
🚪 7 P 🅂 ⬛ All major cards

LA ROUVENAZ
$$

RUE DU MARCHÉ 1
1820 MONTREUX
TEL 021 963 27 36
FAX 021 963 43 94
E-mail: rouvenaz@bluewin.ch
www.montreux.ch/rouve
naz-hotel
This simple, family-run B&B
is a surprisingly affordable
option in the center of
Montreux. It adjoins a wine
bar and a popular Italian
restaurant, which specializes
in seafood, in particular
moules frites (mussels and
chips) and impressive shellfish
platters.
🚪 7 P 🅂 ⬛ All major cards

RESTAURANT

DU MONTAGNARD
$–$$

ROUTE DU VALLON 2
1832 VILLARD SUR CHAMBY
TEL 021 964 36 84
FAX 021 964 83 49
E-mail: office@montagnard.ch
www.montagnard.ch
Away from the well-beaten
tourist track, this characterful chalet-style restaurant,
high above Montreux, serves
generous portions of hearty
soups, terrines, escargots,
fondues, and other seasonal
Vaudois dishes in a converted
barn with exposed stone walls
and rustic wooden beams.

🪑 120 🕐 Closed Mon. &
Tues. P ⬛ MC, V

VEVEY

HOTEL

DES TROIS
COURONNES
$$$$$

RUE D'ITALIE 49
1800 VEVEY
TEL 021 923 32 00
FAX 021 923 33 99
E-mail: info@hoteltroiscou
ronnes.ch
www.hoteltroiscouronnes.ch
Beside the lake in Vevey's
Vieille Ville, this palatial belle
époque hotel and spa remains
true to Swiss tradition with its
luxurious rooms, exceptional
service, and attention to detail.
It also contains a world-class
spa and wellness center, featuring a beautiful indoor pool
with underwater music.
🚪 71 P 🅂 ⬛ ⬛ ⬛ ⬛
⬛ All major cards

RESTAURANTS

DENIS MARTIN
$$$$

RUE DU CHÂTEAU 2
1800 VEVEY
TEL 021 921 12 10
E-mail: restaurantdenis
martin@bluewin.ch
www.denismartin.ch
Expect exceptional, highly-
creative cuisine at the
eponymous restaurant of one
of the leading chefs in French-
speaking Switzerland. The
spearhead of Swiss molecular
cooking, Martin's innova-
tive and sometimes amusing
menus have earned him two
Michelin stars.
🪑 50 🕐 Closed Sun. & Mon.
🅂 ⬛ ⬛ All major cards

LE MAZOT
$

RUE DU CONSEIL 7

PRICES

HOTELS
The cost of a double room
with private bathroom in
peak season is given by
$ signs.

$$$$$	Over $550
$$$$	$351–$550
$$$	$251–$350
$$	$125–$250
$	Under $125

RESTAURANTS
The average cost of a two-
course meal for one person,
excluding tip or drinks, is
given by $ signs.

$$$$$	Over $175
$$$$	$126–$175
$$$	$91–$125
$$	$50–$90
$	Under $50

TEL 021 921 78 22
1800 VEVEY
A cozy, friendly wood-
paneled bistro at the heart
of the appealing old town. It
specializes in juicy beef and
horse steaks, fondues, *croûtes
au fromage*, and regional fish
dishes. Local wines are poured
from pewter pitchers.
🪑 35 🕐 Closed Wed. & Sun.
lunch ⬛ MC, V

■ BASEL &
NORTHWEST
SWITZERLAND

BASEL

HOTELS

GRAND HOTEL LES
TROIS ROIS
$$$$$

BLUMENRAIN 8, 4001 BASEL

🏨 Hotel 🍴 Restaurant 🚪 No. of Guest Rooms 🪑 No. of Seats P Parking 🕐 Closed ⬛ Elevator

TEL 061 260 50 50
FAX 061 260 50 60
E-mail: info@lestroisrois.com
www.lestroisrois.com
On the banks of the Rhine in the heart of Basel, this luxurious grande dame of the Swiss hospitality industry counts among Europe's oldest city hotels. Over the centuries it has hosted such luminaries as Napoleon, Goethe, Sartre, Picasso, the Dalai Lama, and Queen Elizabeth II. Each room and suite is individually decorated, and the choice of culinary delights—which includes the two-Michelin-starred restaurant **Cheval Blanc**—is fit for a king.
[i] 101 🔒 🚭 🅰 🏊 All major cards

🏨 HOTEL KRAFFT
$$$$
RHEINGASSE 12
4058 BASEL
TEL 061 690 91 30
FAX 061 690 91 31
E-mail: info@hotelkrafft.ch
www.krafftbasel.ch /en/inde
.html
Three medieval craftsmen's houses have been converted to create this stylish, historic city hotel on the Rhine promenade in Kleinbasel. The rooms are smart, unclut-tered, and high-tech, with polished wooden floors. The service is impeccable, and the restaurant and terrace command grand views of the river and the impressive skyline of Grossbasel. Ask for a room overlooking the Rhine.
[i] 48 🔒 🚭 🏊 All major cards

🏨 HOTEL D
$$$
BLUMENRAIN 19
4051 BASEL
TEL 061 272 20 20
FAX 061 272 20 21
E-mail: sleep@hoteld.ch
www.hoteld.ch/uk
Basel's first boutique hotel opened in 2010 and offers its

guests affordable state-of-the-art luxury in the city center. Each of the comfortable yet minimalist rooms features free Wi-Fi, an iPod dock, and back-lit LCD televisions with laptop connections. There is also a sauna and fitness studio.
[i] 48 🔒 🚭 🅰 🏋 🏊 AE, MC, V

🍴 HOTEL BRASSERIE AU VIOLON
$$
IM LOHNHOF 4
4051 BASEL
TEL 061 269 87 11
FAX 061 269 87 12
E-mail: info@au-violon.com
www.au-violon.com
This charming hotel offers the ultimate escape—with simple, stylish rooms fashioned from the prison cells of the former city jail. Centrally located in the Old Town, the building was also once a convent. Its highly rated brasserie is particularly pleasant during summer months with al fresco dining under a big maple tree in the fountain-splashed courtyard.
[i] 20 🔒 🚭 🏊 AE, MC, V

RESTAURANTS

🍴 STUCKI
$$$
BRUDERHOLZALLEE 42
4059 BASEL
TEL 061 361 82 22
FAX 061 361 82 03
E-mail: info@stuckibasel.ch
www.stuckibasel.ch
A modern, elegant restaurant, set in a mansion amid flower-filled gardens. It is helmed by one of Switzerland's few Michelin-starred female chefs, Tanja Grandits. Her light seasonal dishes, created with an imaginative twist and with particular attention to fragrance, color, and texture, are a feast for the senses.

🪑 80 🕐 Closed Sun. & Mon. 🚭 🏊 AE, MC, V

🍴 BEROWER PARK
$$
BASELSTRASSE 77
4125 RIEHEN
TEL 061 645 97 70
FAX 061 645 97 60
E-mail: restaurant@beyeler
.com
www.beyeler.com
This elegant restaurant in the historic Villa Berower is in the grounds of the world-famous Fondation Beyeler gallery (see p. 90). Choose a table in the garden and tuck into fine Mediterranean cuisine, with a backdrop of cows grazing in the surrounding countryside.
🪑 85 🚭 🏊 All major cards

🍴 ZUM SCHMALE WURF
$$
RHEINGASSE 10
4058 BASEL
TEL 061 683 33 25
FAX 061 683 33 27
E-mail: info@schmalewurf.ch
www.schmalewurf.ch
Given its appealing location beside the Rhine, and its lively, sunny riverside terrace, this trendy yet classic restaurant is surprisingly affordable. The cuisine is primarily Italian with a regional touch. Expect such specials as mouthwatering antipasti, homemade gnocchi, and mussels with garlic in a white wine sauce.
🪑 46 🚭 🏊 MC, V

🍴 CAFÉ PAPIERMÜHLE
$
BASLER PAPIERMÜHLE
ST ALBAN TAL 35
4052 BASEL
TEL 061 272 48 48
E-mail: restaurant@papier
muehle.ch
www.papiermuehle.ch
This small museum café in Basel's "Little Venice" district is a popular brunch spot for locals who pop in after a

pleasant walk along the St. Alban Rheinweg riverside path. For a light lunch, the homemade soups, salads, quiches, and regional specialties are recommended. Weather permitting, you can sit outside on the terrace beside the old mill stream.
🕐 Closed Mon. 🆂 🆎 MC, V

FRIBOURG

HOTELS

SOMETHING SPECIAL

🏨 AUBERGE AUX 4 VENTS
🍴 $$–$$$
ROUTE DE GRANDFEY 124
1702 FRIBOURG
TEL 026 347 36 00
FAX 026 347 36 10
www.auberge.aux4vents.ch
A quirky boutique hotel in a picturesque 17th-century country house overlooking the city of Fribourg. There are just eight themed rooms, each with individual décor ranging from ultra-modern to rustic baroque. Room three (Bleu) even has a bathtub on rails for al fresco bathing on a secluded balcony. There is an outdoor swimming pool, set in beautiful, flower-filled gardens, and the restaurant serves wholesome, seasonal dishes using home-grown produce.
🛈 8 🅿 🆂 🛋 🆎 MC, V

🏨 HOTEL DES ALPES
🍴 $$
HAUPTSTRASSE 29
3186 DÜDINGEN
TEL 026 493 32 40
FAX 026 493 32 86
E-mail: info@desalpes.org
www.desalpes.org
On the outskirts of Fribourg on the main A12 road to Bern, this small friendly hotel is beside the train station in the town of Düdingen. It offers clean, simply decorated rooms

and an excellent restaurant based on fresh, organic regional produce.
🛈 6 🅿 🆂 🆎 AE, DC, MC, V

GRUYÈRES

🏨 HOSTELLERIE ST.-GEORGES
$$–$$$
1663 GRUYÈRES
TEL 026 921 19 33
FAX 026 921 25 52
E-mail: hostellerie-st-georges@swissonline.ch
www.chevaliers-gruyeres.ch
With their embroidered bed linens and regional furnishings, the bedrooms of this traditional-style hotel in the center of Gruyères village are brimming with Swiss homeliness, as well as having all modern amenities. Choose a room overlooking the village, or a more peaceful one with views over the rolling Pre-Alps. There is also an excellent rotisserie-style restaurant serving traditional cuisine, a sunny terrace, and a café.
🛈 34 🆂 🆎 All major cards

LE LOCLE

🏨 LA MAISON DU BOIS
$
GRAND-RUE 22
2400 LE LOCLE
TEL 079 342 25 37
E-mail: maisondubois@bluewin.ch
www.maisondubois.ch
Wind the clocks back at Le Locle, the cradle of Swiss watchmaking. This characterful 18th-century house once belonged to a watchmaking company that created their timepieces on the very workbench which now carries the breakfast buffet.
🪑 5 🆂 AE, MC, V

MOLÉSON-SUR-GRUYÈRES

SOMETHING SPECIAL

🍴 FROMAGERIE D'ALPAGE
$–$$
PLACE DE L'AIGLE 12
1663 MOLÉSON-SUR-GRUYÈRES
TEL 026 921 10 44
www.fromagerie-alpage.ch
A simple, albeit touristic, chalet restaurant with benches and trestle tables and a sunny hillside terrace just above Moléson village. Their local specialties are truly delicious, and include *soupe du chalet* (chalet soup); *croûte au fromage* (melted cheese and wine on bread); platters of cheeses and cold cuts; and raclettes and fondues, all finished off with meringues and double Gruyères cream. There are cheese-making demonstrations at 10 a.m. (see p. 108).
🪑 60 🕐 Closed Oct.–Apr.
🆂 🆎 MC, V

NEUCHÂTEL

HOTELS

🏨 PALAFITTE
$$$$$
ROUTE DES GOUTTES-D'OR 2
2000 NEUCHÂTEL
TEL 032 723 02 02
FAX 032 723 02 03
E-mail: reservation@palafitte.ch
www.palafitte.ch
A unique five-star hotel comprising a series of sleek, modern suites built on stilts. It appears to float above the water on the edge of Lac de Neuchâtel. Each suite features cutting-edge, contemporary design to complement the glassy lake and angular alpine backdrop.
🛈 40 🆂 🆔 🆎 All major cards

SOMETHING SPECIAL

🏨 A MAISON DU PRUSSIEN

$$$–$$$$

RUE DES TUNNELS 11
2000 NEUCHÂTEL
TEL 032 730 54 54
FAX 032 730 21 43
www.hotel-prussien.ch

This tranquil, romantic hideaway is set in a sensitively restored former brewery and ancient watermill west of the town center. The sumptuous country-style bedrooms are each individually furnished, with stylish architectural features of wood and stone. A gourmet restaurant adjoins the hotel.

🛏 10 🟥 🔇 AE, MC, V

🏨 L'AUBIER

$

RUE DU CHÂTEAU 1
2000 NEUCHÂTEL
TEL 032 710 18 58
FAX 032 710 18 59
E-mail: lecafe@aubier.ch
www.aubier.ch

This tiny, friendly café-hotel is excellent value, given its superb location in the heart of the old town. Breakfast is served in the popular ground floor café, which specializes in exclusively organic produce. This includes wines, herbal teas, handmade syrups, and delicious cheeses—all from the L'Aubier Eco-Hotel and biodynamic farm at Montezillon in the foothills of the Jura mountains.

ℹ️ 9 🟩 🔇 AE, V

YVERDON-LES-BAINS

🏨 GRAND HOTEL DES BAINS

$$$$

AVENUE DES BAINS 22
1401 YVERDON-LES-BAINS
TEL 024 424 64 64

FAX 024 424 64 65
E-mail: reservation@grandhotelyverdon.ch
www.grandhotelyverdon.ch

An appealing blend of historic architecture and contemporary interior features greets guests at this luxury spa hotel, set in its own parkland, with a thermal swimming pool, a private wellness suite, spa treatments and massages, and direct access to the town's public Centre Thermal (see p. 97).

ℹ️ 120 🅿️ 🟩 🔇 🏊 🎾 🔇 All major cards

◼ BERN & BERNESE OBERLAND

ADELBODEN

🏨 THE CAMBRIAN

🍽 **$$$**

DORFSTRASSE 7
3715 ADELBODEN
TEL 033 673 8383
FAX 033 673 8380
E-mail: info@thecambriana
delboden.com
www.thecambrianadelboden
.com

One of the delights of this luxury hotel and award-winning spa just outside Adelboden is its little added extras to make you feel at home. The top-notch restaurant features "new alpine" cuisine—a contemporary interpretation of mountain classics.

ℹ️ 71 🅿️ 🟩 🔇 🏊 🏊 🎾
🔇 All major cards

BERN

HOTELS

🏨 BELLEVUE PALACE

🍽 **$$$$$**

KOCHERGASSE 3-6
3000 BERN 7
TEL 031 320 45 45
FAX 031 320 46 46
E-mail: info@bellevue-palace.ch

www.bellevue-palace.ch/
meta/home

Next to the Bundeshaus, the seat of the Swiss government, this luxurious belle époque hotel has welcomed guests for over a hundred years. It has grand salons and spacious bedrooms overlooking the Jungfrau and the Bernese Alps. The service is impeccable, and a meal eaten al fresco on the romantic **Bellevue Terrasse**, high above the Aare River, is one of the finest dining experiences in Bern.

ℹ️ 126 🟩 🔇 🔇 🔇 All major cards

🏨 BELLE EPOQUE

🍽 **$$$**

GERECHTIGKEITSGASSE 18
3011 BERN
TEL 031 311 43 36
FAX 031 311 39 36
www.belle-epoque.ch

A charming, friendly four-star hotel at the heart of the Altstadt, furnished with original art nouveau paintings, furnishings, and floral fabrics. Its popular bar and restaurant features occasional live jazz on Sunday evenings.

ℹ️ 17 🟩 🔇 🔇 All major cards

🏨 NYDECK

$$

GERECHTIGKEITSGASSE 1
3011 BERN
TEL 031 311 86 86
FAX 031 312 20 54
E-mail: info@hotelnydeck.ch
www.hotelnydeck.ch.

Thanks to its central yet quiet location on one of the oldest in Bern's Altstadt, this friendly bed and breakfast hotel is a popular choice. Its rooms are simple and clean and all have en suite facilities, while the lively café bar, pavement terrace, and pizzeria are great for people-watching.

ℹ️ 12 🟩 🔇 All major cards

🟩 Nonsmoking 🔇 Air-conditioning 🏊 Indoor Pool 🏊 Outdoor Pool 🎾 Health Club 🔇 Credit Cards

RESTAURANTS

🍴 KORNHAUSKELLER
$$$-$$$$
KORNHAUSPLATZ 18
3000 BERN 7
TEL 031 327 72 72
FAX 031 327 72 71
E-mail: kornhaus@bindella.ch
www.kornhauskeller.ch
This atmospheric converted granary feels more like an underground church than a restaurant with its vaulted ceilings, candlelight, and frescoes. It rates among Bern's finest eateries, serving primarily Mediterranean and traditional Bernese cuisine. Upstairs, the Kornhaus Café is a popular after-work meeting point with a bar and a large terrace.
🔧 240 🆂 🅰 All major cards

🍴 SCHWELLENMÄTTELI
$$$
DALMAZIQUAI 11
3013 BERN
TEL 031 350 50 01
www.schwellenmaetteli.ch
Join the smart set at this striking restaurant on Bern's very own "Riviera" on the Aare River. Enjoy fusion cuisine and eye-popping brunch buffets, either in the traditional **Casa**, or in the cutting-edge **Terrasse** restaurant, with its large wooden deck. In winter, there is also a fondue hut (Wed.–Sat.). In summer it's hard to beat the ultra-cool Kultur-Lounge garden for riverside cocktails.
🔧 Casa 70; Terrasse 120
🕐 Closed Sun. 🆂 🅰 All major cards

🍴 CASA NOVO
$$
LÄUFERPLATZ 6
3011 BERN
TEL 031 992 44 44
E-mail: info@casa-novo.ch
www.casa-novo.ch
Situated by the Aare, with a romantic terrace lit by fairy lights, this airy, stylish restaurant and Vinothek serves light tapas dishes, refined Mediterranean cuisine, and an excellent selection of Swiss and European wines.
🔧 55 🕐 Closed Mon. & Sun. from Oct.–April 🆂 🅰 AE, MC, V

🍴 KLÖTZLIKELLER
$
GERECHTIGKEITSGASSE 62
3011 BERN
TEL 031 311 74 56 OR
031 311 97 10
www.kloetzlikeller.ch.
Bern's oldest wine tavern, dating from 1635, serves a wide choice of wines by the glass, accompanied by delicious cold cuts, cheese platters, local fare, and seasonal specialties.
🔧 60 🕐 Closed Sun. & Mon. in summer 🆂 🅰 MC, V

BIEL/BIENNE

SOMETHING SPECIAL

🏨 HOTEL-RESTAURANT
🍴 ST. PETERSINSEL
$$$
ST. PETERSINSEL
3235 ERLACH
TEL 032 338 11 14
FAX 032 338 25 82
E-mail: welcome@st-peters insel.ch
www.st-petersinsel.ch
St. Peter's Island is a rural hideaway, accessible by boat from Erlach, Lüscherz, and Biel. Set in beautiful grounds, the stylish rooms are of ecclesiastical simplicity, and the elegant restaurant serves fresh Bielersee fish and wines from the surrounding vineyards.
🛏 15 🕐 Closed Nov.–mid-March 🆂 🅰 All major cards

PRICES

HOTELS
The cost of a double room with private bathroom in peak season is given by $ signs.

$$$$$	Over $550
$$$$	$351–$550
$$$	$251–$350
$$	$125–$250
$	Under $125

RESTAURANTS
The average cost of a two-course meal for one person, excluding tip or drinks, is given by $ signs.

$$$$$	Over $175
$$$$	$126–$175
$$$	$91–$125
$$	$50–$90
$	Under $50

BRIENZ

🏨 GRANDHOTEL GIESSBACH
$$$
3855 BRIENZ
TEL 033 952 25 25
FAX 033 952 25 30
www.giessbach.ch
A grand and atmospheric retreat from the bustle of everyday life, this elegantly-restored *fin de siècle* hotel enjoys a unique setting amid wooded slopes overlooking Brienzersee. It is reached by its own funicular from the lakeshore beside the Giessbach waterfalls.
🛏 70 🕐 Closed mid-Oct.–late April 🅿 🛗 🆂 🅰 AE, MC, V

DÜRRENROTH (EMMENTAL)

SOMETHING SPECIAL

ROMANTIK BÄREN DÜRRENROTH
$$
3465 DÜRRENROTH
TEL 062 959 00 88
FAX 062 959 01 22
E-mail: info@baeren-duer renroth.ch
www.baeren-duerrenroth.ch
The hotel occupies three late baroque buildings at the heart of Emmental. Together with the Gothic church and village square, they form a "monument of national importance." Most of the individually decorated bedrooms and suites are in a stone country house. There is also an intimate wine-cellar bar, flower-festooned gardens, and an award-winning restaurant serving regional specialties. Simpler rooms in a converted stable building provide a more affordable option for guests on a limited budget.
❶ 28 🅿 ➡ Ⓢ 🗟 AE, MC, V

GRINDELWALD

GLETSCHERGARTEN
$$$
3818 GRINDELWALD
TEL 033 853 17 21
FAX 033 853 29 57
E-mail: info@hotel-gletscher garten.ch
www.hotel-gletschergarten.ch
This flower-clad century-old chalet on the main street remains largely untouched by time, with its warm welcome, homely rooms, log fires, and peaceful setting.
❶ 50 🅿 ➡ Ⓢ 🗟 DC, MC, V

ONKEL TOM'S HÜTTE
$
IM GRABEN 4
3818 GRINDELWALD

TEL 033 853 52 39
Wood-fired pizzas and copious salads to energize skiers and boarders, in a cozy wooden cabin near the Firstbahn cable car. The wine selection is impressive too.
🕒 Closed Mon., June, & Nov.
🗟 MC, V

GUTTANNEN (GRIMSEL PASS)

GRIMSEL HOSPIZ
$$$
3864 GUTTANNEN
TEL 033 982 46 11
FAX 033 982 46 05
E-mail: welcome@grimsel hotels.ch
www.grimselwelt.ch
An inn has welcomed travelers here since 1142 when it was registered as Switzerland's first inn. The current Grimsel Hospice, built in 1932, was fêted as Europe's first hotel with electric heating. It has recently undergone some major renovations and now offers guests comfy armchairs, blazing log fires, and every imaginable comfort, although its bleak and rocky setting remains unchanged.
❶ 28 🕒 Closed May, Nov., & Dec. 🅿 ➡ Ⓢ 🗟 AE, MC, V

GSTAAD

GRAND HOTEL BELLEVUE
$$$$$
3780 GSTAAD
TEL 033 748 00 00
FAX 033 748 00 01
E-mail: info@bellevue-gstaad .ch
www.bellevue-gstaad.ch
An opulent five-star hotel in stunning parkland near the pedestrian zone of Gstaad. It features contemporary guest rooms, sophisticated dining, a top-notch spa, an in-house cinema, a piano bar, and a snug carnotzet wine bar.

❶ 57 🅿 🍽 Ⓢ 🗟 🛡
🗟 All major cards

POSTHOTEL RÖSSLI
$$$
PROMENADE 10
3780 GSTAAD
TEL 033 748 42 42
FAX 033 748 42 43
E-mail: info@posthotelroes sli.ch
www.posthotelroessli.ch
This cozy, family-run enterprise is the oldest hotel in town, built in 1845 and centrally positioned. The comfortable, pine-clad rooms have been modernized recently, and the two restaurants share a menu of tasty Swiss dishes, including their specialty fondue.
❶ 36 🅿 Ⓢ 🗟 MC, V

BERGHAUS EGGLI
$
TSCHAANEREWEG 8 (AT THE TOP OF THE EGGLI CABLE CAR)
3780 GSTAAD
TEL 033 748 96 12
FAX 033 748 96 13
E-mail: rest.eggli@gstaad.ch
A popular alpine chalet-restaurant with a large south-facing terrace overlooking the Bernese, Valaisan, Vaudois, and Fribourg Alps. Enjoy mountaintop fondue, raclette and wine evenings, and live folk music on Sundays, before skiing back to the resort.
🔵 300 Ⓢ

INTERLAKEN

HOTELS

VICTORIA-JUNGFRAU GRAND HOTEL & SPA
$$$$$
HÖHEWEG 41
3800 INTERLAKEN
TEL 033 828 28 28
FAX 033 828 28 80
E-mail: interlaken@victoria-jungfrau.ch

www.victoria-jungfrau.ch/en
You will enjoy a wonderful view of the Jungfrau from this grand 19th-century building. Today, it rates as Interlaken's top hotel, steeped in luxury, with ornamental gardens, a supervised kindergarten, a tennis center, and a spa.

🛈 212 🅿 Ⓢ 🖥 🛌 🍴 🛗
🅢 All major cards

🏨 ALPHORN
$$
ROTHORNSTRASSE 29A
3800 INTERLAKEN
TEL 033 822 30 51
FAX 033 823 30 69
E-mail: info@hotel-alphorn.ch
www.hotel-alphorn.ch
Excellent value for money, this simple but friendly B&B near the train station, just three minutes walk from the town center, is a popular, affordable choice for families. Completely renovated in 2011.

🛈 13 🅿 🛗 🅢 AE, MC, V

KALTACKER (EMMENTAL)

🏨 LANDGASTHOF LUEG
$$
LUEG 535
3413 KALTACKER
TEL 034 435 18 81
FAX 034 435 18 82
E-mail: info@lueg.ch
www.lueg.ch
You will find luxury with an amusing twist at this pretty country hotel. The tasteful decor of each room has a different theme, ranging from golfing and hunting to angels and roses. Enjoy the gastronomic Emmentaler cuisine and explore the scenic surroundings using the Lueg's own hiking maps.

🛈 21 🅿 🛗 Ⓢ 🅢 AE, MC, V

KANDERSTEG

🏨 WALDHOTEL DOLDENHORN
$$$
3718 KANDERSTEG
TEL 033 675 81 81
E-mail: info@doldenhorn.ch
www.doldenhorn.ch/e/index
.php
This four-star oasis of calm is situated at the far end of the Kander Valley, surrounded by country meadows and rugged mountain landscape. Its quaint, rustic facade belies a luxurious interior, with modern bedrooms, cozy lounges, gourmet dining, and a sumptuous spa.

🛈 42 🅿 🛗 Ⓢ 🖥 🍴 🅢 All major cards

KLEINE SCHEIDEGG

SOMETHING SPECIAL

🏨 HÔTEL BELLEVUE DES ALPES
$$$$
3801 KLEINE SCHEIDEGG
TEL 033 855 12 12
FAX 033 855 12 94
www.welcome@scheidegg-hotels.ch
www.scheidegg-hotels.ch
Appointed Swiss Historic Hotel of the Year 2011, this is the most beautifully preserved *fin de siècle* mountain hotel in the Alps. Once the last tourist train has departed from the Jungfrau, this traditional 19th-century hotel at the foot of the Eiger is a veritable oasis of alpine peace. The atmospheric wood-paneled bar is hung with photos of the heroic climbers who have scaled the Eiger's north face over the decades.

🛈 50 🅢 MC, V

MEIRINGEN

🏨 PARKHOTEL DU SAUVAGE

$$$
BAHNHOFSTRASSE 30
3860 MEIRINGEN
TEL 033 972 18 80
FAX 033 972 18 81
E-mail: info@sauvage.ch
www.sauvage.ch/en/Offers/
News/Welcome
The Hotel Englisherhof, where Sherlock Holmes stayed in Arthur Conan Doyle's fictional detective tales, was based on this beautiful art nouveau hotel in the heart of the Haslital. It is near the spectacular Reichenbach Falls, where Holmes fell to his death. The bedrooms are modern, but the reception rooms of the hotel still evoke the spirit of the 1880s.

🛈 71 🅿 🛗 Ⓢ 🅢 All major cards

MÜRREN

🏨 ALPENRUH
$$
3825 MÜRREN
TEL 033 856 88 00
FAX 033 856 88 88
E-mail: alpenruh@schilthorn
.ch
www.alpenruh-muerren
.ch/en
A picture-perfect Alpine chalet hotel, with beautiful interiors and inspirational views across the Lauterbrunnen Valley to the Jungfrau, Eiger, and Mönch. Conveniently situated for skiers by the Schilthorn cable car.

🛈 26 🛗 Ⓢ 🅢 All major cards

🍴 PIZ GLORIA
$
3825 MÜRREN
TEL 033 82 60 007
FAX 033 82 60 009
E-mail: info@schilthorn.ch
www.schilthorn.ch
Atop the Schilthorn (9,800 feet/2,970 m), this revolving restaurant features in the 007 movie *On Her Majesty's Secret Service*, and is the start point for

ski racing's oldest amateur top-to-bottom race, the Inferno Downhill. Expect breathtaking 360° alpine views.

🏕 408 🚭 🏊 All major cards

SOLOTHURN

🏨 HOTEL AN DER AARE
$$
OBERER WINKEL 2
4500 SOLOTHURN
TEL 032 626 24 00
FAX 032 626 24 10
E-mail: info@hotelaare.ch
www.hotelaare.ch
This stylish hotel combines modern amenities with 18th-century architecture. On the banks of the Aare River in the town center, with a beautiful waterside terrace. Excellent breakfast buffet.

🛏 16 🅿 🚭 🏊 All major cards

■ ALPES VAUDOISES & VALAIS

CHÂTEAU D'OEX

🏨 HOSTELLERIE BON
🍴 ACCUEIL
$$
LA FRASSE
1660 CHÂTEAU-D'OEX
TEL 026 924 63 20
FAX 026 924 51 26
www.bonaccueil.ch
Request a room in the old part of this authentic 18th-century chalet, with beautiful wood-paneled rooms and traditional country-style furnishings. Well-situated for pre-alpine walks in summer and easy access to the Glacier 300 ski area, there is also a candlelit restaurant serving Mediterranean-inspired and Swiss fare, and a cozy cellar bar.

🛏 17 🅿 🚭 🏊 All major cards

CRANS-MONTANA

HOTELS

🏨 HOSTELLERIE DU PAS
🍴 DE L'OURS
$$$$$
41 RUE DU PAS DE L'OURS
3963 CRANS-MONTANA
027 485 93 33
027 485 93 34
E-mail: pasdelours@relaischateaux.com
www.pasdelours.ch
Deluxe accommodation in an authentic mountain chalet with a warm, cozy ambiance. Two top-notch restaurants, including the gourmet L'Ours (closed Sun. eve, Mon., & Tues. lunch), with exquisite seasonal cuisine created by Michelin-starred Provencal chef Franck Renaud. The spa offers pampering packages.

🛏 15 🕒 Closed May & Nov.
🅿 🚭 🚭 🏊 🚿 🎾 🏊 All major cards

🏨 HOTEL DU LAC
$$
3963 CRANS-MONTANA
TEL 027 481 34 14
FAX 027 481 51 80
E-mail: hotel-du-lac@bluewin.ch
www.hoteldulac-crans-montana.ch/en/home.html
One of the more affordable options in the Crans-Montana region, this small, friendly, chalet-style hotel boasts a picturesque setting beside Lake Grenon, and offers simple, modern half-board accommodation. It also has a Turkish bath and sauna, an adjoining internet café, and rental facilities for pedalos, snowshoes, and mountain bikes.

🛏 30 🅿 🚭 🏊 🎾 🏊 AE, MC, V

LES DIABLERETS

🍴 BOTTA 3000
$$

TEL 024 492 09 31
FAX 024 492 09 41
www.glacier3000.ch/
This ultramodern, cuboid restaurant atop the Glacier 3000 ski zone is a veritable tour de force of Alpine design, created by the eminent Ticinese architect Mario Botta. Easily accessed by cable car, the food features specialties from the three cantons of Vaud, Bern, and Valais. The view from the sun terrace embraces 24 peaks higher than 13,000 feet (4,000 m).

🏕 270 🚭 🏊 All major cards

LEYSIN

🏨 LE GRAND CHALET
$
1854 LEYSIN
TEL 024 493 01 01
FAX 024 494 16 14
E-mail: hotel.grand-chalet@bluewin.ch
www.grand-chalet.ch/english/index.html
This traditional-style, family-run chalet is ideally placed at the top of the village, near the train station and the ski lifts, and commands grand views of the Alpes Vaudoises, Valais, and the French Alps beyond. Its large outdoor hot-tub sooths the aching muscles of skiers in winter—and walkers and mountain bikers in summer.

🛏 30 🅿 🚭 🚭 🏊 All major cards

🍴 KUKLOS
$
1854 LEYSIN
TEL 024 494 31 41
FAX 024 494 31 40
www.teleleysin.ch
Eye-catching and ultra-modern Kuklos (meaning circle in Greek) is a revolving restaurant at 6,719 feet (2,048 m), with impressive Alpine views that span the Eiger to the Matterhorn and

🚭 Nonsmoking ❄ Air-conditioning 🏊 Indoor Pool 🏊 Outdoor Pool 🎾 Health Club 🏊 Credit Cards

Mont Blanc. Its sleek, mirrored edifice reflects the surrounding mountains, thereby cleverly blending into the landscape. Its sun terrace is popular year-round with skiers and walkers. In summer it is an inspirational venue for classical and folk music concerts.

🛏 250 Ⓢ ♿ All major cards

SAAS ALMAGELL

🏨 HOTEL PIRMIN ZURBRIGGEN
$$
3905 SAAS ALMAGELL
TEL 027 957 23 01
FAX 027 957 33 13
E-mail: pirmin.zurbriggen@rhone.ch
www.wellnesshotel-zurbriggen.ch/en
A stylish hotel and spa complex at the heart of the Saastal, with easy access to the ski slopes. In winter, special ski excursions can be arranged in the company of "Swiss Skier of the Twentieth Century" Pirmin Zurbriggen (b. 1963), who grew up in the valley and whose family runs the hotel.

🛏 20 🛗 Ⓢ ♨ 🍴 ♿ MC, V

SAAS-FEE

🏨 ALPHUBEL
$$$
3906 SAAS-FEE
TEL 027 958 63 63
FAX 027 958 63 64
E-mail: hotel.alphubel@saas-fee.ch
www.hotelalphubel.ch/en/home
This friendly hotel is a popular choice for families, with a large adventure garden. Year-round entertainment includes night-time tobogganing in winter, guided nature trails, and hiking and mountain tours in summer.

🛏 35 🛗 Ⓢ ♿ All major cards

🍴 FLETSCHHORN
$$$
WALDHOTEL FLETSCHHORN
3906 SAAS FEE
TEL 027 9572131
FAX 027 9572187
E-mail: info@fletschhorn.ch
www.fletschhorn.ch/english/index.html
One of Switzerland's top restaurants, with one Michelin star, attached to a gourmet cookery school. It is worth walking the short distance outside the resort center to taste the exquisite alpine cuisine of the exceptional chef, Markus Neff.

🛏 60 🕐 Closed mid-Apr.–mid-June & mid-Nov.–mid-Dec. Ⓢ 🚹 ♿ All major cards

SIERRE

SOMETHING SPECIAL

🍴 DIDIER DE COURTEN
$$$$
HOTEL TERMINUS
1 RUE DU BOURG
3960 SIERRE
TEL 027 455 13 51
FAX 027 456 44 91
E-mail: info@hotel-terminus.ch
www.hotel-terminus.ch/en.html
The two-Michelin-starred eponymous restaurant of local chef Didier de Courten serves inspirational fusion cuisine in an elegant dining room or on a patio under the shade of plane trees. With its colors, flavors, and fragrances from around the world, each dish is a feast for the senses, and there is an impressive selection of fine Swiss wines.

🛏 50 🕐 Closed Sun. & Mon; also late Dec.–mid-Jan. & July–early Aug. 🅿 Ⓢ 🚹 ♿ AE, MC, V

PRICES

HOTELS
The cost of a double room with private bathroom in peak season is given by $ signs.

$$$$$	Over $550
$$$$	$351–$550
$$$	$251–$350
$$	$125–$250
$	Under $125

RESTAURANTS
The average cost of a two-course meal for one person, excluding tip or drinks, is given by $ signs.

$$$$$	Over $175
$$$$	$126–$175
$$$	$91–$125
$$	$50–$90
$	Under $50

ST LUC

HOTELS

🏨 BELLA-TOLA
🍴 **$$$$**
3961 ST-LUC
TEL 027 475 14 44
FAX 027 475 29 98
E-mail: info@bellatola.ch
www.bellatola.ch/en
An elegant, country-style hotel with beautiful antiques, pinewood parquet flooring, and opulent bedrooms. It is complemented by a stunning spa complex. Homely touches include a log fire, afternoon tea, and homemade chocolates. Ask for a south-facing room with a balcony and views toward the Matterhorn. Within the historic hotel, the cozy, wood-paneled **Tzambron** Alpine restaurant serves

a wide array of regional cheese specialties, accompanied by an excellent choice of local wines.
ⓘ 32 🕒 Closed May–June & Nov. 🄿 🔁 🆂 🔲 🔲
🔲 MC, V

SOMETHING SPECIAL

🏨 WEISSHORN
🍴 $$$
3961 ST-LUC
TEL 027 475 11 06
FAX 027 475 11 05
E-mail: info@weisshorn.ch
www.weisshorn.ch
Isolated at an altitude of 7,667 feet (2,337 m), this mountain hotel is accessible only on foot (the shortest route is from St. Luc). The climb is richly rewarded by simple pine-clad bedrooms, shared bathrooms, and a restaurant with spectacular views across the Val d'Anniviers to the Rhône valley and beyond. Half board only.
ⓘ 33 🕒 Closed Sun. & Mon. during April–May & Nov.
🆂 🔲 MC, V

VERBIER

HOTELS

🏨 THE LODGE
$$$$$
CHEMIN DE PLÉNADZEU
1936 VERBIER
TEL 027 775 22 44; (877) 577 8777 (U.S.)
E-mail: enquiriesusa@virgin limitededition.com
www.thelodge.virgin.com
Unadulterated luxury year-round can be found at Richard Branson's alpine escape, which opened in 2007. It is a picturesque chalet hidden in the woods just off one of Verbier's acclaimed ski runs. Facilities include an indoor heated pool, spa, and mini ice-rink.
ⓘ 9 🄿 🔁 🆂 🆂 🔲 🔲
🔲 All major cards

🏨 CHALET D'ADRIEN
$$$$
CHEMIN DES CREUX
1936 VERBIER
TEL 027 771 62 00
FAX 037 771 62 24
e-mail: info@chalet-adrien .com
www.chalet-adrien.com/en
Indulge yourself in deluxe Alpine style at this beautiful five-star chalet overlooking the resort near the Savoleyres lifts. Soothe aching muscles after a day on the slopes in the stylish spa, fitness suite, or rooftop swimming pool.
ⓘ 29 🄿 🔁 🆂 🆂 🔲 🔲
🔲 All major cards

🏨 MIRABEAU
$$
RUE DE LA TINTAZ
1936 VERBIER
TEL 027 771 63 35
FAX 027 771 63 30
E-mail: mirabeau@verbier.ch
www.mirabeauhotel.ch
In high season, you can ski straight to the door of this quiet, friendly B&B near the Médran cable station. There is a sauna, steam room, bar, and a cozy log fire in the evenings.
ⓘ 25 🄿 🔁 🆂 🆂 D, MC, V

ZERMATT

HOTELS

🏨 RIFFELALP RESORT
$$$$$
3920 ZERMATT
TEL 027 699 05 55
FAX 027 699 05 50
E-mail: reservation@riffelalp .com
www.riffelalp.com/the_ resort.html
Enjoy the high life at this ski-in, ski-out hotel at 7,290 feet (2,222 m), with magnificent alpine views (especially of the Matterhorn), and five-star amenities including well-appointed guest rooms, a

sumptuous spa, and the highest outdoor pool in Europe. In winter, the hotel offers a ski guiding service.
ⓘ 72 🕒 Closed mid-April–late May, Oct., & Nov. 🔁 🆂 🔲
🔲 🔲 🔲 All major cards

🏨 MONTE ROSA
$$$
BAHNHOFSTRASSE 80
3920 ZERMATT
TEL 027 966 03 33
FAX 027 966 03 30
E-mail: mr.reservation@ seilerhotels.ch
www.monterosazermatt.ch
This tradition-steeped hotel was founded in 1839. Today it combines luxury with a congenial home-away-from-home atmosphere and draws a loyal clientele. The spa at the neighboring Mont Cervin sister hotel is free to all guests.
ⓘ 41 🕒 Closed mid-April–mid-Jun. & Oct.–mid-Dec.
🔁 🆂 🆂 🔲 🔲 All major cards

RESTAURANT

🍴 STOCKHORN GRILL
$$$
RIEDSTRASSE
3920 ZERMATT
TEL 027 967 1747
www.grill-stockhorn.ch
With its delicious specialty meats grilled over a wood fire, and other tasty Swiss fare, the Stockhorn Grill—owned by the legendary Matterhorn guide Emil Julen—appeals to both locals and visitors. There is also simple, surprisingly affordable accommodation.
🔲 137 🕒 Mon., mid-May–mid-Jun., & mid-Oct.–mid-Nov. 🆂 🔲 All major cards

▥ LUZERN & CENTRAL SWITZERLAND

EINSIEDELN

🏨 LINDE
🍴 $$$

SCHMIEDENSTRASSE 29
8840 EINSIEDELN
TEL 055 418 48 48
FAX 055 418 48 49

E-mail: hotel@linde-einsie
deln.ch
www.linde-einsiedeln.ch
A centrally located hotel
overlooking the monastery.
The rooms are not particularly
inspiring. Choose between
reasonably priced "pilgrim"
and standard rooms or treat
yourself to a luxurious junior
suite. There is a roof terrace
and free wireless internet
access in all rooms. A good
buffet breakfast is included in
the room rate. The restaurant
has been awarded 14 Gault-
Millau points.
🛈 17 🅿 🔁 🚫 🛇 All major
cards

ENGLEBERG

HOTELS

🏨 EUROPÄISCHER HOF EUROPE
$$$

DORFSTRASSE 40
6390 ENGELBERG
TEL 041 639 75 75
FAX 041 639 75 76
E-mail: info@hoteleurope.ch
www.hoteleurope.ch
A belle époque hotel dating
from 1905, which combines
art nouveau charm with modern amenities. It is in a quiet
location convenient for the rail
station and overlooks an area
of garden. Every room has a
balcony with a mountain view.
🛈 68 🅿 🔁 🚫 🛋 🛇 All
major cards

🏨 SPANNORT
🍴 $$$

DORFSTRASSE 28
6391 ENGELBERG
TEL 041 637 26 26
FAX 041 637 44 77
E-mail: info@spannort.ch
www.spannort.ch
A traditional Swiss hotel and
wood-paneled restaurant
serving excellent regional
cuisine. The staff are friendly
and welcoming. Some of the
rooms have balconies with
views of the mountains.
🛈 20 🅿 🔁 🚫 🛇 All major
cards

RESTAURANT

🍴 CHUCHICHÄSCHTLI
$$

KLOSTERSTRASE 11
6390 ENGELBERG
TEL 041 637 16 74
FAX 041 637 16 72
E-mail: info@chuchichae
schtli-engelberg.ch
www.chuchichaeschtli-engel
berg.ch
Beneath a basic hotel, this
restaurant has the ambience
of an Alpine chalet with
gingham curtains. It specializes
in fondue and other traditional
dishes.
➕ 65 🚫 🛇 MC, V

LUZERN

HOTELS

🏨 PALACE LUZERN
🍴 $$$$$

HALDENSTRASSE 10
6002 LUZERN
TEL 041 416 16 16
FAX 041 416 10 00
E-mail: info@palace-luzern.ch
www.palace-luzern.ch
Overlooking the lake and the
mountains around Pilatus,
the Palace Luzern combines
old-world charm with the
most modern comforts in an
ambience of stylish elegance.

Tastefully renovated rooms,
dating from the founding
year of the hotel more than a
century ago, are a captivating
contrast to the new gourmet
Jasper restaurant which has
one Michelin star. The authentic belle époque ambience
of **Les Artistes** serves light
international cuisine, inspired
by national and regional
specialties.
🛈 168 🅿 🔁 🚫 🛋 🛇 All
major cards

🏨 SCHWEIZERHOF
🍴 $$$$$

SCHWEIZERHOFQUAI 3
6002 LUZERN
TEL 041 410 04 10
FAX 041 410 29 71
E-mail: info@schweizerhof-
luzern.ch
www.schweizerhof-luzern.ch
Located on the lake prom-
enade, the grand dame of the
city's top hotels has welcomed
royal and distinguished visitors
since 1845, including Tolstoy,
Wagner, and Ludwig II. The
renovated **Galerie** restaurant
specializes in fish cuisine while
the **Pavillon** offers seasonal,
international à la carte menus
as well as local Swiss specialties. In summer there is dining
on the sun terrace in the shade
of palm trees.
🛈 101 🅿 🔁 🚫 🛋 🛇 All
major cards

🏨 ART DECO MONTANA
🍴 $$$$

ADLIGENSWILERSTRASSE 22
6002 LUZERN
TEL 041 419 00 00
FAX 041 419 00 01
E-mail: info@hotel-
montana.ch
www.hotel-montana.ch
Opened in 1910, the hotel
has magnificent views over
the lake thanks to its position
up the hillside, reached by its
own funicular. The hotel has a
strong art deco theme with an
outstanding bar and restaurant

with regular jazz evenings lending an appropriate atmosphere. The menu in the **Scala** restaurant is influenced by south Switzerland, Italy, France, and Greece, and includes daily new variations of freshly made pasta.

🛈 55 🅿 ⬆ 🅢 🛡 🅐 AE, DC, MC, V

🏨 DES BALANCES
$$$$
WEINMARKT
6004 LUZERN
TEL 041 418 28 28
FAX 041 418 28 38
E-mail: info@balances.ch
www.balances.ch
Dating from 1807 and located in the heart of Luzern's old town, the hotel has a magnificent facade in the style of Holbein and bedrooms overlooking the Reuss River and the Jesuit church.

🛈 56 🅿 ⬆ 🅢 🅐 🅐 AE, MC, V

SOMETHING SPECIAL

🏨 WILDEN MANN
$$$$
BAHNHOFSTRASSE 30
6000 LUZERN
TEL 041 210 16 86
FAX 041 210 16 29
E-mail: mail@wilden-mann.ch
www.wilden-mann.ch
Seven sensitively renovated town houses, the oldest dating from 1517, have been combined to create a hotel of great character. Its walls are covered in historic paintings and prints of local scenes. Rich sauces are to the fore in the historic *stübe*, which purports to be the city's oldest public dining room, its beams decorated by coats of arms. In summer, tables spill out on to a terrace in a pedestrian square.

🛈 50 ⬆ 🅢 🅐 🅐 All major cards

🏨 ZUM WEISSEN KREUZ
🍽 $$$
FURRENGASSE 19
6004 LUZERN
TEL 041 418 82 20
FAX 041 418 82 30
E-mail: contact@altstad thotelluzern.ch
www.hotel-wkreuz.ch
Located near the Reuss River in a traffic-free part of the old town. The hotel has a newly designed modern interior and all nonsmoking bedrooms. The restaurant has a wood-fired oven and offers 45 different types of pizza, while the haute cuisine Chrüzli restaurant is a more intimate affair.

🛈 21 ⬆ 🅢 🅢 🅐 All major cards

🏨 JAILHOTEL LÖWENGRABEN
$$
LÖWENGRABEN 18
6004 LUZERN
TEL 041 410 78 30
FAX 0 41 410 78 32
E-mail: hotel@jailhotel.ch
www.jailhotel.ch
The Hotel Löwengraben has been reconstructed out of a former town prison built in 1862 and in use until 1998. Sixty original cells have been remodeled into bedrooms for one to four people. They are comfortable, but their origin is unmistakable.

🛈 60 🅢 🅐 MC, V

RESTAURANTS

🍽 NIX'S IN DER LATERNE
$$$
REUSSTEG 9
6003 LUZERN
TEL 041 240 25 43
E-mail: info@nixinderlat erne.ch
www.nixinderlaterne.ch
Attractive corner restaurant with a lovely oriel window overlooking the river and an outside seating area away

from traffic noise. Local ingredients are used whenever possible and daily specials are chalked on a blackboard.

🔧 60 🅢 🅐 All major cards

🍽 OLD SWISS HOUSE
$$$
LÖWENPLATZ 4
6004 LUZERN
TEL 041 410 61 71
FAX 041 410 17 38
E-mail: info@oldswisshouse.ch
www.oldswisshouse.ch/en/index.html
Expect unrivaled 17th-century ambience at this family-run eatery, with main courses including lake fish, beef stroganoff, and Wiener schnitzel pan-fried at your table. Extensive wine list.

🔧 80 🕐 Closed Mon. & Feb.
🅢 🅐 AE, DC, MC, V

🍽 HELVETIA
$$
WALDSTATTERSTRASSE 9
6003 LUZERN
TEL 041 210 44 50
www.helvetialuzern.ch
A popular lunchtime restaurant with locals, sometimes serving unusual fare such as ostrich steak in peppercorn sauce. Wi-Fi available.

🔧 105 🅢 🅐 AE, DC, MC, V

MOUNT RIGI

HOTELS

🏨 RIGI KULM
$$$
6410 RIGI KULM
TEL 041 880 18 88
FAX 041 855 00 55
E-mail: hotel@rigikulm.ch
www.rigikulm.ch
There has been a hotel on the Rigi for almost 200 years, providing guests with the opportunity to watch sunset and sunrise from the summit of this famous mountain, an

activity parodied by Mark Twain in *A Tramp Abroad*. The current hotel with its summer terrace restaurant was built in the 1950s but used some furnishings from its predecessor to give it the charm of a typical mountain hotel. The rooms have been recently refurbished in a modern idiom.

 33 P 😊 ⑤ ⑤ 👁 All major cards

 BERGSONNE
🍴 **$$**
6356 RIGI KALTBAD
TEL 041 399 80 10
FAX 041 399 80 20
info.rigi@wvrt.ch
www.bergsonne.ch
This family-run hotel in the car-free resort of Rigi Kaltbad has magnificent views over the lake and the Alps. The rooms are decorated with paintings by local artists, there is a library, and the decor tells you that you are in Switzerland and in the mountains. The hotel is renowned for its gastronomy, with a menu changing every day, using fresh seasonal ingredients. Special events are held such as a fish festival, and a menu is available which focuses on nutritional value.

① 17 P 😊 ⑤ 👁 MC, V

SCHWYZ

🏨 **WYSSES RÖSSLI**
🍴 **$$**
HAUPTPLATZ 3
6430 SCHWYZ
TEL 041 811 19 22
E-mail: info@wrsz.ch
www.roessli-schwyz.ch
A historic hotel in the old town. Its two restaurants are well known for their seasonal specialties.

① 28 😊 ⑤ 👁 MC, V

STANS

🏨 **ENGEL**
🍴 **$$**
DORFPLATZ 1
6370 STANS
TEL 041 619 10 10
FAX 041 619 10 11
E-mail: info@engelstans.ch
www.engelstans.ch
This handsome historic hotel in the town center is an unusual mix of ultramodern design and period features. It has a garden terrace offering traditional local fare and a gourmet *stübli*.

① 18 P 😊 ⑤ 👁 MC, V

VITZNAU

HOTELS

🏨 **VITZNAUERHOF**
🍴 **$$$$$**
SEESTRASSE 80
6354 VITZNAU
TEL 041 399 77 77
FAX 041 399 76 66
E-mail: info@vitznauerhof.ch
www.vitznauerhof.ch/intro
.php
This delightful Jugendstil-style hotel was opened in 1901 on the shore of Vierwald-stättersee and has recently reopened after a long upgrade and restoration to provide 21st-century amenities such as the MedinWell Spa. The public rooms and lake-facing bedrooms have outstanding views, and there are three restaurants: the **Inspiration,** the gourmet restaurant **Sens,** and the **Panorama** garden restaurant. The last opens in fine weather on a terrace beside the water and serves Mediterranean cuisine, grilled specialties, and antipasti.

① 53 P 😊 ⑤ ⑤ 🍷 👁 All major cards

PRICES

HOTELS
The cost of a double room with private bathroom in peak season is given by $ signs.

$$$$$	Over $550
$$$$	$351–$550
$$$	$251–$350
$$	$125–$250
$	Under $125

RESTAURANTS
The average cost of a two-course meal for one person, excluding tip or drinks, is given by $ signs.

$$$$$	Over $175
$$$$	$126–$175
$$$	$91–$125
$$	$50–$90
$	Under $50

🏨 **HOBBY HOTEL**
🍴 **VITZNAU**
$$
SCHIFFSTATION
6354 VITZNAU
TEL 041 397 10 33
FAX 041 397 21 55
E-mail: ferein@hobbyhotel.ch
www.hobbyhotel.ch
Situated next door to the steamer pier and the funiculars up Mount Rigi. This Swiss Historic Hotel was built as part of the station complex of the Vitznau-Rigibahn railway (Europe's first mountain railway) in 1873. Later modifications and extensions transformed the hotel's size and appearance. The restaurant **Rondel,** built over the lake, provides guests with a stunning view, especially at sunset. The Hobby Hotel offers guests creative courses in arts and crafts as well as exhibition

space for their works.

① 23 🅿 ⊜ ⑤ 🅢 MC, V

WEGGIS

HOTELS

🏢 PARK WEGGIS
$$$$$
HERTENSTEINSTRASSE 34
6353 WEGGIS
TEL 041 392 05 05
FAX 041 392 05 28
E-mail: weggis@relais
chateaux.com
www.relaischateaux.com/
weggis

Overloking the lake of Vierwaldstättersee, this luxuriously
appointed hotel features a spa
and wellness center. Its six
exotic wood and natural stone
cottages sit in the middle of
a Japanese garden. The hotel
is staffed by specially trained
therapists from Tibet, India, and
Switzerland. There is an outdoor pool, and various water
sports are available. The hotel
even has a classic Chevrolet
Impala of 1959 for guests' use.

① 52 🅿 ⊜ ⑤ 🅢 🗷 🍸
🅢 All major cards

🏢 SEEHOTEL GOTTHARD
🍽 SCHONAU
$$$
GOTTHARDSTRASSE 11
6353 WEGGIS
TEL 041 390 21 14
FAX 041 390 09 14
E-mail: gotthard@gotthard-
weggis.ch
www.gotthard-weggis.ch

This family-run hotel on the
shore of Vierwaldstättersee has
rooms with beautiful views and
offers free access to wellness facilities (April–mid-Oct.) with a
heated outdoor pool. It is three
minutes' walk from the boat
pier. There are four restaurants,
one of which is in the lovely
garden by the lake.

① 17 🅿 ⊜ ⑤ 🗷 🍸 🅢 All
major cards

🏢 SEEHOF HOTEL DU LAC
🍽 $$
GOTTHARDSTRASSSE 4
6353 WEGGIS
TEL 041 390 11 51
FAX 041 390 11 19
E-mail: info@hotel-du-lac.ch
www.hotel-du-lac.ch

A small hotel in a central
location on the lake shore
just two minutes' walk from
the boat station. The **Garden**
restaurant is an idyllic spot,
offering various fondues, local
fish dishes, and traditional
meals. Free wireless internet in
public areas.

① 52 🅿 ⊜ ⑤ 🅢 MC, V

ZÜRICH & ZÜRICHSEE

KÜSNACHT

🏢 SONNE
🍽 $$$
SEESTRASSE 120
8700 KÜSNACHT
TEL 044 914 18 18
FAX 044 914 18 00
E-mail: seehotel-sonne@
romantikhotels.com
www.sonne.ch

An atmospheric hotel, situated directly on the Zürichsee
(just 10 minutes from the
city center by S-Bahn) and
offering every comfort. Sonne
offers fine dining, fine art
(paintings and sculptures by
such artists as Giacometti
and Warhol), cozy lounges, a
"wellness oasis," beer garden,
and pier.

① 40 🅿 ⊜ ⑤ 🅢 🍸 🅢 AE,
MC, V

🍽 RICO'S KUNSTSTUBEN
$$$$$
SEESTRASSE 160
3700 KÜSNACHT
TEL 044 910 07 15
FAX 044 910 04 95
E-mail: info@kunststuben
.com

www.kunststuben.com
Since 2010, Rico Zandonella—
the Ticinese protégé of
Horst Petermann (one of
Switzerland's most reputed
chefs)—has taken the helm
of Petermann's celebrated
restaurant, which for years
ranked as the nation's best.
Newly renovated, the brightly
colored interior now reflects
the bold flamboyance of
Rico's "new Mediterranean"
cuisine.

🕒 Closed Sun. & Mon. 🅿 ⑤
🅢 AE, MC, V

RAPPERSWIL

🏢 JAKOB
$$
HAUPTPLATZ 11
8640 RAPPERSWIL
TEL 055 220 00 50
FAX 055 220 00 55
E-mail: info@jakob-hotel.ch
www.jakob-hotel.ch

A simple stylish hotel with a
trendy bar, a classic bistro, and
vaulted wine cellar. However,
rooms can be noisy every
second Thursday nights when
live jazz concerts are staged in
the lounge.

① 20 🅿 ⊜ ⑤ 🅢 All major
cards

UETLIBERG

🏢 UTO KULM
$
8143 UETLIBERG
TEL 044 457 66 66
FAX 044 457 66 99
E-mail: info@utokulm.ch
www.utokulm.ch/en/home

A rural retreat, with sweeping views over Zürich and
the lake, and sophisticated,
minimalist furnishings. Reserve
the romantic "tower suite"
for that special occasion, with
a wood-burning stove and
heart-shaped jacuzzi bath.

① 55 ⊜ ⑤ 🅢 🅢 AE, MC, V

WINTERTHUR

🏨 PARK HOTEL WINTERTHUR
$$$
STADTHAUSSTRASSE 4
8402 WINTERTHUR
TEL 052 265 02 65
FAX 052 265 02 75
E-mail: welcome@phwin.ch
www.phwin.ch
Central yet tranquilly situated in beautiful parkland just a stone's throw from the Altstadt, this classic-modern hotel appeals to business visitors as well as tourists.

🛏 69 🅿 ⬍ 🅂 🅂 🅂 🅂 All major cards

🍴 CAFÉ AM RÖMERHOLZ
$
HALDENSTRASSE 95
8400 WINTERTHUR
TEL 052 269 27 43
Pause awhile with a delicious homemade cake and coffee, or a light lunch snack in this light, airy café at the Sammlung Reinhart "am Römerholz" gallery (see p. 206), or on the sunny terrace outside, overlooking beautiful parkland.

🪑 40 🕐 Closed Mon. 🅿 🅂
🅂 No cards

ZÜRICH

HOTELS

🏨 BAUR AU LAC
$$$$$
TALSTRASSE 1
8001 ZÜRICH
TEL 044 220 50 20
FAX 044 220 50 44
E-mail: info@bauraulac.ch
www.bauraulac.ch/en/intro
.html
One of the nation's grandest hotels, famed for its revered tradition of unsurpassed quality, luxury, and old-world elegance. Set in its own park overlooking the lake and the Alps, it is just steps away from the glamorous shops of Bahnhofstrasse, the city's celebrated shopping boulevard.

🛏 120 🅿 ⬍ 🅂 🅂 🅂 AE, DC, MC, V

🏨 DOLDER GRAND
🍴 $$$$$
KURHAUSSTRASSE 65
8032 ZÜRICH
TEL 044 456 60 00
FAX 044 456 60 01
E-mail: info@thedoldergrand
.com
www.thedoldergrand.com
High in the hills and backing onto woods, a golf course, tennis courts, and an ice-rink (in winter), this 19th-century "city resort" was radically renovated in 2008 by British architect Norman Foster. The result is a perfect fusion of tradition and modernity, with high-tech bedrooms and suites. There is sophisticated dining (including a two-starred Michelin restaurant), a state-of-the-art spa, and unsurpassed views of the city, lake, and Alps.

🛏 173 🅿 ⬍ 🅂 🅂 🅂 🅂 🅂
🅂 AE, MC, V

🏨 ROMANTIK FLORHOF
$$$$
FLORHOFGASSE 4
8001 ZÜRICH
TEL 044 250 26 26
FAX 044 250 26 27
E-mail: info@florhof.ch
www.florhof.ch
A traditional, country-style hotel near the Kunsthaus and the city center. It is in a 16th-century former merchant's home with a secluded garden terrace. It features personal service and luxury amenities.

🛏 35 🅿 ⬍ 🅂 🅂 🅂 AE, DC, MC, V

🏨 SORRELL RÜTLI
$$$
ZÄHRINGERSTRASSE 43
8001 Zürich
TEL 044 254 58 00
FAX 044 254 5801
E-mail: info@rutli.ch
www.rutli.ch/en/home.asp
At the entrance to the characterful Niederdorf district, and well placed for shops, restaurants, and museums. This centrally located hotel is newly renovated with practical, modern bedrooms and a relaxing jacuzzi room.

🛏 58 ⬍ 🅂 🅂 🅂 AE, MC, V

🏨 LEONECK
$$
LEONHARDSTRASSE 1
8001 ZÜRICH
TEL 044 254 22 22
FAX 044 254 2000
E-mail: info@leoneck.ch
www.leoneck.ch/en/index
.html
Eccentric but stylish, this offbeat hotel is decorated in "Swiss ethno" style. Its cheerful bedrooms are individually decorated by local artists, with cow motifs throughout. Free Wi-Fi, and excellent value given its central location, just a stone's throw from the Niederdorf district.

🛏 80 ⬍ 🅂 All major cards

🏨 KAFISCHNAPS
$
KORNHAUSSTRASSE 57
8037 ZÜRICH
E-mail: contact@kafischnaps
.ch
www.kafischnaps.ch
A small B&B with five simple, stylish rooms named (and decorated) for the classic Swiss after-dinner liqueurs: Williams Pear, Plum, Quince, Purple Plum, and Cherry. All five are served in the lively neighborhood café-bar beneath. Reservations online or through Zürich's tourist office.

🛏 5 🅂 MC, V

RESTAURANTS

🍴 ZUNFTHAUS ZUR WAAGE
$$$$

MÜNSTERHOF 8
8001 ZÜRICH
TEL 044 216 99 66
FAX 044 216 99 67
E-mail: secretariat.waag@
bluewin.ch
www.zunfthaus-zur-waag
.ch/?lang=en
A classy Swiss restaurant in a beautiful 17th-century guild-house, with exceptional service; and wood-paneled dining rooms set with white linen tablecloths and candles. Be sure to try Zürich's trademark dish, *Züri gschnetzlets* (veal in a cream and mushroom sauce) served with delicious *rösti* potatoes.
🛏 194 🚭 🏧 AE, MC, V

🍴 SEGANTINI
$$

ANKERSTRASSE 120
8004 ZÜRICH
TEL 044 241 07 00
www.segantini.ch
A gourmet restaurant in Zürich's fashionable fourth district, named for Italian artist Giovanni Segantini and run by one of his descendants. The striking interior of bright silk fabrics and striking mirror work is echoed in the simple, bold flavors of the fine Italian cuisine. There is also a tiny shady deck for al fresco dining in summer.
🛏 32 🕐 Closed Sun. & Mon.
🚭 🏧 AE, MC, V

🍴 ADLER'S SWISS CHUCHI
$

ROSENGASSE 10
8001 ZÜRICH
TEL 044 266 96 96
FAX 044 266 96 69
E-mail: info@hotel-adler.ch
www.hotel-adler.ch/en
The specialty in this friendly, alpine-style restaurant is fondues and raclette dishes, as well as a wide variety of authentic Swiss dishes for non-cheese lovers.
🛏 80 🚭 🏧 AE, MC, V

🍴 CRAZY COW
$

LEONHARDSTRASSE 1
8001 ZÜRICH
TEL 044 261 4055
FAX 044 261 4059
E-mail: zuerich@crazycow.ch
www.crazycow.ch
This lighthearted restaurant attracts a lively crowd with its zany cartoon decorations of cows, mountains, Toblerone, and other Swiss kitsch—and its witty entertainment of Swiss-themed video clips. The menu (written in amusing Swiss dialect with English translations) comprises generous portions of *rösti, alpen macaroni,* and other rustic Swiss fare.
🛏 140 🚭 🏧 AE, DC, MC, V

🍴 HILTL
$

SIHLSTRASSE 28
8001 ZÜRICH
TEL 044 227 70 00
FAX 044 227 70 07
E-mail: info@hiltl.ch
www.hiltl.ch/en/index.php
Founded in 1898 as Europe's first vegetarian restaurant, Hiltl has gone from strength to strength. With its delicious salad bar and mouthwatering curries, it remains Zürich's top vegetarian eatery.
🛏 420 🚭 🏧 AE, MC, V

🍴 ZEUGHAUSKELLER
$

IN GASSEN,
BAHNHOFSTRASSE 28A
TEL 044 221 26 90
www.zeughauskeller.ch
Expect a lively atmosphere in this old-fashioned, Bavarian-style beer hall, housed in a converted 15th-century arsenal. The menu features hearty portions of traditional Zürcher fare, including 15 different sausage dishes, and an impressive selection of beers.
🛏 240 🚭 🏧 AE, MC, V

▧ NORTHEAST SWITZERLAND

APPENZELL

HOTELS

🏨 ROMANTIK SÄNTIS
🍴 $$$

LANDSGEMEINDEPLATZ 3
9050 APPENZELL
TEL 071 788 11 11
FAX 071 788 11 10
E-mail: info@saentis-appenzell.ch
www.saentis-appenzell.ch
On the main square in a traditional-style building with a beautifully painted facade, Appenzell's top hotel is comfortable and welcoming, with two restaurants serving regional fare, a small wellness center, and a sunny terrace. Ask for a room with a four-poster bed.
🛏 37 🅿 ⇄ 🚭 🏊 🏧 All major cards

🏨 FREUDENBERG
$

RIEDSTRASSE 57
9050 APPENZELL
TEL 071 787 12 40
FAX 071 787 86 42
E-mail: info@hotel-freuden berg.ch
www.hotel-freudenberg.ch
A friendly family-run hotel on a hill on the outskirts of Appenzell, with plenty of rustic charm. You will find lace curtains, pillowy duvets, and beautiful hand-painted furniture.
🛏 7 🅿 ⇄ 🚭 🏧 AE, MC, V

ARBON

HOTEL BRÄUEREI
FROHSINN
$$

ROMANSHORNERSTRASSE 15
9320 ARBON
TEL 071 447 84 84
FAX 071 446 41 42
E-mail: info@frohsinn-arbon.ch
www.frohsinn-arbon.ch

A small half-timbered hotel by Bodensee with its own brewery, bowling alley, and three restaurants. One of the restaurants is the informal **Bräukeller,** which serves hearty regional cuisine. In summer the beer garden offers lake views from beneath its shady chestnut trees.

🛈 13 🅿 🚫 🏔 AE, MC, V

BRAUNWALD

🏨 MÄRCHENHOTEL
BELLEVUE
$$

8784 BRAUNWALD
TEL 055 653 71 71
FAX 055 643 10 00
E-mail: info@maerchen hotel.ch
www.maerchenhotel.ch

The Bellevue certainly lives up to its name with its spectacular panoramas. However, it is perhaps best known for its hotelier who has been telling fairy stories to spellbound children here daily since 1976. There are other activities (including a crèche, an indoor pool, and treasure hunts) to amuse the kids so that their parents can have a well-deserved break. Half board only.

😴 🚫 🛌 🏔 🏔 MC, V

GLARUS

🍴 WIRTSCHAFT
SONNEGG
$

BEIM SONNENHÜGEL
8750 GLARUS
TEL 055 640 11 92
FAX 055 640 81 06
E-mail: sonnegg@bluewin.ch

A tiny restaurant with a well-stocked wine cellar, specializing in French and classic Swiss cuisine, using the very best of local, seasonal, market-fresh produce. The sunny terrace affords fine views of Vorder-glärnisch mountain.

🛋 30 🕐 Closed Tues. & Wed.
🚫 🏔 All major cards

GONTEN

🍴 BÄREN
$$

9108 GONTEN
TEL 071 795 40 10
FAX 071 795 40 19
E-mail: info@hotel-baeren-gonten.ch
www.hotel-baeren-gonten.ch

The region's most famous restaurant has remained in the same family for five generations and specializes in old original Appenzeller cuisine, having rediscovered and refined many forgotten recipes over the years. The restaurant has been awarded 15 GaultMillau points.

🛋 30 🕐 Closed Sun. eve. & Mon. 🅿 🚫 🏔 MC, V

RORSCHACH

🏨 SCHLOSS WARTEGG
$$$

9490 RORSACHERBERG
TEL 071 858 62 62
FAX 071 858 62 60
E-mail: schloss@wartegg.ch
www.wartegg.ch

This 16th-century former royal Austrian castle is set in beautiful grounds on a hillside above Rorschach. It has been converted into a smart, modern hotel and spa and boasts light, airy rooms, a large organic castle garden, a garden restaurant, and exceptional views across the Bodensee.

PRICES

HOTELS
The cost of a double room with private bathroom in peak season is given by **$** signs.

$$$$$	Over $550
$$$$	$351–$550
$$$	$251–$350
$$	$125–$250
$	Under $125

RESTAURANTS
The average cost of a two-course meal for one person, excluding tip or drinks, is given by $ signs.

$$$$$	Over $175
$$$$	$126–$175
$$$	$91–$125
$$	$50–$90
$	Under $50

🛈 24 rooms 🅿 🚫 🛌 🏔 All major cards

SCHAFFHAUSEN

🏨 FISCHERZUNFT
$$$

RHEINQUAI 8
8200 SCHAFFHAUSEN
TEL 052 632 05 05
FAX 052 632 05 13
E-mail: info@fischerzunft.ch
www.fischerzunft.ch

A luxurious hotel on the Rhine. It has one of the region's finest restaurants (awarded one Michelin star) with exceptional Euro-Asiatic haute cuisine. Try the Menu Yin-Yang for an exotic culinary voyage around the world.

🛈 10 🕐 Closed Mon. & Tues.
🅿 🚫 🏔 AE, DC, MC, V

STEIN-AM-RHEIN

🍽 RHEINFELS
$$

8260 STEIN-AM-RHEIN
TEL 052 741 21 44
FAX 052 741 25 22
E-mail: rheinfels@bluewin.ch
www.rheinfels.ch
A fine 16th-century Rhineside inn serving delicious fish dishes in a beautiful wood-paneled dining room. Views over the Rhine.

🛏 120 🕐 Closed Wed. (except July–Aug.) & Jan.–Feb.
🚭 🈸 AE, MC, V

■ GRAUBÜNDEN

AROSA

HOTELS

🏨 TSCHUGGEN GRAND
🍽 $$$$$

SONNENBERGSTRASSE
7050 AROSA
TEL 081 378 99 99
FAX 081 378 99 90
E-mail: info@tschuggen.ch
www.tschuggenhotelgroup.ch
Arosa's flagship hotel was transformed by a futuristic spa designed by Swiss architect Mario Botta in 2006, which offers Thalasso therapy, Indoceane and Ayurveda treatments, and a range of massages and beauty treatments. Its four levels are lit by nine glass sails that create an extraordinary effect at dusk when set against the dark conifers behind the spa. Three restaurants serve classic French dishes, refined Mediterranean cuisine and regional Swiss fare.

🛏 129 🕐 Closed mid-April– mid-May 🅿 🚭 🈸 🛎 🏊
🛗 🈸 All major cards

🏨 ASTORIA
🍽 $$

ALTEINSTRASSE
7050 AROSA

TEL 081 378 72 72
E-mail: hotel@astoria-arosa .ch
www.astoria-arosa.ch
This family-run hotel is just 300 yards (270 m) from the cable car and rail station. The bedrooms have flat-screen TVs and free Wi-Fi. Guests can eat in the Astoria-Stübli which offers a five-course evening menu with a huge buffet of fresh salads. There is also a rustic-style bar and a sun terrace with uninterrupted views of the mountains. Facilities include two jacuzzis, two infrared cabins, a sauna, fitness room, and games room.

🛏 15 🅿 🚭 🈸 🛎 🛗 🈸 AE, MC, V

RESTAURANT

🍽 VETTERSTUBLI
$$

SEEBLICKSTRASSE
7050 AROSA
TEL 081 378 80 00
FAX 081 378 80 08
www.arosa-vetter-hotel.ch
A restaurant that lists its local suppliers is always a good sign, and high-quality local produce is the basis of the fine Italian-influenced dishes at this characterful restaurant with red-and-white checked tablecloths.

🛏 60 🅿 🚭 🈸 All major cards

BERGUN

🏨 KURHAUS BERGÜN
🍽 $

7482 AROSA
TEL 081 407 22 22
FAX 081 407 22 33
E-mail: info@kurhausber guen.ch
www.kurhausberguen.ch
Located in the pristine landscape of the Albula Valley, this former wellness hotel dating from 1906 is a unique combination of hotel and

apartments. In 2002 its guests bought it as a public limited company, and it has since been renovated, step by step. Its unusual collection of art nouveau lighting fixtures has won an award. The spacious design makes it ideal for families. The restaurant **La Peida** is complemented by a breathtaking ballroom.

🛏 62 🅿 🚭 🈸 🈸 AE, MC, V

CHUR

🏨 ROMANTIK STERN
$$$

REICHSGASSE 11
7000 CHUR
TEL 081 258 57 57
FAX 081 258 57 58
E-mail: stern@romantik hotels.com
www.stern-chur.ch
Now in its fourth century, the Stern is Chur's most characterful hotel with imaginatively designed rooms and a traditional restaurant serving regional cuisine. Both public rooms and bedrooms use pine to create a cozy atmosphere. If you arrive by train, the hotel can arrange for you to be picked up in its classic 1933 Buick.

🛏 65 🅿 🚭 🈸 🈸 AE, DC, MC, V

🍽 ZUM ALTEN ZOLLHAUS
$$

MALIXERSTRASSE 1
7000 CHUR
TEL 081 252 33 98
FAX 081 252 11 37
E-mail: info@zollhaus-chur .ch
www.zollhaus-chur.ch
Three restaurants in one historic building. The Bündnerstube has served traditional Swiss cuisine since 1900, while the Pizzeria Verdi offers traditional and simple Italian food. The Mandarin restaurant serves Chinese and Thai dishes.

 🚭 Nonsmoking 🈸 Air-conditioning 🏊 Indoor Pool 🏊 Outdoor Pool 🛎 Health Club 🈸 Credit Cards

🔢 130 🕐 Mandarin closed Mon. 🅰️ AE, MC, V

DAVOS

🏨 WALDHOTEL BELLEVUE
$$$
BUOLSTRASSE 3
7270 DAVOS
TEL 081 415 15 15
FAX 081 415 15 16
E-mail: info@waldhotel-davos.ch
www.waldhotel-davos.ch
Perched on a mountain ledge commanding stunning views over the town and valley to the distant peaks, the hotel was once a sanatorium made famous by German writer and Nobel prizewinner Thomas Mann. Every south-facing room has a panoramic balcony, and the gastronomic restaurant also makes a feast of the view. A luxurious indoor salt water pool heated to a pleasant 91°F (33°C) forms part of the Wellness Pavilion.
🛏️ 50 🕐 Closed mid-Oct.–Nov. & May–mid-Jun. 🅿️ 🛗 📶 💺 🍴 📺 🅰️ AE, MC, V

🍴 RISTORANTE DA DAMIANO
$$
PROMENADE 95
7270 DAVOS
TEL 081 413 61 28
E-mail: info@da-damiano.ch
www.da-damiano.ch
This Italian restaurant has a wide selection of pizzas but also seasonal specialties including a varied game menu in the fall, which features deer, boar, and wild duck.
🔢 40 🅿️ 📶 🅰️ MC, V

DISENTIS

HOTELS

🏨 WALDHAUS FLIMS
🍴 $$$$$
VIA DIL PARC 3
7018 DISENTIS
TEL 081 928 48 48
FAX 081 928 48 58
E-mail: info@waldhaus-flims.ch
www.waldhaus-flims.ch
This enchanting hotel stands in Switzerland's largest hotel park, providing a setting of unrivaled seclusion. The three hotel buildings—Grand Hotel Waldhaus, Hotel Belmont, and Villa Silvana—have different styles to suit different clientele. They are interlinked by covered walkways and underground passages to the Pavillion, the lively heart of the resort and the meeting point for social get-togethers. Depending on the season, there are up to seven restaurants, including the gourmet Epoca. English afternoon tea is served in the Waldhaus Bar to the accompaniment of piano music.
🛏️ 150 🅿️ 🛗 📶 💺 🍴 📺 🅰️ All major cards

🏨 CUCAGNA
$$
OBERALPSTRASSE 10
7180 DISENTIS
TEL 081 929 55 55
FAX 081 929 55 00
E-mail: info@cucagna.ch
www.cucagna.ch
Just five minutes' walk from the center of Disentis and cable cars. This stylish modern hotel offers spacious bedrooms and a restaurant serving Swiss and international cuisine, regional dishes, and a breakfast buffet. Facilities include a heated outdoor pool and a Finnish log cabin sauna with an infrared cabin.

🛏️ 35 🅿️ 🛗 📶 💺 📺 🅰️ AE, DC, MC, V

FLIMS/LAAX/FALERA

HOTELS

🏨 ROMANTIK SCHWEIZERHOF
$$$$
RUDI DADENS 1
7018 FLIMS-WALDHAUS
TEL 081 928 10 10
FAX 081 928 10 11
E-mail: schweizerhof-flims@romantikhotels.com
www.schweizerhof-flims.ch
Set in wooded grounds, the rooms in this period hotel with its striking pink facade mostly have wonderful views of forest and mountains. There is a French accent to the cooking, which uses predominantly fresh local produce. Half-board guests have the option of a five-course meal every evening. There is also an indoor pool, caldarium, Finnish sauna, and solarium.
🛏️ 50 🕐 Closed mid-Oct.–early Dec. & April–May 🅿️ 🛗 📶 💺 🍴 📺 🅰️ AE, MC, V

🏨 SIGNINA
$$
7032 LAAX
TEL 081 927 90 00
FAX 081 927 90 01
E-mail: info@hotelsignina.com
www.signinahotel.com
Part of the award-winning Laax Rocks Resort (which takes its name and its rough-hewn stone identity from the surrounding landscape). This ultramodern chalet-style hotel is adjacent to the base station in Laax and is ideal for skiers in winter and walkers in summer. The minimalist rooms feature natural materials and textiles to create a

warm ambience. Free Wi-Fi.

🛈 91 P ⊜ ⊜ ⊜ ⊜
🕭 DC, MC, V

RESTAURANT

🍴 GRANDIS
$$$
ROCKS RESORT
7032 LAAX
TEL 081 936 00 36
www.grandislaax.ch
An open-flame grill is used
here to cook outstanding
quality local meat with per-
fect judgment, or authentic
raclette cooked over an open
fire. Modern décor. Excellent
service.
🍴 48 P ⊜ 🕭 All major
cards

KLOSTERS

🏨 WALSERHOF
$$$$$
LANDSTRASSE 141
7250 KLOSTERS
TEL 081 410 29 29
FAX 081 410 29 39
E-mail: info@walserhof.ch
www.walserhof.ch
This traditional chalet-style
hotel is small and intimate,
finished to a very high
standard and with a lovely
garden. Its outstanding
restaurant is decorated with
historic carvings and has a
stone oven. Warm colors
combine with pine and fir
to give a traditional feel to
the rooms, which have large
beds and pine wardrobes.
Some overlook a toboggan
run.
🛈 14 P ⊜ ⊜ ⊜ 🕭 MC, V

🍴 THE RUSTICO HOTEL
$$
LANDSTRASSE 194
7250 KLOSTERS
TEL 081 410 22 88
FAX 081 410 22 80
info@rusticohotel.com
This cozy restaurant has oc-

casional themed menus, such
as game and truffle dinners,
to add variety to its regular
fare, with some dishes influenced by Southeast Asian
cuisines. Attractively priced
lunch menu.
🍴 32 🕒 Closed mid-April–
mid-June P ⊜ 🕭 AE, MC, V

LENZERHEIDE

🏨 SCHWEIZERHOF
$$$/$$$$
7078 LENZERHEIDE
TEL 081 385 25 25
FAX 081 385 26 26
E-mail: info@schweizerhof-
lenzerheide.ch
www.schweizerhof-lenzer-
heide.ch
Contemporary design
combined with natural
materials and a striking blend
of new and nostalgic in five
different grades of bedroom,
plus a hammam. The hotel
also boasts green credentials
such as a sophisticated heat
recovery system.
🛈 83 P ⊜ ⊜ 🕅 🕭 All
major cards

PONTRESINA

HOTELS

🏨 WALTHER
🍴 $$$$$
VIA MAISTRA 215
7504 PONTRESINA
TEL 081 839 36 36
FAX 081 839 36 37
E-mail: walther@relais
chateaux.com
www.hotelwalther.ch
Now in its second century
and run by the third
generation, this hotel retains
an elegant atmosphere and
such architectural gems as
the waterfall and the sauna
in an igloo made of massive
Andeer granite. One of
the three restaurants has
15 GaultMillau points and

another specializes in dishes
from Graubünden. Besides
the spa there are whirlpools,
and a children's playground.
🛈 70 P ⊜ ⊜ ⊜ 🕭 🕅
🕭 All major cards

🏨 MULLER-CHESA
MANDRA
$$$$
VIA MAISTRA 100
7504 PONTRESINA
TEL 081 839 30 00
FAX 081 839 30 30
E-mail: info@hotel-
mueller.ch
www.hotel-mueller.ch
This hotel has different
types of Zen-style rooms
with pastel tones and
natural materials to create
a serene atmosphere. The
well-equipped rooms are
decorated in a modern style.
There are three restaurants:
an Italian with delicacies
from Bolzano-Alto Adige; a
pine-paneled *stüva* with à la
carte menu; and the similar
Stüvetta.
🛈 23 P ⊜ ⊜ ⊜ 🕭 AE,
MC, V

ST. MORITZ

HOTELS

🏨 KEMPINSKI GRAND
HOTEL DES BAINS
$$$$$
VIA MEZDI 27
7500 ST. MORITZ
TEL 081 838 38 38
E-mail: info.stmoritz@
kempinski.com
www.kempinski-stmoritz
.com
Located in St. Moritz Bad,
opposite the Corviglia cable
car, this luxurious hotel has
exceptional leisure facilities.
These include an indoor
heated pool with views of
the surrounding mountains,
Kempinski Spa, a beauty
salon, and a well-equipped

---

gym. A large club caters for children from two upward, with a wide range of fun and educational activities, including supervised early children's tea.
ⓘ 184 🅿 🕐 Closed mid-April–early June & mid-Oct.–Nov. 🔁 🚫 🔄 🛏 📺 🚭 AE, DC, MC, V

🏨 CRYSTAL HOTEL
🍴 $$$$

VIA TRAUNTER PLAZZAS 1
7500 ST. MORITZ
TEL 081 836 26 26 |
FAX 081 836 26 27
E-mail: stay@crystalhotel.ch
www.crystalhotel.ch
The ultramodern Hotel Crystal is just a few steps away from the Corviglia Mountain cable car and the pedestrian zone with its bars, cafés, restaurants, and shops. All rooms have marble bathrooms and are furnished in traditional Swiss-style Engadine pine. Il Ristorante Grissini offers gourmet Italian cuisine. Crystal Wellfit features a sauna, steam baths, fitness equipment, and a massage service.
ⓘ 84 🅿 🔁 🚫 🔄 🚭 AE, DC, MC, V

🏨 WALDHAUS AM SEE
$$$

VIA DIM LEJ 6
7500 ST. MORITZ
TEL 081 836 60 00
FAX 081 836 60 60
E-mail: info@waldhaus-am-see.ch
www.waldhaus-am-see.ch
Beautifully situated on a quiet hill overlooking the lake, the hotel offers weekly summer packages. Restaurant specialties include fresh fish, grilled meats, and fondue. The hotel is renowned for its astonishing selection of whiskies.
ⓘ 54 🅿 🔁 🚫 🔄 🚭 AE, DC, MC, V

RESTAURANTS

🍴 LA MARMITE
$$$–$$$$

CORVIGLIA BERGSTATION
7500 ST. MORITZ
TEL 081 833 63 55
FAX 081 833 85 81
E-mail: info@mathisfod.ch
www.mathisfood.ch
Only accessible by cog railroad, at 8,156 feet (2,486 m), La Marmite is probably the highest gourmet restaurant in Europe. Outside, the appearance is starkly modernist; inside, the decor is traditionally Swiss and simple. Enjoy the stunning mountain view, celebrity spotting, and a high-end menu lovingly created by chef Reto Mathis. Try venison in truffle reduction, lobster bisque, or tuna sashimi with black truffles and salmon caviar.
🔼 241 🚭 AE, MC, V

🍴 RESTAURANT BAR CASCADE
$$$

VIA SOMPLAZ 6
7500 ST. MORITZ
TEL 081 833 33 44
E-mail: mail@cascade-stmoritz.ch
The imposing counter in this art nouveau restaurant is a popular place for an aperitif. The elegantly presented cuisine is refined Italian with seasonal specialties.
🔼 46 🕐 Closed late April–early Dec. 🚫 🚭 AE, MC, V

SCUOL

HOTELS

SOMETHING SPECIAL

🏨 HOTEL PARADIES
$$$$

7551 FTAN
TEL 081 861 08 08

PRICES

HOTELS
The cost of a double room with private bathroom in peak season is given by $ signs.

$$$$$	Over $550
$$$$	$351–$550
$$$	$251–$350
$$	$125–$250
$	Under $125

RESTAURANTS
The average cost of a two-course meal for one person, excluding tip or drinks, is given by $ signs.

$$$$$	Over $175
$$$$	$126–$175
$$$	$91–$125
$$	$50–$90
$	Under $50

FAX 081 861 08 09
E-mail: paradies@relais chateaux.com
www.relaischateaux.com/paradies
Perched above the spa town of Scuol, this luxury hideaway has stupendous views over the mountains of the Lower Engadine and the fairytale castle of Tarasp. The hotel is furnished with antiques and works of art by celebrated Engadine artists. There is a small but beautifully finished spa, and the surrounding country invites walks, cross-country skiing, and bicycle tours. Baby sitting and children's menus are available.
ⓘ 23 🅿 🕐 Late Apr.–late May 🔁 🚫 🔄 🛏 📺 🚭 All major cards

🏨 Hotel 🍴 Restaurant ⓘ No. of Guest Rooms 🔼 No. of Seats 🅿 Parking 🕐 Closed 🔁 Elevator

🏨 HOTEL GUARDAVAL
🍴 $$
VI 383
7550 SCUOL
TEL 081 864 13 21
E-mail: info@guardaval-
scuol.ch
www.guardaval-scuol.ch
This boutique 19th-century
hotel has cozy log fires
and views over the Lower
Engadine. The individually
designed and decorated
rooms feature bright colors
and modern design elements
alongside the traditional
Engadine features. Authentic
regional cuisine in the restaurant uses largely local and
organic products.
🛈 36 🅿 🔄 🅂 🅂 🆈 🄰 AE,
MC, V

SILS

🏨 MARIA
🍴 $$$
7514 SILS
TEL 081 832 61 00
FAX 081 832 61 01
E-mail: info@hotel-maria.ch
www.hotel-maria.ch
In a quiet location ideal for
walkers, this traditional-style
hotel has two restaurants, the
Italian-influenced **Arvensaal**
and the traditionally rustic
Stüve serving à la carte dishes.
➕40 🅿 🔄 🅂 🄰 MC, V

ZUOZ

🏨 POSTHOTEL
🍴 ENGIADINA
$$$
7524 ZUOZ
TEL 081 851 54 54
FAX 081 851 12 45
E-mail: mail@hotel
engiadina.ch
www.hotelengiadina.ch
Standing amid imposing
patrician and farmhouses
dating from the 16th century,
the Posthotel first opened its

doors to guests in 1876. It has
four room types and a choice
of two à la carte restaurants.
In summer there is a flower-
filled garden and a heated
outdoor swimming pool.
➕40🅿🔄🅂🄰🄰 All
major cards

◼ TICINO

AIROLO

🏨 FORNI
🍴 $$
VIA STAZIONE
6780 AIROLO
TEL 091 869 12 70
FAX 091 869 15 23
E-mail: info@forni.ch
www.forni.ch/index_e.html
Conveniently situated for the
railway station at the southern end of the Gotthard
Tunnel, this simple hotel has
comfortable rooms and an
excellent Italian restaurant
with a gourmet menu.
🛈20 🅿🔄🅂🄰MC, V

ASCONA

HOTELS

🏨 CASTELLO DEL SOLE
🍴 $$$$$
VIA MURACCIO 142
6612 ASCONA
TEL 091 791 02 02
FAX 091 792 11 18
E-mail: castellosole@realis
chateaux.com
www.relaischateaux.com/
castellosole
This oasis of tranquillity
resembles a manor house in a
parklike setting with a private
beach on Lake Maggiore. The
gourmet restaurant features
Italian-Mediterranean cuisine,
and there is a large, exclusive
spa. Additionally, the hotel
boasts both indoor and
outdoor swimming pools,
a sauna, hammam, and
solarium. Babysitting services

and a children's menu are
available.
🛈 85 🅿 🕒 Closed winter
🅂 🅂 🅂 🆉 🆉 🆈 🄰 AE,
DC, MC, V

🏨 EDEN ROC
$$$$
VIA ALBARELLE 16
6612 ASCONA
TEL 091 785 71 71
FAX 091 785 71 43
E-mail: info@edenroc.ch
www.edenroc.ch
One of Switzerland's great
hotels is in a glorious position
beside the lake, with waterfront gardens and a pool. The
hotel decor was styled by
Carlo Rampazzi to create one
of the most distinctive hotels
in the country.
🛈95 🅿 🔄 🅂 🆉 🆉 🆈
🄰 AE, DC, MC, V

RESTAURANTS

🍴 DELTA BEACH
LOUNGE
$$$
VIA DELTA 137-141
6612 ASCONA
TEL 091 785 77 85
FAX 091 785 77 35 l
E-mail: info@parkhoteldelta
.ch
www.deltabeachlounge.ch
Part of the Park Hotel, this
chic, romantic lounge bar/
restaurant on the shore of
Lake Maggiore offers creative
crossover cuisine and live jazz
in the former Spa Hall. The
latter was designed in the
Bauhaus style in 1930.
➕70 🕒 Closed early Jan.–
mid-March 🄰 AE, MC, V

🍴 SEVEN
$$
VIA MOSCIA 2
6612 ASCONA
TEL: 091 780 77 77
E-mail: info@seven-ascona
.ch
www.seven-ascona.ch

Top chef Ivo Adam has brought the skills that twice won him the title of World Cookery Champion with the Swiss national team. His restaurant looks along the promenade. The open-air harborfront area is a good place to watch the boats come and go—it even has sun-loungers.
🛏 90 🕐 Closed Mon. in Jan. & Feb. ♿ ⬛ MC, V

BELLINZONA

🏨 UNIONE
🍽 $$$
VIA G. GUISAN 1
6500 BELLINZONA
TEL 091 825 55 77
FAX 091 825 94 60
E-mail: info@hotel-unione
.ch
www.hotel-unione.ch
Close to the Castelgrande fortification, this family-run hotel has newly renovated rooms. The restaurant provides traditional home-made local, à la carte, and international cuisine.
ℹ 41 🕐 Closed Sun. & mid-Dec.–mid-Jan. ⬛⬛⬛
⬛ All major cards

GANDRIA

🏨 MOOSMANN
🍽 $$
6978 GANDRIA
TEL 091 971 72 61
FAX 091 972 71 32
E-mail: hotel_moosmann@
bluewin.ch
www.hotel-moosmann-
gandria.ch
This hotel boasts a sublime and blissfully quiet location on the edge of the lake in a car-free village. It is best reached by boat from Lugano, just 3 miles (5 km) away. The rooms were renovated recently, and there is an excellent restaurant.
ℹ 29 ⬛ MC, V

GOTTHARD PASS

🏨 ALBERGO SAN GOTTARDO
$$
SAN GOTTARDO OSPIZIO
6780 AIROLO
TEL 041 91 869 12 35
FAX 041 91 869 18 11
E-mail: hotel@gotthard-
hospiz.ch
www.gotthard-hospiz.ch
A unique refuge near the summit and lake of the Gotthard Pass, with basic but comfortable bedrooms and a restaurant. The National Gotthard Museum is adjacent.
ℹ 26 🅿 🕐 Closed Nov.–Apr. ⬛ MC, V

LOCARNO

HOTELS

🏨 HOTEL BELVEDERE
🍽 $$$
VIA AI MONTI 44
6601 LOCARNO
TEL 091 751 03 63
FAX 091 751 52 39
E-mail: info@belvedere-
locarno.com
www.belvedere-locarno.com
On a hillside, just five minutes' walk from Piazza Grande, this hotel occupies a 16th-century former nobleman's residence. The interior is decorated with granite from the valley, expertly carved pear wood, and warm colors. There are two international restaurants: L'Affresco with La Veranda; and the gastronomic La Locanda with its garden terrace. During the summer, grill specialties are served at the al fresco Grotto Al Sasso next to the outdoor pool in the garden.
ℹ 81 🅿⬛⬛⬛⬛⬛⬛⬛
⬛ All major cards

🏨 DELL'ANGELO
🍽 $$
PIAZZA GRANDE 1
6601 LOCARNO
TEL 091 751 81 75
FAX 091 751 82 56
E-mail: info@hotel-dell-
angelo.ch
www.hotel-dell-angelo.ch
In a renovated historic building in the heart of town, this hotel offers a family atmosphere and a restaurant serving traditional Ticinese and Italian cuisine (pizzeria with wood-burning oven). The cellar is stocked with regional and classic wines. The hotel also has a delightful garden restaurant in summer.
ℹ 55 🅿⬛⬛⬛ All major cards

🏨 DU LAC GARNI
$$
VIA RAMOGNA 3
6600 LOCARNO
TEL 091 751 29 21
FAX 091 751 60 71
E-mail: info@du-lac-locarno
.ch
www.du-lac-locarno.ch
In a quiet location with small but well-equipped rooms. There is free Wi-Fi in the bedrooms. There are two bikes for use, free. Du Lac Garni does not have a restaurant, but there are plenty close by.
ℹ 30 🅿⬛⬛⬛⬛ MC, V

🏨 MILLENIUM GARNI
$$
VIA DOGANA NUOVA 2
6600 LOCARNO
TEL 091 759 67 67
FAX 091 759 67 68
E-mail: info@millennium-
hotel.ch
www.millennium-hotel.ch
Until 2000 this small air-conditioned B&B hotel on the edge of Lake Maggiore was Locarno's custom house. The individually decorated rooms are dedicated to

famous jazz artists. It is just two minutes' walk from Piazza Grande.

[1] 11 [P] [symbols] DC, MC, V

RESTAURANT

SOMETHING SPECIAL

RISTORANTE DA ENZO
$$
PONTE BROLLA
6652 LOCARNO
TEL 091 796 14 75
FAX 091 796 13 92
www.ristorantedaenzo.ch
No visit to Ticino is complete without a visit to a grotto—one of the quiet off-the-beaten-track restaurants with a tree-shaded garden and simple tables and benches. This is one of the best, easily reached by a short train journey from Locarno to Ponte Brolla. Beside the gray stone house is a series of arched openings into the hillside, topped by a balustrade on which life-sized stone figures are arranged as though in conversation. Typical dishes might be salad with mushrooms and sweetbreads and a local fish accompanied by black rice, spinach, and baby tomatoes.
120 [P] Closed mid-Jan.–end Feb.; Wed. & Sun. evenings AE, MC, V

LUGANO

HOTELS

VILLA PRINCIPE LEOPOLDO & RESIDENCE
$$$$$
VIA MONTALBANO 5
6900 LUGANO
TEL 091 985 88 55
FAX 091 985 88 25
E-mail: info@leopoldohotel.com
www.leopoldohotel.com
Gloriously situated above

Lake Lugano, this magnificent villa was built for Prince Leopold von Hohenzollern. The Villa has a strong Italian atmosphere and retains marble fireplaces and fine works of art. There is also a spa, swimming pool, and access to sports including horse-riding, waterskiing, and polo.
[1] 75 [P] [symbols] All major cards

PARCO PARADISO
$$$$
VIA CARONA 27
6900 LUGANO
TEL 091 993 11 11
FAX 091 993 10 11
E-mail: info@parco-paradiso.com
www.parco-paradiso.com
This family-friendly hotel near the Museum of Modern Art offers good views of Lugano and the lake. All bedrooms have balconies, CD, and DVD players, and hypoallergenic bedding is available upon request. **La Favola** restaurant offers a daily menu with tables on the terrace in summer. The Japanese restaurant **Tsukimi-Tei** offers Teppanyaki dishes from Tuesday to Saturday. Further amenities include an indoor pool, sauna, fitness facility, and steam room.
[1] 65 [P] [symbols] AE, MC, V

CONTINENTAL PARK HOTEL
$$$
VIA BASILEA 28
6903 LUGANO
TEL 091 966 11 12
FAX 091 966 12 13
E-mail: info@continental-parkhotel.ch
www.continentalpark.ch
A historic family-run hotel near the main railway station and the town center. It is surrounded by a large palm park with swimming pool, vineyard, and the hotel's own

distillery. Bedrooms (renovation completed in 2010) are air-conditioned. Free internet.
[1] 100 [P] [symbols] AE, DC, MC, V

ALBERGO PESTALOZZI
$$
PIAZZA INDEPENDENZA 9
6901 LUGANO
TEL 091 921 46 46
FAX 091 922 20 45
E-mail: pestalo@bluewin.ch
www.pestalozzi-lugano.ch
A family-run, traditional hotel in the center of Lugano, just 150 yards (135 m) from the lake. Some rooms have air-conditioning. The restaurant serves Ticinese specialties and vegetarian dishes.
[1] 55 [P] [symbols] AE, MC, V

MELIDE

SOMETHING SPECIAL

ART DECO HOTEL DEL LAGO
$$$
LUNGOLAGO G. MOTTA 9
6815 MELIDE
TEL 091 649 70 41
FAX 091 649 89 15
welcome@hotel-dellago.ch
www.hotel-dellago.ch
An extremely stylish, chilled-out boutique hotel with a variety of price-banded rooms, an excellent seafood restaurant, and fantastic views over the lake. Some rooms have a jacuzzi and steam bath. Homemade produce and local grappa.
[1] 21 [P] [symbols] All major cards

Shopping

Shopping opportunities in Switzerland are almost never-ending. The country is renowned for products ranging from chocolate to cheeses, watches to Swiss Army knives, and sports equipment to handmade crafts. Then, of course, in the big cities you will find stores where the finest clothing and jewelry may be purchased.

Switzerland prides itself on its high-quality goods and innovative ideas. Even ordinary practical products can be beautifully designed and can make excellent gift ideas. Many items are endorsed with the well-known "Swiss made" quality label. Shops range from tiny independent boutiques to glitzy department stores. Local markets, with their mouthwatering array of fresh local fruit and vegetables, breads, cheeses, honey, and local wines are ideal for picnic purchases. And the celebrated Christmas markets (most notably in Basel, Bern, and Zürich) offer a host of gourmet treats, including mulled wine and gingerbread, alongside seasonal decorations and crafts.

Shopping hours are governed by cantonal law and vary from region to region. Most stores are generally open from 8 a.m. to 6:30 p.m. on weekdays, with a 90-minute to three-hour break for lunch outside of the cities and large towns. On Saturday, opening hours are usually 8.30 a.m. to 4 p.m. or 5 p.m. Some shops close on Monday mornings, and some cities (including Zürich, Geneva, and Bern) have late-night shopping until 8 p.m. on Thursdays. Shops are generally closed on Sundays, although many tourist outlets and the shopping malls next to large train stations usually open.

Foreign visitors are entitled to a tax refund with purchases in excess of CHF300 (including VAT) provided the goods leave the country within 30 days. Ask for a Tax Refund Cheque when paying. Then get it stamped by Swiss customs officials on departure from

Switzerland and claim your refund from a Global Blue customer service desk *(see www.global-blue.com for further details).*

Antiques, Books, & Collectibles

Erasmushaus
Bäumleingasse 18
4051 Basel
Tel 061 228 99 44
www.erasmushaus.ch
Switzerland's oldest antiquarian bookseller.

Orell Füssli
Bahnhofstrasse 30
8001 Zürich
Tel 044 455 56 17
www.books.ch/home/orell fuesslifiliale/bookshop
The largest English-language bookshop in Europe.

The Travel Bookshop
Rindermarkt 20
8001 Zürich
Tel 044 252 38 83
www.travelbookshop.ch
Specialist travel books and one of Europe's most comprehensive map collections.

Wishbone
Klosterstrasse 7
6002 Luzern
Tel 076 595 13 05
www.wishbone-antiques.ch
Furniture, mirrors, chandeliers, lamps, silver, crystal, china, and linen. Closed Mon.

Arts, Crafts, & Swiss Souvenirs
Caran d'Ache
place du Bourg du Four 8

1204 Geneva
Tel 022 310 90 00
Swiss-made high-quality pencils, crayons, and luxury writing instruments.

Urs Ettlin
Via Rosatsch 7
7500 St. Moritz
Tel 081 832 17 07
www.antiquitaeten-stmoritz.ch
Swiss costumes and handcrafted furniture.

Schweizer Heimatwerk
Uraniastrasse 1
8001 Zürich
033 222 19 55
www.heimatwerk.ch
Upscale contemporary handicrafts. There are other branches in Bern, Interlaken, Saanen, Zewisimmen, and Gstaad.

Jobin
Hauptstrasse 111
3855 Brienz
Tel 033 952 13 00
www.jobin.ch
Musical boxes (made here since 1865), Brienzer cuckoo clocks, and other hand-carved items.

Johann Wanner Weihnachtshaus
Spalenberg 14
4051 Basel
Tel 061 261 48 26
Queen Elizabeth of England and U.S. presidents are among customers at this, the world's largest manufacturer of handmade Christmas decorations.

Kunstgewerbe-Dörig
Poststrasse 6
9050 Appenzell

Tel 071 787 11 82
www.myappenzell.com
Ornate metal engravings,
saddlework, and leather
studwork from one of Appenzell's last traditional Alpine
saddlers.

Verrerie Bertin
rue St. Joseph 4
1227 Carouge–Geneva
022 343 10 43
Exquisite handcrafted glass
beads, vases, and giftware from
Geneva's only glassblower.

Chocolate
Confiseur Bachmann
Schwanenplatz 7
6002 Luzern
Tel 041 410 91 44
www.confiserie.ch
Longest showcase of pralines
in Switzerland, with over 250
specialty chocolates. Open daily,
including Sun.

Fuchs
Getwingstrasse 24
3920 Zermatt
Tel 027 967 20 63
www.fuchs-zermatt.ch
Beautifully crafted Matterhorn-
shaped chocolates.

Philippe Pascoët
rue St. Joseph 12
1227 Carouge–Geneva
Tel 022 301 20 58
E-mail: Boutiques@pascoet.com
www.pascoet.com
Exquisite chocolates. Try the
range infused with herbs and
teas. Closed Mon. July & Aug.

Schuh
Höheweg 56
3800 Interlaken
Tel 033 888 80 50
www.schuh-interlaken.ch
Demonstrations and tastings
(daily at 5 p.m. and 6 p.m.)
from one of the nation's oldest
chocolate manufacturers.

Confiserie Sprüngli
Bahnhofstrasse 21
Zürich
Tel 044 224 46 46
www.spruengli.ch
One of the nation's most
celebrated chocolatiers.

Teuscher
rue du Rhône 2
1204 Geneva
Tel 022 310 87 78
www.teuscher.com
Truffles are the specialty of this
famous family business.

Villars
route de la Fonderie 2
1701 Fribourg
Tel 026 426 65 49
www.chocolat-villars.com
Reduced-price chocolate straight
from the factory outlet.

Fashion, Accessories & Clothing
Alprausch
Bahnhofstrasse 33
3860 Meiringen
Tel 033 971 07 85
www.alprausch.com
Alpine chic, trendy urban
fashions and snow-wear.

Bally
Bahnhofstrasse 66
8001 Zürich
Tel 044 224 39 39
www.bally.com
The world's largest outlet of the
famous Swiss shoe manufacturer.

Freitag
Geroldstrasse 17
8005 Zürich
Tel 044 366 95 20
www.freitag.ch
Ultracool accessories made from
recycled junk.

Marta
Via Nassa 66
6900 Lugano

Tel 091 923 5869
Beautifully designed nightware
and clothes.

Food & Drink
Chäs Vreneli
Münsterhof 7
8001 Zürich
Tel 044 221 32 81
www.chaes-vreneli.ch
A tiny cheese shop with a massive
selection of regional cheeses.

Confiserie Albert Meier
Alpenstrasse 16
6300 Zug
Tel 041 711 10 49
www.diezugerkirschtorte.ch
The place to purchase the local
specialty, *zuger kirschtorte*–a delicious almond cake saturated with
kirsch (cherry brandy).

Gabbani Wine and Food
Via Pessina 12
6900 Lugano
Tel 091 911 30 90
www.gabbani.com
Outstanding delicatessen selling
regional produce and ingredients
since 1937.

Hanselmann
Via Maistra 8
7500 St. Moritz
Tel 081 833 38 64
www.hanselmann.ch
Famous café and patisserie with
legendary Engadine nut-torte.
Open daily, including Sun.

Läckerli Huus
Gerbergasse 57
4001 Basel
www.laeckerli-huus.ch
Scrumptious Läckerli biscuits
are a Basler specialty, made with
spices, honey, hazelnuts, and
citrus peel.

Laiterie Gougler
rue de Lausanne 83
1700 Fribourg
Tel 026 341 73 00

www.laiterie-gougler.ch
Wine, cheeses, fondue mixes,
meringues, cream, and other delicacies from the Gruyères region.

Lavaux Vinorama
route du lac 2
1071 Rivaz
Tel 021 946 31 31
www.lavaux-vinorama.ch
Over 200 different wines from
more than 150 local producers,
for tasting and purchase. Closed
Mon. & Tues. in Jan.–June &
Nov.–Dec. Open Sun.

Design & Interiors
Einzigart
Josefstrasse 36
8005 Zurich
Tel 044 440 46 00
www.einzigart.ch
Amusing gadgets created by local
designers. Closed Mon.

Füglistaller
Bäumleingasse 14
4001 Basel
Tel 061 260 78 10
www.fueglistaller.ch
Stylish Swiss kitchen accessories,
including raclette cheese grills
and fondue sets.

Neumarkt 17
Neumarkt 17
8001 Zürich
Tel 044 254 38 38
www.neumarkt17.ch
Chic interior design and contemporary furnishings. Closed Mon.

**Selvaggio Gallery
of Architecture**
Vicolo Ghiriglioni 3
6612 Ascona
Tel 091 785 19 10
www.selvaggio.ch
Designer Carlo Rampazzi's shop,
selling vibrantly colorful and
arresting creations.

Sibler
Münsterhof 16

8001 Zürich
Tel 044 211 55 50
Design shop that turns mundane
items into witty gift ideas.

Perfumes & Toiletries
Autour du Bain
rue St. Joseph 12
1227 Carouge–Geneva
Tel 022 300 53 73
www.autourdubain.com
Beautiful, handmade organic
soaps and bath products.

Théodora
grand-rue 38
1204 Geneva
Tel 022 310 38 75
A classy boutique specializing in
traditional "haute parfumerie."
Closed Mon.

Sportswear & Equipment
Transa
Zürcherstrasse 7
8400 Winterthur
Tel 052 238 01 00
www.transa.ch/de/shop-
winterthur
Specialist outdoor clothing,
shoes, and sports equipment.

Victorinox
Schmiedgasse 57
6438 Ibach
Tel 022 318 63 40
www.victorinox.com
Swiss Army knifes with mind-
boggling arrays of handy utensils.

Toys
Albert Schild
Bahnhofstrasse 19
3800 Interlaken
Tel 033 822 34 34
www.swisssouvenir.ch
Swiss-made traditional wooden
toys and souvenirs.

Watches & Jewelry
Beyer
Bahnhofstrasse 31

8001 Zürich
Tel 043 344 63 63
www.beyer-ch.com
Celebrated chronometry store,
with a clock museum in the basement. Closed a.m.

Bucherer
Schwanenplatz 5
6002 Luzern
Tel 041 369 77 00
Largest branch of Switzerland's
famed jewelry and watch retailer.
Open daily, including Sun.

Jaeger-Lecoultre
rue du Rhône 2
1204 Genève
Tel 022 310 61 50
Seductive jewelry and watches on
Geneva's most exclusive shopping
boulevard.

Junod
place St. Francois 8
1003 Lausanne
Tel 021 312 83 66
www.junod-lausanne.ch
One of the oldest jewelers in
French-speaking Switzerland.

Jean Kazès
rue St. Joseph 21
1227 Carouge–Geneva
Tel 022 343 30 91
Traditional watchmaker's workshop, full of eccentric devices.

Swatch
Bahnhofstrasse 94
8001 Zürich
Tel 044 221 28 66
The first ever shop of the most
successful wristwatch brand.
Seasonal collections.

Swiss Lion
Löwenplatz 11
2004 Luzern
Tel 041 410 61 81
www.swisslion.ch
Wide range of watches and
Victorinox products. Open daily,
including Sun.

Entertainment

Given the small size of the nation, Switzerland offers a surprising amount and range of entertainment throughout the year. Geneva, Zürich, and Luzern are the main cultural hubs. Visitors can enjoy world-class opera, ballet, dance, and theatrical performances ranging from classical to the avant-garde. Whenever you visit, there will be concerts and music festivals to enjoy.

To find out what's on when, contact the nearest tourist office or check in a local newspaper. Tickets for most events can be obtained directly at the venue, or from such ticket handling agents as FNAC (www.fnac.ch) and Ticket-Corner (www.ticketcorner.ch), but note that these are German-language sites.

Theater

Berner Puppentheater
Gerechtigkeitsgasse 31
3011 Bern
Tel (031) 311 95 85
www.berner-puppentheater.ch
Puppet theater for adults and children, housed in a former wine cellar.

Kleintheater Luzern
Bundesplatz 14
6003 Luzern
Tel 041 210 33 50
www.kleintheater.ch
Each year over 200 visiting artists from world of theater, cabaret, music, literature, and dance perform here.

Luzerner Theater
Theaterstrasse 2
6003 Luzern
Tel 041 228 14 14
www.luzerner-theater.ch
The only theater in central Switzerland presenting opera, plays, and dance.

Mummenschanz
Trogenerstrasse 80
9450 Altstätten (near St. Gallen)
Tel 071 755 55 47
www.mummenschanz.com/en
Famous touring theater company,

world-renowned for their mime and masked theater productions.

Narrenpacktheater
Kramgasse 30
3011 Bern
Tel 031 352 05 17
www.narrenpack.ch
Traditional and modern folk theater.

Schauspielhaus
Zeltweg 5
8032 Zürich
Tel 044 258 70 70
www.schauspielhaus.ch
Switzerland's largest and most prestigious theater. Classical and contemporary repertoire. Closed for most of July & Aug.

Schiffbau
Schiffbaustrasse 4 (off Hard-strasse)
8005 Zürich
Tel 044 258 77 77
www.schauspielhaus.ch
A second stage for Zürich's Schauspielhaus, in a warehouse once used for building ships. Closed for most of July & Aug.

Teatro di Locarno
Largo Zorzi 1
6600 Locarno
Tel 091 756 61 60
www.teatrodilocarno.ch
Principal Italian-language theater with wide range of productions.

Teatro Sociale Bellinzona
Piazza Governo 11
6500 Bellinzona
Tel 091 820 24 44
www.teatrosociale.ch.
Varied program of plays and

musicals in a theater modeled on Milan's celebrated La Scala opera house. Closed in summer.

Tell Freilichtspiele (Tell Open-Air Theater)
Tellbüro, Höheweg 37
3800 Interlaken
Tel 033 822 37 22
www.tellspiele.ch
Schiller's famous William Tell story is staged daily in summer in woods near Interlaken (see p. 52).

Theater Basel
Elisabethanstrasse 16
4051 Basel
Tel 061 295 11 33
www.theater-basel
A large theater company staging theater, opera, and ballet. Closed for most of July & Aug.

Theater an der Effingerstrasse
Effingerstrasse 14
3000 Bern
Tel 031 382 72 72
www.dastheater-effingerstr.ch/
A popular venue for alternative theater. Closed July & Aug.

Theater St. Gallen
Museumstrasse 2/24
9004 St. Gallen
Tel 071 242 06 06
www.theatersg.ch
Striking modern arts complex for theater, concerts, and ballet.

Théâtre de Vidy
avenue Jaques-Dalcroxe 5
1007 Lausanne
Tel 021 619 45 45
www.vidy.ch
Renowned, innovative French-speaking productions.

Classical Music, Opera & Dance

Béjart Ballet Lausanne
chemin du Presbytère 22
1004 Lausanne
Tel 021 641 64 64
www.bejart.ch/fr/en-2
World-famous dance company,
founded by the late French
choreographer Maurice Béjart
(see p. 52).

Grand Théâtre de Genève
place Neuve 5
1204 Geneva
Tel 022 418 31 30
www.geneveopera.ch
Opera and ballet season from
September to July (see p. 60).

Kultur-Casino Bern
Herrengasse 30
3011 Bern
Tel 031 328 02 28
www.kultur-casino.ch
Tel 031 328 24 24
Home to Bern Symphony
Orchestra, one of Switzerland's
very best.

**Kultur-und Kongresszentrum
Luzern (KKL)**
Europaplatz 1
6005 Luzern
Tel 041 226 70 70
www.kkl-luzern.ch
Futuristic concert hall with near
perfect acoustics (see p. 170)

Musikkollegium Winterthur
Rychenbergstrasse 94
8400 Winterthur
Tel 052 268 15 60
www.musikkollegium.ch/en
/html
An orchestra acclaimed for its
contemporary classical repertoire.

Opernhaus Zürich
Falkenstrasse 1
8008 Zürich
Tel 044 268 64 00
www.opernhaus.ch

One of Europe's leading opera-
houses (see p. 200), and home to
the Zürcher Ballet. Closed Aug.

Stadtcasino
Am Barfüsserplatz
4051 Basel
Tel 061 273 73 73
www.casinobasel.ch
www.konzerte-basel.ch
Main venue for the Basel
Symphony Orchestra (www
.sinfonieorchestrabasel.ch) and
Basel Chamber Orchestra
(www.kammerorchesterbasel.ch).

Stadttheater Bern
Kornhausplatz 20
3011 Bern
Tel 031 329 52 52
www.stadttheaterbern.ch
Bern's main theater has a resident
opera company and a contemporary dance troupe.

Tonhalle St. Gallen
Museumstrasse 25
9000 St. Gallen
Tel 071 242 06 06
www.theaterstgallen.ch
A magnificent art nouveau setting for concerts by the St. Gallen
Symphony orchestra. Closed
much of July & Aug.

Tonhalle Zürich
Claridenstrasse 7
8002 Zürich
Tel 044 206 34 40
www.tonhalle.ch
World-class concert hall, with an
extensive classical concert program by the Tonhalle Orchester,
the Zürcher Kammerorchester,
and visiting ensembles. Closed
much of July & Aug.

Victoria Hall
rue du Général-Dufour 14
1204 Geneva
Tel 022 418 35 00
www.ville-ge.ch/culture/
victoria_hall/en/index.html
Geneva's main classical music

venue; residence of the Orchestra
de la Suisse Romande (www.osr
.ch). Closed much of July & Aug.

Jazz

Casino Barrière de Montreux
rue du Théâtre 9
1820 Montreux
Tel 021 962 83 83
www.casinodemontreux.ch
A major venue for the celebrated
Jazz Festival (see p. 83).

Gabs Lounge
rue de Zürich 12
1201 Geneva
Tel 022 732 31 32
www.gabslounge.com
Popular locals' haunt for live jazz,
swing, blues, and boogie-woogie.

Le Chat Noir
rue Vautier 13
1227 Carouge
Tel 022 307 10 40
www.chatnoir.ch/
One of Geneva's top jazz haunts,
situated in historic Carouge.

Le Chorus
avenue de Mon-Repos 3
1005 Lausanne
Tel 021 323 22 33
www.chorus.ch
Lively cellar club, famed for its
live jazz and jam sessions. Closed
July, Aug., & Sept.

Marian's Jazzroom
Hotel Innere Enge, Engestrasse 54
3012 Bern
Tel 031 309 61 11
www.mariansjazzroom.ch
Top notch jazz club featuring
international names in jazz
and blues. Closed most of
July & Aug.

**Montreux Music & Convention
Center**
grand-rue 95
1820 Montreux
Tel 021 962 20 00
www.montreuxcongres.ch

The main venue for the Montreux Jazz Festival (see p. 83).

Moods
Schiffbaustrasse 6
8005 Zürich
Tel 044 276 80 00
www.moods.ch
Zürich's top jazz club features regular live jazz, funk, and blues.

Widder
Widder Hotel
Rennweg 7
8001 Zürich
Tel 044 224 25 26
www.widderhotel.ch
A cozy piano bar with live jazz most weeks.

Cinema
Arthouse Le Paris
Gottfried-Keller Strasse 7
8001 Zürich
Tel 044 250 55 60
www.arthouse.ch/kino/leparis
Varied arthouse program centered around festival winners.

Festival Internazionale del Film
Piazza Grande
6600 Locarno
Tel 091 756 21 21
www.pardo.ch
Locarno's main square is transformed into Europe's largest open-air cinema every August for a 10-day festival of mostly European films.

La Scala
rue des Eaux-Vives 23
1207 Geneva
Tel 022 736 04 22
www.les-scala.ch
Popular arthouse cinema, specializing in movies from around the world.

OrangeCinema
www.orangecinema.ch
Temporary open-air movie screens (July–Aug.) erected by the lake in Geneva (Port-Noir)

and Zürich (Zürichhorn); at Bern's Grosse Schanze; and in Münsterplatz in Basel.

Nightclubs
Bierhalle Wolf
Limmatquai 132
8001 Zürich
Tel 044 251 01 30
www.bierhalle-wolf.ch
Authentic Germanic-style beer cellar with live oompah music.

Club 1
Via Cantonale 1
6900 Lugano
Tel 078 909 75 50
House, R&B, 70s, and 80s nights. Closed Mon. & Tues.

Das Schwarze Scharf
Frankenstrasse 2
6003 Luzern
Tel 041 210 43 35
www.dasschwarzeschaf.ch
Stylish nightclub with themed music nights.

Delta Beach Lounge
Park Delta Hotel
Via Delta 137–141
6612 Ascona
Tel 091 785 77 85
www.parkhoteldelta.ch
Popular lounge with large terrace overlooking the lake, jazz, R&B, piano evenings, and DJ nights.

Farm Club
Route de la Poste
1936 Verbier
Tel 027 775 20 10
www.farmclub.ch
Verbier's leading nightclub.

Kaufleuten
Pelikanstrasse 18
8001 Zürich
Tel 044 225 33 22
www.kaufleuten.com
Rub shoulders with Tina Turner, Prince, and other celebrities at one of Zürich's most sophisticated nightclubs.

King's Club, Badrutt's Palace
Via Serlas 27
7500 St. Moritz
Tel 081 837 10 00
www.badruttspalace.com
International stars and dance floor reflecting disco style of the 70s. Themed nights.

Le Piano Bar
Hotel Le Mirador Kempinski
Chemin de l'Hôtel du Mirador 5
Chardonne
1801 Mont-Pèlerin
Tel 021 925 11 11
www.mirador.com/kempinski
Sophisticated cocktail bar, serving more than 70 varieties of champagne, high above Vevey and Lake Geneva.

MAD (Moulin à Danses)
rue de Genève 23
1003 Lausanne
Tel 021 340 69 69
www.mad.ch
Lausanne's number one dance club, with top DJs and wild party nights on five floors.

New Orleans Club
Quartiere Maghetti
6900 Lugano
Tel 091 921 44 77
www.neworleansclublugano.com
Hip-hop and R&B club. Closed Sun., Mon., & Tues.

Privilege
Piazza Dante 8
6900 Lugano
Tel 0789 427 886
www.privilegelugano.ch
House, 70s, 80s, dance, and Italian music.

Pur Pur
Seefeldstrasse 9
8008 Zürich
Tel 044 419 20 66
www.purpurzurich.ch
Hip Moroccan-style lounge-bar with music ranging from "chill-out" to "Ibiza reunion."

Tours & Outdoor Activities

Because Switzerland is well-endowed with mountains and lakes, it's no surprise that it has a phenomenal variety of winter sports and watersports. For keen cyclists the mountain roads present a must-do challenge, while the less energetic can still enjoy beautiful routes without the scary gradients. Add an interesting array of tours, ballooning, and golf, and no traveler is going to be at a loss for something exciting to do.

TOURS

Food & Wine Tours

Au Clos de la Republique
Ruelle du Petit-Crêt
1098 Epesses
Tel 021 799 14 44
www.patrick-fonjallaz.ch
The Fonjallaz family have produced wine here for 13 generations since the 16th century. View their vines and taste their wine. Open Tues.–Thurs.

Fromagerie d'Alpage
1663 Moléson-sur-Gruyères
Tel 026 921 10 44
www.fromagerie-alpage.ch
Join the Cheese Nature Trail between Moléson-sur-Gruyères and Pringy. Information panels tell the secrets of cheese-making. Finish up in a show dairy.

Engelberg Cheese
Klosterhof
Klosterstrasse 3
6390 Engelberg
Tel 041 639 77 77
www.schaukaeserei-engelberg
.ch/main-en.html
Visit a cheese dairy in a working monastery. Watch the monks shape the cheeses by hand. Cheese-making from 11 a.m.– 4 p.m. Mon.–Sat. Closed Sun.

Field to Table
Ente Turistico Valposchiavo
7742 Poschiavo
Tel 081 844 05 71
www.valposchiavo.ch
Over two days, follow a grain of buckwheat on a guided gourmet excursion in Graubünden.

Tastings, accommodations, and breakfast included. May–Oct.

Lavaux Wine Train
Gare du Lavaux Express
1096 Cully
Tel 021 799 54 54
www.lavauxexpress.ch
A guided journey through vineyards, stopping for tastings. Departs from the lake landing stage at Lutry or Cully. April–Oct.

Food & Carriage Rides

Rössli-Fahrten
Bahnhofstrasse 60
8553 Hüttlingen
Tel 052 765 10 96
www.roessli-fahrten.ch
Tour the countryside in a horse-drawn carriage.

Segway Tours

Segway City Tours
Tel 0848 734 929
www.segwaycitytours.ch
Sightseeing tours of Zürich, including Segway training. Driver's licence required.

Steam Train Rides

Rosa Dampffahrten
Appenzeller Bahnen AG
Bahnhof Heiden
9410 Heiden
Tel 071 891 18 52
www.appenzellerbahnen.ch
Nostalgic steam train rides from Rorschach to Heiden.

Wildlife Tours

Liberty Bird
RB Reise Beratung
Belpstrasse 47
3000 Bern

Tel 031 382 22 26
www.liberty-bird.com
Professional local guides show individuals and groups Swiss bird specialties. Based in Bern.

Emetten Wildlife Path
Tourismus Beckenried-Klewenalp
Seestrasse 1
6375 Beckenried
041 620 31 70
www.tourismus-beckenried.ch
Close to Vierwaldstättersee, guided tours in the mountains along a 7-mile (11 km) path at dawn. Look for chamois, ibex, marmots, eagles, and other birds. Summer only.

OUTDOOR ACTIVITIES

Ballooning & Paragliding

Ballon Château-d'Oex
SkyEvent SA
La Place
1660 Château-d'Oex
Tel 026 924 22 20
www.volenballon.ch
For memorable mountain vistas over the Alpine capital of hot-air ballooning.

Fly-Xperience
Tel 078 648 20 68
info@fly-xperience.com
www.fly-xperience.com
Try your hand at tandem paragliding high above Lake Geneva (departures from Villeneuve rail station, allow 1.5 hrs).

Rappi Ballon
Lindenhofstrasse 16
8640 Rapperswil

Tel 079 420 59 59
www.rappiballon.ch
Balloon tours over Zürichsee.

Cycling & Mountain Biking

Bike Arena
Parkhotel Schoenegg
3818 Grindelwald
Tel 033 854 18 18
www.bikearena.ch
Guided tours for all levels in the Jungfrau region.

Bike Tech AG
Schwende 1
4950 Huttwil
Tel 062 959 55 55
www.flyer.ch
"Flyer" e-bike holidays, rentals, day trips, and tours.

Rentabike
www.rentabike.ch
Nationwide bike hire (city bikes, mountain bikes, tandems, and e-bikes), from many resorts including Basel, Fribourg, and Yverdons-les-Bains.

SwissTrails GmbH
Chlupfstrasse 8
8165 Oberweningen
Tel 043 422 60 22
www.swisstrails.ch
Touring, racing, mountain, and electric bikes for hire or as part of a package tour with luggage transported.

Golf

Golf Club Crans-sur-Sierre
Tel 027 485 97 97
www.golfcrans.ch
18 holes, par 72. Some say this is the world's most scenic tournament course.

Golf Club de Genève
Route de la Capite 70
1223 Cologny-Genève
Tel 022 707 48 00
18-holes, par-72 course.

Golf Club Küssnacht am Rigi
6403 Küssnacht am Rigi
Tel 041 854 40 20
www.gck.ch
This 18-hole course has been praised for its "specially environment-friendly layout."

"Hot-Pot" Bathing

Berglialp Matt
8766 Matt
Tel 055 642 14 92
www.molkenbad.ch
Al fresco barrel-bathing in therapeutic herbal, honey, and whey baths.

Star-gazing

Observatoire Robert-A. Naef
Route du Petit-Épendes 45
1731 Ependes
Tel 026 413 10 99
info@observatoire-naef.ch
www.obesrvatoire-naef.ch
Viewings every Friday evening.

Watersports

Centre Nautique Les Vikings
Avenue des Pins 34
1462 Yvonand
Tel 079 342 90 50
lesvikings@bluewin.ch
www.lesvikings.ch
Sailing boat, pedalo, and small motorboat rental; sailing and windsurfing lessons.

Ciels Bleus
Place du Vieux-Port
1006 Ouchy–Lausanne
Tel 076 366 39 49
www.bateauecole.ch
Boat hire, sailing, and water-skiing school.

Kanuschule Scuol Outdoor Engadin
Punt 42
7550 Scuol
Tel 081 860 02 06
www.outdoor-engadin.ch
Canoeing on the Inn River in the beautiful Lower Engadine.

Lang Sailing
Seestrasse 24
8712 St:afa
Tel 044 928 18 18
www.sail.ch
Sailing lessons or boat hire on Zürichsee.

Winter Sports

Bergün Filisur Tourismus
Hauptstrasse 83
7482 Bergün/Bravuogn
Tel 081 407 11 52
www.berguen-filisur.ch
Switzerland's first floodlit toboggan run—and Europe's longest—extends for 4 miles (6 km) from Preda to Bergün. Trains carry you and the sledges back up the mountain.

Kronberg Bobbahn
Jakobsbad
Tel 071 794 12 89
www.kronberg.ch
Summer toboggan track at the foot of Kronberg mountain. Also a rope park, Seilpark Jakobsbad.

Siberia Sports
Clos-Rognon
2406 La Brévine
Tel 032 935 13 24
Fax 032 935 13 30
siberia-sports@bluewin.ch
www.siberiasports.ch
Cross-country ski equipment and snowshoes for hire. Also accompanied evening snowshoe tours.

Tobogganing Park
Place des Feuilles
1854 Leysin
Tel 024 494 28 88
www.tobogganing.ch
Snow-tubing venue in winter only, depending on snow.

INDEX

ILLUSTRATIONS CREDITS

2-3, Robert Harding/Photolibrary; 4, Shutterstock; 8, Bon Appetit/Alamy; 11, Fedor Selivanov/Shutterstock; 12, Look-foto/Photolibrary; 15, Stuart Dee/Photographers Choice/Getty Images; 16, Getty Images; 18, Robert Sprich/EPA/Corbis; 20-21, Prisma Bildagentur AG/Alamy; 22, Arnd Wiegmann/Reuters/Corbis; 24-25, Alistair Scott/Alamy; 27, Michael Peuckert/Imageboker/Photolibrary; 28-29, Cornelia Doerr/Age Fotostock/Photolibrary; 33, Luis Castaneda/Age Fotostock/Photolibrary; 36, The Art Archive/Alamy; 39, akg-images/Alamy; 40-41, Prisma Bildagentur AG/Alamy; 43, Andy Christiani; 45, Sigi Tischler/Keystone/Corbis; 46-47, Hemis/Alamy; 48, Prisma Bildagentur AG/Alamy; 51, Guenter Fischer/Imagebroker/Photolibrary; 53, Imagebroker/Alamy; 54-55, JTB/Photolibrary; 56, Konrad Wothe/Look-foto/Photolibrary; 60, Peter Richardson/Robert Harding/Photolibrary; 63, Patrick Forget/Saga/Photolibrary; 64, Patrick Forget/Saga/Photolibrary; 66, Guenter Fischer/Imagebroker/Photolibrary; 69, Patrick Forget/Saga/Photolibrary; 70, Tips Italia/Photolibrary; 72, Imagebroker/Alamy; 75, Ingolf Pompe/Look-foto/Photolibrary; 76, Norbert Eisele-Hein/Imagebroker/Photolibrary; 78, White Smoke/Shutterstock; 80, Martin Moxter/Imagebroker/Photolibrary; 82, Gamma-Rapho/Getty Images; 84, Walter Bibikow/Mauritius/Photolibrary; 86, Hervé Gyssels/Photolibrary; 88, P. Narayan/Age Fotostock/Photolibrary; 91, Prisma Bildagentur AG/Alamy; 92, Ingolf Pompe/Look-foto/Photolibrary; 94, Paul Raftery/View pictures/Photolibrary; 96, Martin Moxter/Imagebroker/Photolibrary; 98, Jean-Lou Zemmermann/Bios/Photolibrary; 100, J. Charles Gerard/Photolibrary; 101, Werner Dieterich/Imagebroker/Photolibrary; 103, Michael Szonyi/Imagebroker/Photolibrary; 104, Hemis/Alamy; 107, Franck Guiziou/Hemis/Photolibrary; 109, Media Colours/Alamy; 110, Louis Bertrand/Age Fotostock/Photolibrary; 112, JTB/Photolibrary; 116, Andy Christiani; 118, Andy Christiani; 120, S. Kennedy Taylor/Getty Images; 123, Blaine Harrington III/Corbis; 124, Norbert Eisele-Hein/Imagebroker/Photolibrary; 126, Fedor Selivanov/Shutterstock; 128, Fresh Food Images/Photolibrary; 130, Ingolf Pompe/Look-foto/Photolibrary; 133, Paul Thompson/Ticket/Photolibrary; 134, Gavin Hellier/Robert Harding/Photolibrary; 136, Glyn Thomas/Age Fotostock; 138, Geoffrey Taunton/Alamy; 141, Prisma Bildagentur AG/Alamy; 142, David Noton Photography/Alamy; 144,

Daniel Boschung/Corbis; 146, istockphoto/Thinkstock; 149, Guenter Fischer/Imagebroker/Photolibrary; 150, Jevgenija Pigonze/Imagebroker/Photolibrary; 152, David Wei/Alamy; 155, Norbert Eisele-Hein/Imagebroker/Photolibrary; 156, Andre Jenny/Alamy; 158, Eddie Gerald/Alamy; 162, Andy Christiani; 166, Andy Christiani; 168, Blickwinkel/Alamy; 169, Barbara Boensch/Imagebroker/Photolibrary; 170, Martin Ruetschi/Corbis; 173, Prisma Bildagentur AG/Alamy; 174, Hans Georg Eiben/F1 Online/Photolibrary; 176, Ingolf Pompe/Hemis/Photolibrary; 178, Bildarchiv Monheim GmbH/Alamy; 181, Ingolf Pompe/Look-foto/Photolibrary; 182, Steve Vidler/Photolibrary; 185, Prisma Bildagentur AG/Alamy; 186, Ingolf Pompe/Look-foto/Getty Images; 190, Ludovic Maisant/Hemis/Corbis; 193, travelstock44/Alamy; 195, travelstock44/Photolibrary; 196, Richard T. Nowitz/Corbis; 198, travelstock44/Alamy; 200, Ludovic Maisant/Hemis/Corbis; 202, Thomas Sbampato/Imagebroker/Photolibrary; 205, Massimo Borchi/Atlantide Phototravel/Corbis; 206, Interfoto/Alamy; 208, Prisma Bildagentur AG/Alamy; 211, Prisma Bildagentur AG/Alamy; 212, Shutterstock; 215, Eisbahnwadi Wadenswil/Swiss Tourism; 216, travelstock44/Alamy; 218, Nick Biemans/Shutterstock; 220, Werner Dieterich/Alamy; 223, Werner Dieterich/Alamy; 224, Prisma Bildagentur AG/Alamy; 226, Shutterstock; 228, Andy Christiani; 230, Ken Welsh/Age Fotostock/Photolibrary; 233, Peter Wey/Shutterstock; 234, Peter Arnold Travel/Photolibrary; 236, Olaf Boders/OSF/Photolibrary; 238, Interfoto/Alamy; 240, Rudy Mareel/Shutterstock; 242, Rafael Rojas/Bios/Photolibrary; 245, JTB/Photolibrary; 246, Prisma Bildagentur AG/Alamy; 248 Ervin Monn/Shutterstock; 251, Tips Italia/Photolibrary; 252, Angelo Cavalli/Age Fotostock; 254, Robert Harding/Alamy; 256, Darryl Leniuk/Getty Images; 259, Tibor Bognar/Alamy; 260, Michael Szonyi/Imagebroker/Photolibrary; 262, Shutterstock; 264, travelstock44/Alamy; 266, Shutterstock; 268, Andreas Strauss/Age Fotostock/Photolibrary; 270, Dallas and John Heaton/Photolibrary.

Special thanks to Photolibrary and Alamy for their spectacular images and to Andy Christiani for his photographic contribution. Windmill Books has made every attempt to contact the copyright holder. If anyone has any information please email smortimer@windmillbooks.co.uk